1990

Death, Dying, and the Biological Revolution

Death, Dying, and the

Biological Revolution

Our Last Quest for Responsibility

Revised Edition

Robert M. Veatch

Yale University Press
New Haven and London

Copyright © 1989 by Robert M. Veatch.
All rights reserved.
This book may not be reproduced, in whole
or in part, including illustrations, in
any form (beyond that copying permitted by
Sections 107 and 108 of the U.S. Copyright
Law and except by reviewers for the public
press), without written permission from the
publishers.

Set in Electra type by
Brevis Press, Bethany, Connecticut.
Printed in the United States of America by
Vail-Ballou Press, Binghamton, New York.

Library of Congress Catalog Card Number: 88–50434
International Standard Book Numbers: 0–300–04364–3 (cloth)
0–300–04365–1 (pbk.)

The paper in this book meets the guidelines for
permanence and durability of the Committee on
Production Guidelines for Book Longevity of the
Council on Library Resources.

10 9 8 7 6 5 4 3 2 1

Contents

Preface

It is sometimes said that there is no progress in ethics. Anyone who believes that ought to study the history of the care of the terminally ill. In the days of ancient Greece Hippocratic physicians were advised that they need not take on terminally ill patients (because it was bad for their reputations as healers). The mortally afflicted infant was, for Aristotle, best disposed of by discarding it.

If the movement in the long sweep of history is dramatic, however, the recent changes that have taken place in the ethics of terminal care are equally breathtaking. In 1976, when the first edition of this volume was published, a young woman named Karen Quinlan had just had her case decided by the New Jersey Supreme Court. That decision established the tentative and limited authority of a loving family to stop high technology respiratory support for a woman who was, with great certainty, irreversibly comatose. One state, California, had hesitatingly passed a Natural Death Act giving persons who had been certified terminally ill for fourteen days a very limited set of rights to refuse treatment. A few states had passed laws authorizing the pronouncement of death based on brain-related criteria. Still the vast majority of physicians held that it was their Hippocratic duty to withhold potentially traumatic news of a diagnosis of terminal illness from patients in order to protect those patients from a decision-making responsibility that they supposedly could not handle. A handful of heart transplants had taken place, but there was a self-imposed moratorium on this procedure because of the serious problems of rejection.

No one was yet thinking seriously about states passing laws that would give well-motivated persons the right to fulfill their familial responsibility to make medical decisions for their incompetent members. No one had begun to imagine the possibility of applying the principles of responsible refusal of treatment to simple, everyday medical technologies such as medically administered nutrition and intravenous fluids. No one anticipated that physicians were about to abandon their Hippocratic paternalism and adopt, almost unanimously, the position that one of the moral requirements of medical professionals was to deal honestly with patients, even terminally ill patients. No one imagined the era of the Baby Does, of the Elizabeth Bouvias, or of Baby Fae. No one was thinking about the day when the rejection phenomenon could be sufficiently controlled that organs would be in such scarce supply that we would begin public policy debate about "required requests," "routine inquiries," "opting out," and cash markets for human organs.

Today all of these things have come about. But the questions raised in volumes on the ethics of terminal care were structured for a simpler era, one in which the nuances of these problems were not recognized. Indeed, essays on dealing with terminal care written only a decade ago reveal not so much moral mistakes as moral simplicity.

It is in the face of this rapid change (if not progress) that I have undertaken the overdue task of completely rewriting my 1976 study of the ethical and public policy issues stimulated by the biological revolution. What I said in the preface to the first edition still states the task well. My objective has not been to write a philosophical analysis of the ethics of death and dying—or at least not that alone. Rather, it has been much broader. At the Institute of Society, Ethics and the Life Sciences (now the Hastings Center), where I was for ten years, and at the Kennedy Institute of Ethics, where I have been for the past eight, we are convinced that the best hope for gaining insight into the complex dilemmas posed by the technological and biological revolutions is an eclectic spirit combining contributions from many disciplines. This volume, in its revised edition as well as its first, is written in that spirit. I begin with a theoretical reflection—sometimes philosophical, sometimes more theological—and move through a maze of technical medical and legal facts toward an examination of alternative public and personal policy.

In a simpler day we often knew, or thought we knew, what our objectives were for medicine. Someone dying of pneumonia, who had heard that some drug would restore health, needed to know what the drug was or at least how to get it. No obvious moral problem arose. It was clear what would produce the best consequences and, for the most part, what was the right thing to do. Now, however, with miraculous but only partially successful interventions, such as those given to Karen Quinlan, it is not at all clear what alternative actions will have the best consequences. It is even less clear what is morally right. The biological revolution poses new problems for us: what a good life is, what our rights are, and what our responsibilities are in the process of our dying.

These questions of rights and responsibility in our final days are crucial—literally matters of life and death. Yet it would be unfair to say that those difficult questions alone are the subject of this book. Many years ago I became interested in the social and ethical problems of death and dying not merely because they were themselves important questions, but because dealing with those questions produced a context for struggling with even more basic questions. To ask the meaning of death is, in an indirect way, to ask the meaning of life. To ask what are the rights of the dying is to ask what are the rights of the living. To decide the nature of questions in the care of the dying— who is an expert and who shall control the decision making—is to decide even more fundamental questions about expertise and decision making. If individuals and societies are to retain their freedom and dignity, their responsibility, in the living of their lives, then they must do so in their last quest for responsibility.

Although those objectives remain the same in this new edition, both the issues and the ethical analysis of them have become more complex. Virtually every detail of every chapter has been reassessed. Often major sections have been rewritten, with considerable material added to cover both increased ethical and policy complexity. That accounts for the substantial increase in length over the earlier edition. At the same time, I have cut out those items from the earlier edition that were outdated and those that no longer seemed as important.

This edition brings up to date the massive case law that has appeared since the earlier edition, and it incorporates the rapid progress in statutory laws dealing with the definition of death as well as "natural death acts." In the interim I have had the opportunity to publish a much more systematic theory of medical ethics. During the research for that volume my own theoretical positions became clearer to me. Those developments have been incorporated throughout the volume. The reader will find this particularly in the use of a more explicitly deontological ethical theory in which ethical principles that do not simply emphasize producing good consequences in aggregate (principles like truth telling, promise keeping, and justice) collectively take precedence over maximizing good consequences. In this edition I also develop the notion that there is a deontological duty to avoid the active killing of another human being, and I attempt to show how that makes sense of our intuitions regarding the distinction between active killing and forgoing treatment.

I also apply this general ethical theory to the problem of justice in allocating resources to the terminally ill and to those who will benefit from the use of their body parts. In particular I incorporate the notion that aggregate good consequences can never justify overriding other ethical principles, but that justice sometimes can. And this notion has led me to ask whether those who might benefit from limiting scarce medical resources that are available to the terminally ill are better off or worse off than the terminally ill person. It has led me to answer questions of the allocation of transplantable organs by asking who has the greatest need. But it also has led me to distinguish between need at a moment in time and need over a life time, a distinction that has a major impact on both the problem of allocating organs and that of funding research on the extension of the human life span.

In chapters 3 through 6, I develop in greater detail the notion of familial responsibility for decisions about terminally ill incompetents. I introduce the distinction between bonded and nonbonded guardians and the idea of limited familial autonomy, which I increasingly see as crucial for dealing with the policy problems of surrogate decision making.

I take up the issues of nutrition and hydration in greater detail, examine the moral reasons underlying the radical shift in physicians' attitudes about the disclosure of terminal illness, and develop the policy issues of organ allocation and procurement more than in the first edition. People have both the right and the responsibility for decisions concerning terminal illness for themselves and their loved ones. It is still our last quest for responsibility.

A major rewriting of a project undertaken over a decade ago is something I undertook hesitantly. It would not have been possible without the enormous help of some very capable and dedicated people. I am particularly grateful for the research and administrative support given by Carol Mason and Karen Roberts. The professional staff of the Kennedy Institute of Ethics library, the National Reference Center for Bioethics, has been extremely competent and helpful. I am grateful to my colleagues at the Kennedy Institute of Ethics for their assistance in reading and rereading portions of the manuscript of this edition.

Is Death Moral? An Introduction

The patient, twenty-three-weeks pregnant, was rushed to the emergency room convulsing in seizures. She had been an epileptic since childhood, but medication had controlled her seizures reasonably well. Now she showed decerebrate posturing and random eye movement. The working diagnosis was meningoencephalitis. Seventeen days later her pupils were fixed and dilated. Reflexes were absent. The next day an EEG showed no cerebral activity; she was unresponsive to pain. In short, she met all the standard criteria to indicate her brain was dead. Still her lungs continued to respire on a ventilator, and her heart continued to beat (because of the oxygen from the mechanically supported lungs). The fetal heart rate continued to be normal. A sonogram showed a living, twenty-five-week-old fetus. The hospital's success rate in delivering a fetus this young by cesarean section was poor. Another week or two would greatly increase the chance of saving the baby. The woman was unmarried. Her elderly mother was the next of kin.[1]

Some crucial decisions had to be made. One possibility was to consider her dead, and to proceed to use her newly dead body as an incubator to save the living fetus. To do so would require great medical skill. It would also require some moral and public policy decisions. It would require assuming that an individual is dead when his or her brain is dead. It would require figuring out who, if anyone, had the authority to authorize the use of the body for this purpose. It would require a decision that the body should be used to save the fetus rather than as a source of organs for transplant to save others dying of heart, kidney, or liver failure.

Although the clinicians assumed this woman was dead, the law in the state where the patient had her seizure did not, at the time, explicitly hold that persons with dead brains were dead. That suggests a second way of interpreting the case. If the woman was still alive (although with a dead brain), a decision would have to made whether to continue supporting her life through aggressive medical means. In forty jurisdictions in the United States, laws permit persons to write instructions authorizing nontreatment in cases of terminal illness. In other jurisdictions they probably have a common law right to do so. If this woman was not dead, she was certainly terminally ill. But even if she had written such an instruction, should she have been able to have treatment stopped in spite of her pregnancy? Some states with such laws say the law does not apply in cases where the woman is pregnant. On the other hand, she would have had the legal right to abort the fetus, at least up to the point of viability. Should she have also written instructions to abort so that she could then have had treatment stopped? Were the clinicians, her mother, the father of the fetus, or someone else—like a judge—the ones who should have had the authority to decide whether to continue life support (assuming she was alive) or to continue supporting heart and lung function in her corpse (assuming she was dead)?

If she were dead, the use of her body would seem to be covered by the Uniform Anatomical Gift Act, which governs the use of the newly dead in all American jurisdictions in regard to the recovery of body organs for transplant, as well as other uses of the body for research, education, and therapy. In this case the law would apply to the possibility of using the mother's newly dead body for therapy for the fetus. If this woman was dead, the law is clear that, unless she had specified her desires about the use of her body, her next of kin had the authority to do so. If, on the other hand, she was considered alive, it is not so clear who had authority. In states where living will legislation has been passed, it depends on what the law specifies. In some jurisdictions, the next of kin is the presumed guardian with authority to make medical decisions for incompetent patients. In some states, even if the next of kin is the presumed guardian, treatment cannot be refused while the woman is pregnant. Nowhere is authority given to the fetus's father, even though the father may have certain obligations to serve the interests of the fetus. Also none of this gives any authority to the clinicians.

Modern medical technology has given us remarkable powers to intervene in the dying process, but it has also created new moral dilemmas in the care of the dying and the dead. In the case of this pregnant woman with a dead brain there were some important scientific and medical questions to be answered. It was important to know that there was a much smaller chance of saving the fetus if the delivery took place at twenty-three weeks rather than at twenty-six weeks. It was important to know what risks the fetus was exposed to during the seizures and during the effort to prolong maternal bodily functions. But even if these scientific questions were answered, we would still have been a long way from knowing what to do in this case. We literally did not know whether this woman was alive or dead and, in either case, it was not obvious whether medical treatment to support her bodily processes should have continued. In other words, the biological revolution has raised ethical and social issues so fundamental and controversial that the debate can no longer be contained within hospital walls. The public as well as professionals—physicians and philosophers and lawyers—must confront these issues.

Is Death Moral in a Technological Age?

Death has always been inevitable—a "fact of life." But where humans were once helpless onlookers in the presence of death, we are now increasingly able to intervene in the process, using technological resources to direct or delay the inevitable.

A surgeon has removed the heart from a living human being and maintained him for sixty-five hours by mechanical devices while waiting for a suitable heart for transplantation. A human being's cells can be kept alive virtually indefinitely through the use of artificial respirators, artificial cardiac pacemakers, and intravenous feeding with artificial food—giving rise to what many would call an artificial human being. A man's body has been frozen immediately after death to await discovery of a cure for his particular disease with a faith in technology that someday we shall be able to thaw him out and cure him.

Efforts like these make it appear that we are engaged in a struggle against death itself, that, as never before, we look upon it as an evil. We are mobilizing technology in an all-out war against it, and we are assuming that, if not death itself, at least certain types of deaths are conquerable. We are being forced to ask the question, "Is death moral in a technological age?"

Each year about fifty million people die throughout the world, In the United States slightly over two million people die each year. A casual look at American records of causes of death reveals a predominance of lingering death, that is, death anticipated over months or years. One report indicated that chronic conditions are the cause of 87 percent of all deaths.[2] Another study found that half of the population dies of an illness diagnosed at least twenty-nine months earlier.[3] That implies that in the United States alone, perhaps four million people are now in the process of dying. The exact number depends upon what we mean by *dying*. Yet, if in this confusing time we cannot agree on a definition of death, we have hardly begun to ask what it means to be dying.[4]

Communicable diseases of childhood and rapid infectious diseases do not cause enough deaths to warrant tabulation in most lists. Among the causes of rapid death only accidents, suicides, and homicides (and some cardiovascular diseases) ever claim a place on the lists, and even they are sometimes the result of some of the most horrible biomedical interventions. All other deaths in the list are chronic. Until recently they were often masked by early death from now vanquished organisms, but now we confront chronic death in ever increasing proportions.

We can anticipate not only that the cause of death will be different, but the place as well. The scene of a family gathered in the bedroom of the dying is now little more than a poignant memory. Seventy-three percent of adult Americans dying in 1965 had hospital or other institutional care during the last year of their lives.[5] A recent estimate suggests that figure has increased slightly, to 75 percent.[6] And the chances of dying in an institution have increased dramatically. In 1937, 37 percent of all deaths in the United States occurred in hospitals or other institutions; in 1958, it had risen to 61 percent.[7] In 1983 the President's Commission for the Study of Ethical Problems in Medicine and Biomedical and Behavioral Research estimated the figure was 80 percent.[8]

Average life expectancy at birth has risen from 47.3 years in 1900 to about 75 years now, largely because of the precipitous decline in deaths of children and young adults.

There is a great deal of controversy and confusion over the costs of terminal care.[9] A study of data from the mid-1960s found that the median cost of hospital bills for those who died was three times greater than for those who did not.[10] Similar results were found in a study published in 1981.[11] In a study of patients who died during 1978, Lubitz and Prihoda found that 27.9 percent of Medicare expenditures went for patients who died, in spite of the fact that those patients accounted for only 5.9 percent of Medicare beneficiaries.[12] Deaths from cancer, for example, generate particularly traumatic cost statistics. For cancer patients under age sixty-five, expenditures averaged

$21,219 for the last year, of which $15,936 came in the last six months of life and $6,161 in the last month.[13] Lubitz and Prihoda, in their study of all Medicare beneficiaries, found a similar pattern of extensive expenses during the last days of life.[14]

In short, people have radically changed their style of dying. Scientific advance has meant that more die in institutions, die older, take longer to die, and spend more money doing it. Somehow in the emergence of our technologized, expertized society, we even seem to have developed the bizarre notion that we need "permission to die."[15] On hospital floors and in medical magazines medical professionals are asking whether they should let the dying go ahead and die. Citizens who are winning a prolonged struggle for individual freedoms from oppressive governments may at the same time be losing that freedom to a technocratic elite. They now have to ask if there is a "right to die." What was once inevitable now must be defended as one's moral right.

This new potential for controlling life means there is a new potential for controlling death. This technological power makes many deaths either tragic accidents or, where social injustice permits inadequate health care services, intolerable outrages. Responsibility must now be borne for deaths that could have been prevented had adequate health care services been available. As humans first learned to control infectious diseases, then social diseases, and now chronic illness, they seem now to close in on death itself, leading some to treat it as an immoral power to be driven from the community like the Salem witch.

Is Death Moral or Technical?

In one sense, then, the impact of modern biomedical technology has made mortality itself in the eyes of some an immorality. In another sense, the question "Is Death Moral?" still remains to be answered. Was the debate about whether the pregnant woman was alive or dead a dispute over technical medical facts or was it a debate about morality? While technology has given us greater power to control death, paradoxically it has also generated confusion over the once simple concepts of life and death, over whether an individual is alive or dead.

On May 7, 1968, the heart of Clarence Nicks was removed and transplanted into the chest of John Stuckwish, a sixty-two-year-old man suffering from a severe heart condition. Nicks had been beaten by a group of assailants in a brawl. His breathing had stopped and his brain waves were flat. He would not regain brain function. He was pronounced dead by one physician. Another disagreed, claiming Nicks was not yet dead since his heart was still beating—although its continuation required the introduction of artificial respiration. It is not difficult to imagine what the assailants' legal counsel chose as a defense against the charge of murder: according to them, the victim was not dead until the heart was removed. If anyone was responsible for the immediate cause of death, it was the physician who removed the heart.

The physicians were surprised at the disagreement among their colleagues. They were for the first time forced to ask what the real meaning of death is. There was little disagreement over the technical facts, yet substantial disagreement over what ought to be done. In what sense is death a "fact" at all? In what sense is death a technical issue to be decided by experts with appropriate scientific training? In what sense is it a moral or philosophical or theological question to be decided by criteria of a radically different kind? That death can be a matter of moral judgment rather than of biological fact seems strange. That possibility will be explored in chapter 1 of this book.

It is not enough, however, to speculate about the philosophical meaning of death. The pregnant woman with a dead brain was in an intensive care unit. The medical staff had to know whether to continue support. In chapter 2 I shall ask the questions about practical policy. Exactly when should public policy permit or require death to be pronounced? Who should determine when death should be pronounced, and by what concept, locus, and criteria? Most, but not all states have now adopted laws permitting or requiring the use of so-called "brain definitions of death." I shall explore some of the pitfalls of such legislation and see why the debate has not subsided. More fundamentally, I shall ask exactly who has the right to select a concept of death for a particular patient?

Is a Particular Death Moral?

It is striking that regardless of whether we decide to call the pregnant woman with the dead brain alive or dead a set of difficult and important questions remains. Moreover, in either case the questions are rather similar. Among those who consider her dead, disagreement could persist. They could decide to continue treating the new and respiring corpse aggressively, using it as an incubator with the hope of saving a fetus's life. Or they could decide that it would be more appropriate to cease treatment of the corpse even though it meant the death of the fetus. The answer will depend on what they perceive as the morality of the use of the newly dead body.

Among those who consider her alive, there could also be a dispute over whether to continue treatment. Someone could decide to let her die, knowing that it would mean the death of her fetus. Or that person could decide to treat aggressively, maintaining her alive with the hope of increasing the chance of saving her fetus.

Even if we conclude that it is morally acceptable to die in a technological age, and even if we conclude that the definition of death is a moral rather than a technical or biological problem, still we must ask whether a particular death—a particular way of dying—is moral. A tragically large percentage of people in the world will do their dying in what many would consider outrageously immoral ways. Some will die through starvation, war, drugs, and the blight of poverty; others because they cannot obtain needed medical care. Still others will do their dying in an atmosphere of mystery where they know their own condition only vaguely or are given medical treatment that they or their agents are desperately trying to refuse.

Certain philosophical distinctions must be made in attempting to resolve issues of medical morality. They arise most commonly in what some call the euthanasia debate. *Euthanasia*, however, is a very confusing term. To some it means literally "a good death." To others it means a morally outrageous death. When one term has such contradictory meanings it is probably better that it disappear from the language. I shall generally avoid it. The questions in that debate, however, cannot be avoided. Is there, for instance, a moral difference between actively killing dying patents and forgoing treatment, between direct and indirect killing, or between stopping treatment and deciding not to start? Is it morally acceptable to relieve pain or induce sleep with drugs whose side effects may hasten death? Is this the same as actively killing the patient? Is stopping a treatment morally more like actively killing or like not starting the treatment in the first place? Is there a difference between "ordinary" and "extraordinary" treatments, and if there is, has it any practical significance? What is the distinction between a medical treatment that saves life and one that merely forestalls death? These questions will be dealt with in chapter 3.

THE PATIENT'S RIGHT TO REFUSE TREATMENT

It is an unfortunate aspect of modern medical ethics that these questions are frequently asked in a way that assumes the decisions will be made by someone acting on the patient's behalf. Our technocracy even assigns experts to decide the life and death of the terminal patient. A fundamental thesis of this book is that, especially in issues as basic as these, the patient must be the one who decides. The question should never be, "When should we stop treating this patient?" as if the patient were an object to be repaired or discarded. Rather the question must be, "When, if ever, should it be morally and/or legally possible for the patient to decide to refuse medical treatment even if that may mean that dying will no longer be prolonged?" In chapter 4 I examine cases where competent patients have tried to refuse medical treatment, often to the point of legal battles. In chapter 5 I take up the more complex situation of surrogate decision making for incompetent patients.

We shall see that in spite of the seeming inconsistency in court opinions, a few basic principles appear to account for every decision. New public policy is emerging to ensure humane and dignified treatment of the dying. In chapters 4 and 5 I attempt to provide a framework for deciding the legality and morality of refusing treatment based on a small number of concepts and guidelines. We shall see that we are much closer to having clear policy than most people realize.

It is not enough, however, to explore the legal side of refusing treatment; it is not even enough to propose some guidelines for changes in our case law. Only the force of an informed and concerned public will insure that our public policy regarding death and dying is examined and modified. Cases such as that of Karen Ann Quinlan have generated enormous amounts of press coverage and public debate.[16] We are now asking if we can continue the current practice of permitting individual physicians standing at the bedside to decide whether a patient shall live or die. Committees are being proposed—sometimes called God Squads—to take the burden off the individual physician. Advance directives patterned after the Living Will are being drafted for people to use to instruct their family, friends, physician, lawyer, or clergyman about their wishes for their own terminal care. In chapter 6 I offer an analysis of these policy alternatives. It contains a set of criteria for writing one's own advanced directive as well as a sample directive for guidance in that writing. It also contains an assessment of current state statutes and a set of criteria for an ideal statute to facilitate decisions by competent persons or by surrogates for incompetents.

TELLING THE DYING PATIENT

The particular deaths of some patients are morally questionable, not because of medical treatment or its lack, but because critical information has been withheld from them. They may suspect a fatal diagnosis or be informed through other channels, but too often they are not given a clear picture of their condition.

During the 1970s the pattern of physician disclosure of terminal illness underwent a dramatic change. In a 1961 study, 88 percent of physicians claimed that they would tend not to tell cancer patients their diagnosis even though it was "certain" and "treatment may be possible (but) the prognosis is grave."[17] Yet most lay people (82–98 percent) apparently wanted to be told if they had cancer.[18] By the 1980s that pattern had changed radically. The reasons for the earlier differences between physicians and lay people and for the moral change will be examined in chapter 7. We shall see that while the change has been dramatic, not all physicians now favor full disclosure and, even when they do, some critical problems can emerge, not the least of which is the possibility that the patient or family of the patient may not want the truth disclosed.

TRANSPLANTS AND OTHER USES OF SPARE PARTS

When patients such as the pregnant woman have dead brains, a dispute over their mortal status arises, at least in part, because the dying (or already dead) individual possesses some now possibly spare parts which have life and death significance for others. Joseph Fletcher has called it a "shameful waste of human tissue" simply to let patients pass from hospital bed to coffin without tapping the vital resources remaining in their bodies.[19] But should the need for body parts for transplantation or other uses such as incubators be relevant to the issue of who is to die and who is to call them dead?

Although transplantation gets most of the publicity surrounding the responsible care and use of the new corpse, other uses are envisioned. The Uniform Anatomical Gift Act, now passed in all fifty states, specifies that a body donated under its provisions may be used for "medical or dental education, research, advancement of medical or dental science, therapy or transplantation." Some proposed uses of newly dead bodies, however, are controversial, and it must be asked whether certain ingenious techniques being developed are either morally tolerable or practically necessary.

The human body has traditionally been considered a "temple of God" and treated with sacred awe by even the most secular, and the defensive humor of first-year medical students entering the anatomy laboratory only betrays their uneasiness at treating this temple so irreverently.[20] Once again, the question of policy must be resolved: Who should authorize the use of human flesh and blood and under what circumstances?

In the early years of organ transplantation there was a sustained debate between those who wanted to treat the newly dead body as a social resource to be salvaged without explicit permission from the individual or next of kin, and those who held that bodies should be used for medical purposes only after they are explicitly given for that purpose. The gift model won the day. Now, however, as transplantation has become more routine and we are on the way toward solving the problem of rejection, organs are more valuable than ever. It is also increasingly clear that there is a persistent shortage, much of which is the result of the fact that people who have no objection in principle to having their organs used after their deaths have never made the donation formal. Because of this, various schemes such as requiring requests of the next of kin after death have become fashionable. In chapter 8 I shall look at these schemes and the reasons why they should be opposed.

Organs will have to be allocated for the foreseeable future. Although the allocation of organs on the basis of social usefulness was tried, practical and moral problems have led to a consensus in favor of the use of "medical criteria." But what, exactly, does that mean? In chapter 8 we shall also see that medical criteria may sometimes be simply social criteria in disguise. We shall also see that a policy decision needs to be made distinguishing medical usefulness and medical need. I shall develop arguments against the common wisdom that medical usefulness is the proper basis for allocating organs from the newly dead.

NATURAL DEATH AND THE INCREASE OF LIFE SPAN

All of the issues generated by the biological revolution result from new ways we have found to intervene into what is now thought of as premature death. At best we are creating opportunities to get more and more people up to what is thought of as their normal life span—perhaps to ninety or one hundred years. Simultaneously, however, biological researchers are also exploring the basic processes of aging and the notion of "dying of old age." They are beginning to question what leads to this natural death. As we enable more people to reach the normal life span for the species, we begin to think about the more ambitious possibility of tampering with that life span, of getting people to live to, say, one hundred-twenty or one hundred-fifty, if they are not struck down by disease, accident, or violence.

I close this volume with an exploration of the conceptual, moral, and public policy issues raised by this more radical revolution ahead. I shall raise conceptual questions: does it make sense any longer to refer to some deaths as "natural" or to "dying of old age"? I shall also raise moral questions: is it wrong to tamper with nature; is it ethical to begin the basic research that has the possibility of making a fundamental change in the nature of the species? I shall finally raise the policy questions: how much public and private funding should go toward this kind of research and what are its priorities in comparison with interventions to prolong the lives of persons who do not now reach the currently normal life span? These are the issues of chapter 9.

In all these discussions, certain moral principles are central. These themes underlie the arguments of this book:

1. Patients' control of decisions affecting their death and dying;
2. preservation of patients' freedom and dignity;
3. rejection of the assumption that moral policy expertise is the exclusive prerogative of technical experts;
4. substitution of the patient's agent, normally the next of kin, when the individual is unable to act;
5. modification of public policy to allow individual autonomy and dignity to the greatest extent tolerable to the moral sense of society; and
6. radical subordination of social utility to social justice and the balancing of social justice against individual autonomy.

It is strange that we have to ask whether the dying continue to have rights of their own. It is sad that at the same time individuals are winning political and legal victories for freedom and justice, they must surrender their moral autonomy to a technocratic elite. By confronting the moral and policy crisis precipitated by the biological revolution in human death and dying, we can hope to advance human freedom and justice and once again make at least some people's dying a moral experience.

A Historical Perspective on the Meaning of Death

The business of death and dying, of life in the last of it, has not always commanded the same attention from the philosopher, theologian, and political theorist that it does in the day of the biological revolution. Most so-called primitive societies, from what we know of them, had a limited perspective of death. Their myths and symbols were intimately related to the realities of the actual world, of the immediate surroundings.[21] Death was not considered a necessary attribute of the human condition.[22] Consciousness of death requires a separation of individual identity from that of the tribe. A concept of death must be the product of a long-developing cultural system, of a set of myths, rituals, and symbols giving perspective on an event modern people assume to be inevitable. To the extent that death was imagined at all by early man, it was seen as the result of evil powers inflicted by human or spiritual enemies.

When more highly structured cultures emerged with more complex cosmologies and otherworldly perspectives, death began to play a major part in the constructive symbolism of the society, and humans began the philosophical struggle to come to terms with their own deaths. From this point on, the debate dominates Eastern and Western philosophy in myriad forms—the Eastern doctrines of transmigration and ultimate release from the world,[23] for example, or the notions of the immortality of the soul found in the Egyptian *Book of the Dead*[24] and in Greek thought.[25]

The older Hebraic strand of the Judeo-Christian tradition showed remarkably little interest in the question of death. The inevitability of death in a world created by an all-powerful and benevolent suzerain was considered perplexing, true, but virtually no attention was given to the problem of human fate after worldly death. Only in the later accounts, in Ezekiel's vision of the Valley of the Dry Bones coming to life and the explicit reference to the resurrection of the dead in Daniel, were there intimations of the struggle that was to play so dominant a role in Greek and Christian thought.

In Western philosophical thought, death became a major theme, capturing the imagination of the great thinkers of the day. But in the philosophical debates of fifth and fourth century Greece (which really continue into modern times), the main concern was the period after death, not death itself or the period of dying. The great argument was whether some form of life existed after death (the view of archaic societies such as the Babylonians, and also of Homer, Pythagoras, Plato, Seneca, and the later strands of the Judeo-Christian tradition) or whether life ended in annihilation (the view suggested in Heraclitus and found more clearly in Aristotle, Lucretius, Marcus Aurelius, Averroes, Montaigne, and the eighteenth-century rationalists). Those who believed in life after death disagreed about the nature of that existence: the Eastern and Pythagorean transmigration of the soul competed with the Platonic immortality of the soul, and the Judeo-Christian resurrection of the body.[26]

The premodern philosophical mind found death fascinating because of its cosmological significance for the human's relation to the transcendent, but it also devoted thought to the social and ethical problems of death and dying.[27] Questions on the meaning of death and the appropriate care of the dying often arose in the context of rather mundane matters of governmental and social relations. Aristotle discussed the killing of deformed infants while instructing the legislator how to govern well.[28] He saw suicide as an act related not fundamentally to oneself but to the state.[29]

In the *Phaedo*, Socrates ponders the absolute prohibition on suicide, concluding that although the philosopher is one who is ready and willing to die, he must await God's call. The *Republic* began by pondering the fate of man after death and questioned the expansion of "strange and new-fangled" names and treatments for disease. Plato saw Herodicus as the corrupter of the tradition of Asclepius:

> But Herodicus, being a trainer, and himself of a sickly constitution, by a combination of training and doctoring found out a way of torturing first and chiefly himself, and secondly the rest of the world . . . by the invention of lingering death; for he had a mortal disease which he perpetually tended, and as recovery was out of the question, he passed his entire life as a valetudinarian; he could do nothing but attend upon himself, and he was in constant torment whenever he departed in anything from his usual regimen, and so dying hard, by the help of science he struggled on to old age.[30]

In contrast, Plato had Socrates say of Asclepius:

> bodies which disease had penetrated through and through he would not have attempted to cure by gradual processes of evacuation and infusion: he did not want to lengthen out good-for-nothing lives, or to have weak fathers begetting weaker sons;—if a man was not able to live in the ordinary way he had no business to cure him[31]

What is striking is the oblique treatment of the subject in classical literature. Epicureans and Stoics, who find so little to agree on, seem quite compatible on the subject of suicide, although they approve it for quite different reasons. Marcus Aurelius and Seneca, especially, make suicide a major theme, a release from the burdens of the world: "For mere living is not good, but living well. Accordingly, the wise man will live as long as he ought, not as long as he can."[32] And though for the Stoic, suicide may offer solace to a body tormented with disease, there is yet no specific development of the ethics of the treatment of the dying, such as will be seen in, say, the Roman Catholic moral theology of the sixteenth century and later.

In the Middle Ages a series of handbooks on the *ars moriendi*, the art of dying, began to signal a shift in attention to the moral and social problems of the dying. The books were part of a movement that also gave rise to a series of hospices for the care of the dying at religious centers throughout Europe. (These are the historical precursors of the present day hospices such as St. Christopher's in England and the hundreds of American hospices that have emerged in the last decade.) There remained, however, a distinct focus on preparing properly for the transition to the world beyond, to the life of real and everlasting significance. It was the psychology of dying rather than the social and ethical aspects of death and dying in this world that were important.

The Contemporary Interest in Death

The modern spirit in the West, characterized so clearly by Max Weber and more recently by Talcott Parsons as intraworldly, instrumental, and activist, has a new attitude toward death.[33] Modern people (and Americans particularly) tend to focus on the active and rational control of day-to-day events. This orientation is basic both to technological society and to the biomedical attack on death.

It cannot exactly be said that the total annihilation view of death has won out. There are still spokesmen for existence after death: Spinoza, Leibniz, Kant, Fichte, Schelling, Bergson, and, in the twentieth century, Whitehead, Kierkegaard, or Marcel, as well as most interpreters of orthodox Christianity. Still, concern for what follows this earthly life has become less pressing to secular people. Rather, we seem to be fascinated by the rational solution of worldly problems, including the problem of death. This activist approach to nature produced the biological revolution, which in turn has made possible the attack on death. But there are at least two additional reasons for the current interest in public policy for dealing with death and its problems.

First, as with ecology, civil rights, overpopulation, or any other cause, many deep-seated and unmet needs must be involved when a topic attracts wide public concern. People are seeking ultimate answers about the nature of the human species and the meaning of life in the face of the social crises and chaos of the past decade. As we come closer to controlling our biological processes through new biomedical technological breakthroughs, death stands as an ultimate abyss, a final unknown. Medical research has conquered a few infectious diseases—smallpox, salmonella, syphilis, polio, pellagra, and even the plague—but not one piece of medical research has ever told us a thing about the meaning of death. It stands before us as something completely outside the scientific point of view, probably more awe-inspiring than ever before.

Thus death is both an enemy to be conquered by our activist faith in human ability to solve problems and an unknown of infinite proportions. There is in our culture a simultaneous obsession with the phenomenon of death and a compulsion to conceal it. To use the religious term, death is taboo. This concurrent preoccupation with and avoidance of the subject of death reveals that even the most secularized of us still treats death as a sacred event, and as an ultimate dread. To bring the subject into the open will permit profound questions to be raised, thereby giving perspective on our situation and allowing us to deal with the fundamental problems facing our society.

Second, we are in the midst of not only a biological revolution but also a social one that began with the rise of individualism. This movement appeared in embryo in the fourteenth century, grew among the radical religious sectarians and spiritualists of the sixteenth century, and reached maturity among the liberal political philosophies of the eighteenth century. The banners of personal freedom and the right of individuals to hold and act on their own values were advanced by political revolutions of eighteenth-century France and America. The instrumental activism that spawned our technological society has also produced the social egalitarianism that now resists vesting authority over life and death in the medical specialist.

This book should be seen then, in relation to these twin revolutions, the biological and the social. Death is of interest in part because it offers people—ordinary people— their last chance to express their human potential to determine their own destinies. It is not a belated contribution to the philosophical debate about the possibility and nature of a life after death. It is not another exploration of the psychology of the dying. Understanding the dying process through social science techniques is part of the intense modern drive to grasp and rationalize experience in this world; it may well contribute to the humane care of the dying, although this is an art that cannot entirely be reduced to a science. To the extent that it can be learned, however, there are others who have addressed the psychological issues.

Nor will this book be a theology of death. Death as a sacred event will always be subject to theological analysis. Although this volume may be seen by some as a medical book, my intention is to deal with ethics, philosophy, sociology, law, and public policy—and with people first and foremost. My concern is our struggle for freedom and justice in a world increasingly moved by a technological priesthood. I want to probe the new social and ethical problems of death and dying that have been generated by those revolutions.

The questions at stake are, as I have said, fundamentally philosophical or ethical. That they arise in a medical context should not lead anyone to conclude that they are the exclusive purview of the scientific expert. They are in but not of the realm of science. I shall attempt to clarify the issues on a theoretical level, then proceed with matters of practical policy. This approach goes against the scholarly tradition of the scientific era, in which it once was fashionable to say that such pursuits were morally neutral, tools to be put to good or evil purpose by others. There is a certain naive simplicity about this view that is attractive to scientific minds who would just as soon skirt the complex ethical issues. It is true that the same atomic theory produces the bomb and potential medical cures. The same genetic theory permits selective change in a fetus's genetic code to avoid a potentially fatal genetic disease or to produce a monstrosity. The same technology lets us save a drowning child whose breathing has stopped and prolong the dying of a semicomatose octogenarian whose time has long since come.

Yet the claim of the "pure scientist" (including the philosophers and policy research- ers) that scientific facts can be isolated from the moral judgments necessary to make use of the facts is no longer tenable.[34] In the first place, ethical and other values are essential ingredients in what is normally considered the purely investigatory stage, the mere gathering of data and testing of hypotheses. Values are involved at every step: in selecting a significant problem for study, forming meaningful hypotheses, choosing methods, selecting analytical tests (levels of significance, for instance), and, most im- portant, deciding what is worth reporting. All scientific investigators must also decide at the research stage whether their proposed research is morally tolerable, whatever the morality of the use made of the results. The research process itself is therefore not morally neutral, any more than are the technological applications of that research.

In addition, new technologies seem to feed back into the basic value orientations of the culture. In the Judeo-Christian tradition, people are duty-bound to "have dominion over the earth and subdue it"—to have what might be called a control mentality, which has generated the technological revolution and in turn is spurred on by technological progress. Technology feeds and feeds on the control mentality. People are no longer able to return to the simple solutions of the past. They are no longer able to participate in a simple religious healing ceremony supported by their communities or to let nature do its own healing without their domination. Cannon's *Wisdom of the Body* has been superseded by the wisdom of the technocracy.

Second, technology shifts the bulk of decision making to those who have technolog- ical expertise. Not long ago anyone could decide to conceive a child or brew an herbal tea or walk off into the wilderness. But now few couples would think of going through a pre- and post-natal period without following doctor's orders. We have lost almost entirely the art of self-medication, ceding these operations to the medical priests. Now countless hopelessly ill and suffering patients literally cannot avoid death-prolonging intervention. This may occur, ironically, while others who desperately need medical interventions lack the social and economic keys to unlock the chambers where tech- nology's priests practice their life-saving craft. If technology does nothing more, it radically shifts the locus of decision making.

If it is the case that the biological sciences as well as the analysis of philosophy, theology, and the social sciences cannot really be value free, but only "value disguis- ing," then we not only can, but must carry our discussion on to the crucial policy questions and make at least a first effort to form some answers. Whether readers agree with those answers, they will at least know the framework of values that went into the analysis of the more theoretical questions. Those questions are of interest not only because of the literally life and death issues that are at stake, but also because hidden among them are the even more fundamental issues society must face: the nature of the human, the nature of authority, and the nature of our last quest for freedom in a technological society.

1 | Defining Death Anew

Technical and Ethical Problems

_____

At 5:41 on the morning of Sunday, November 10, 1985, Philadelphia Flyers' star goaltender Pelle Lindbergh drove his $117,000 red Porsche into a concrete wall in front of a Somerdale, New Jersey, school. He and two companions were trapped in the car. Lindbergh suffered massive injuries to the brain and spinal cord, a broken hip, jaw, and two bones in his left leg. *The Washington Post* ran a story the next day with the headline "Flyers Goalie Lindbergh Is Declared Brain Dead." The same day the *New York Times* reported that Lindbergh "was brain dead and had no hope for recovery." The coverage of the story for the next two days continued to refer to him as "brain dead," yet spoke of him as "being kept alive on life-support systems," as "hovering near death," and as having "no chance to survive." One account reported that he was declared "clinically dead" on Monday. Finally, in stories dated Tuesday, two days after the accident and the apparent declaration of "brain death," it was reported that surgeons removed his organs for transplant "at his family's request." The *Times* reported on Wednesday that he "died yesterday afternoon at the conclusion of a five hour operation to remove his organs for transplant."[1]

What can it mean to say that a person is declared "brain dead" on Sunday morning, "clinically dead" on Monday, and "dead" on Tuesday afternoon? If he really was not dead until Tuesday afternoon, what caused his death? Was it the removal of his vital organs? Did surgeons kill him when they removed them?

Were the writers of these stories aware of the fact that the state of New Jersey had not passed legislation authorizing the pronouncement of death based on brain criteria? Were they aware that one New Jersey court case involving a homicide ruled that the victim who was "brain dead" did not expire until after a respirator was stopped?[2] Were they purposely calling Lindbergh "alive" because they thought there was not adequate legal basis in the state of New Jersey to call someone dead because he has a dead brain? Did they contemplate the possibility that he could have been taken from the hospital in New Jersey across the nearby state line to a hospital in Pennsylvania where there is statutory authorization for pronouncing death based on the lack of brain function? If he had been moved, would Lindbergh then have died the moment he crossed the state line? And, what would have happened if he had been returned to New Jersey after being pronounced dead?

Two decades ago, scholars and clinicians began thinking seriously about whether persons without brain function should be considered alive or dead, but society still seems confused about the definition of death. For most of human history, of course, people have not been concerned with this issue at all. They have had a clear enough idea to be able to transact the business of death: to cover the corpse, bury the dead, mourn, read wills, and transfer authority. But now that technology permits us to treat the body organ by organ, cell by cell, we are forced to develop a more precise understanding of what it means to call a person dead. At the same time, in the contemporary world, these decisions involve a complex interaction between the technical aspects (the business involving stethoscopes, electroencephalograms, and intricately determined medical diagnoses and prognoses) and the more fundamental philosophical considerations that determine whether a person in a particular condition should be called dead.

The debate over the definition of death has become increasingly heated in recent years because a great deal is at stake. But even the meaning of the word *definition* is ambiguous. Both empirical and philosophical questions are involved. Some of the issues, for example, are matters of neurological fact and as such, and within limits, are appropriately interpreted by medical experts. Important though these kinds of judgment are, however, they can be called definitions only in an operational sense. They must be separated from those issues that probe the meaning of life (including such ethical or religious questions as when we should begin treating people the way we treat dead people). The philosophical issue that needs to be defined is: What is lost at the point of death that is essential to human nature? It is only by carefully differentiating among the various levels of the debate, then, that we can hope to avoid serious philosophical errors.

Four separate levels in this debate must be distinguished. First, there is the purely formal analysis of the term *death*, an analysis that gives the structure and specifies the framework that must be given content. Second, there is the concept of death, which attempts to fill the content of the formal definition. At this level the question is: What is so essentially significant about life that its loss is termed death? Third, there is the question of the locus of death: Where in the organism ought one to look to determine whether death has occurred? Fourth, one must ask the question of the criteria of death: What technical tests must be applied at the locus to determine if an individual is living or dead?

Serious mistakes have been made in slipping from one level of the debate to another and in presuming that expertise on one level necessarily implies expertise on another. These problems began to emerge early in the debate. They can be seen in the historically important Report of the Ad Hoc Committee of the Harvard Medical School to Examine the Definition of Brain Death, entitled "A Definition of Irreversible Coma."[3] The title suggests that the committee members intend simply to report empirical measures that are criteria for predicting an irreversible coma. Yet the name of the committee seems to point more to the question of locus. The committee was established to examine the death of the brain. The implication is that the empirical indications of irreversible coma are also indications of "brain death." We now know that to be mistaken even at the empirical level, but the committee's confusions were even more serious. In the first sentence of the report the committee members claim that their "primary purpose is to define irreversible coma as a new criterion for death." They have now shifted so that they are interested in "death." They must be presuming a philosophical concept of death—that a person in an irreversible coma should be considered dead—but they neither argue this nor state it as a presumption.

Even the composition of the Harvard committee signals some uncertainty of purpose. If empirical criteria were the principal concern, the inclusion of nonscientists on the panel was strange. If the philosophical concept of death was the main concern, medically trained people were overrepresented. As it happened, the committee did not deal at all with the conceptual matter of what it really means to be dead, yet that was the important policy issue raised in the shift to a brain-oriented definition of death. The committee and its interpreters have confused the questions at different levels.

The Formal Definition of Death

A strictly formal definition of death might be the following:

Death means a complete change in the status of a living entity characterized by the irreversible loss of those characteristics that are essentially significant to it.

Such a definition would apply equally well to a human being, a nonhuman animal, a plant, an organ, a cell, or even metaphorically to a society or to any temporally limited entity like a research project, a sports event, or a language. To define the death of a human being, we must recognize its essential human characteristics. It is quite inadequate to limit the discussion to the death of the heart or the brain.

In fact it should be clear that terms such as *brain death* and *heart death* are systematically ambiguous. They can mean the death of the individual based on the irreversible destruction of the brain or heart. But they can also mean the death of the organ in a still living person. Since the living person with a dead heart or brain may be treated quite differently legally, ethically, and psychologically from a dead person, the terms *brain death* and *heart death* should no longer be used. In this volume when I want to refer to the death of a person (as a whole), I shall refer to the death of that person based on brain (or heart) criteria. When I simply want to refer to the irreversible destruction of the brain or heart function, I shall use that language, avoiding completely the confusing terms *brain death* and *heart death*.

Henry Beecher, the distinguished physician who chaired the Harvard committee that proposed a definition of irreversible coma, said that "at whatever level we choose . . . , it is an arbitrary decision."[4] But he went on: "It is best to choose a level where although the brain is dead, usefulness of other organs is still present." Now, clearly he was no longer making an "arbitrary decision," but one based on benefits for policy. Like the rest of us, he realized that death already has a well-established meaning. And though it is the task of the current debate to clarify the meaning of death for a few rare and difficult cases, much of it in fact has taken place because of its important implication for policy.

And no matter how tenuous some of the fine distinctions of this debate may seem, the long-range consequences for policymaking as well as for individual action hinge on its outcome. For example, socially we behave in a different way when we decide that a living person has become a corpse, adopting a newly appropriate manner that can be called death behavior. Some of the things we do are connected with the traditional rituals surrounding death. We pronounce death, go into mourning, begin preparing for a funeral, conduct an autopsy, and read a will. But other actions now include making decisions introduced by the technological revolution, such as allowing organs to be removed that could not have been removed earlier. In addition, death changes the roles of others as well as their actions, as is evident in the example where Lyndon Johnson told of the awful feeling of being elevated to the presidency upon hearing of the death of President Kennedy. In effect, we are saying that the dead person has so changed in essence that entirely different behavior is not only permitted but required.

We could of course decide that there is no one point where all or most of these behaviors are appropriate. In an earlier time when many critical bodily changes took place in rapid succession there would have been no practical purpose in differentiating the moment at which mourning should begin, organs could be removed, or transfer of political office should take place. Our new technical capacities, however, can now stretch out the dying process. Indeed, Robert S. Morison argues that death must be viewed as a process. "The life of a complex vertebrate like man," he has written, "is not a clearly defined entity with sharp discontinuities at both ends."[5] If that is true, then it may no longer have any meaning or purpose to determine what death means and when it occurs.

However, it is possible that society has good reason for retaining the notion that there is a quantum change in the status of individuals at a fixed moment and that at that moment a whole series of behaviors becomes legitimate. Leon Kass argues in a reply to Morison that, while dying is often a continuous process, death itself is not:

> What dies is the organism as a whole. It is this death, the death of the individual human being, that is important for physicians and for the community, not the "death" of organs or cells, which are mere parts.[6]

Still, we must assess carefully whether all the behavior we normally associate with death really should continue to be linked to the decision to call someone dead. It is important to realize, for instance, that stopping medical treatment need not be directly linked to that judgment. Some kinds of treatment might well be stopped at a much earlier stage. Even conservative thinkers, traditional Roman Catholic medical ethicists for example, consider it appropriate to stop certain procedures—especially those labeled heroic, extraordinary, or simply useless—before an individual dies. This certainly is not the same as saying the patient is dead. Others hold that treatment should continue until the patient is indeed considered dead.

There may also be good reasons for continuing a treatment after death. It is done routinely when there is a need to preserve organs or when some other use of a still-respiring cadaver is contemplated. The Uniform Anatomical Gift Act authorizes the use of the dead body not only for transplantation, but also for other therapeutic uses as well as for research and teaching. As I have shown, some people think it is appropriate to maintain treatment of pregnant women who have irreversible loss of brain function in order, in effect, to use the corpse as an incubator.[7]

The reports in the Lindbergh case are ambiguous. One interpretation is that Lindbergh in fact died when his brain function was destroyed. If that situation pertained, clinicians, with the permission of the next of kin, could reasonably maintain respiratory support and other bodily functions for the purpose of maintaining organs. Treatment, then, would be continued on the corpse of a deceased person. Many people discussing the case (including the reporters covering it) apparently did not adopt this position, however. They continued to speak in the present tense about Mr. Lindbergh. They talked of him being kept alive. Moreover, according to reports, physicians did not pronounce death until after the heart was removed, implying that they were working within the traditional concept of death based on loss of heart function. Legally they probably had to adopt this position if they believed they were in a jurisdiction that had not authorized death pronouncement based on brain function loss.

In a much earlier case that raised similar questions, a man named Bruce Tucker was left without brain function in a Richmond, Virginia, hospital following a fall.[8] In this and similar cases the physicians turned off the respirator and waited until heart function stopped before pronouncing death, only then authorizing the removal of organs. In a jurisdiction that bases death on loss of heart function there may be no other course. That policy may have the practical consequences of exposing transplantable organs to some risk of damage. The only alternative short of changing the basis for death pronouncement, however, would be to legalize organ removal from living, permanently comatose or vegetative patients under certain conditions.

The only way to answer important, practical policy questions such as these is to ask directly what it is that is essential to being human, what it is that morally requires us to treat a human being as alive. Answering those questions and determining when it is appropriate to treat someone as dead will provide what I call the concept of death.[9]

The Concept of Death

To ask what is essentially significant to a human being is a philosophical question— a question of ethical and other values. Many features have been suggested to be the one that makes human beings unique—their opposable thumbs, their possession of rational souls, their ability to form cultures and manipulate symbol systems, their upright posture, their being created in the image of God, and so on. Any concept of death will depend directly upon how one evaluates these qualities. Four choices seem to me to cover the most plausible approaches.

IRREVERSIBLE LOSS OF FLOW OF VITAL FLUIDS

At first it would appear that the irreversible cessation of heart and lung activity would represent a simple and straightforward statement of the traditional understanding of the concept of death in Western culture. Yet upon reflection this cannot be. If patients permanently lose control of their lungs and are supported by mechanical respirators, they are still living persons as long as they continue to get oxygen. If modern technology produced an efficient, compact heart-lung machine capable of being carried on the back or in a pocket, people using such devices would not be considered dead, even though both heart and lungs were permanently nonfunctioning. Some might consider such a technological person an affront to human dignity; some might argue that such a device should never be connected to a human; but even they would, in all likelihood, agree that such people were alive.

What the traditional concept of death centered on was not the heart and lungs as such, but the flow of vital fluids, that is, the breath and the blood. This movement of liquids and gases at the cellular and organismic level is a distinguishing characteristic of living things. According to this view, the human organism, like other living organisms, dies when there is an irreversible cessation of the flow of these fluids.

IRREVERSIBLE LOSS OF THE SOUL FROM THE BODY

There is a long-standing tradition, sometimes called vitalism, that holds the essence of humans to be independent of the chemical reactions and electrical forces that account for the flow of the bodily fluids. Aristotle and the Greeks spoke of the soul as the animating principle of life. The human being, according to Aristotle, differs from other living creatures in possessing a rational soul as well as vegetative and animal souls. This idea later became especially pronounced in the dualistic philosophy of gnosticism, where salvation was seen as the escape of the enslaved soul from the body. Christianity in its Pauline and later Western forms shares the view that the soul is an essential element in the living human. While Paul and some later theologian-scholars including Erasmus and Luther sometimes held a tripartite anthropology that included spirit as well as body and soul, a central element in all their thought seems to be animation of the body by a noncorporeal force. In Christianity, however, in contrast with the gnostic tradition, the body is a crucial element—not a prison from which the soul escapes, but a significant part of the person. This will become important later in this discussion. The soul remains a central element in the concept of the human in most folk religions today.

The departure of the soul might be seen by believers as occurring at about the time that the fluids stop flowing. But it would be a mistake to equate these two concepts of death, as according to the first fluid stops from natural, if unexplained, causes, and death means nothing more than that stopping of the flow, which is essential to being treated as alive. According to the second view, the fluid stops flowing at the time the soul departs, and it stops because the soul is no longer present. Here the essential thing is the loss of the soul, not the loss of the fluid flow.

THE IRREVERSIBLE LOSS OF THE CAPACITY FOR BODILY INTEGRATION

In the debate between those who held a traditional religious notion of the animating force of the soul and those who had the more naturalistic concept of the irreversible loss of the flow of bodily fluids, the trend to secularism and empiricism made the loss of fluid flow more and more the operative concept of death in society. But human intervention in the dying process through cardiac pacemakers, respirators, intravenous medication and feeding, and extravenous purification of the blood has forced a sharper examination of the naturalistic concept of death. It is now possible to manipulate the dying process so that some parts of the body cease to function while other parts are maintained indefinitely. This has given rise to disagreements within the naturalistic camp itself. In its report, the Harvard Ad Hoc Committee to Examine the Definition of Brain Death gave two reasons for its undertaking. First, the committee members argued that improvements in resuscitative and supportive measures sometimes had only partial success, putting a great burden on "patients who suffer permanent loss of intellect, on their families, on the hospitals, and on those in need of hospital beds already occupied by these comatose patients." Second, they argued that "obsolete criteria for the definition of death can lead to controversy in obtaining organs for transplantation."

These points have proved more controversial than they may have seemed at the time. In the first place, the only consideration of the patient among the reasons given for changing the definition of death was the suggestion that a comatose patient can feel a "great burden." That is somewhat puzzling since most people would hold that comatose persons do not have the capacity to perceive or to suffer burdens. Perhaps there is an "assault on the memory of the individual" or an "affront to dignity," but it is not a burden in the straightforward sense.

If the individual himself or herself cannot perceive burden, then all the benefits of the change in definition will come to other individuals or to society at large. It is a strange argument to hold that people who were previously considered alive should now be considered dead solely because it is useful to others to consider them such. With regard to the committee's first reason for undertaking a redefinition, then, all the benefits of the change in definition will come to other individuals.

The introduction of transplant concerns into the discussion has attracted particular criticism. Paul Ramsey, among others, has argued against making the issue of transplant a reason for changing the definition of death: "If no person's death should for this purpose be hastened, then the definition of death should not for this purpose be updated, or the procedures for stating that a man has died be revised as a means of affording easier access to organs."[10]

The need for organs cannot be a legitimate reason for adopting a new concept of death. This does not mean that the search for a new concept of death must be abandoned or even that the need for organs is not a relevant factor. Henry Beecher argued:

"There is indeed a life-saving potential in the new definition, for, when accepted, it will lead to greater availability than formerly of essential organs in viable condition, for transplantation, and thus countless lives now inevitably lost will be saved."[11]

When he said this is one of the reasons for accepting a new definition, he made an ambiguous statement. If he meant that it is a reason for adopting the new concept, he was making an unacceptable compromise with the value of the individual human being. If, however, he meant that this is a reason for undertaking the task of philosophical examination of the meaning of death, that is something quite different. It would indeed be morally outrageous if "countless lives" were lost simply because society was too lazy to undertake the philosophical task of reexamining and clarifying its precise understanding of death.

Nevertheless, this reason for undertaking the reexamination of the concept of death must still be subordinated to the primary one. Just as it is wrong to treat a living person as dead, it is morally wrong to treat dead people as alive. It is certainly morally relevant that others may benefit from a clarity of definition. This is true even without consideration of transplantation and is a legitimate reason for undertaking the reexamination. I would argue, however, that even if no one were to benefit, it would still be a moral affront to the dignity of the individual to treat a corpse as if it were a living person.

We now must consider whether concepts of death that focus on the flow of fluids or the departure of the soul are philosophically appropriate. The reason that the question arises as a practical matter is fear of a "false positive" determination that human life is present. There are several ways of handling doubtful cases. Many would argue that when there is moral or philosophical doubt about whether someone is dead, it would be (morally) safer to act as if the individual were alive. An intermediate position is that we may follow a course of action whose morality is in doubt if (and only if) it is more likely to be than not. Another position, called probabilism, offers the most leeway, holding that a "probable opinion" may be followed even though the contrary opinion is also probable or even more probable. In the case under consideration, the probabilist could consider the individual dead even though moral doubt, even perhaps serious doubt, remained. Holders of the more rigorous positions would argue that we should take the morally safer course and consider the person alive even though the heart, lungs, and fluid flow had permanently stopped functioning.

Even the probabilist, however, traditionally has placed restrictions on legitimizing actions supported by a probable opinion, for instance, when a life may be saved by taking one of the probable courses of action. This is clearly the sort of case involved in trying to decide whether to treat an individual as dead.

Thus, when modifying our traditional concept of death to pronounce dead some individuals who would under older concepts be considered alive (that is, those with heart and lung but no brain function), the problem of moral doubt must be resolved. Three basic approaches can be used. First, one may argue that there is really no doubt to deal with, since the older concepts of death, which depend on fluid flow or departure of the soul, are now so implausible that they are not even viable candidates. This seems a difficult argument to sustain in view of the apparent continued acceptance of precisely these concepts by some portion of the public. Even the physicians in the Lindbergh case apparently harbored some lingering doubts about the newer concept, because they did not pronounce death when the brain had irreversibly ceased functioning, but only after they had turned off the respirator. Several state legislatures have, in fact, rejected brain-oriented alternatives.

Second, one might reject the exception to the probabilist rule in cases where a life may be saved. Since many would argue that the newer concepts of death are morally probable, even more probable than the older concepts, simply rejecting the exception in life-saving cases would justify the use of the newer concepts. This seems morally risky, however. We should continue to err in the direction of protecting the lives of individual patients, particularly those who are helpless, in need of protection, or from ethnic and income groups traditionally ill-treated by the health care system.

The real problem with treating the concept of death debate as a problem of moral doubt is that it assumes that only one moral norm—preserve life wherever possible—should be applied. Thus it is hard to avoid the conclusion that we should err on the side of assuming that the doubtfully living person is alive. There are, however, also sound moral reasons for treating individuals with no brain function as if they were dead. Benefit to others is one such reason, but the crucial point is that it is an affront to the memory of individual persons to treat them as alive if they are dead.

This leads to a third solution, the one that is most plausible: to treat the situation as one of perplexed conscience. There are two relevant and important moral principles at stake: preservation of an individual life and preservation of the dignity of an individual by being able to distinguish a dead person from a living one. The introduction of a moral obligation to treat the dead as dead leaves one perplexed. It creates moral pressures in each direction. The defenders of the older concepts, which may lead to false pronouncements of living, must defend their action as well. It seems to me that only when such positive moral pressure is introduced on both sides of the argument can we plausibly overcome the claim that we must take the morally safer course. We must consider that it may be not only right to call persons dead, but also wrong to call them alive. This will still mean minimizing the life-saving exception, but at least at this point there will be a positive moral argument for doing so. It is, thus, quite difficult to justify any divergence from the older, more traditional concepts of death, but the case for a neurologically centered concept can be made.

At first it would appear that the irreversible loss of brain activity is the concept of death held by those no longer satisfied with the vitalistic concept of the departure of the soul or the animalistic concept of the irreversible cessation of fluid flow. This is why the name *brain death* is frequently, if ambiguously, given to the new proposals, but the term is unfortunate for two reasons.

First, as we have seen, it is not the heart and lungs as such that are essentially significant but rather the vital functions—the flow of fluids—that we believe according to the best empirical human physiology to be associated with these organs. An "artificial brain" is not possible at present, but a walking, talking, thinking individual who had one would certainly be considered living. It is not the collection of physical tissues called the brain, but rather their functions—consciousness; motor control; sensory feeling; ability to reason; control over bodily functions including respiration and circulation; major integrating reflexes controlling blood pressure, ion levels, and pupil size; and so forth—that are given essential significance by those who advocate adoption of a new concept of death or clarification of the old one. In short they see the body's capacity for integrating its functions as the essentially significant indication of life. [12] Although there are occasional suggestions that it is the anatomical structure of the brain that is important, [13] now almost anyone arguing for a brain-oriented definition of death will accept that it is not technically the death of the brain that is critical, but the irreversible loss of the functions normally carried on by the brain.

Second, as I suggested earlier, we are not interested in the death of particular cells, organs, or organ systems, but in the death of the person as a whole—the point at which the person as a whole undergoes a quantum change through the loss of characteristics held to be essentially significant—and so terms such as brain death or heart death should be avoided. At the public policy level, this has practical consequences. A statute adopted in Kansas in 1970 specifically referred to "alternative definitions of death" and said that they are "to be used for all purposes in this state . . . ." According to this language, which resulted from talking of brain and heart death, a person in Kansas could simultaneously be dead according to one definition and alive according to another. When a distinction must be made, it should be made directly on the basis of the philosophical significance of the functions mentioned above rather than on the importance of the tissue collection called the brain. For purposes of simplicity I shall use the phrase *the capacity for bodily integration* to refer to the total list of integrating mechanisms possessed by the body. A case for these mechanisms being the ones that are essential to humanness can indeed be made. Humans are more than the flowing of fluids. They are complex, integrated organisms with capacities for internal regulation. With and only with these integrating mechanisms is homo sapiens really human.

There appear to be two general aspects to this concept of what is essentially significant: first, a capacity for integrating one's internal bodily environment (which is done for the most part unconsciously through highly complex homeostatic, feedback mechanisms) and, second, a capacity for integrating one's self, including one's body, with the social environment through consciousness, which permits interaction with other persons. Together these offer a more profound understanding of the nature of the human than does the simple flow of bodily fluids. Whether it is a more profound concept than that which focuses simply on the presence or absence of the soul, it is clearly a very different one. The ultimate test between the two is that of meaningfulness and plausibility. For many in modern secular society, the concept of loss of capacity for bodily integration seems a more meaningful and accurate description of the essential significance of the human and of what is lost at the time of death. According to this view, when individuals lose all of these "truly vital" capacities we should call them dead and behave accordingly.

At this point the debate may just about have been won by the defenders of the neurologically oriented concept. For the most part the public sees the main dispute as being between partisans of the functions of the heart and the brain. Even cases and the major articles in the scientific and philosophical journals have for the most part confined themselves to contrasting these two rather crudely defined positions. If these were the only alternatives, the discussion probably would be nearing an end. There are, however, some critical questions that began to emerge about a decade ago, provoked by the recognition that it may be possible in rare cases for a person to have the higher brain centers destroyed but still retain lower brain functions including spontaneous respiration.[14] This has led to the question of just what brain functions are essentially significant to man's nature. A fourth major concept of death thus emerges.

THE IRREVERSIBLE LOSS OF THE CAPACITY FOR CONSCIOUSNESS OR SOCIAL INTERACTION

The fourth major alternative for a concept of death draws on the characteristics of the third concept and has often been confused with it. Henry Beecher offers a summary of what he considers to be essential to man's nature: ". . . the individual's personality, his conscious life, his uniqueness, his capacity for remembering, judging, reasoning, acting, enjoying, worrying, and so on."[15]

Beecher goes on immediately to ask the anatomical question of locus. He concludes that these functions reside in the brain and that when the brain no longer functions, the individual is dead. What is remarkable is that Beecher's list, with the possible exception of "uniqueness," is composed entirely of functions explicitly related to consciousness and the capacity to relate to one's social environment through interaction with others. All the functions that give the capacity to integrate one's internal bodily environment through unconscious, complex, homeostatic reflex mechanisms—respiration, circulation, and major integrating reflexes—are omitted. In fact, when asked what was essentially significant to man's living, Beecher replied simply, "Consciousness."

Thus a fourth possible concept of death is the irreversible loss of the capacity for mental or social functioning. If a group of hypothetical human beings had irreversibly lost the capacity for consciousness or social interaction, they would have lost the essential character of humanness and, according to this definition, they would be dead even if they had capacity for integration of bodily function.

Even if one moves to the so-called higher functions and away from the mere capacity to integrate bodily functions through reflex mechanisms, it is still not clear precisely what is ultimately valued as essential. We must have a more careful specification of mental or social function. Are these two capacities synonymous and, if not, what is the relationship between them? Before taking up that question, I must first make clear what is meant by capacity.

The Meaning of Capacity

Holders of this concept of death and related concepts of the human essence specifically do not say that individuals must be valued by others in order to be human. This would place life at the mercy of other human beings who may well be cruel or insensitive.

Nor does this concept imply that the essence of humanness is the fact of social interaction with others, as this would also place a person at the mercy of others. The infant raised in complete isolation from other human contact would still be human, provided that the child retained the capacity for social interaction. This view of what is essentially significant to humanness makes no quantitative or qualitative judgments. It need not lead to the view that those who have more capacity for social integration are more human. The concepts of life and death are essentially bipolar, threshhold concepts. People should either be treated as living or they should not.

One of the real dangers of shifting from the third concept of death to the fourth is that the fourth, in focusing exclusively on the capacity for mental or social function, lends itself much more readily to quantitative and qualitative considerations. When the focus is on the complete capacity for bodily integration, including the ability of the body to carry out spontaneous respiratory activity and major reflexes, it is quite easy to maintain that if any such integrating function is present the person is alive. But when the question begins to be, "What kinds of integrating capacity are really significant?" one finds oneself on the slippery slope of evaluating different kinds of consciousness or social interaction. If consciousness is what counts, does a long-term, catatonic schizophrenic or a patient with extreme senile dementia really have the capacity for consciousness? To position oneself for such a slide down the slope of evaluating the degree of capacity for social interaction is extremely dangerous. It seems to me morally obligatory to stay off the slopes.

Specifying Mental and Social Function

Precisely what are the functions considered to be ultimately significant to human life according to this concept? There are several possibilities.

Rationality. The capacity for rationality is one candidate. The human capacity for reasoning is so unique and important that some would suggest it is the critical element in human nature. But certainly infants lack any such capacity, and they are considered living human beings.

Nor is possession of the potential for reasoning what is important. Including potential might resolve the problem of infants, but it does not explain why those who have no potential for rationality (such as the permanently backward psychotic or the senile individual) are considered to be humanly living in a real if not full sense and to be entitled to the protection of civil and moral law.

There is some confusion here because some philosophers are inclined to make a great deal out of labeling some human beings "persons.." Their view seems to be that among those who are living human beings some are persons.[16] Persons are those who can reason, manipulate symbol systems, or otherwise partake in moral discourse. In this narrow, technical sense persons are seen by the proponents of this usage as morally in a different category from other living humans. For them a person apparently is a rightsbearing human being by definition while some other humans are not.

I have consistently avoided this usage. Whenever I use the term *person*, it is synonymous with living human beings, and I leave open the question of whether all living humans are equally bearers of rights. In pressing the meaningfulness of the definition of death debate, however, I imply that it is plausible to think of all living human beings as standing in a moral position different from that of those who are dead. To wit, living human beings deserve to be treated differently from those who are dead, as subject to the moral and legal protections of the society such as those granted by the Constitution. They are individuals for whom death behaviors are not yet appropriate. That leaves entirely open the questions of whether there is some subgroup of living humans who have additional moral status and why they would be given that status, whether it be because they have the capacity to reason, to manipulate symbol systems, or to generate claims. It strikes me that it is hard to defend the position that some such subgroup exists, but that is not a problem for a discussion of the definitions of life and death.

Consciousness. Consciousness is a second candidate for that critical function that qualifies one to be treated as living. If the rationalist tradition is reflected in the previous notion, then the empiricist philosophical tradition seems to be represented in the emphasis on consciousness. What may be of central significance is the capacity for experience. This would include the infant and the individual who lacks the capacity for rationality, and it focuses attention on the capacity for sensory awareness, summarized as consciousness. Yet, this is a very individualistic understanding of the human's nature. It describes what is essentially significant to the human life without any reference to other human beings.

Personal Identity. A third possibility has been proposed by philosophers Michael B. Green and Daniel Wikler[17] and has been considered by the President's Commission.[18] They argue that it is personal identity that is critical in deciding when a person is dead. Their position is that "a given person ceases to exist with the destruction of whatever processes there are which normally underlie that person's psychological continuity and connectedness."[19]

They go on to argue against my position. They suggest that I am making an essentially moral argument for a so-called higher-brain conception of death. In this they are certainly correct. I have repeatedly claimed that all that is at stake in the public policy debate over the definition of death is determining when death behaviors are appropriate.

They claim that this is "ontological gerrymandering," or arranging a concept of death to fit moral judgments. They argue against doing this by apparently reducing moral judgments to judgments about subjective value. Instead they want what they refer to as an ontological argument for the concept of death, which simply clarifies the concept without going on to reach moral conclusions. They cite as an example the possibility that some society valuing sports might find it congenial to classify the lame as dead.[20] Since it is clearly absurd to do so, they apparently believe that they have demonstrated that the definition of death is not a matter of moral judgment.

Perhaps Green and Wikler have too modest a notion of the ontological status of moral judgments. I would analyze the problem of the lame as follows. The question being debated is a moral one: should lame persons be treated like the dead? The answer is clearly negative, and it is a moral answer. That, however, does not make it less ontological. If one believes that moral judgments should be viewed as if they had ontological grounding in reality rather than being merely subjective expressions of a society's values, then one could say of the society that wanted to treat the lame as dead that they have made a mistake. Although they do not value the lame, they are wrong to the extent that they treat them as though they were dead. I would claim they are morally wrong just as Green and Wikler would claim they are conceptually wrong. This has nothing whatsoever to do with the empirical question of whether a society, in fact, values certain of its members. The concept of being dead, for me, can be reduced to being in a state in which one is appropriately treated the way dead people are treated.

Green and Wikler go on to argue that an individual is appropriately considered dead when personal identity (that is, psychological continuity and connectedness) is destroyed. Insofar as being dead precipitates what I have called death behavior, I am sure Green and Wikler are wrong in equating irreversible loss of personal identity and death. The test case is that of a (possibly hypothetical) individual—call him Jones—who suffers a severe head trauma that leaves him with permanent amnesia. These are, in fact, the kinds of cases Green and Wikler address in their article.

Suppose that Jones eventually recovers consciousness, but it is established that there is a total and irreversible break in psychological continuity and connectedness. He does recover, however, to the point where he can leave the hospital and, after substantial education in language and the skills of living, return to society. The question that Green and Wikler should have difficulty answering in a way that squares with intuitions is whether Jones has died and a new person (say, Smith) has been created. They must say that Jones has died and that a new and different person comes out of the hospital.

I have no problem if they want to claim that according to their theory of personal identity a new person with a new identity emerges, but that question is not really the same as debating whether an individual has died. I am only interested in whether any of the behaviors that society appropriately initiates upon death would be appropriate for Jones. Would we, for example, read his will and transfer his assets to his beneficiaries, leaving Smith destitute? Would mourning be initiated by relatives who would show no interest in or commitment to Smith, a new and different person who is a stranger? I am convinced that Jones's relatives would have no problem remaining identified with him and that no traditional death behaviors would be appropriate. If Green and Wikler want to say that there is a destruction of personal identity, fine, but they surely cannot say that Jones has died. Anyone who did so would be confusing irreversible loss of personal identity with death.

Social Interaction. Social interaction is a fourth candidate. The Western tradition in both its Judeo-Christian and Greek manifestations has long held that the human is essentially a social or political animal. Perhaps the human's capacity or potential for social interaction has such ultimate significance that its loss is considered death. The claim here is a radical one. It is not merely that human life would be boring or miserable lived in total isolation. It is rather that the essence of being human would be lost. I believe that anyone who stands in this tradition must ultimately maintain that it is the capacity for social interaction that is essential for being treated as living.

Is this in any sense different from the capacity for consciousness? Certainly it is conceptually different and places a very different emphasis on the human's essential role. Yet it may well be that the two functions, experience and social interaction, are completely coterminous. For all practical purposes it may make no difference whether we speak of the critical characteristic as capacity for consciousness, or social interaction. Thus even though it is crucial for a philosophical understanding of the human's nature to distinguish between these two functions, it may not be necessary for deciding when an individual has died. Thus, for our purposes we can say that the fourth concept of death is one in which the essential element that is lost is the capacity for consciousness or social interaction or both.

The concept presents one further problem. The Western tradition, which emphasizes social interaction, also emphasizes, as we have seen, the importance of the body. Consider the admittedly remote possibility that the electrical impulses of the brain could be transferred by recording devices onto magnetic computer tape. Would that tape together with some kind of minimum sensory device be a living human being and would erasure of the tape be considered murder? If the body is really essential, then we might well decide that such a creature would not be a living human being.

This may help explain why Jones, the victim of permanent amnesia, did not die but is still Jones. He still has the same body, to which his family would relate. As long as he did not have another person's identity (the sort of case envisioned in the brain transplant scenarios), I think no one would have difficulty treating the conscious individual with bodily continuity as the same individual. (Whether he is the same person or not is irrelevant.) It also helps explain why we are so repulsed at the thought of a brain transplant. Assuming the consciousness of one person is merged with the body of another, a moral monster would be created, one having all of the components of living people, but containing the bodily trace of one person and the mental trace of another. If continuity of bodily and mental functions is critical then the merging of two produces a chimera. It is not merely the continuation of one person (the one who supplied the mental component) in a new body as some modern day gnostics would have us believe.

Where does this leave us? The earlier concepts of death—the irreversible loss of the soul and the irreversible stopping of the flow of vital body fluids—strike me as quite implausible. The soul as an independent nonphysical entity that is necessary and sufficient for a person to be considered alive is a relic from the era of dichotomized anthropologies. Animalistic fluid flow is simply too base a function to be the human essence. The capacity for bodily integration is more plausible, but I suspect it is attractive primarily because it includes those higher functions that we normally take to be central—consciousness, the ability to think and feel and relate to others. When the reflex networks that regulate such things as blood pressure and respiration are separated from the higher functions, I am led to conclude that it is the higher functions that are so essential that their loss ought to be taken as the death of the individual. While consciousness is certainly important, the human's social nature and embodiment seem to me to be the truly essential characteristics. I therefore believe that death is most appropriately thought of as the irreversible loss of the embodied capacity for social interaction.

Until about the late 1970s, it appeared that the initial battle between the concept of death based on fluid flow and that based on integrative function would be won by the latter, with a subsequent debate between that view and the idea that it is the capacity for mental and social functions that is vital. At that time, however, the debate got even more complicated. We began to realize that there were actually many different nuances among each of these positions. Some were arguing for the destruction of actual ana-tomical structures while others were concerned about functional losses. Some were convinced that individuals should be treated as alive if there were cellular level functions while others considered function at that level irrelevant. They held that as long as supercellular, organ system functions were irretrievably lost, the person ought to be considered dead. Among those emphasizing integrating capacities, there began a dispute about exactly which integrating capacities were critical. Did spinal cord integration count? If not, did simple cranial reflexes count? The Harvard report gave criteria for a wide range of functions. It is not obvious that all of those included in the Harvard list are essential but that no others are. Likewise, among those who emphasize capacities for consciousness and social interaction, a wide range of capacities could be included or excluded.

What at first appeared to be a two-way feud—between the heart and brain, to put it crudely—shifted into a three-way dispute by adding what is loosely called the higher-brain formulations. It is now apparent, however, that there is a very large, potentially infinite, number of positions about what has to be lost before a person should be treated as dead. The permutation of the anatomy versus function dispute, of the cellular versus supercellular dispute, and of the wide range of subtle distinctions among each of the major conceptual positions leads to a very large number of positions of which none is overwhelmingly convincing. While I am satisfied that function is more critical than anatomy, that cellular level functioning counts for nothing, and that some version of the consciousness and social interaction position is correct, it is clear since the report of the President's Commission on the Study for Ethical Problems in Medicine and Biomedical and Behavioral Research that my position will not soon be supported by consensus nor will any other position in the debate. What is being debated has nothing all to do with matters of fact, but rather matters of what is essential to require being treated in particular ways. If we are careful in specifying the options, no position might command the allegiance of more than a small minority. That leads me to advocate a range of discretion for individuals to pick their own concept of death, a theme that will be developed later.

Unfortunately, the members of the President's Commission, the most significant public body looking at this question, did not agree. It is worth examining their position. First, they argued that adopting my formulation requires "accepting one particular concept of those things that are essential to being a person, while there is no general agreement on this very fundamental point among philosophers."[21] They went on to suggest that this might require treating some who are arguably nonpersons, such as the severely senile, as dead. This is true of anyone who would equate being dead to losing the characteristics of personhood. Tristram Engelhardt, whom the commissioners also cited, is possibly guilty of this.[22] Clearly, this is not my position. As I have argued above, I am not equating loss of personhood with death, only the loss of what is essential to being treated as a living human being. That leaves open the possibility that some people who are not persons according to some philosophical theories of personhood could still be living human beings.

Second, the commission suggested that adopting a "higher brain" formulation for those who are in a permanent vegetative state, such as Karen Quinlan, would make them "just as dead as a corpse in the traditional sense." They went on to say that the "Commission rejects this conclusion and the further implication that such patients could be buried or otherwise treated as dead persons."[23]

There are two problems here. First, they argue by intuition that we would not bury a spontaneously respiring patient in a permanent vegetative state and that therefore she could not be dead. It does not follow, however, from the fact that we would not bury people that they are not dead. Consider, for example, the patient on a respirator with IV lines whose heart stops beating to the point that it cannot be started. Such a person is surely dead, yet we would not bury him with the respirator running and the IV lines in place. For aesthetic reasons we would first remove the interventions. We might also wait for relatives to arrive. There are many good reasons for brief delays in burying a corpse.

In the case of the spontaneously respiring cadaver we might plausibly wait until respiration ceases for similar aesthetic reasons. The mere fact that we would not bury him or her does not establish that the individual is not dead. What is left is the commission's claim that it rejects the conclusion that such persons are "just as dead." That, of course, is no argument at all.

The commission went on to suggest policy consequences of adopting the higher brain formulation. It claimed that "at present, neither basic neurophysiology nor medical technique suffices to translate the 'higher brain' formulation into policy." This may or may not be true. The question is one of whether neuroscientists can measure the irreversible loss of consciousness. Whether that loss can at present be measured, however, is irrelevant to the question of whether it represents the proper conception of what it means to be dead. If a person is dead when and only when there is an irreversible loss of consciousness and ability to interact socially, then it makes no sense to pronounce him dead on some other basis. It may be, as we shall see, that some more conservative criteria (such as loss of all brain function) will have to be used to pronounce death, but this would only be because that was the best measure we had for knowing that consciousness is lost, not because it measures the loss of integrative function or anything else.

The commission's final reason for avoiding a higher brain formulation was that it "would depart radically from the traditional standards." While that is probably true, it is hardly a reason for avoiding the correct answer. In fact, a good case can be made that even adopting a concept of death related to loss of integrative function is also a radical departure. It is only because the commissioners apparently accepted Alex Capron's implausible claim that there is no change in the concept of death when moving from the heart oriented to the whole-brain-oriented conception that they could claim that only moving to a higher brain formulation is a radical departure.

If that is true the most powerful arguments that the commission musters for the now more conservative concept of death related to whole brain function loss is that it is easier to measure. This argument can hardly bear the weight of the counterarguments taken from Judeo-Christian and secular traditions to the effect that the human is necessarily the integration of physical, mental, and social functioning.

The Locus of Death

Thus far, whenever the temptation arose to formulate a concept of death by referring to organs or tissues such as the heart, lungs, brain, or cerebral cortex, I have carefully resisted. Now I must ask, "Where does one look if one wants to know whether a person is dead or alive?" This question at last leads into the field of anatomy and physiology. Each concept of death formulated in the previous section raises a corresponding question of where to look to see if death has occurred. This level of the definitional problem may be called the locus of death. Yet, the term *locus* must be used carefully, as we are concerned about the death of the individual as a whole, not a specific part. Nevertheless, differing concepts of death will lead us to look at different body functions and the structures normally associated with those functions in order to diagnose the death of the person as a whole. This task can be undertaken only after the conceptual question is resolved.

Moreover, when we speak of looking at a particular anatomical site, we must keep in mind the possibility that at some point in the future some mechanical device could be constructed as a substitute for that anatomical structure. So we are really asking what the anatomical site is that, at our present stage of biomedical development, will give us insight into whether the critical function is irretrievably lost. With these qualifications, we can ask what are the different loci corresponding to the different concepts.

THE LOCUS OF VITAL FLUID FLOW

The loci corresponding to the irreversible loss of vital fluid flow are clearly the heart and blood vessels, the lungs and respiratory tract. At least according to our contemporary empirical knowledge of physiology and anatomy, these are the vital organs and organ systems to which the tests should be applied to determine if a person has died. Should a new Harvey reveal evidence to the contrary, those who hold to the concept of the irreversible loss of vital fluid flow would presumably be willing to change the site of their observations in diagnosing death.

THE LOCUS OF THE SOUL

The locus, or the "seat," of the soul has not been dealt with definitively since the day of Descartes. In his essay, "The Passions of the Soul," Descartes pursues the question of the soul's dwelling place in the body, arguing that the soul is united to all the portions of the body conjointly, but concluding, nevertheless, that

> in examining the matter with care, it seems as though I had clearly ascertained that the part of the body in which the soul exercises its functions immediately is in no wise the heart, not the whole of the brain, but merely the most inward of all its parts, to wit, a certain very small gland which is situated in the middle of its substance. . . .[24]

Descartes is clearly asking the question of locus, but his conclusion that the soul resides in the pineal body raises physiological and theological problems that most of us are unable to comprehend.

The fact that the Greek term *pneuma* has the dual meaning of both breath and soul or spirit could be interpreted to imply that the presence of this animating force is closely related to (perhaps synonymous with) breath. This give us another clue about where holders of the irreversible loss of the soul concept of death might look to determine the presence or absence of life.

THE LOCUS OF INTEGRATING CAPACITY

The locus for loss of capacity for bodily integration is a more familiar concept today. The anatomist and physiologist would be sure that its locus is the central nervous system, as Sherrington has ingrained into the biomedical tradition. Neurophysiologists asked to find this locus might reasonably request a more specific instruction, however. They are aware that the autonomic nervous system and spinal cord play roles in the integrating capacity, both as transmitters of nervous impulses and as the central analyzers for certain simple acts of integration (for example, a withdrawal reflex mediated through the spinal cord). They would have to know whether one was interested in such simple reflexes.

Beecher gives us the answer quite specifically for his personal concept of death: he says spinal reflexes are to be omitted.[25] This leaves the brain as the place to look to determine whether an individual is dead according to the third concept of death. The brain's highly complex circuitry provides the minimal essentials for the body's real integrating capacity. This third concept quite specifically includes unconscious homeostatic and higher reflex mechanisms such as spontaneous respiration and pupil reflexes. Thus, anatomically, according to our reading of neurophysiology, we are dealing with the whole brain, including the cerebellum, medulla, and brainstem. This is the basis for calling the third concept of death "brain death," although I have already discussed objections to this term.

Where to seek the locus for irreversible loss of the capacity for consciousness and social interaction, the fourth concept of death, is quite another matter. We have eliminated unconscious reflex mechanisms. The answer is clearly not the whole brain—it is much too massive. Determining this locus certainly requires greater scientific understanding, but evidence points strongly to the neocortex or outer surface of the brain.[26] Indeed, if this is the locus of consciousness, the presence or absence of activity in the rest of the brain will be immaterial.

Nevertheless, one cannot actually equate the presence of consciousness with the presence of neocortical activity, even at the present state of technology, because there is every reason to believe that certain sections of the neocortex (for example, those responsible for motor function) could be intact and still such a person would be completely lacking any capacity for consciousness or social interaction. A more complex question is whether it is possible to have a capacity for consciousness or social interaction when *all* neocortical tissue is destroyed. Is it possible that other portions of the brain, the thalamic region, for example, could take over and provide some rudimentary consciousness? These are complex empirical questions best left to neurophysiologists. For that reason I and others, including the members of the President's Commission, have preferred purposely to speak more vaguely of a "higher brain" locus of this concept of death rather than being overly concrete in using terms such as "cerebral," "cortical," or "neocortical."

In any case, one must identify certain brain regions that are necessary in order for there to be a capacity for consciousness and social interaction. We may have to err on the safe side by identifying too large a region for the purpose of empirical measurement of death. For example, we could be quite conservative and hold that the entire brain must be destroyed in order to be sure that the capacity for consciousness and social interaction is lost. This would lead to a series of tests for pronouncing death that were identical to those supported by holders of the concept of death based on loss of integrating capacities, but that would only be an accident of the imperfect state of our neurological knowledge, and it would change as more precise knowledge emerged in the future. For the holders of the higher-brain-oriented concept of death to insist that the entire brain must be destroyed in order to be confident that the sites responsible for consciousness are destroyed exposes us to the potential error of considering individuals alive who are actually dead based on the irreversible loss of capacity for consciousness and social interaction. It permits the conclusion that a person has these capacities when only brainstem functions remain.

The Criteria of Death

Having determined a concept of death, which is rooted in a philosophical analysis of the nature of the human species, and a locus of death, which links this philosophical understanding to the anatomy and physiology of the human body, I am finally ready to ask the operational question, what tests or measurements should be applied to determine if an individual is living or dead? At this point I move into a more technical realm in which the answer will depend primarily on the data gathered from the biomedical sciences.

MEASURING FLUID FLOW LOSS

I begin with the first concept of death, irreversible loss of vital fluid flow, and ask what criteria can be used to measure the activity of the heart and lungs, the blood vessels and respiratory tract. The methods are simple: visual observation of respiration, perhaps by the use of the classic mirror held at the nostrils; feeling the pulse; and listening for the heart beat. More technical measures are also now available to the trained clinician: the electrocardiogram and direct measures of oxygen and carbon dioxide levels in the blood.

MEASURING THE LOSS OF THE SOUL

If Descartes's conclusion that the locus of the soul is in the pineal body is correct, the logical question would be "How does one know when the pineal body has irreversibly ceased to function?" or more precisely "How does one know when the soul has irreversibly departed from the gland?" This matter remains baffling for the modern neurophysiologist. If, however, holders of the soul-departing concept of death associate the soul with the breath, as suggested by the word pneuma, this might give us another clue. If respiration and breath are the locus of the soul, then the techniques discussed above as applying to respiration might also be the appropriate criteria for determining the loss of the soul.

MEASURING LOSS OF INTEGRATING CAPACITY

I have identified the (whole) brain as the locus associated with the third concept of death, the irreversible loss of the capacity for bodily integration. The empirical task of identifying criteria in this case is to develop accurate predictions of the complete and irreversible loss of brain activity. This search for criteria was the real task carried out by the Harvard Ad Hoc Committee; the simple criteria it proposed became for some years the most widely recognized in the United States:

1. Unreceptivity and unresponsivity
2. No movements or breathing
3. No reflexes
4. Flat electroencephalogram.

The report stated that the fourth criterion is "of great confirmatory value." It also called for the repetition of these tests twenty-four hours later. Two types of cases were specifically excluded: hypothermia (body temperature below 90°F) and the presence of central nervous system depressants such as barbiturates.[27]

Several other major sets of criteria have since been proposed to diagnose the condition of irreversible loss of brain function. In addition to the prerequisites established in the Harvard criteria, most other sets have required the absence of cardiovascular shock and/ or the presence of an irreparable lesion.

In 1971 the University of Minnesota Health Sciences Center published the so-called Minnesota criteria. They differ from the Harvard criteria by not recommending a confirmatory EEG and by not requiring the absence of movement in response to painful stimuli. They specify testing for the presence of spontaneous respiration for a period of four minutes at a time, and they only require the absence of brainstem reflexes. Additionally they lower the time limit for the results to remain unchanged to a minimum of twelve hours.[28]

Like the Harvard criteria, the criteria adopted in 1976 by the Minnesota Medical Association (MMA) require total unresponsiveness to intense stimulation as well as the absence of spontaneous movements. They specify a three minute period for testing the absence of spontaneous respiration, and, like the earlier University of Minnesota criteria, they require only the absence of brainstem reflexes and specify that the pupils be fixed in midposition, greater than 5.0 mm in diameter (that is, they do not require the dilated pupils of the Harvard criteria). The MMA criteria also require two separate evaluations of the patient with a minimum of twelve hours between examinations. They suggest that the EEG and cerebral angiography may provide confirmatory data although they are not essential.[29]

In 1977, in a collaborative study organized by the National Institute of Neurological Diseases and Stroke (NINDS) of the National Institutes of Health and headed by Earl Walker, a set of brain-based criteria for determining death was published. In addition to the necessary deep coma with cerebral unresponsivity and apnea, the Walker group required that pupils be dilated, that cephalic reflexes be absent, and that electrocerebral silence be found on an EEG examination. All of these conditions must be present for thirty minutes at least six hours following the onset of coma and apnea. The group also proposed as a confirmatory measure a test demonstrating the absence of cerebral blood flow.[30]

In 1981 a group of medical consultants to the President's Commission proposed a set of criteria including the standard condition of deep coma and the now accepted absence of brainstem reflexes including adequate testing for apnea. Clinical indicators for the cessation of all brain functions must be present for at least six hours and confirmation of clinical findings by EEG is desirable. Further testing for the absence of cerebral blood flow can aid in the diagnosis.[31]

Numerous other sets of criteria exist as well, and these generally fall into one of five categories: clinical criteria alone,[32] clinical with EEG confirmation either optional or mandatory,[33] clinical with cerebral angiography,[34] clinical with metabolic confirmatory tests,[35] or clinical with combinations of confirmatory tests.[36]

European observers seem to have placed more emphasis on diagnosing the death of the brain by demonstrating the absence of circulation in the brain,[37] which can be measured by angiography, radioisotopes, or sonic techniques.[38] This diagnostic criterion reduces the duration of time required to determine the death of the brain since the absence of cerebral blood flow for twenty-five to thirty minutes predicates a dead brain regardless of the etiology.[39]

Sets of criteria analogous to those developed in the United States have been proposed in other countries as well. In 1971 the National Board of Health in Finland, the first country legally to accept death according to brain criteria, required permanently fixed and dilated pupils, the absence of spontaneous respiration, and the complete absence of cranial nerve reactions as verification of the irreversible loss of brain functions. In addition it held that EEG or cerebral angiography must confirm the diagnosis in cases where doubt remains.[40] The Swedish Medical Society in 1972 established a rigorous set of criteria that requires, in addition to the presence of unresponsive coma and apnea, the absence of brain functions including brainstem reflexes, an isoelectric EEG, and the absence of cerebral blood flow on an angiogram for a period of twenty-five minutes.[41] In addition to Finland and Sweden, Germany in 1968,[42] the Netherlands in 1971,[43] Japan in 1973,[44] the United Kingdom in 1976[45] and 1979,[46] and, in less explicit form, Canada in 1981[47] have all formulated similar sets of criteria.

Neither Sweden nor Japan has specific statutory recognition of such criteria as a basis for declaring death, and such criteria have not been accepted medically even in the absence of such legislation. Sweden and Poland, however, apparently use the criteria to justify withdrawing ventilatory support although cardiac arrest must occur before death can be pronounced. According to one survey, three countries of the twenty-eight responding used cardiac arrest as the determinant of death.[48] In eleven countries it was medical practice to declare death on the basis of brain criteria although there were no specific laws to that effect.[49] Eleven countries (in addition to the United States and Puerto Rico, which was reported separately) reported specific statutory recognition of brain based criteria for defining death in at least some of their legal jurisdictions.[50] Finally the majority of the countries indicated that clinical tests formed the basis for diagnosing the death of the brain while ten also required an EEG and/or cerebral angiogram.

There is a substantial consensus among neurological scientists that these various sets of criteria accurately measure the irreversible loss of brain function. The choice among alternative sets rests in large part on matters of convenience in administering tests and in concern that some of the older criteria may be too conservative, failing to identify some individuals who have actually irreversibly lost brain function. When one searches the literature to examine upon what this confidence in the sets of criteria rests, however, the evidence is not presented as clearly as one would like. For example, the original Harvard committee report did not suggest conclusively that its criteria accurately measured irreversible coma. The most convincing evidence presented in the literature involves 128 patients to whom these criteria were applied. In each case, autopsy results showed the brain to be "obviously destroyed."[51]

In a study of 2,650 patients with isoelectric EEGs, twenty-three cases were reported of recovery of cerebral activity after electrocerebral silence. Of those, eleven were errors about recovery or of mistaking low voltage activity for true silence. Nine cases could not be followed up because records could not be located or because clinicians failed to reply. That left only three recoveries of cerebral function, and they were all cases of patients who received anesthetic doses of CNS depressants and therefore outside the class of patients covered by the Harvard criteria.[52] While this seems to demonstrate that cerebral function is unlikely to return once (in the absence of drug intoxication) EEGs are isoelectric, it does not show that there is a complete absence of all brain function. Moreover, these data cannot be used to support absence of cerebral function based on any sets of criteria that do not incorporate EEG evidence.

In some cases, studies use the fact that there was no recovery of *mental* function to support the claim that brain function has been lost, although this premise is surely faulty. In other cases support for brain criteria is based on the fact that patients meeting some criteria rapidly lose circulatory and respiratory function. That evidence could be used to support the claim that people meeting the criteria will soon be dead based on these other functions, but it cannot be used to show that brain function is irreversibly lost.

The 1971 Minnesota criteria are supported by the evidence from autopsies on twenty-five patients. Some of them showed maceration of the brain tissue to the point that no tissue was available for examination. On the other hand, in a number of cases there was no change in the brainstem tissue.[53] This is hardly definitive evidence that the loss of brain function was irreversible.

The main report from the NINDS collaborative study does not provide any evidence that patients who meet the proposed criteria, in fact, have irreversibly lost all brain function. It cites more technical papers,[54] but, unfortunately, those papers do not deal with the data presented in the primary study. In the primary report, the collaborative group concludes that of 503 patients studied, 187 met the criteria for neurologically defined death. It then adds rather unreassuringly that "185 of these died, all *presumably* with dead brains. This 99% accuracy seems adequate for basic criteria."[55] It seems that once again the end point is that the patients meeting the criteria did, in fact, "die" apparently meaning their heart function ceased. Note, especially, that there is only a "presumption" that the brains were dead. More provocatively, apparently two patients did not even "die." It is not clear that all people would be satisfied with 99 percent accuracy in deciding that someone has died. Once again the data do not quite make the case.

The medical consultants to the President's Commission also cite no evidence that their criteria accurately identify patients who have irreversibly lost brain function.[56] Some studies present EEG and other data, but often using criteria that are not the same as those in any of the standard sets.[57] We are left with rather unsatisfying results. Most of the data do not quite show that persons meeting a given set of criteria have, in fact, irreversibly lost brain function. They show that patients lose heart function soon, or that they do not "recover." Autopsy data are probably the most convincing. Even more convincing, though, is that over the years not one patient who has met the various criteria and then been maintained, for whatever reason, has been documented as having recovered brain function. Although this is not an elegant argument, it is a reassuring one.

MEASURING LOSS OF CAPACITY FOR CONSCIOUSNESS

The alternate sets of criteria are normally applied to measuring loss of brain function, but it appears that many of these authors, especially the earlier ones, did not intend to distinguish them from those for measuring the narrower loss of cerebral function.

It should be clear that the above criteria measure loss of all brain activity, including spontaneous respiration and brainstem reflexes, and not simply loss of consciousness. Exactly what is measured is an entirely empirical matter. Establishing a system to measure irreversible loss of the capacity for consciousness or social interaction is far more difficult.

What then is the relationship between the more inclusive criteria, such as those favored first by the Harvard committee and more recently by the consultants to the President's Commission, and the simple use of electrocerebral silence as measured by an isoelectric or flat electroencephalogram? The former might be appropriate for those who associate death with the disappearance of any neurological function of the entire brain. For those who hold the narrower concept based simply on consciousness or capacity for social interaction, however, the Harvard criteria and the criteria of the medical consultants to the President's Commission may present exactly the same problem as the more conservative heart and lung-oriented criteria, by which every patient whose circulatory and respiratory function had ceased was indeed dead. Some patients, dead according to the loss of bodily integrating capacity concept of death (for which the brain is the corresponding locus), would be found alive according to heart and lung-oriented criteria. It might also happen that some patients who would be declared dead according to the irreversible loss of consciousness and social interaction concept would instead be found to be alive according to the more inclusive brain-oriented criteria.[58]

In the *Lancet*, the British physician J. B. Brierley and his colleagues report a similar situation.[59] In two cases in which patients had undergone cardiac arrest resulting in brain damage, "the electroencephalogram (strictly defined) was isoelectric throughout. Spontaneous respiration was resumed almost at once in case 2, but not until day 21 in case 1."[60] They report that the first patient did not "die" until five months later (p. 561), whereas the second patient "died on day 153" (p. 562). Presumably in both cases they were using the traditional heart and lung locus and correlated criteria for pronouncing death. Subsequent detailed neuropathological analysis confirmed that the "neocortex was dead while certain brainstem and spinal centers remained intact" (p. 560). These intact centers specifically involved the functions of spontaneous breathing and reflexes: eye-opening, yawning, and "certain reflex activities at brainstem and spinal cord levels" (p. 560). As evidence that lower brain activity remained, they report that an electro-retinogram (measuring electrical activity of the eye) in the first patient was normal on the thirteenth day (p. 561). After the forty-ninth day the pupils still reacted to light, and there was spontaneous respiration.

If this evidence is sound, it strongly suggests that it is empirically as well as theoretically possible to have irreversible loss of cortical function (and therefore loss of consciousness) while lower brain functions remain intact. This leaves us with the empirical question of the proper criteria for the irreversible loss of consciousness, which is thought to have its locus in the neocortex of the cerebrum. Brierley and his colleagues suggest that the EEG alone (excluding the other three criteria of the Harvard report) measures the activity of the neocortex.[61] Presumably this test must also meet the carefully specified conditions of amplifier gain, repetition of the test after a given time period, and exclusion of the exceptional cases, if it is to be used as the criterion for death according to our fourth concept, irreversible loss of capacity for social interaction. It would seem that the 2,650 cases of flat EEG without recovery that are cited to support the Harvard criteria would also be persuasive preliminary empirical evidence for the use of the EEG alone as empirical evidence for the irreversible loss of consciousness and social interaction. What these cases would have to include for the data to be definitive would be a significant number of Brierley-type patients where the EEG criteria were met without the other Harvard criteria being met—a question for the neurophysiologists to resolve.

A problem that arose with the heart-lung and Harvard criteria is also related to the use of electroencephalogram, angiography, or other techniques for measuring cerebral function as a criterion for the irreversible loss of consciousness: the possibility of a false positive diagnosis of life. Could a person have electroencephalographic activity but still have no capacity for consciousness or social interaction? Whether this is possible is difficult to say, but at least theoretically the motor cortex could be functioning and presumably be recorded on an electroencephalogram without the individual having any capacity for consciousness. Even the narrowest criterion of the electroencephalogram alone may therefore give false positive diagnoses of life for holders of the consciousness/social interaction concept.

For the higher-brain-oriented definitions of death, then, careful diagnosis of other severe brain conditions may be important as a way of diagnosing death in addition to its important use in deciding when it is appropriate to stop treatment so that the patient may die. There are many severe brain pathologies short of total and irreversible loss of all brain function and even short of the total loss of cortical function that could be indicators of death for those who adhere to a higher-brain-oriented concept of death, among which are both coma and a persistent vegetative state(PVS).

The President's Commission defines coma as the "inability to (1) open eyes, (2) obey verbal command and (3) utter recognizable words," but the Commission in its study of the outcome of comatose patients seems also to include PVS patients, who are not in a coma by this definition. The term *persistent vegetative state* is used to denote a condition of severe, irreversible damage to higher brain centers, that is, to cerebral hemispheres and the midbrain, usually resulting from a prolonged interruption of blood flow.[62] It is characterized by a loss of "personality, memory, purposive action, social interaction, sentience, thought," emotion, and cognition.[63] In such a state, only vegetative functions and reflexes persist. Patients with PVS are usually described as "wakeful, but devoid of conscious content"[64] (and thus they are not comatose). Unlike comatose patients, those with PVS still retain arousal mechanisms.[65]

The President's Commission report, entitled "Studies of Outcome in Comatose, Artificially-Respirated Patients," is not as careful in differentiating such patients as it is in other sections of its reports.[66] In classifying eventual outcomes in its study, it implies that there is no condition between PVS and death. It does not deal with patients in true coma or those with no cortical function who nevertheless retain brainstem function.

In that study, some patients were identified who eventually recovered to the point of being considered alive by any definition of death. Some had "severe, moderate, or mild disability" or even "good recovery." Others, however, were in a persistent vegetative state and did not recover. The critical question is whether some of the PVS patients can be accurately diagnosed in advance to have a truly permanent vegetative condition. If they can, then for a holder of a higher-brain-oriented definition of death, they ought to be viewed as dead.

While it is clear that some PVS patients do recover consciousness,[67] many do not. In a study conducted by Walshe et al., twenty-nine institutionalized patients who had PVS were monitored over a three-year period.[68] During that time, none of the patients improved and ten "died." The President's Commission, after examining available evidence, concluded that it "was assured that physicians with experience in this area can reliably determine that some patients' loss of consciousness is permanent."[69] If such a condition can be diagnosed with relative accuracy, patients with it would be considered dead by holders of higher-brain oriented concepts of death whether those patients have irreversible cortical function loss, irreversible coma, permanent vegetative state, or any other brain pathology.

Complexities in Matching Concepts with Loci and Criteria

It has been my method throughout this chapter to identify four major concepts of death and then to determine, primarily by examining the empirical evidence, what the corresponding loci and criteria might be. But there are good reasons, primarily pragmatic and empirical, why the holders of a particular concept of death might not want to adopt the corresponding criteria as the means of determining the status of a given patient. As a matter of policy, for example, we would not want to have to apply complex brain-oriented criteria before pronouncing death on a clearly dead body.

Reliance on the circulatory and respiratory criteria in cases where the individual is obviously dead can be justified in one of two ways. First, there is the formula of the original Kansas statute, in which two concepts of death are operational, either of which is satisfactory. This solution, however, is philosophically unsound, since it means that a patient could be simultaneously dead and alive. If the philosophical arguments for either of the neurological concepts are convincing, and I think they are, we should not have to fall back on the fluid-flow concept for pronouncing death even in the ordinary case.

A second way to account for the use of the heart and lung oriented criteria while holding a brain-oriented concept is to conclude that they do indeed correlate empirically with the neurological concepts. If there is no circulatory or respiratory activity for a sufficient time, there is invariably a loss of capacity for bodily integration or capacity for consciousness or social interaction, and this qualifies as a definitive diagnosis of death even for the neurologically oriented concepts. Their use is thus a shortcut; if these criteria are met, one need not go on to the brain-oriented criteria for the purpose of pronouncing death. This would appear to be a sound rationale for continuing the use of the criteria of respiratory and circulatory activity in ordinary cases.

There is one other way to account for the use of circulatory and respiratory function tests to pronounce death based on irreversible loss of brain function. This is the strategy used first by Alex Capron and Leon Kass[70] and then adopted by the President's Commission,[71] of which Capron was executive secretary. They maintain that the traditional criteria for death (linked to heart and lung function) were, in fact, always thought of as ways of testing for lack of integrating capacity of the brain. They reject the idea that the traditional use of these measures had anything to do with the idea that a person was alive when vital fluids were flowing regardless of the state of the neurological functions. They hold that when we shifted to use more direct measures of brain function, we were merely using more sophisticated techniques. That leads them to conclude that no significant conceptual shift took place when a brain-oriented definition of death was adopted. We simply supplemented the old criteria.

While that interpretation is logically coherent, it flies in the face of common usage and common sense. For millennia, no one spoke of death being based on neurological functions. Everyone associated it with loss of capacity for the flow of vital fluids. In fact, a significant minority of people today, including some physicians,[72] continues to believe that persons with fluid flow capacity, but no brain function, are alive.

A second practical difficulty is inherent in correlating concepts and criteria. Consider why one might not wish at this time to adopt the EEG alone as a definitive criterion for pronouncing death. There are two plausible reasons. First, there will be those who do not accept the correlated concept of death. They reject the irreversible loss of the capacity for consciousness or social interaction in favor of the irreversible loss of capacity for bodily integration or for fluid flow. Second, there are those who accept the concept of irreversible loss of consciousness or social interaction, but still are not convinced that the EEG unfailingly predicts this. If and when they can be convinced that the EEG alone accurately predicts this irreversible loss without any false diagnosis of death, they will adopt it as the criterion. In the meantime they would logically continue to advocate the concept while adhering to the more conservative criteria that appear to measure the loss of all brain function. Since the distinction is a new one and the empirical evidence may not yet be convincing, it is to be expected that many holders of the higher-brain-oriented concept will prefer the more conservative criteria for determining death.

There is a third practical difficulty. It is now commonplace to suggest that the conceptual question is one requiring philosophical, ethical, and/or public policy judgments. That is why it is almost universally recognized that choosing a concept of death cannot be a matter left to those with technical neurological or cardiological knowledge. It has been suggested by Capron and Kass as well as by the President's Commission that for the purposes of public policy it is not necessary to reach social agreement on the precise concept of death. They suggest that all that is necessary is agreement on what I have called the locus, that is on the sites to be examined for pronouncing death. This could mean that holders of concepts of death with slightly different metaphysical or theological nuances could still reach agreement about public policy if they held concepts that led them to the same locus for pronouncing death.

Moreover, there is also general agreement that what I have called criteria need not be chosen by the public. It is widely held that the criteria (what the commission calls the measures) can and should be left up to those with empirical expertise in the neurological sciences. They argue that such questions as whether to use angiography to determine that brain function has been lost are not questions that could be answered by a lay person and that the detailed technical procedures could easily change with time.

There is a great deal of truth to this claim, but there is also a problem. It is clear that a great deal of technical knowledge is needed to determine what criteria predict irreversible loss of critical functions, but it is also increasingly clear that these questions cannot be answered without drawing on some normative framework. An example will illustrate this point.

Consider the alternative sets of criteria now available for measuring the loss of total brain function, including the Harvard criteria and the report of the consultants to the President's Commission. Before any criterion is chosen by any one of these groups, some complex judgments must be made. Consider, for example, the questions of how many times and for how long a period the various neurological tests must be repeated. The Harvard committee proposed twenty-four hours[73] while the Minnesota Medical Association proposed twelve hours[74] The President's Commission, however, suggests that neurological tests be repeated after six hours.[75] These differences are, in part, accounted for by empirical changes over time. The supporters of more recent proposals have generally felt comfortable relying on shorter periods of EEG confirmation.

For any given length of time, there is some finite probability that if the tests were repeated over a longer period, activity would return. Choosing *any* cutoff runs the risk (even though infinitessimally small) that the person could be judged to have irreversibly lost function when, in fact, it was only a reversible loss. The more a person fears making this kind of error, the longer he or she will want the tests to be repeated.

On the other hand, extending the length of time will mean that there will be a longer period when persons who have really suffered irreversible loss of function will be in limbo, still being treated as alive while confirmatory tests are awaited. The more one fears the moral error of treating the dead as if they were alive, the more one will favor a shorter time for confirmatory tests.

It should now be clear that choosing the length of time depends not only on empirical matters, but on moral judgment. If one had no concern at all about treating dead persons as alive, the tests could be repeated endlessly. If one had no concern about treating living persons as dead, one would not need to repeat tests at all. Choosing the "correct" length of time for repeating the tests requires a moral judgment about the relative importance of the two kinds of error. That is a totally nonscientific question, and yet it is a judgment that each of the committees proposing criteria has made.

If the committee members, generally neurological experts, and lay people held similar views about balancing these two kinds of moral error, there would be little problem. There is some reason to suspect, however, that neurological experts are not typical in the way they compare the importance of the two errors. For example, it may well be true that neurologists place unusual importance on mental functions. In comparison with others in the society, they may reason that the error of treating someone as dead who is still living is not very serious because those persons mistakenly considered dead would almost always be severely impaired neurologically, or "as good as dead."

This is speculation, of course, but the members of the committees must make these evaluative choices in selecting which criteria to recommend. There is no reason to believe that they make the trade off in the same way the general population would. Even apparently technical tasks, such as choosing measurements to predict irreversible loss of brain function, are, in fact, and at least partially, evaluative tasks.

Having examined the theoretical distinctions associated with different concepts of death, as well as their related loci, and the empirical criteria for determining when death has occurred according to any one of the concepts, I now turn attention to the critical policy question. Which concept, locus, and criteria should be used, as a matter of public policy, to pronounce a human being dead?

2 | Defining Death Anew

Policy Options

While we philosophize about the meaning of death, people are being pronounced dead (or alive) by physicians. In some instances, those physicians may be choosing a definition of death based only on their own beliefs and values. Forty-six states and the District of Columbia have legislation or case law authorizing—in fact, usually requiring—the use of brain criteria for death pronouncement. The other four still operate under common law that bases the pronouncement of death on the loss of "all vital functions." Physicians in these four states are nevertheless taking it upon themselves to use a brain-oriented concept of death. Others, even those in states with legal authorization to use brain criteria, are reluctant to use newer concepts of death, fearing they may offend the patient's family or some district attorney.

Worse yet, some physicians believe that persons are really dead when the higher brain functions are irreversibly lost, and others are confused about the difference between higher brain and whole brain formulations. Certainly, serious problems are raised if they are allowed to pick a concept of death based solely on their own beliefs and values without regard to public legal authorization of that concept's use. This could lead not only to these "liberal" physicians using higher brain formulations, but also to physicians using whole brain formulations in states that have not authorized their use. It could also involve conservative physicians using heart and lung criteria in jurisdictions requiring the use of brain criteria for pronouncing death. All of these extralegal practices raise important public policy questions, especially since one individual can be considered dead in one state but would be considered alive if he or she were moved only a few miles away into another state.

Some order must be brought to this confusion. A public policy must be developed that will enable us to know when people should be treated as alive or dead. If it is true that there are several levels of debate over the definition of death, it may be that different public actions will be required at each level. It would be foolish to rely on a Gallup poll or a group of legislators to produce the empirical measures for predicting that a patient will not regain consciousness. It is just as irrational to rely on the personal opinions of health professionals to choose a concept of death. Even with the qualifications raised in chapter one, empirical matters are nonetheless largely scientific and can be left in the hands of the relevant professional groups, at least until there is some evidence that their consensus is being shaped in a unique way by their beliefs and values. The basic concept of death ought to be determined in a public forum such as a state legislature.

The question of whether to treat a person who will never regain consciousness as dead—that is, what concept of death is correct—is a philosophical one that can be answered independent of medical training or healing skills. The options are more numerous than they once were. Once, de facto public policy was that the physician should (even must) pronounce death when the patient dies. Everyone knew when that was: when the individual's vital bodily fluids were no longer circulating, as determined by looking at heart and lung function. The new pluralism requires that we now move beyond this traditional policy. In this chapter I shall look at four of the policy proposals that are now receiving serious consideration.

First, many have argued that medical professionals should be free to use whichever definition of death they deem appropriate. Others take a second position, that physicians should be required by law to pronounce death when the individual's brain is completely destroyed. A third proposal reflects a different concept of death; holders of this view would pronounce death when there is irreversible loss of the capacity of consciousness or social interaction.

The debate among these approaches leads me to offer a fourth proposal, which, although it has not yet received much consideration in the public debate, may be the most reasonable and workable solution. In a pluralistic world, different philosophical interpretations may well have to operate simultaneously. We may wish to give patients and their agents some choice in deciding the meaning of death in their own cases. If we are dealing with philosophical choices about what is essential to human living, we may have to tolerate philosophical pluralism.

Of course there is a fifth alternative: the traditional concept, locus, and criteria of death focusing on the functioning of the heart and lungs could be reaffirmed. If we are to continue to use this older concept, however, we must choose consciously to establish it as a public policy. As yet no such choice has been made. In the remainder of this chapter I discuss the four new policy alternatives that offer some hope of resolving this chaotic situation.

Medical Professional Choice

At first it seems obvious and reasonable to let the choice of a definition of death rest with physicians. A number of medical professionals, including Vincent J. Collins[1] and the World Medical Association,[2] have endorsed this perspective. "With scientific advances and new methods of resuscitation always coming up," said the group's president, Sir Leonard Mallen, "it would be silly of us to give a definition which could be outmoded within half an hour."

This bestowing of the decision making authority on the physician is implied in the often-cited Black's Law Dictionary definition of death: "The cessation of life; the ceasing to exist; *defined by physicians* as a total stoppage of the circulation of the blood, and a cessation of the animal and vital functions consequent thereupon, such as respiration, pulse, etc." (italics added). The question now raised by advocates of newer notions of death is, what if physicians decide to define death otherwise? If the physicians' old view of death was accorded legal standing, why should not any new medical consensus have legal significance?

Other authorities are also willing to give special weight to physicians' opinions about what counts as significant for life.[3] Pope Pius XII, at a 1957 meeting of the International Congress of Anesthesiologists, recognized that what was at stake was determining when a body no longer has its "vital functions." This the pope distinguished from "the simple life of the organs." But then he said, "It remains for the doctor . . . to give a clear and precise definition of 'death' and the 'moment of death' . . . ."[4] It is not clear whether he was ceding to the medical community the role of determining what bodily functions are really vital or simply the more limited technical task of making empirical observations about various body functions. Some lawyers such as Henry H. Foster[5] and Deborah Cowie[6] also endorse the notion of physicians choosing among definitions.

Allowing physicians to determine death according to accepted medical practice based on brain criteria *or* heart and lung criteria effectively permits them to choose a concept of death according to their own philosophies. Medical science may someday discover new specific criteria for evaluating the functioning of a particular part of the brain or even of the functioning of the circulatory and respiratory system, but this is measurement. How could medical research possibly *discover* that death should be pronounced when brain function rather than heart function has stopped irreversibly? Proposals urging physicians to select a definition of death are really dangerous invitations for medical professionals to exercise their philosophical judgments at the expense of nonconsenting or even unwilling patients. Even so, some philosophers have also expressed faith that the medical community should make such decisions. Dallas High, for example, has written that what is needed is a "medical-legal consensus" together with "the bona fides of the wider public," rather than a legislative determination. He concludes "I do not believe that further legislation is needed at this time. . . ."[7]

One could conceivably oppose legislation because there are other, more effective public mechanisms for deciding: court decisions, executive agency directives, or an informal public consensus created without overt governmental actions. But that means something much more than "the bona fides of the wider public"; it requires direct public action. It may be that High simply means that the medical profession is as good at the task of philosophical and social policy choices as the rest of humanity, and that if it is left alone it will reach essentially the same decision that an informed public would. If that is his position, however, it needs to be stated explicitly.

Let us assume for a moment that the biologist or physician may have some special skill in resolving the policy question. Would not the consensus of the profession as a whole still be more meaningful than the opinions of individual professionals, who may have biases that affect their judgment? An individual physician may have a particular attachment to the body's blood pump because of extraneous factors. Should he be permitted to keep a corpse's heart pumping blood for months or years just because of his own individual, and perhaps outdated, philosophy?

Thus some have proposed that in a given locality a committee of physicians, a board at the local hospital, or the medical society as a group should have the authority to determine the concept of death to be used.[8] An article by David G. Warren in the *Health Law Bulletin* has proposed a statute specifying only that the method used for determining death shall be "one approved by the state medical society."[9] This proposal is too sweeping in at least two respects. If it means only that the state medical society should determine the criteria to be used for measuring the presence or absence of functions in the organs associated with a particular concept of death, it would seem preferable to entrust this task to specialists—neurophysiologists, cardiologists, or others—depending on the tests to be made. But the proposal actually would place *all* authority in the hands of the medical society, not simply the selection of criteria. This might effectively eliminate biases of individual physicians by substituting the consensus of the medical profession or some subgroup. But it still leaves open the question of why an individual should have to be pronounced dead or alive because those trained in biology and medicine favor the philosophical concept of life that focuses upon fluid flow or integrating capacities or consciousness.

Placing responsibility on the individual physician or the profession as a whole for deciding what the definition of death should be is the result of inadequate analysis. The medical professional undoubtedly has special skills for determining and applying the specific criteria that measure whether particular body functions have irreversibly ceased. But the crucial policy question is at the conceptual level: should the individual in irreversible coma be treated as dead? No medical answers to this question are possible. If I am to be pronounced dead by the use of a philosophical or theological concept that I do not share, I at least have a right to careful due process. In the states that do not authorize brain-oriented criteria for pronouncing death physicians who take it upon themselves to use those criteria not only run the risk of criminal or civil prosecution but, in my opinion, should be so prosecuted.

At the same time, a more conservative physician who happens to practice in a state defining death as the irreversible loss of all brain function should not be permitted to refuse to pronounce death simply because he believes that his patient will not be dead until the heart stops. It should be just as illegal to fail to use brain criteria in a state requiring their use as it is to use them in jurisdictions that do not authorize their use.

Anyone who believes that no harm can come from allowing individual physicians to choose their own definition of death should consider the implications for physicians who hold personal concepts of death that are "more liberal" than either the whole brain or heart-and-lung oriented formulations. It is clear that some neurologists, for example, really believe that persons are dead when they irreversibly lose higher brain functions even though lower brain functions remain. Some physicians may hold that persons can be dead even when some higher brain functions remain. If they are authorized to pick their own definitions of death, then people could easily be pronounced dead who are breathing on their own and who retain other lower, or even higher, brain functions. In spite of the fact that some physicians and many philosophers writing on the subject favor such a formulation, no jurisdiction in the world now permits death to be pronounced under such circumstances. Individually selected definitions of death simply cannot be tolerated.

A Statutory Definition of (Whole) Brain Death

THE KANSAS PROPOSAL

In 1968 Kansas became the first state to pass a law permitting the procuring of organs for transplantation.[10] The transplanters at the University of Kansas Medical Center faced a dilemma because a year earlier a court case had affirmed the traditional definition of death. With some overstatement of the problem, Dr. Loren Taylor noted that they were able to procure organs at the same time case law was interpreted as precluding organ transplantation.[11]

That same year, however, M. M. Halley and W. F. Harvey proposed a statutory definition of death thereby initiating the debate about the proper formulation.[12] In 1970, as a result of prodding from the transplanters, Kansas passed the first statutory definition of death. Maryland next passed an almost identical bill.[13] Subsequently thirty-nine states and the District of Columbia passed statutes incorporating some brain-oriented definition of death.[14] In addition, several of these states also have pertinent case law, while seven other states[15] authorize brain-based death pronouncement by judicial decision alone.

CRITERIA FOR A STATUTE

Criticisms of the earlier bills have led to gradual refinement in the statutory model. What has emerged are various criteria for a good brain-oriented bill.[16]

A Single Definition of Death

Some of the early legislative proposals implied that there could be different definitions of death for different purposes. For example, some held that if persons are candidates to be organ donors for transplant, then they could be pronounced dead based on irreversible loss of brain function, but that otherwise they should be declared dead based on heart and lung function. This could lead to some serious practical problems.[17] If, for instance, a potential organ donor were declared dead and then the potential recipient died, thus eliminating the possibility of organ donation, would the potential donor have been revivified?

More fundamentally, it seems to make no sense that persons should be alive or dead depending on what use is to be made of the corpse. Now it is generally agreed that a single concept of death ought to apply regardless of potential use of the corpse, although it is still possible that different criteria can be used. For example, some statutes permit use of heart and lung criteria in simple cases, reserving brain criteria for special cases where heart and lung functions are artificially maintained.[18] What is important, however, is that the heart and lung criteria are now being used as predictors that brain function is irreversibly destroyed, not as predictors that circulatory and respiratory function is lost.

The Death of the Organism as a Whole

Any good definition of death should apply to the organism as a whole. For public policy purposes we are not, at this point, interested in measuring that the brain or the heart or the lungs have "died." A dead brain or a dead cerebrum in a still living organism may be important for making other critical decisions, such as whether to let the individual die, but it is not important to the definition of death. By the same token, we are not interested in the death of cells or organs; we are interested in when we can treat what was formerly the body of a person as a corpse.

The Focus on the Locus of Death

For policy purposes it is generally agreed that legislation or other broad policy pronouncements should not deal with levels that are either too specific or too general. This means that criteria for death should probably not be included in the legislation. They may well change frequently as the empirical science develops and are therefore technical matters that can be left to the consensus of the relevant professional groups. It is only if there is some reason to believe that the consensus is being influenced substantially by the values held by the professional group as a whole that the public would need to become involved. If, as in the example in chapter 1, neurologists chose too short or too long a time period for repeating measurement because they had an atypical way of relating the danger of mistakenly deciding brain function was destroyed to the danger of mistakenly deciding it was not destroyed, then it would be appropriate for society to adjust the criteria. But other than when these values become significant, the criteria should be left to professional consensus.

There can also be a problem if the legislative effort is aimed at the conceptual level. No legislation attempts to determine whether it is integrative function or something else under the control of the brain that is critical. Rather, those people who agree that it is the function of the whole brain have formed a coalition to support the whole brain locus to support a whole-brain-oriented concept of death. Those who favor other concepts of death could form similar coalitions. The effectiveness of such groups, of course, would depend on their ability to overcome internal disagreements among their own members—among holders of the higher-brain-oriented concepts, for example, over exactly which tissues must be functional. For now, however, what is appropriate is legislation specifying the locus for pronouncing death.

The Possibility of Conflict of Interest

Some early critics called for a requirement that the physician pronouncing death be different from the one who might use organs from the deceased for transplantation.[19] If the only use of a brain-oriented definition were to obtain organs for transplant, this would make sense. However, many have argued that the definition of death should be

independent of the use of the cadaver. What would be appropriate is a general requirement that the one pronouncing death should have no conflict of interest that could
distort the judgment that criteria have been met. That would cover the use of the organs
for transplant and any other potential conflict of interest.

A BETTER (WHOLE BRAIN) STATUTE

The first proposal for a statute defining death based on a whole-brain concept that
took many of these concerns into account was that of Alexander Capron and Leon
Kass, a lawyer and a physician who developed their proposal in the early 1970s working
closely with the Death and Dying Research Group of the Institute of Society, Ethics
and the Life Sciences.

The Capron-Kass Proposal

They did not like the Kansas law's close link with the transplantation issue, and they
were particularly distressed at the implication that there are alternative forms of death
appropriate for different situations. But they were still in favor of legislation. The
questions at stake, in their opinion, were crucial matters that call for public involve-
ment. "Physicians *qua* physicians are not expert on these philosophical questions nor
are they expert on the question of which physiological functions decisively identify the
'living, human organism'."[20] The legislative route, they argued, would permit the public
to play a more active decision making role. It would also dispel both lay and professional
doubt and provide needed assurance for physicians and patients' families that the new
definition could be used without fear of a legal suit.

On the basis of these guidelines they proposed a new draft statute as an alternative
to the laws in Kansas and Maryland.[21] It captures all of the virtues and has none of the
problems of the Kansas statute. It does not require two physicians to participate in
determining death, and it does not provide that the death-pronouncing physician be
separate from the physician interested in the potential cadaver's organs—but these
requirements seem superfluous for a general public policy for determining when an
individual is dead.

The American Bar Association Model Law

In 1975 the American Bar Association endorsed a simple alternative that defines death
solely in terms of the loss of brain function. This version was adopted verbatim in
Montana and Tennessee. Illinois, California, and Georgia adopted it with minor mod-
ifications: "For all legal purposes, a human body, with irreversible cessation of total
brain function, according to usual and customary standards of medical practice, shall
be considered dead."[22]

The most serious problem with this version is that it might be taken to imply that
brain function tests would actually have to be performed in all cases rather than relying
on loss of heart and lung function as an indicator of irreversible cessation of total brain

function. This could force needless neurological tests in cases where the individual is obviously dead.

The Uniform Brain Death Act

In 1978 the National Conference of Commissioners on Uniform State Laws adopted the Uniform Brain Death Act. This version has been adopted verbatim in Nevada and, with modification, in West Virginia. It is more explicit in emphasizing that the brain-stem as well as cortical function must be lost for an individual to be dead. [23]

Uniform Determination of Death Act

The confusion generated by the proliferation of models led the President's Commission to generate still another wording, the Uniform Determination of Death Act. This version has now been endorsed not only by the commission, but also by the American Bar Association, the American Medical Association, and the National Conference of Commissioners on Uniform State Laws in place of their earlier versions. It reintroduces the explicit recognition that loss of circulatory and respiratory functions can be used as an indicator of death:

> An individual who has sustained either (1) irreversible cessation of circulatory and res-
> piratory functions, or (2) irreversible cessation of all functions of the entire brain, in-
> cluding the brain stem, is dead. A determination of death must be made in accordance
> with accepted medical standards. [24]

Critics of the proposed statutes for determining death have either emphasized diffi-culties in technical wording or made misguided appeals for vesting decision-making authority in physicians or medical professional groups. These, however, are not the only problems. In order to accept a statute such as the Uniform Determination of Death Act, it is first necessary to accept the underlying policy judgment that irreversible destruction of the entire brain is indeed death—that an individual should be treated as dead when, and only when, the entire brain will never again be able to function. [25] Some of us continue to have doubts about that basic judgment.

A Higher-Brain-Oriented Statute

There has been great concern that statutes designed to legalize and regularize the use of brain-oriented criteria may not be sufficiently flexible to keep up with changes in this rapidly developing area. Those who place their faith in medical discretion fear that a statute would not permit the adoption of new techniques and procedures. For the most part they are wrong, since none of the proposed statutes specifies any particular criteria, techniques, or procedures. But our concepts are evolving rapidly, too. Even today most people writing in the field, including competent scientists and physicians, are careless in distinguishing between the functions of the whole brain and the higher brain. Much of the discussion does not make the distinction between lower brain functions, such as those that control spontaneous respiration, and those higher brain functions giving rise to consciousness and individual personality.

If a person without the capacities that are thought to reside in the higher brain centers should really be considered dead, then an amendment to the whole-brain-oriented statutes is in order. The change could be a simple one: simply strike the word *brain* and replace it with *cerebral*.

Actually, the change may not be that simple. It is clear that the higher brain functions identified in chapter one as a possible basis for a concept of death (that is, consciousness and social interaction) are not coterminus with the existence of cerebral activity. The law might call for death to be pronounced when there is the irreversible loss of all cerebral function, with its authors acknowledging that this formulation is not precise because certain cerebral functions (other than consciousness or ability to interact socially) might be present, leading to a false diagnosis of life. Alternatively, the drafters of the law could shift to using conceptual terms, speaking of death being pronounced when there is irreversible loss of capacity for consciousness and/or social interaction. This approach, however, would necessitate agreement on the more philosophical conceptual issues rather than a mere coalition around a particular brain locus.

Such a change in specifying the locus or the general concept for determining death may or may not have practical significance for the clinician who pronounces death. The question of criteria is an empirical one, and the answer will change periodically. It may be that the only way of knowing for sure that the higher function is irreversibly lost is to use exactly the same tests as those for determining that the whole brain has lost its power to function, that is, the criteria of the consultants to the President's Commission or something similar. But it may also be that other tests—such as EEG alone—could predict with certainty when individuals have irreversibly lost higher function even if they retain some lower brain functions.

There may be reasons for sticking with the old-fashioned statutes based on whole-brain conceptions of death. Only a few people will be dead according to a higher-brain concept but alive according to a whole-brain concept. There may be some risk of making an empirical error in applying higher-brain criteria and pronouncing someone dead who could still regain some form of consciousness. Some moral doubt may remain about the legitimacy of pronouncing someone dead who retains lower brain function. But these same problems arise with the whole-brain-oriented statutes as well. Once the judgment has been made that false positive diagnoses of life are a serious problem, there is a strong case for moving on from the whole brain to a higher-brain focus.

A Statute for a Confused Society

There is still another option. Part of the current confusion reflects sincere and reasonable disagreement within society over which philosophical concept of death is the proper one.

A persistent, significant minority, including many Orthodox Jews, continues to hold that individuals should be treated as alive until all vital functions, including circulatory and respiratory functions, cease. On the other hand, a significant number of people, especially scholars working in philosophy and neurological scientists, is gravitating toward some higher brain formulation. Moreover, even among those who identify with the whole-brain-oriented concept, there are subtle disagreements: over the exact functions that must be eliminated; over whether anatomical destruction of tissues must take place or only loss of function; and over whether cellular functions count. It is now apparent that there are really not only two or three positions, but countless variations that are likely never to be resolved.

As with many philosophical and religious disagreements in our society, we have a well-established method for dealing with diversity. It is to allow free and individual choice as long as it does not directly infringe on the freedom of others and does not radically offend the common morality. When dealing with a philosophical conflict so basic that it is literally a matter of life and death, the best solution may be individual freedom to choose among different philosophical concepts within the range of what is tolerable to all the interests involved.

There have been rare and tentative hints at this solution in the literature. A 1968 general definition of human death proposed by Halley and Harvey had an apparent option clause:

Death is irreversible cessation of all of the following: (1) total cerebral function, (2) spontaneous function of the respiratory system, and (3) spontaneous function of the circulatory system.
   Special circumstances may, however, justify the pronouncement of death when consultation consistent with established professional standards have [sic] been obtained and when valid consent to withhold or stop resuscitation measures have been given by the appropriate relative or legal guardian.[26]

They abandoned this "consent" formula, however, in later versions of their proposal.[27]

Halley and Harvey have been criticized for their mistake in making the state of being dead (rather than the acceptance of imminent death) depend on the "consent of a relative or guardian."[28] It seems likely that they did indeed confuse the state of being dead with the state in which a decision could justifiably be made by a relative or guardian to stop resuscitation and let a person die. But I do not see that their perhaps naive formulation makes "the state of being dead" dependent upon consent of a relative. It makes the state of being *pronounced* dead dependent upon consent. Being dead or alive may be quite independent of the wishes of relatives, but the treatment of persons as if they were dead or alive can logically still be a matter of choice of a relative or even a prior choice of the individual. There are two possibilities: (1) we could require every individual (or the next of kin or other legal guardians) to choose from acceptable definitions of death, or (2) we could adopt one definition to be followed unless caregivers are instructed otherwise. The second approach seems more practical.

There are, in fact, several objections to the idea of limited choice among definitions of death. Has individualism run amok? Do we really want to be so antinomian, so anarchical, that any individual no matter how malicious or foolish can specify any meaning of death that the rest of society would then be obliged to honor? What if Aunt Bertha says she knows Uncle Charlie's brain is completely destroyed and his heart is not beating and his lungs are not functioning, but she still thinks there is hope—she does not want death pronounced for a few more days? Worse yet, what if a grown son who has long since abandoned his senile, mentally ill, and institutionalized father decides that his father's life has lost whatever makes it essentially human and chooses to have him called dead even though his heart, lungs, and higher brain centers continue to function? Clearly society cannot permit every individual literally to choose any concept of death. For the same reason, the shortsighted acceptance of death as meaning whatever physicians choose for it to mean is wrong. A physician agreeing with either Aunt Bertha or the coldhearted son should certainly be challenged by society and its judicial system.

There are also practical problems in requiring every individual or guardian to make such a choice. Many people simply will not do so while competent. Many guardians will not understand the complex questions being raised. Some individuals will not have guardians available to make these choices. The more practical solution is to specify some general standard for death that should be used for all legal purposes unless the individual, while competent, or a guardian in the case that the individual has not spoken while competent, selects some other, reasonable definition of death.

With this approach it will not matter a great deal which of the plausible definitions of death is chosen. It could be one focusing on the locus of the heart, the whole brain, or the higher brain. Any person not accepting this so-called default position would then have the option of choosing some other definition. It would probably make sense to choose the default position held by the largest group in the jurisdiction. And while it should be clear that no single position attracts a majority of the population, it also seems that, at the present time, the greatest support appears to be for the whole-brain-oriented definition. One might also argue that the safest course would be to choose the heart-oriented position, forcing dissenters to register for one of the other positions. I am inclined to favor a default based on the higher brain position, because I think it is the right formulation. Some such discretion is necessary, however, if a society is not going to violate the consciences of a significant majority of its population.

The President's Commission, partially at my urging, considered incorporating a conscience clause in the selection of a definition of death and rejected this possibility.[29] Its members argued that "unfortunate and mischievous results are easily imaginable." In the report, however, they do not cite any such results. They only cite an earlier article by the commission's executive director.[30] That article states specifically that the "mischief that would be worked by a conscience clause of the sort recommended by Dr. Veatch is probably not great."[31] It goes on to illustrate potential problems, but only through cases where a guardian was acting with obvious conflict of interest and where guardians opt for extreme and unacceptable definitions of death of the sort discussed above. Capron cites the example of a man who shoots his wife and tries to avoid a murder charge by opting for a definition of death that would keep his wife "alive" until the murder charge could be avoided. The law deals frequently with the problem of removing guardians who have a conflict of interest. It would have no more difficulty removing a guardian making a malicious choice regarding a definition of death than removing a malicious guardian making any other medical or economic choice, including the decision to refuse medical treatment now permitted under many state laws.

The President's Commission, in fact, discusses some of the adjustments that could be made in public policy to permit individual discretion. It endorses a policy of maintaining a dead individual on a ventilator for several hours after death in deference to family wishes or in order for the family to decide whether to donate the deceased's organs.[32] I am assuming that the commission is not endorsing a trick—a policy of pronouncing death, but letting the family believe falsely that their loved one is still alive legally. If what they are endorsing is a policy of tolerating ventilation of what the family knows to be a corpse, why not change the description so that the individual is called alive during that period? This would show greater respect for the family's position while involving all medical personnel in exactly the same behaviors.

There may be more subtle problems with a conscience clause. Under present public policy, individual discretion in opting for an alternative definition of death could affect the time of life insurance payment. It could require health insurance to fund care for what would, under the default definition, be a corpse. Even these problems are not likely to be serious, however. For example, if a higher brain concept of death were chosen as the default position, conscientious selection of an alternative definition would delay life insurance payments. This, however, is likely to be a self-limiting problem, an option chosen only by a small number of truly conscientious objectors against their economic interest.

The problem of Medicare and other health insurance coverage continuing for persons who opt for more conservative definitions of death is unlikely to be serious either. For a person dead by whole brain criteria, but who has opted for a heart-and-lung-oriented definition of death, present technology only permits support of the individual medically for a short time, a matter of days. Moreover, there are ways to solve the health insurance problem even if society opted for a higher-brain default position. With such a position, a person conscientiously opting for a heart-and-lung definition could be maintained indefinitely, thereby generating considerable costs for the insurance company. The most straightforward way to overcome this would be to specify insurance limits on the treatment of permanently vegetative living patients. This would have the effect of limiting coverage for those who choose the alternative definition of death. In any case the insurance problem is no different when conscience is respected than when the family is permitted to have ventilation continue on the corpse. In either case a decision needs to be made about who will pay for that extra period of care.

Capron and the commission write as if there is some important reason why "society has a basic interest in defining for all people a uniform basis on which to decide who is alive—and consequently subject to all the protections and benefits of the law—and who is dead."[33] In one sense they are correct. It would be nice if all people were treated as dead if, and only if, they really were in the condition in which they ought to be treated as dead. By the same token it would be nice if people were allowed to die if, and only if, they were in a state in which they ought to be allowed to die. However, there has now emerged a substantial consensus that individual deviations from objective metaphysical moral standards ought to be tolerated in the name of individual conscience. People are now given substantial discretion in deciding whether to refuse life-prolonging medical treatment. Any confusion or mischief that could arise in permitting limited discretion in choosing a definition of death could also arise in permitting decisions to refuse treatment. A person who would opt for a higher-brain-oriented definition of death could, if prohibited from being called dead, still refuse life support, in which case he would be dead almost as soon. States have dealt with the fact that life insurance payments will be hastened by legislating that, even in these cases, payments shall be made at death. If a person opted for being considered alive until heart and lung function ceased, the health insurance problems would be no different from cases where decisions are made to continue medical support. The law could either require that individual's health insurance to cover the modest extra cost or could exclude coverage for persons with dead brains. In short, all the confusion in public policy that could be created by giving an individual discretion in defining death already exists in giving that individual discretion in deciding when to stop treatment. Provided certain steps are taken to protect society from the most serious consequences of individual discretion, it is better to respect individual conscience in moral matters than to ride roughshod over people's consciences.

There must, then, be discretion in choosing among plausible concepts of death as well as limits on individual freedom. At this moment in history the reasonable choices are those focusing on respiration and circulation, on the body's integrating capacities, and on consciousness and related social interaction. Allowing individual choice among these alternatives, but not beyond them, may be the only way around this social policy impasse.

To develop model legislation, we can begin with the Uniform Determination of Death Act and make several changes to avoid the problems I have discussed. First, a higher-brain locus for determining if a person is dead can be incorporated by simply changing the wording. On the presumption that no person who has lost cerebral function retains any of the higher functions about which we are concerned, we can adopt the cerebral locus in the statute knowing that it is only an approximation and probably a conservative one at that. Second, it seems to me reasonable to insist, in general terms appropriate for a statutory definition, that there be no significant conflict of interest. Finally, wording should be added to permit freedom of choice within reasonable limits. These changes would create the following statute specifying the standards for determining that a person has died:

> An individual who has sustained (1) irreversible cessation of circulatory and respiratory functions, or (2) irreversible cessation of cerebral brain functions is dead. A determination of death must be made in accordance with accepted medical standards.
>
> However, no individual shall be considered dead even with the announced opinion of a physician solely on the basis of irreversible cessation of cerebral functions if he or she, while competent, has explicitly asked to be pronounced dead based on irreversible ces-

sation of all functions of the entire brain or based on irreversible cessation of circulatory and respiratory functions. Also, unless an individual has, while competent, asked to have irreversible cessation of cerebral function used as a basis for pronouncing death or has asked that either irreversible cessation of the entire brain or irreversible cessation of circulatory and respiratory function be used, the legal guardian or next of kin may opt for any one of the alternative definitions.

It is further provided that no physician shall pronounce the death of any individual in any case where there is significant conflict of interest with his obligation to serve the patient (including commitment to any other patients, research, or teaching programs that might directly benefit from pronouncing the patient dead).

3 | Dying Morally

The Ethics of Choosing
Not to Prolong Dying

Although the debate over the definition of death has captured much attention in the past decade, it is not a critical issue for the care of most critically ill patients, who are not yet dead by any definition. They are nevertheless persons about whom serious ethical questions are being asked. Does there come a point in life when it is no longer appropriate to continue the struggle to live? If so, what actions are acceptable?

There is a vast literature on the distinct but related issues of "euthanasia," "mercy killing," treating in a way that risks life, allowing to die, deciding to cease treatment, and exercising the right to refuse treatment. Formulators of any public policy dealing with these issues will consciously or unconsciously have to make distinctions among these meanings or have a confusing policy. For thorough ethical analysis, however, it is vital to have these distinctions spelled out. I shall survey these issues in this chapter before examining the legal status of the right to refuse treatment in the next two chapters and the public policy alternatives in chapter 6.

Actions and Omissions

On March 4, 1985, Roswell Gilbert went to lunch with his wife of fifty-one years. She was suffering from Alzheimer's disease and osteoporosis that left her disoriented and in pain. Sometimes her behavior had become bizarre. A witness reported hearing her say, "I'm in pain. I want to die." Upon returning to their apartment, Mr. Gilbert gave his wife a sedative. He is quoted as saying in response to her plea for someone to help her die, "Who's that somebody but me? I guess I got cold as ice. I took the gun off the shelf, put a bullet in it and shot her. Then I felt her pulse. I thought, 'Oh my God, I loused it up.' I put in another bullet and shot her again." In May of that year he was convicted of first degree murder and given a life sentence.[1]

THE LEGAL STATUS OF KILLING THE DYING

To date, at least twenty-six cases of the active killing of dying or seriously ill patients have been decided by American courts.[2] Fourteen of the cases resulted in convictions. Eight of the accused were found guilty of manslaughter and four of second degree murder, deferred murder, or attempted murder. Two other individuals, Gilbert and an attorney named John Noxon, were convicted of murder in the first degree. Noxon was found guilty of having electrocuted his six-month-old mongoloid son by wrapping a lamp cord around his neck. He was sentenced to death, a sentence later commuted to life and then to six years.

There have been twelve acquittals, but seven were on grounds of temporary insanity. Three other cases, one of which involved a nurse, were never brought to trial because of confusion in the evidence or inability to establish the cause of death. Two other acquittals have been handed down in the case of Vincent Montemorano and Herman Sander, the only two physicians tried for the active killing of dying patients, where "mercy killing" might have been involved.

In 1950 Dr. Sander was charged with the murder of Mrs. Abbie Borroto, who was dying of cancer. He had dictated into the hospital record the notation, "Patient was given 10 cc. of air intravenously four times. Expired within ten minutes after this was started." In the trial, however, there was expert medical testimony that the patient may not have died from the air bubble injections. It was argued that the cause of death was not clear—that she might have already been dead at the time of the injections; that the forty cubic centimeters of air would not have been sufficient to cause the death; and that some autopsy findings indicated death was not sudden. The jury apparently accepted these grounds and acquitted Dr. Sander. Similar arguments were offered in defense of Dr. Montemoreno, who had been accused of injecting a lethal dose of potassium chloride into a terminally ill cancer patient.

It is striking that the two physicians and the nurse were acquitted without resorting to an insanity defense while virtually all the lay people had to resort to such pleas. Dr. Sander had the support of a petition signed by 90 percent of his townspeople, including the husband of the woman he was accused of murdering. The extent to which these factors played on the sympathies of the jury in this and the "temporary insanity" cases is not clear. The key conclusion is that the courts have never found anyone responsible for actively killing a sick person, yet on the grounds of "mercy" found the accused not guilty. In spite of this string of acquittals, standards for ruling insanity are tightening, and in the future it may be more difficult to get acquittal on this basis.

In the case of withdrawing treatment, the legal situation is more complex, although patterns do exist. In the following discussion, however, I shall attempt to clarify the moral differences, if any, between these two kinds of behavior.

THE ETHICS OF KILLING AND OF FORGOING TREATMENT

The distinction between killing and allowing to die is often debated in medical ethics. But the terms are not always used precisely, with the result that the distinction between actions and omissions is often conflated with that between "direct" and "indirect" killing. They are not really the same. As we shall see later in the chapter, direct killing is killing that is intended. Still, it is possible that with some omissions killing may be directly intended, while with some actions it is not. A health professional who purposely failed to initiate resuscitation because the patient was difficult to care for and because the health professional wanted to dispose of the patient would have directly killed by omission. Likewise, a death during surgery in which the aorta is cut by accident is a death that resulted from action by the surgeon, but not one that is directly intended.

Nevertheless, some authors use the term *direct* when they mean *active killing*. Thus although Joseph Fletcher uses the terms *direct* and *indirect*, he appears really to be attacking the distinction between actions and omissions when he says (apparently stating his own position):

> To others this seems a cloudy and tenuous distinction. Either way the intention is the same, the same end is willed and sought. And the means used do not justify the end in one case if not the other, nor are the means used anything that *can* be justified or "made sense of" except in relation to the gracious purpose in view.[3]

The pragmatist may indeed ask what difference it makes whether an action is taken to cause death or a treatment is omitted so that death takes place. In either case the patient dies. Is it not philosophical obscurantism to dwell on the differences?

The "pragmatic" view is challenged by Roman Catholic and other religious traditions as well as by secular philosophers who emphasize the importance of the distinction. The Roman Catholic Church stands firm on this position even though the code also says that "neither the physician nor the patient is obliged to use extraordinary means" of medical treatment. An elderly Catholic man, for example, was dying of widespread cancer. Reflecting on the patient's course of treatment, which had included irradiation and several operations, his clearly concerned but tough-minded secular physician re- marked that proposed further surgery really could not do a thing for him. He then added, "If he weren't Catholic I don't think I would operate." He apparently assumed that Catholics oppose all decisions to omit treatment as well as active interventions to kill. A morally concerned physician ignorant of the ethical position of a major religious group was inflicting both physical and moral injury on his patient.[4]

At least five critical differences between the active termination of a patient's life and forgoing treatment have been cited. The first three turn out to be poor reasons to hold on to the moral distinction between omissions and commissions. The last two reasons are more difficult to set aside. Let us look at the moral implications.

Actions and Omissions Are Psychologically Different

First, it is argued that actions and omissions are psychologically different. We feel differently about the active killing of a terminally ill individual than we do about forgoing treatment and letting nature take its course. These feelings are particularly relevant if we are concerned about the consequences of our actions. Many feel that more guilt would attend the action than the omission.

But what is the origin of this difference? If guilt feelings are an indication of our moral perception of rightness and wrongness, then it may be that active killing actually is more wrong. On the other hand, we may feel more guilt simply because we have traditionally believed that there is a moral difference between the two courses (which, of course, would be circular reasoning). While no doubt there is a perceived difference, we must still determine whether that perception is valid.

There is another problem with this argument. Decisions to prolong the dying process may produce a long period of suffering and deterioration which can also result in considerable feelings of guilt. Mr. Gilbert, for example, may have felt greater guilt if he had let his wife continue to live while her condition declined. If guilt feelings are used as the basis for establishing a moral difference between actions and omissions, then this evidence might be used to show that active killing is morally preferable. If psychological feelings are to be the basis for arguing that actions and omissions are morally different, it must first be established that there are indeed consistent patterns of difference in those feelings, and then it must be proved that the difference can be attributed to a real moral difference, rather than to traditional, but invalid moral beliefs. In short, while a psychological difference may exist, it is probably not conclusive evidence for either side.

Active Killing Conflicts with the Role of the Physician

Second, it is argued that the duty of physicians is to preserve life. Allowing them the role of killers—even of the dying—would conflict with their proper role. Sometimes this role is even expressed with hyperbole—"to preserve life at all costs." It is not clear where this expression of gross biological vitalism comes from. Francis Bacon called it a new duty added to the physician's traditional obligation. In the Hippocratic Oath, physicians pledge that they "will neither give a deadly drug to anybody if asked for it, nor . . . make a suggestion to this effect." Some interpret this to forbid supplying the sick with poisons for suicide.[5] Others interpret it as a simple prohibition on murder. However the phrase is interpreted, it is difficult to make it the basis of a moral distinction between actively killing patients and simply letting them die.

In any event, the primary injunction of the oath is that physicians should do what they think will benefit their patients or protect them from harm. But whether stated positively or negatively, it is an open question whether refusing to hasten death will always benefit the patient or avoid harm. Even physicians who would strive to preserve life at all costs probably would feel obliged to avoid not only actions that kill, but life-shortening omissions as well. That not all physicians share this norm is demonstrated in a study in which 18 percent of the physicians surveyed favored "positive euthanasia."[6] Another study indicated that 27 percent would practice "positive euthanasia" if it were permitted.[7]

Suppose, however, that most physicians did agree that their duty was to preserve life and somehow that led them to oppose active killing, but not omissions of treatment. Should that make any difference to the rest of us? This sort of policy question cannot be left to the members of one profession to settle. Independent of what physicians believe, therefore, the rest of society must decide whether the physician's role should be kept separate from the task of hastening death. A good case can be made either way. If active killing were to be practiced at all, it would seem that the appropriate person to carry it out would be those in the best position to know the prognosis and have access to the most humane techniques. Yet we commonly believe that it is necessary some-times to set apart special classes of individuals to exercise unique moral duties. It is probably a safer course for society to recognize that the physician should be in a special role oriented to the preservation of life and health, at least until contrary directions are given.

This conclusion, however, only implies that physicians should not be the ones who hasten death. We still have not established a general moral distinction between com-missions and omissions that result in death. Even if we thought that the norm to preserve life permitted omissions and prohibited commissions by physicians, it would say nothing about the more numerous cases of active killing by parents or spouses for reasons of mercy. It would not speak to the morality of Mr. Gilbert's action. Grounding the ethics of the commission-omission distinction on the role of the physician involves a number of presumptions: that the physician should be the one to serve as the hastener of death; that society sees the role of the physician as the preserver of life; that com-missions conflict with that principle but omissions do not; and, that we would not be able to set up mechanisms for releasing the physician from that special role in special cases. Many, if not all, of these presumptions seem tenuous. Even if we conclude that physicians should never actively kill, others in society could be given that role. We could create the role of euthanizer just as we have created the role of executioner. This would spare the physician from active killing. If commissions and omissions are to be considered morally different, additional arguments are necessary.

There Is a Difference in Intent

A third argument is that there is a difference in intent between commissions and omissions. The relevance of intention is perplexing, however; indeed it is not even clear that such a difference exists. The active injection of an air bubble or potassium chloride into a patient in order to reduce a health professional's work load has the unambiguous intention of producing death, yet the simple omission of treatment may have precisely the same purpose. Furthermore, some actions such as open heart surgery or treatment with high doses of a toxic drug may kill the patient when the intent was precisely the opposite.

One step in clarifying the importance of intention is to distinguish between the rightness of the act and the worthiness of the actor's motive. At least since Kant we have distinguished between moral worth of agents and the rightness of their actions.[8] If the physician gives what is intended to be a life-saving drug, based on previous experience with the drug at a particular dosage level, and the recipient has an unusual and fatal reaction to it, the physician could be said to have done the wrong thing but would not be blameworthy unless some usual or reasonable test was omitted that might have disclosed the peculiar toxic response. The physician's intentions were good, we would say, even if the act were the wrong one. Intentions may thus be morally significant, at least in establishing blame or praiseworthiness, but they still may not establish an adequate basis for preferring omissions over commissions.

The Consequences Differ

One of the most powerful arguments against the omission/commission distinction rests on the claim made by Fletcher and others that whether one actively kills or merely omits treatment, the result will be the same—the death of the patient. This has led many who believe that ethics is a matter of consequences to conclude that the bare difference between the omission and the commission of an act cannot be morally decisive in situations of terminal illness where that decision leads to the death of the patient.

One of the scholars cited most frequently in this argument is James Rachels. Writing in the *New England Journal of Medicine*[9] and in more detail in an essay entitled "Euthanasia, Killing, and Letting Die,"[10] Rachels argues that

> as far as . . . ending the patient's life is concerned, it does not matter whether the euthanasia is active or passive: *in either case*, the patient ends up dead sooner than he or she otherwise would. And, if the results are the same, why should it matter so much which method is used?[11]

Rachels buttresses his argument with several clinical examples, including the standard one in which a patient in intractable pain is inevitably dying and would die somewhat sooner if "allowed to die," but much sooner if killed actively. Rachels concedes the consistency of someone (such as some Orthodox Jews) who would not accept any course that diminishes the patient's time to live by either omitting treatment or actively killing. However, he finds incomprehensible the intermediate position, the view that it is appropriate to cease fighting death and thereby shorten the patient's suffering while at the same time it is morally wrong actively to kill, thereby shortening the suffering even more. He favors the view that if forgoing treatment is acceptable then actively killing is as well. The bare difference between acting and refraining, he argues, makes no difference.

He further asks us to compare two pairs of relatives, each pair comprising a six-year-old child and his adult cousin.[12] In each case the adult is malicious and would like to have his cousin dead because he would then gain a large inheritance. In the first case, Smith sneaks into the bathroom while the child is bathing and drowns the child, thus killing him. In the second case, Jones intends to do the same, but as he enters the bathroom, the boy slips, hitting his head so that he falls face down in the water. Jones simply fails to pull the boy out of the water, and the boy drowns. Rachels concludes that both acts are equally reprehensible and so, since the only difference is that one involved active killing and the other allowing to die, there is no moral difference between the two kinds of behavior.

The question raised is whether Rachels is correct in concluding that because these two acts seem equally reprehensible, there is no moral difference in principle between killing and letting die. The method used here is an argument by example. He expects us to conclude that if a pair of examples leads to the intuition that the individual instances of the behavior are equally reprehensible, then in general there are no moral distinctions to be drawn.

Two kinds of rebuttal have been offered. The first operates from within what appears to be Rachels's normative moral theory. The second, discussed in the next section, relies on deontological normative theory.

Rachels seems to hold that conduct is judged right or wrong based on consequences. In the passage quoted above, Rachels says that "if the results are the same, why should it matter so much which method is used?" Some of his critics accept his normative ethics, his assessment based on consequences, but disagree with him about what the consequences of the two kinds of behavior are.

Individual Consequences. At the first level, in an individual case, letting the terminally ill patient die may have consequences different from actively killing. If, for example, a physician is mistaken in his diagnosis that death is inevitable, "letting die" might result in the survival of the patient, while killing the patient would not. The same can be said in the (hopefully rare) case where the care giver is maliciously trying to eliminate the patient. If the care giver simply steps aside and lets nature take its course, the patient may live while if active killing is the course the patient dies.

These differences in consequences are not terribly impressive, though. Moreover, everything that can be said for giving moral preference to letting die over killing on these grounds can also be used as an argument for preferring aggressive treatment over letting die. In either case, the argument comparing the consequences must also take into account the bad consequences of extending life as well as the good ones. In turn, this would seem to reduce the argument to empirical questions such as how likely the decision makers are to make errors or be malicious, or how well pain can be controlled. Rachels and many other defenders of the moral acceptability of active killing include in their argument the assumption that patients sometimes suffer intractable pain.[13] Others more in tune with the technical aspects of hospice care, such as Robert Twycross, would question whether there is ever pain that is unresponsive to adequate sophisticated pharmacological intervention.[14]

On balance it is not clear whether the projected net consequences of letting the patient die are better or worse than actively killing. Nonetheless, Rachels's claim that the presence of an omission or a commission per se makes no difference is plausible.

Long-term Social Consequences. The defenders of the omission/commission distinction, however, are likely to shift the argument to another level. Some of the more sophisticated of these maintain that it is not really the consequences of the particular, isolated bedside action that are decisive; rather it is the longer course of the consequences of alternative actions or even of alternative sets of moral rules.

One of the possible effects of an individual instance of active killing, even assuming it is justified by its short-term consequences in an individual case, may be that subtle, long-term implications are more difficult to calculate and possibly more ominous. Killing individuals and letting them die, for example, will lead others to be aware that care givers sometimes engage in such behavior. It could also lead to a suspicion that this behavior might happen in other situations. This could have a staggering impact on the human psyche: at the time when people most need comfort from others, they might begin to suspect that they are candidates for merciful active killing or the omission of treatment. Moreover, patterns could be established that would have subtle, harmful effects. Killing and letting die would become more accepted practice. Others who are not necessarily terminally ill or even suffering might become candidates for death. If (and only if) the psychological effects of permitting active killing are worse than those of a policy of accepting some decisions to let die, could we then conclude that the consequences of a policy of active killing are different from the consequences of a policy of letting some people die.

This is the position of those who use the Nazi analogy to argue against active killing. For example, Leo Alexander, a physician who played a central role in the drafting of the Nuremberg Code, saw a dangerous precedent in that period. According to him, the German mass murders

> started with the acceptance of that attitude, basic in the euthanasia movement, that there is such a thing as life not worthy to be lived. This attitude in its early stages concerned itself merely with the severely and chronically sick. Gradually the sphere of those to be included in this category was enlarged to include the socially unproductive, the racially unwanted, and finally all non-Germans. But it is important to realize that the infinitely small wedged-in lever from which this entire trend of mind received its impetus was the attitude toward the nonrehabilitable sick.[15]

Some cannot believe that this could happen in a democratic and freedom-loving country like the United States. There is, in fact, a significant historical debate over whether the Nazi mass murders really began with attitudes toward the nonrehabilitable sick. Some argue that protection and purification of the Aryan stock was the intention from the beginning.[16] A more balanced thesis, one which may well be the most accurate, is that both the ideal of a pure race and the specific precipitating event of a plea of a father for the merciful death of his son were necessary for the mass murders.[17]

Whether the Nazi historical experience required an attitude toward the nonrehabilitable sick as a necessary condition, the critical question is whether such a shift could take place in a contemporary state. In order to test the susceptibility of educated Americans to such a thought, a psychologist, Helge Mansson, asked a group of university students to participate in a research project. They were told that it was designed to develop ways of killing "unfit" persons as a "final solution" to problems of overpopulation and personal misery. During the presentation of the project, it was stated that mercy killing "is considered by most experts as not only being beneficial to the unfit because it puts them out of their misery or lives, but more importantly it will be beneficial to the healthy, fit and more educated segment of the population." Participants were told that the only problems were to determine which method of killing should be used, who should do the killing, and who should decide when killing should be resorted to. The students were also informed that "the findings of our studies will be applied to humans once the system has been perfected." Of the 570 students, 326 approved of the project. When applied to minority groups the acceptance rate was even higher.[18]

In a recent, intriguing, and powerful study of psychology of the Nazi physicians Robert Jay Lifton has concluded that the sociopsychological conditions leading to murderous behavior were extremely powerful. "No individual self is inherently evil, murderous, genocidal. Yet under certain conditions virtually any self is capable of becoming all of these."[19] He claims, "Under certain conditions, just about anyone can join a collective call to eliminate every last one of the alleged group of carriers of the 'germ of death.'"[20]

It is not enough, however, to show that there are subtle, long-term social consequences of behavior. In order to use these consequences as a basis for arguing that there is a moral difference in principle between active killing and letting die, one must also show that these consequences differ in the two cases. That, in fact, is what consequentialist defenders of the distinction try to do. They maintain that letting die is self-limiting; only certain members of the society will die if left untreated. On the other hand merciful killing could potentially include all humans within its scope. Large groups who are leading pitiful existences, but who are not dying, could come under the scope of a practice of merciful killing: the retarded, the handicapped, the poor, the uneducated, those with politically unattractive commitments. Clearly, the practice of killing whenever the consequences would be good on balance is a practice that is quite different from that of letting die whenever the consequences would be good on balance. In assessing an individual case where the options of active killing and letting die are being considered, a classical consequentialist (such as a utilitarian) must take into account all of the projected consequences including the long-term effects on society as well as the effects on the individual patient.

Rule Consequentialism. Some sophisticated consequentialists part company with those who limit the assessment of consequences of killing and letting die to the individual case by arguing that it is not individual instances of human behavior that should be assessed in terms of the benefits and harms envisioned, but rather broader societal practices (or groups of practices).[21] They would ask what practice, on balance, produces better consequences: a practice that permits active killing, one that permits letting die but not active killing, or one that permits neither? They, along with Rachels, rule out a moral prohibition on both killing and letting die. However, they also rule out accepting active killing on the grounds that active killing would have unacceptable consequences if it became a generally accepted practice. They are "rule utilitarians": They opt for the rule that will have better consequences than any other rule. For this group, the rule permitting some instances of letting die, but no instances of active killing, is the best practice available.[22] It is sometimes said that this defense amounts to a "wedge" or "slippery slope" or "camel's nose under the tent" argument. If active killing of the suffering would lead to active killing of others, that is a relevant consequence, which must be taken into account in evaluating even the first, most apparently justifiable act of this sort.

If, however, one has reason to believe that the distinctions between the active killing of the terminally ill for mercy and the killing of the unwanted for the convenience of society are clear or at least morally sound, then the two kinds of killing can be seen as morally different. For instance, rule utilitarians might reject a rule that permits active killing whenever someone believes net good would come of the killing as well as a rule that prohibits all active killings. They might instead opt for a rule that permits active killing only when it is requested by a competent person, perhaps one who is terminally ill, and only after the circumstances are reviewed by a court or publicly appointed panel to confirm that these are really the wishes of the person who will be killed. Such a rule could also exclude all health care professionals from the role of euthanizer. Alternatively, one could opt for a rule that extends active killing under rigorous due process to incompetents, but only when it is demonstrated overwhelmingly that it is for the good of the incompetent rather than for the good of others.

Logically, one could hold that the principle that active killing for mercy is morally acceptable without also accepting the principle that active killing for the benefit of others—other individuals, ethnic groups, or the race—is also acceptable. Marvin Kohl attempts to refute the use of the wedge argument against active killing by pointing out that the appropriate rule to follow is: do not kill except in cases of voluntary inducement of painless and quick death when the intention and consequences of which are the kindest possible treatment in the actual circumstances for the recipient of the act.[23] His formula clearly separates, at least in theory, killing for kindness and killing for the benefit of others.

At this point there seem to be two forms of the wedge argument. One is the logical form as argued by Kohl: the same rule that supports killing that appears acceptable also supports killing that does not appear acceptable. The rule—kill whenever the good of society justifies it—might justify unacceptable killing of the undesirable, the useless, or the unconscious as well as the intractably suffering. To some that implication is clearly unacceptable and, therefore, since the rule leads from arguably tolerable killings to clearly intolerable ones, the rule must be wrong.

The second form of the wedge argument rests not on a logical point but on an empirical, psychological claim: that one practice, mercifully killing the intractably suffering for their own good, will as a matter of psychology, lead to another—killing the undesirable, the useless, or the unconscious. The defenders of this claim would concede that one does not logically lead to another. They would maintain, however, that society will be so conditioned to accept purposeful death in the one case that it will be psychologically readier to accept it in the second. If the second would be judged a horrendous wrong, then the first practice would be opposed to the extent it leads to the second. It is a claim that is not easily refuted.

A number of consequentialists have concluded that this bad outcome is sufficiently plausible that even merciful killing based on the request of a competent patient and confirmed by public scrutiny and due process should be prohibited. The careful consequentialist will have to concede to Rachels and his colleagues, however, that, on the basis of this argument, it is really not the bare difference between actions and omissions that is decisive; it is the difference in the consequences of the two practices.[24]

This argument from long-term consequences seems to be the best argument thus far for a possible difference between the practice of accepting active killing and the one of accepting some decisions to let people die. It is probably as good an argument as can be made for the difference if one accepts the premise that all that counts in morality is consequences. A fifth, and I think more powerful, case might be possible, however, if one holds to a normative morality that moves beyond consequences. It is here we finally encounter the deontological rebuttal to the claim that if two actions are equally reprehensible there is no moral distinction between them.

Active Killing Is Deontologically Wrong

Rachels's position rests on the assumption that if two actions are equally reprehensible there is no moral difference between them, but this position poses two serious problems. First, assessments of reprehensible behaviors are normally thought to be assessments of character or personal moral blameworthiness. It is easy to conclude that the two men who participated in their cousins' deaths are equally blameworthy. It does not follow that they were equally wrong, much less that there is no moral difference between them.

There is a difference between the assessment of character and the assessment of the morality of actions. A despicable character may nevertheless do what is right (for example, out of fear of getting caught). A person of exemplary character may, out of error, do something that is morally wrong. The assessment of their characters seems to have little bearing on whether their actions were right or wrong. We are forced to conclude with regard to Rachels's example, however, not only that both men are equally despicable characters, but that their actions are equally wrong. Can we conclude, however, that because two actions are equally wrong there is no moral difference between them and that, therefore, there is no moral difference between the two kinds of behavior they represent? Clearly not.

Many people believe that there are a number of things that can make actions wrong, the consequences being only one such reason. People who hold that there are many different wrong-making characteristics of actions are called deontologists. They claim that the mere fact that two instances of behavior are equally wrong on balance does not make them the same.[25] We can imagine a particular lie so wrong that it is as wrong as or worse than some particular murder. If the particular lie is just as wrong as the particular homicide, it does not follow that there is no difference between lying and homicide. It still makes sense to say that generally murder is worse than lying. In fact, one could maintain that lying, however wrong, should not always be prohibited, whereas murder, however sympathetic in a particular case, should always be treated as wrong. In any case, if telling a lie and committing a homicide are two different wrong-making characteristics of actions, then showing that two particular instances are equally reprehensible or even equally wrong tells us nothing about whether the two are different.

What the consequentialists miss—even the sophisticated rule consequentialists—is the possibility that actively killing and merely letting die are different because they involve different wrong-making characteristics. The deontologist would claim that even if the consequences of the practice of active killing are different from and generally worse than the practice of permitting decisions to let some people die, it does not follow that this is the reason that it is morally different to kill actively.

For the deontologist, the basis of the difference between active killing and simply letting die is that killing another human being is a *prima facie* wrong-making characteristic of actions while letting a person die is not. To say that it is a prima facie wrong-making characteristic is to say that it is always a wrong-making element of a behavior. Other elements sometimes identified as prima facie wrongs include telling a lie or breaking a promise or distributing a valuable resource unfairly. This is not to say that behaviors that contain these elements are always wrong. It is to say that they are wrong prima facie, that is, insofar as they contain these elements. Behaviors may simultaneously contain right-making characteristics. Since there may often be complex combinations of prima facie rights and wrongs, whether these behaviors are right or wrong on balance requires some theory for relating these characteristics.[26]

There is a long, unresolved debate over the question of whether there can be any inherent wrong-making characteristics of actions of this sort. Some attempts, not terribly successful, have been made to mount arguments for the existence of these deontological elements in normative ethical theory. This may be because we are, at this point, searching for the most fundamental principles of morality. This starting point cannot be argued for. It must be discovered, assumed, revealed, or found obvious by common sense.

In this problem, consequentialists (such as the utilitarians) face the same dilemma. They hold that the right-making characteristic of an action (or rule) is that it produces good—as much or more good than any alternative action (or rule). If asked to prove or argue for the proposition that the fact that an action produces good is a right-making characteristic, they are hard pressed. In one way or another, they will appeal to common sense or claim that it is obvious to all rational observers. Reductionists press the position that production of good is the only such obvious right-making characteristic. Others—the deontologists—claim that there are other characteristics that must be incorporated as well if we are plausibly to make sense of the world. The list ought to be as short as possible, but it is no more reasonable to exclude some characteristic that must be present than it is to include one that can be omitted. The standard short list that deontologists consider wrong-making includes, along with lying, breaking promises, failing to respect autonomy, failing to show gratitude, failing to make reparation for a wrong, and treating people unjustly.[27]

I am increasingly convinced that the killing of human beings must be added to that list. That conclusion, I would suggest, is, in principle, not one that can be argued (any more than the conclusion that producing good is right-making can be). For those in religious traditions such as Orthodox Judaism, Buddhism, Hinduism, and most of Christianity the conclusion can be grounded in scriptural text and revelation. For those working in more secular systems, it is harder to explain where the basic assumptions of a philosophical system are formed. I think there is good historical evidence that secular thinkers absorb such notions from more religious cultural precursors. However these basic principles are derived, there is a widespread (but not universal) inclusion of the inherent wrongness of killing on the list, and it is almost as widespread as the inclusion of the production of good as a right-making characteristic. Those who do not accept this will have to revert to the consequentialist arguments to determine the moral status of active killing for mercy. Deontologists have available another moral option, a prima facie principle prohibiting killing.

The next critical question is whether letting people die is a behavior that is exactly like killing them and, therefore, covered under a prima facie principle prohibiting killing. I think not. Deciding whether to intervene to prevent a death depends on variables that are not present in deciding to intervene to kill. When one kills one always enters the nexus of responsibility. When one lets die, one does not. For the moment, I shall limit the discussion to interventions by health care professionals. A physician, for example, can treat a patient only with the consent of the patient or the patient's surrogate. To intervene otherwise is to violate the autonomy of the patient—to commit a battery. Without the permission of the patient or the surrogate for the patient, health professionals do not have the authority to intervene to prevent a death, let alone the duty to do so. They are not in the nexus of responsibility. With regard to most human beings at any given time a health professional has not been authorized to intervene. This is particularly true in cases where a patient has specifically refused a treatment. Thus the health care professional is often outside the sphere of responsibility when it comes to interventions to delay dying. By contrast, the same professional is always responsible for active interventions, including the action of killing. To the extent that those actions involve violations of prima facie principles, they always include an element that makes them wrong.

The establishment of a relationship of responsibility is complex in the case of letting die. In Hippocratic ethics, the physician has a duty to benefit the patient, only *after* he has agreed to accept that person as a patient. In Judeo-Christian ethics and secular liberalism, on the other hand, a fiduciary relationship is established when and only when the patient has accepted the professional's offer of commitment and has reciprocated the commitment. It is at that point that a covenant is established. The patient may plausibly accept the fiduciary relationship with the condition that certain treatment not be rendered. A professional who refrains from intervening, who lets die when the patient has refused treatment, is "guilty" only of failure to commit battery. But the professional who kills such a patient, even with the patient's permission, has violated at least the prima facie duty to avoid killing a human being. From the deontological point of view, therefore, the two behaviors are radically different morally.

What, however, of health care professionals who have been invited into the patient's world, who have become responsible for the care of the patient? Some patients might establish a covenant with health care providers that would be open-ended—in effect, giving a blank check that authorizes the provider to do anything that the provider deems appropriate. They conceivably would offer a contract that would give the provider authority to continue treatment even if the patient later decided he wanted to stop the relationship. Such contracts with a provider, especially the ones that are irrevocable, are both legally and ethically suspect. Indeed, it is highly unlikely that a rational person would make such an authorization, and it is even more unlikely that such authorizations could be irrevocable. Were such an arrangement made, however, the provider could not maintain that he or she was not responsible for decisions to forgo treatment. In this situation, the health care professional would function like a lay surrogate (a next-of-kin or designated proxy) who has the responsibility to act in the best interest of the patient.[28]

The more interesting moral puzzle turns out to be whether surrogates who clearly have a duty to serve the best interests of the incompetent patient can be any more justified in ordering nontreatment than they can in actively killing. At this point, it will not do to argue that letting die is only a failure to commit battery while killing is a violation of a prima facie duty, yet something analogous still holds. The fiduciary has a responsibility for the welfare of the individual. In the case of a decision about death-prolonging treatment, this moral principle generates the prima facie duty to promote the patient's best interest.

If the fiduciary did not intervene when to do so would be in the patient's best interest, the appropriate moral charge would be a violation of the prima facie duty to benefit, that is a violation of the principle of beneficence. If the fiduciary has also made a promise to provide life-prolonging treatment to the patient, failure to do so is a violation of the prima facie duty to keep promises. In either case, this still is morally different from active killing, which is a violation of the prima facie duty to avoid killing.

However, not everything that can be done to prolong the dying process can be said to promote the patient's best interest. Failure to intervene in such cases is not a wrong at all. In fact, if intervening would hurt the patient, then failing to intervene is avoiding harm. It is following the principle of nonmaleficence.

All of this leads to the conclusion that letting die is not a wrong at all unless it is a violation of beneficence or promise keeping, while killing is always a violation of the duty to avoid killing. Even when intervening to prolong life is a net good for the patient and the decision maker has a fiduciary duty to promote the patient's best interest, it is still morally different from actively killing.

I am convinced that failure to benefit someone is morally much less serious than violating nonconsequentialist principles such as the duty not to kill. The principle of beneficence is morally different from the other principles on the deontologist's list of duties. It seems clear that even in the case of persons with whom a covenant of responsibility has been established (normally, lay surrogates), there are many times when benefit need not be produced—for example, when maximizing benefit would come at the expense of failing to benefit someone else to whom a special duty is owed. The parent who fails to benefit one child in order to benefit another understands the notion well. The subordination of the duty to benefit is even clearer in the case of persons to whom we have no relationship of responsibility. We all let starving people die daily. While this may be a prima facie wrong, it is surely less a wrong than violation of one of the nonconsequential prima facie principles. In fact, I have elsewhere argued that the principle of beneficence must always be subordinated to all the nonconsequentialist prima facie principles.[29] This includes the principle of respecting autonomy as well as of avoiding killing.

This leads me to the conclusion that while active killing is always a violation of the prima facie principle to avoid killing another human being, letting die, when the decision maker is outside the nexus of responsibility, is nothing more than fulfilling the prima facie principle of respecting autonomy. And even if the decision maker is in the nexus of responsibility, letting die may be merely following the dictates of the principle of beneficence and nonmaleficence. In other cases, when the person would be better off being treated, it may be merely the failure to be beneficent with this person in order to fulfill other obligations.

In those cases where a relationship of responsibility has been established, the good of the patient would be served, and no counterveiling prima facie obligation would be violated by preserving life, then, and only then, would letting die be a terrible wrong. In some rare cases it would be as wrong as actively killing. It would still not be the same as actively killing, at least to the deontologist, but it would be as wrong in the specific case. In the cases discussed above, Rachels has managed to present examples that would lead to this special situation: where a clear relationship of responsibility exists on the part of the adult letting his cousin die as well as on the part of the one who actively kills; where intervention clearly would be for the good of the child, and where no counterveiling prima facie obligation exists. Then and only then can he conclude that letting die is as wrong as killing. Even then it is not the same. It is failure in the fiduciary obligation to promote the welfare of the child; it is not a failure to fulfill the duty to avoid killing.

THE POSSIBLE MORALITY OF ACTIVE KILLING

Thus far I am led to a tentative conclusion that active killing seems different from letting die for two reasons: the consequences of the practices may be different and, more importantly, they involve different ethical principles. However, none of these arguments about the differences between active killing and letting die can lead to the conclusion that active killing is always wrong on balance. Even if avoiding killing is always a prima facie moral duty, whether it is one's actual duty will depend on the relationship of this duty to other prima facie duties. Since I hold that the nonconsequentialist principles take precedence over merely producing benefits and avoiding harms, I am led to the conclusion that the good of the patient will not justify mercy killing.

There are two important corollaries. First, if the prima facie duty to benefit is not subordinated to the duty to avoid killing, but is balanced against it, as many philosophers would hold, then in some cases where great good would be done by mercifully killing, then perhaps sometimes the duty to benefit will outweigh the duty to avoid killing. In such cases killing would be right on balance even though a prima facie wrong. That stance, however, seems to open the door to other killings, including ones that seem clearly unacceptable.

Second, even if the duty to benefit is subordinated to other nonconsequentialist duties, possibly when these other duties come into conflict among themselves, a balancing of competing claims must take place. In that case the principle of avoiding killing possibly would have to give way. This would occur in a more limited number of cases than if benefits can be taken into account. It is hard to imagine cases where one would have to kill mercifully in order to respect autonomy or tell the truth. Possibly it could come into conflict with the duty to keep promises, such as a case where one had promised to kill another if pain became intractable. Even then, however, the conflict would rest on the legitimacy of a promise to engage in a behavior that conflicted with other principles. Promises to lie or treat people unfairly or kill may be void from the beginning if they violate other duties.

The most plausible case for a conflict of principles is probably grounded in justice. If justice requires that we act so as to improve the situation of the least well off, and a dying person in intractable pain is among the least well off, then justice might require killing. And then the duty to promote justice would be in conflict with the duty to avoid killing, a conflict that could only be resolved by balancing the two competing duties. Assuming that merely letting such a person die would not prevent as much suffering, then on balance, in this rare circumstance, active killing could be more moral.

George Fletcher argues that the distinction between actively assisting in the death of the patient and allowing the dying to die has a parallel in the American legal system in the different ways that culpability is assigned to "causing" or "permitting" harm to be done to others. In cases where there is an act to cause harm, liability for the proscribed harm is readily assigned once the agent who has carried out the act has been identified. In cases of omission, however, liability is not so readily assigned.[30] In the case of an omission, liability will depend upon "the relationship between the parties."[31]

THE CASE FOR A DIFFERENCE: PRACTICAL CONSIDERATIONS

Even if an argument can be made for the moral acceptability of active killing, and even for preferring it in the rare case, it is still an open question whether such active killing should be made legal. As I have shown, pervasive and serious consequences can attend the principle that it is acceptable to kill patients for whom life is not worth living. Without being concerned about the extension of this principle to those other than the dying, we still have reason to be cautious. And because of the power of drugs to control pain, which makes the need for active intervention to spare the patient suffering extremely rare, we may want the active killing of dying patients to remain illegal even in those exceptional cases where it might be morally justified. This situation is inescapable in a society governed by the crude instrument of the law.

Consider the analogy of the "red light rule." It is really not necessary for every car to stop at every red light under every conceivable condition. One could cautiously continue through a red light if no car were in sight in order to save time. There can be no doubt that the rule "always stop at every red light" is crude. A better one (if it were followed scrupulously) might be "stop and wait for every red light unless the road is clear." Yet, obviously the rule "stop unless the road is clear" will not work because too many mistakes will be made. It is better in the long run to follow the apparently less efficient rule, even if we occasionally waste time.

A similar situation applies in those cases where active killing of the dying might be morally justified. The courts would probably be lenient toward a parent who drove through a red light to speed a critically ill child to the hospital. It may be that civil disobedience is also the appropriate course in the case of the rare patient who is irreversibly dying in extreme pain. If the active hastening of death has to be justified by an appeal to civil disobedience, the courts may continue to show leniency in their judgments, but we may also continue to examine those cases carefully and thoroughly.

Stopping Versus Not Starting Treatments

Should Mrs. Gilbert suddenly have caught an infection or suffered a cardiac arrest, Mr. Gilbert would have had the option of letting the ailment take its course without intervening. Mrs. Gilbert was relatively healthy. She was not on a ventilator or receiving hemodialysis. She was not suffering from heart disease that produced a need for CPR. The situation of other patients is often different. They are either in need of temporary and intermittent life-saving interventions or on permanent life-support systems such as ventilators. Consider the incompetent patient who has never expressed any wishes about terminal care and who is being maintained in intensive care by the use of a respirator. Would the surrogate decision makers have the option of turning off the respirator, or do they have to wait until pneumonia or some other new problem develops so that they can omit treatment and let the patient die?

If there is a moral difference between actions and omissions, especially if that difference is such that as a matter of policy active killing is never legal, it might at first appear that the only acceptable course is to wait until the respirator-dependent patient develops some new complication for which treatment can be omitted.

From the standpoint of the five distinctions between action to end life and the simple avoidance of treatment, stopping a treatment that has been started has some characteristics of each. There seems to be some difference of opinion on whether the psychological impact of stopping is more akin to active killing than to not starting a treatment. Paul Ramsey, for instance, observes that medical professionals tend to see stopping an ongoing treatment (like a respirator) as similar to active killing, but that ethicists and moral theologians treat it like not starting treatment in the first place. The link between the psychological impact of a decision and the rightness or wrongness is difficult to establish, however.

In terms of the consequences stopping a treatment seems more like a decision to omit treatment. That is, where active killing could cause many who are not terminally ill to die, the withdrawal of treatment would lead to death only in a narrower class of patients, more or less the ones who might have died from having treatment omitted in the first place. The impact on societal attitudes about killing are harder to assess. Some might argue that active intervention to withdraw ongoing medical support of life could prepare the way for more controversial actions, just as injecting an air bubble or potassium might. On the other hand, virtually all ongoing therapies are in fact stopped from time to time in order to clean or replace equipment or to see how the patient will do without it. For example, momentary withdrawal of a respirator is standard practice. If one equated purposeful stopping of treatment with active killing rather than with omission of treatment, then one could take advantage of these temporary cessations of treatment to decide to omit restoration of the treatment.

From the point of view of deontological duties, the arguments that apply to omissions of treatment seem to apply to withdrawals as well. Even if a patient has exercised autonomy by consenting to treatment, normally that consent should be seen as limited in duration to the extent that consent can be withdrawn at any time. If a respirator-dependent patient withdraws consent, continued treatment would be a violation of the autonomy of the patient in precisely the same way that initiating treatment without consent would be. Even the patient (or the surrogate or other responsible agent) may be motivated only by the intention of beneficence or protection from harm, which may legitimately be separate from the intention of killing, a distinction that I shall take up in the next section.

There is, then, a broad consensus that stopping treatment should be viewed morally not as an action to kill, but as akin to omission of treatment. Thus the President's Commission for the Study of Ethical Problems in Medicine and Biomedical and Behavioral Research has concluded that "neither law nor public policy should mark a difference in moral seriousness between stopping and not starting treatment."[32] It points out that it would be relevant to take into account the possibility that starting a treatment creates an expectation that it will be continued.[33] On the other hand, again arguing in a consequentialist mode, it suggests that making withdrawing more serious than failing to initiate treatment could lead to serious problems. Often before a treatment is tried it is not clear whether the treatment will help. If decision makers knew that once treatment was started it would be hard to stop, this could incline them to resist starting, thus leading to unjustified omissions.[34] Although these arguments from consequences may not be definitive reasons for treating withdrawals as morally like omissions, they provide additional support for that conclusion.

Direct Versus Indirect Killing

Another ambiguous class of actions is those that result in death although that was not the direct intention. Consider the possibility that a patient who is being maintained is suffering from anxiety. To induce sleep, phenobarbitol is given, but increasing doses are required until the drug levels reach the point where there is serious risk of respiratory depression and even death. Earlier I observed that sometimes there is an attempt to make a distinction between active killing and omission of treatment on the basis of intention. While that distinction may not have been valid in distinguishing omissions and commissions, intention does become relevant when death is a possible side effect of a treatment, whether surgery or drugs, to relieve pain or anxiety. Catholic literature, for example, states specifically that "it is not euthanasia to give a dying person sedatives and analgesics . . . even though they may deprive the patient of the use of reason, or shorten his life."[35]

The term *indirect killing* or *indirect euthanasia* are sometimes used to refer to the omission of treatment in order to allow the dying patient to die. This language is confusing at best.[36] It is possible for someone to omit treatment specifically to bring about death just as it is possible to kill actively (for example, through an anesthesia accident) even though one's intention is to preserve life.

The distinction between direct and indirect effect has its origins in Roman Catholic ethics, in which an effect is indirect when it is really a side effect, a consequence that is secondary. Within this tradition, for an evil effect to be morally licit, four conditions must be met. They have been summarized by Gerald Kelly as follows:

1. The action, considered by itself and independently of its effects, must not be morally evil.
2. The evil effect must not be the means of producing the good effect.
3. The evil effect is sincerely not intended, but merely tolerated.
4. There must be a proportionate reason for performing the action in spite of its evil consequences.[37]

The framework is one in which an intervention can be divided conceptually into an "action" and several consequences, some of which are good and others evil. It is a framework that accepts the notion that some actions are "intrinsically evil," that is, they cannot be justified in spite of their consequences. Kelly cites murder, by which he means active killing, as one example.[38] In the case of stopping or omitting treatment, there is presumably no reason to assess the action itself as evil. The consequences would include some that were intended, such as relief from the agony of the treatment, which is good, and some that were not, such as the death of the patient, which is considered bad.

The scheme requires that three additional conditions be met beyond the one that the action itself not be evil. The sequence of events is important (criterion two). The evil effect cannot come earlier in the sequence so that it is a means to the good. Thus it is not considered acceptable to attempt to relieve pain by permanently depressing respiration, and then to claim that the death of the patient is an unintended effect. If stopping respiration permanently (death) as a means to relieving pain is considered an evil effect, this order of events, with the death occurring before pain is relieved, makes the effects unacceptable. Some authors in the Catholic tradition claim that any effects that are means to the good effects are "intended."[39] Some critics of the Catholic doctrine question how the mere sequence of events can affect their morality. They argue that if the good effects are proportional to or greater then evil effects, than it should not make any difference in what order they occur.

Another area of contention is whether intention per se can make an action moral or immoral. Other critics would argue that intention should affect the praiseworthiness or blameworthiness of the actor, but not whether the action was right or wrong, especially in cases where the evil is foreseen though not intended. They argue that while an unforseen evil need not be taken into account (for example, an idiosyncratic toxic reaction of a patient that produces death), one that is or should be anticipated (for example, the death of a fetus in the case of the removal of the fallopian tube in an ectopic pregnancy) should not be less significant morally because it is not intended. Either the foreseen event is justified on grounds of proportionality or it is not, regardless of whether it is intended. Of course, if the evil is intended, the actor is blameworthy, but the action is, according to these critics of double effect reasoning, no less moral.

Whether the distinction between direct and indirect effect is of significance in reasoning about the care of terminally ill patients will depend on validity of these criticisms of the doctrine. In any case, the distinction is not the same as the distinction between omission and commission. One can actively kill indirectly and kill directly by omission.

Once again, the President's Commission for the Study of Ethical Problems in Medicine and Biomedical and Behavioral Research has reviewed these issues and rejects the moral importance of the distinction between intended and unintended but foreseen outcomes.[40] The implication can be seen in the debate over giving potentially lethal narcotics for the relief of pain. Both Catholic theology and the President's Commission accept the legitimacy of giving such drugs (assuming, of course, that the purpose is to relieve pain and not to cause death). Presumably the two groups would disagree in the case of a dose that was with great certainty going to cause death although that was not intended. This foreseen, but unintended death would apparently be acceptable according to the doctrine of double effect, but not according to persons who consider unintended, but foreseen consequences the moral equivalent of intended ones. Of course, both groups would accept giving such medication when the lethal effect was a possible, but not an expected outcome.

Reasonable and Unreasonable Treatments

Those who decide that a patient is alive and who also decide that they are opposed to hastening death actively must finally face a critical question: When, if ever, is it moral to forgo treatment? Does it make any difference whether a dying patient refuses radical experimental surgery, an expensive but not experimental cardiac valve operation, a mechanical respirator, or an intravenous feeding? Does it make any difference whether the patient is in the last hours of severely metastasized cancer or the early days of a certainly fatal but not yet debilitating disease, in the prime of life or over the hill?

The distinction is sometimes made between "ordinary" and "extraordinary" means of medical treatment. Pope Pius XII considers the traditional moral distinction critical:

> But morally one is held to use only ordinary means—according to circumstances of persons, places, times, and culture—that is to say, means that do not involve any grave burden for oneself or another. A more strict obligation would be too burdensome for most men and would render the attainment of the higher, more important good too difficult. Life, health, all temporal activities are in fact subordinated to spiritual ends.

On the other hand, one is not forbidden to take more than the strictly necessary steps to preserve life and health, as long as he does not fail in some more serious duty.[41]

The distinction has found its way into some, but not all, of the public policy proposals dealing with forgoing of treatment. The terms *ordinary* and *extraordinary* are extremely vague and used inconsistently in the literature. They are misleading and should be dropped just as the term *euthanasia* should be. The terms have really meant nothing more than treatments that are unreasonable and reasonable to refuse. At least three different bases for distinguishing the two are found.

CRITERIA FOR DISTINGUISHING BETWEEN
REASONABLE AND UNREASONABLE REFUSAL OF TREATMENT

Jesuit moral theologian Edwin Healy defines extraordinary as "whatever here and now is very costly or very unusual or very painful or very difficult or very dangerous"[42] That Healy includes these factors indicates that the term *extraordinary* implies more than a simple survey of frequency of use under a given condition. Nevertheless, we might expect usualness to correlate closely with these other factors. Thus, this first criterion of the distinction can be summarized, somewhat awkwardly, as "usualness."

Usual vs. Unusual

There are obvious problems with the notion of usualness, however. If usual treatments are morally required and unusual ones not required, the status quo defines the moral requirement. It does not seem reasonable to answer the question "What is required?" by saying "Whatever the physicians tend to be providing." It should be possible to say that even though something is not now being done, it ought to be. Adequate primary health care for urban ghettos and rural areas is unusual. That it is morally expendable because it is unusual seems preposterous. In the same light, it does not seem reasonable to require a treatment simply because it is usually provided. If that were the case, no change in treatment could ever take place. We could never have argued that a usual treatment such as a respirator for a chronically semicomatose accident victim ought to be omitted. Although "usualness" may be helpful in reflecting upon what might be required, it alone cannot possibly tell us precisely what is required.

Simple vs. Complex

Closely related to the question of how common a treatment is, is that of how complex it is. There is some inclination among clinicians to identify morally expendable treatments with those that are technologically complex. A heart transplant or a hemodialysis machine would be expendable, while an IV drip or an antibiotic for an infection would be required because they are so simple.

Like the criterion of usualness, this one seems to be based on a misunderstanding of the term *extraordinary*. It is true that high technology interventions are more likely to be extraordinary in the sense of being statistically unusual, but the complexity of the technology can no more be a reasonable basis for deciding whether to provide a treatment than usualness can.

Reasonable vs. Unreasonable Treatment

What is needed is a set of criteria that tell us when it is reasonable to intervene and when it is unreasonable. The appropriateness of interventions for patients must be based not on their statistical frequency in the general population or their technological complexity, but rather on some more rational criteria. Two such criteria are now being discussed in the secular and theological literature.

Useful vs. Useless. In his statement on the "Prolongation of Life," the pope said that an anesthesiologist is not bound to use modern artificial respiration apparatus in cases that are "considered to be completely hopeless."[43] These insights are often held to establish uselessness as a rational criterion of expendability.

Grave Burden. Pope Pius XII goes beyond affirming that useless treatments are morally expendable. He says that one is held to use only "means that do not involve a grave burden for oneself or another."[44] He recognizes that some treatments may do good, but only at the expense of inflicting serious pain or suffering. This, in fact, reflects a long tradition in Catholic moral theology.[45] The result is that treatments are morally expendable if they are useless and, furthermore, even if they serve some useful purpose, they are still expendable if they involve grave burden.

The inclusion of burdens to others is controversial. Certainly we have reached the point where resources are so scarce that burdens to others justify some limits in special cases. Those are essentially societal decisions that raise questions of distributive justice, however. I think it is more appropriate to talk about patient-centered burdens. This leaves open the possibility that a competent patient may be so focused on the burden to others (his children, for instance) that he incorporates this notion into his own judgment about the refusal of treatment, but that surrogates making decisions for patients should not normally have these issues on their agendas.

The notion of grave burden raises several problems. First, burdens may come from several sources. The most straightforward would be the burden of the treatment itself. The pain from radical surgery, the nausea from chemotherapy, or the anguish of hemodialysis certainly all potentially justify refusing treatment. Sometimes, however, the burden that is envisioned comes not from the treatment, but from the underlying medical condition of the patient. A person racked with pain in the last stages of metastatic cancer who happens to get pneumonia might well consider refusing penicillin to treat the pneumonia on the grounds that "grave burden will result." It is true that the person will experience much more pain if he takes the penicillin than if he does not, but it is not the pharmacological effects of the penicillin that are of concern. It is the resulting life that is burdensome, so burdensome, in fact, that even simple life-prolonging medication might justifiably be refused.

The introduction into the calculation of the burden of the resulting life is somewhat more controversial than simply considering the burden of the treatment itself. It is even more controversial when one realizes that this burden of life must be compared with its benefits. That seems to open the door to assessing how beneficial certain lives are. For example, would adding a year to the life of a productive middle-class worker or homemaker with responsibility for children be considered a greater benefit than adding an equal amount of time to the life of an unemployed alcoholic or a severely retarded citizen and therefore justify greater burden during that year?

There appears to be an emerging consensus that, for purposes of making medical decisions, lives should be presumed to be of equal value. Perhaps individuals considering whether to accept or reject care for themselves should appropriately assess how much benefit they will consider their lives to produce, but this is not the sort of assessment that other persons should be making. Still, to exclude consideration of the medical burdens of the resulting life seems implausible. At least those burdens that are beyond the control of the decision makers (such as pain from cancer) seem to be legitimate when determining the burdens resulting from a treatment.

What can be said of a third kind of burden, one that is "socially generated"? Consider a child born with sickle dwarfism who is also suffering from projectile vomiting. One particular child with these problems was born to low-income parents in a state with extremely few resources committed to support for the mentally handicapped. The projectile vomiting was life-threatening, but could be corrected surgically with relatively little pain and suffering. The treatment would not be gravely burdensome from that standpoint. The sickle dwarfism, of course, would not be corrected, and the result would be a life of mental retardation. We have just concluded, however, that the resulting life should not be used as a basis for concluding that little benefit would be produced from saving the life. In fact, the life of a mentally retarded child may be a quite happy one provided there is adequate and humane support, but in this case it is virtually certain that there will not be such care. The parents lack the resources to provide it, and the jurisdiction in which they live lacks the will to provide adequate, humane support. In such a case we face a fascinating dilemma. Performing the surgery will, with great reliability, lead to a grave burden for the child—not from the surgery and not from any inevitable medical condition, but rather from a virtually inevitable failure on the part of society. Compassionate and dedicated parents, such as the surrogate decision makers for the child, may feel compelled, if they are to promote the welfare of the child, to refuse the surgery on the grounds of grave burden.

Some people are inclined to reject this conclusion. They argue that socially caused burdens should not be a legitimate part of the calculation. They might also point out that if parents could legitimately refuse life-saving treatment because of socially caused, future burdens, then society would have less incentive to correct the social conditions, in this case to improve the quality of care for the handicapped.

This might lead to the conclusion that burdens that are medically inevitable (like cancer pain) are legitimately considered, but socially caused burdens are not. The problem with that conclusion, however, is that it, in effect, makes the child a means to a socially good end—prodding society to improve its care for the needy. If the parents should not consider socially caused burdens, then they, in effect, have a duty to sacrifice their child's welfare for the good of society. That is not what we normally expect of parents. Perhaps, after all, if the socially caused burdens really are inevitable, then a surrogate decision maker who is really committed to the welfare of the patient may have to consider them regardless of their source, provided the burdens are beyond the control of the surrogate.

There is a second kind of problem with the criterion of grave burden. Some treatments may offer both grave burden and even greater benefit. Does it make sense to hold that these treatments are morally optional even though benefits outweigh burdens? Or alternatively, some treatments may present only modest burdens, but virtually no hope of any benefit at all. If they are not totally useless, but not *gravely* burdensome either, are they still morally obligatory?

Proportionality. The combination of the linguistic problems with the terms *ordinary* and *extraordinary* and the conceptual problems with the notion of grave burden has led many of those writing in the religious and the secular literature to substitute a much simpler formulation that seems to accomplish the same thing as the uselessness and grave burden criteria.

The 1980 Vatican Declaration on Euthanasia says, for example:

> In the past, moralists [held] that one is never obliged to use "extraordinary" means. This reply, which as a principle still holds good, is perhaps less clear today, by reason of the imprecision of the term and the rapid progress made in the treatment of sickness. Thus some people prefer to speak of "proportionate" and "disproportionate" means.
>
> In any case, it will be possible to make a correct judgment as to the means by studying the type of treatment to be used, its degree of complexity or risk, its cost and the possibilities of using it, and comparing these elements with the result that can be expected, taking into account the state of the sick person and his or her physical and moral resources.[46]

A similar approach has been adopted by a number of Catholic commentators[47] and the President's Commission.[48]

WHAT TREATMENTS ARE REQUIRED?

The Evaluative Nature of Judgments

Although it may not at first be obvious, judgments of both benefit and harm, of uselessness as well as of burden, are inherently evaluative. There is, in principle, no way that medical science alone can determine that a treatment is either useless or burdensome. Two medically identical patients on hemodialysis may assess the burden quite differently. One may find the thought of being attached to a dialysis machine six to eight hours a day, two to three days a week for the rest of his life excruciating. Both the physical and mental burden may be more than he can bear. A second patient, medically identical, may find the dialysis unpleasant, but not agonizing. Likewise, they may assess the benefits differently. Deciding that the benefits are proportionate requires the inherently nonmedical determination of how valuable it is to continue living. It should be obvious that these are judgments that no outsider should be able to make.

Having extensive medical training—even extensive medical experience with dialysis— will not help in determining whether the dialysis treatments are disproportionately burdensome for a particular patient.

It may be less obvious that uselessness is also a value judgment. Some interventions are so clearly of no value that it is almost as if it were a scientific fact that they had no value. Whether value judgments can have an objective basis raises complex philosophical questions. Even if they can, however, they are not grounded in medical science. Consider the respiratory support of a permanently vegetative patient who would die without a ventilator, but who would live for perhaps years with one. Is the ventilator useful or useless? The answer will depend on whether it serves some useful purpose to preserve vegetative life. An Orthodox Jew and a Roman Catholic ought to give different answers if they are reflecting their own traditions. In any case, it should be obvious that there is no way that medical skill or experience can provide an answer.

What Specific Treatments Are Disproportionally Burdensome?

The evaluative nature of these judgments suggests that it is a mistake to attempt to divide treatments into those that are expendable ("extraordinary") and those that are not. If judgments ought to be based on proportionality, and if proportionality involves assessment not only of the burdens of the treatment but also of the future life based on individually held beliefs and values, then no possible list of expendable treatments could ever be compiled. Some treatments as simple as CPR, antibiotics, medically supplied nutrition and hydration will sometimes be morally inappropriate, because they do not offer proportional benefits. The idea that something this simple can be expendable has become controversial recently. Medical nutrition and hydration are the ultimate in routine, everyday care. But a treatment's being usual or simple is not an appropriate basis for making moral judgments about expendability.

Is Supplying Nutrition Medical? The critics of accepting decisions to forgo nutrition and hydration offer several arguments. The first is that these are not medical procedures, but basic sustenance that all humans need in order to survive.[49] Gilbert Meilaender has argued that

> All living beings need food and water in order to live, but such nourishment does not itself heal or cure disease. When we stop feeding the permanently unconscious patient, we are not withdrawing from the battle against any illness or disease; we are withholding the nourishment that sustains all life.[50]

Some respond by arguing that nasogastric tubes, IVs, or a gastrostomy are not natural means of feeding, but artificial techniques requiring medical skill. Moreover, the medical interventions produce burdens well beyond regular oral feeding.[51] There is a more basic response to Meilaender and his colleagues, however. Regardless of whether a nasogastric tube is "medical," it may be serving no purpose; it may be unduly burdensome.[52] The hidden premise in the Meilaender position seems to be that if a procedure is basic sustenance rather than "medicine," then it should be required even if it is useless or gravely burdensome. It seems that whether something is *medical* care cannot be morally relevant. If it serves some proportionate good, it ought to be provided; otherwise it should not.

By this logic, even oral feeding could conceivably be morally optional as disproportionate. While this conclusion may not be acceptable to some moderates who accept forgoing parenteral and enteral nutrition by arguing that it is medical, it seems hard to defend requiring anything that is useless or gravely burdensome just because it is nonmedical.

Is Nutrition an Important Symbol? Daniel Callahan raises another argument in a partial defense of the moral uniqueness of nutrition and hydration. Beginning with "a stubborn emotional repugnance against discontinuance of nutrition," Callahan argues that feeding the hungry is "the perfect symbol of the fact that human life is inescapably social and communal."[53] The repugnance against starving people to death, Callahan suggests, is an "enduring and central" moral emotion that is linked to an inescapable moral obligation.

Callahan is certainly on to something. Withholding nutrition is linked in some way with a revulsion against starving people. Those defending the legitimacy of forgoing disproportionately burdensome nutrition, however, question the link between the psychological states of being hungry and thirsty, on the one hand, and the physiological states of being nutritionally deprived and dehydrated, on the other. Joanne Lynn has argued that it is crucial to keep the two separate.[54] She and others working clinically in the field maintain that it is quite possible to have blood chemistries indicating radically abnormal nutritional and hydration states and still not feel hungry or thirsty. In fact, providing nutrition and hydration for some such patients can make them distinctly less comfortable.[55]

If that is the case, then it is confusing to speak of someone who is not getting nutrition as starving. Starving implies severe distress, while feeding may in fact be what produces distress. Even if it is important to retain a revulsion against starving people, it seems odd to do it at the expense of inflicting pain and discomfort on people who are not hungry, but only nutritionally abnormal. Callahan's conclusion is a wise one. The symbolic value of feeding cannot require feeding even in cases where it serves no useful purpose, but the revulsion should remain as a way of requiring excruciatingly careful justification for withholding nutrition and hydration. Nevertheless, in some cases forgoing even these basic supports is morally appropriate.

Is Withholding Nutrition a Backdoor Approach to Active Killing? One of the arguments for the possible moral distinction between killing and letting die was based on consequences. If active killing were acceptable, potentially every human being could be a target of such a practice. On the other hand, forgoing treatment would lead to death only in a much smaller number of cases. One (but only one) argument for the distinction rested on this difference in the degree of societal risk.

But if one of the interventions that people may forgo is nutrition and hydration (especially if oral nutrition is included), then anyone at any time could potentially have a death causally linked to a decision to forgo intervention. This should, indeed, give us pause. The imaginable harms of a policy tolerating forgoing nutrition are much like those of tolerating active killing.

This argument would, of course, not work for anyone who believes that the real difference between active killing and forgoing treatment is one rooted in deontological moral principles. For example, if someone held that accepting a patient's decision to forgo treatment is respecting autonomy while killing involves a violation of the prima facie principle of avoiding killing, then the difference would not rest on consequences. For someone holding this position, withholding nutrition could still be within the rights of the competent patient. It would also be acceptable for the properly established surrogate acting within reason. Holders of this view would not be swayed by the consequentialist considerations. They would conclude that, insofar as one is forgoing nutrition and hydration that are not doing proportional good, one is within one's rights.

PROCEDURES FOR DISTINGUISHING IMPERATIVE AND ELECTIVE INTERVENTIONS

We are still left with the problem of distinguishing between imperative and elective procedures. I suggest that we ought to do two things at this point. First, we ought to adopt the patient's perspective, and, second we ought to adopt the language of reasonableness. From these perspectives, we can ask what treatments are reasonable to refuse. The result is a scheme for decision making based on the moral theory developed in this chapter. I will summarize that scheme here and then test it against the increasingly massive American case law concerning refusal of treatment in the next two chapters.

Competent Patients

From the patient's perspective, it should be sufficient for competent patients to refuse treatment for themselves whenever they can offer reasons valid to themselves—that is, out of concern about physical or mental burdens and their personal application of the proportionality criterion.

Incompetent Patients

For the incompetent patient, it is much more difficult to determine what standard should be used. I suggest that a critical distinction needs to be made among different types of incompetent patients, as well as among different types of surrogates.

Formerly Competent Patients. First, some surrogates are acting on behalf of formerly competent patients who have made their wishes known about the kinds of care they would want if they were incompetent. The task for these surrogates is surely to determine what the patient would choose based on the patient's own values as best as that can be determined. Here we are merely extending the principle of autonomy to the formerly competent patient. The surrogate is offering what has been called a "substituted judgment."[56]

Never Competent Patients. If the incompetent patient has never been competent, however, or if the patient was once competent, but has never expressed wishes about terminal care that are (or should be) accessible to the proper surrogate, then it is meaningless to speak of extended autonomy. There is nothing to extend. In these cases, it is now recognized that what a surrogate ought to do is attempt to serve the "best interest" of the incompetent patient.[57]

Kinds of Surrogates

It is common to stop the analysis at this point, but that is a serious mistake. The critical question is what ought to happen when the surrogate makes an unexpected assessment. In the first case the surrogate might make an unexpected substituted judgment, offering an unlikely estimate of what the patient would have wanted based on his or her values. In the second case the surrogate might offer an unlikely estimate of what is in the patient's best interest. Should the surrogate have to make the best assessment in either case?

Nonbonded Surrogates. I have become convinced that a further distinction is necessary. There are two kinds of surrogates. Some are strangers to the patient, appointed by the courts or by other public mechanisms for patients who have no family or friends available for the surrogate role. These surrogates are not previously "bonded" with the surrogate. I shall call them "nonbonded" or "stranger" surrogates. Other surrogates fall naturally into their role because they are the next of kin or they have been designated by the patient using mechanisms to be discussed in chapter 6. These surrogates are previously "bonded" with the patient.

It seems clear that the nonbonded surrogates should have no latitude to draw on their own values in making assessments about what patients would have wanted or what is as objectively as possible in their best interest. Nonbonded surrogates must, according to this analysis, make the best possible assessment.

Bonded Surrogates. What of bonded guardians? At first it seems that they should also make the best possible assessment. Certainly, that is what they should try to do. It is not clear, however, that they must be held to the standard of actually choosing the most plausible assessment. If they were, every parental decision would have to be reviewed to determine that it is really in the child's best interest. It seems unworkable and an unnecessary intrusion on the family to require the best possible decision.

Rather, I would suggest that for bonded guardians we use what I term the *standard of reasonableness*.[58] We have in our society a nebulous but nevertheless widely used "reasonable person" standard, which is receiving increased attention. Most discussion of it has arisen in the context of cases of informed consent, but it is just as useful in the subject of refusing treatment.

In the debate about how much a patient or research subject must be told in order for consent to be informed, the traditional standard was what other competent medical professionals would have disclosed in similar circumstances.[59] Behind that standard was the presumption that there was something inherently medical about deciding how much information a person would want to know. In 1969 a new standard began to be used. It was recognized that reasonable people (the courts still use the term *reasonable man*) could judge whether they would find a piece of information sufficiently meaningful or useful that they would want to know it.[60] Citing this decision, higher courts in several jurisdictions now have held that the reasonable person standard is the one that should be used to determine how much information is to be given.[61] It is the kind of question that does not need medical training to answer.

The same kind of question is involved when one asks whether a bonded guardian has exceeded the limits of reasonableness in deciding whether the patient would have refused treatment (in the case of formerly competent patients who have expressed their wishes) or whether the treatment is in the patient's best interest. While it is important to have medical training to determine the diagnosis, prognosis, and alternative courses of treatment, deciding whether a particular treatment ought to be given (or accepted) is a normative question to be decided on the basis of ethical and other values. It is those value choices that the reasonable person can make without scientific or medical training.

For the incompetent patient—the child, the mentally incompetent, the senile, the comatose—it would seem morally acceptable for the patient's agent to refuse treatment when the judgment is within reason. That means that the surrogate making a substituted judgment would have to be within reason in judging what the patient would have wanted. In the case of the application of the best interest standard, the judgment that the treatment was in the patient's best interest would have to be within reason. I shall look in detail at cases involving refusal of treatment by competent patients and incompetent patients' agents in the next two chapters.

I find, then, that a refusal will be morally acceptable if it is reasoned, in the case of competent patients, or within reason, in the case of agents acting for incompetent patients. But what exactly does the reasonable person consider a reasonable or unreasonable refusal? We have seen that usefulness is one relevant consideration. At the same time, a treatment, even a useful one, ought to be dispensable if it inflicts a severe burden on the patient.

This is not far from the definitions of *ordinary* proposed by Pope Pius XII, Kelly, Healy, or Ramsey, but it avoids that ambiguous term and specifies a set of criteria together with a standard for resolving the specific case. It also eliminates two additional ambiguities. First, Pope Pius XII said that an "extraordinary" treatment is not required, leaving open, at least in that paragraph, the question of whether physicians could morally stop a treatment they found extraordinary (that is, unreasonable) even though the patient or his or her agents might find it reasonable or might not have been consulted about its reasonableness.

Second, the papal statement that treatments are extraordinary if they might impose a grave burden on the patient or another, may dangerously depart from the patient's perspective. While it is reasonable that concern for the welfare of others could well be among the patient's concerns and thus legitimate basis for refusal of treatment, do we really want to say that the agent for an incompetent patient can judge a treatment unreasonable because it is a burden on persons other than the patient (including presumably the agent deciding)? By emphasizing that treatments are unreasonable if they do not give rise to patient-centered objections, we can clearly eliminate such possibilities.

Allowing to Live Versus Allowing to Die

There is a final distinction that must be made before turning to the public policy questions involved in forgoing treatment. This is the distinction between decisions that, in effect, end a life that would otherwise continue until terminated by another cause and those that permit the dying process to continue uninterrupted. The difference is important to the one who must determine the benefits and the burdens of treatment. The maximum possible benefits are radically different in the case of the patient who is inevitably dying rapidly. Nevertheless, the importance of the distinction should not be overemphasized. For one thing, it is possible to have endless arguments over exactly when a patient is dying. Different patients have different probabilities for survival. They also have different life expectancies. For some public policy purposes these are important questions. Hospices, for example, for economic reasons, often want to set limits on the maximum life expectancy of patients they accept for treatment.

For the purposes of making decisions to refuse treatment, however, it may make no difference in principle whether the patient is dying. In either case, the decision maker should refuse treatment when the burdens are disproportionate and accept them when they are not. Authors of policies that try to make more out of the division between the terminally ill and those who are not (such as most state "living will" laws) must not understand the moral basis upon which decision makers refuse treatment. The only other alternative is that they are purposely rejecting the notion that treatments are justifiably refused on grounds of burden so that all treatments that will preserve life must be used. That is a terribly implausible, indeed inhumane, position—one that is rejected by most commentators.

4 | Deciding to Refuse Treatment

The Cases of Competent Patients

Elizabeth Bouvia has had a difficult life. She was, at birth, afflicted with severe cerebral palsy, which has left her a bedridden quadraplegic. According to the court record, except for a few fingers of one hand and some slight head and facial movements, she is immobile. She is totally dependent on others for every aspect of her care. She suffers from continually painful arthritis for which a tube implanted in her chest automatically pumps morphine.[1] According to an earlier court record, in addition to arthritis she has suffered constant pain from her inability to change her own position, from muscle contracture, and from increased spasticity that affects her limbs.[2]

In spite of these severe physical problems, she has accomplished a great deal. She is intelligent and mentally competent. She went to San Diego State University, earned her B.S. degree, married, and became pregnant. Her pregnancy ended in a miscarriage, however, and her husband has since left her. She lived with her parents until her father told her they could no longer care for her. At the time she sought the help of the courts, she had been unable to find a permanent place to live where she could receive the care she needed. She was without financial means.

In September 1983 she sought the right to be cared for at Riverside General Hospital in California while she intentionally starved herself to death. She needed to be hospitalized, she maintained, because of her need for continual medical and nursing assistance as she deteriorated. When the medical staff objected, she sought an injunction against the hospital and its staff to prevent them from feeding her without her consent or from discharging her. She specifically sought to have them enjoined from inserting a nasogastric tube for feeding or performing a gastrostomy. She argued that she had these rights based on her rights of privacy and self-determination.

In refusing to grant her request for an injunction, the court provided a complex and perhaps misunderstood ruling. It made reference to some, by now, standard objections to patient refusals of treatment. It referred to claims that she was not competent or making a free choice, but rejected those claims by holding that she made her own decision to forgo further feedings and that contentions to the contrary were "completely without merit." It went on, though, to cite other arguments that it appeared to view as legitimate. It noted that she was not terminal, that she had a life expectancy of fifteen to twenty years. It noted that third parties, including other patients in the hospital, other persons similarly situated, and health care professionals who would have to assist in her death would be affected, and that society has an interest in preventing suicide. Finally, it referred to the integrity of the medical profession. It even claimed that "the established ethics of the medical profession clearly outweigh and overcome her own rights of self-determination," a claim that could potentially justify forcing treatment on any patient, terminal or not, if only the profession's ethics require it.

The 1983 court decision was taken widely to mean that persons, at least those who are not terminal, do not have the right to refuse nutritional support. Her claim to a right to privacy and self-determination appeared to some to be overcome not only by societal interests in preventing suicide, but even by something as vague and seemingly irrelevant as a private professional group's moral objection to her action.

In fact, the court said something quite different. First, it affirmed that she does have "a fundamental or preferred right to terminate her own life and to terminate medical intervention." In fact, when Ms. Bouvia later left Riverside General Hospital, no legal action was taken to assure that she continued to get adequate nutrition.

The real issue apparently was, as stated by the court, whether she "has the right to end her life with the assistance of society." The court concluded that her right to terminate her own life was overcome by "the strong interests of the State and society." Third parties, such as the health professionals at the hospital could not, in the opinion of this court, be forced to assist her in her chosen plan. The court concluded that if she "voluntarily agrees to stay but declines nutrients in order to sustain her life, the defendants [the hospital staff] now will face the problem of forcing nutrients upon her." It was at this point that the court concluded that force-feeding should be permitted. In effect the court was saying that Elizabeth Bouvia's right of self-determination does not extend to her right to require health professionals to participate in her plan on the hospital turf. Her freedom to act does not imply her right to coerce the assistance of others in her plan.

Following that decision, Ms. Bouvia, in fact, left Riverside General Hospital. She attempted to live under a number of arrangements. Social workers tried, unsuccessfully, to arrange for an apartment so that she could live on her own with visiting nurses to care for her. Still her condition worsened. She got to the point that she could not retain solids. Her weight dropped to between sixty-five and seventy pounds. She was rehospitalized, this time at High Desert Hospital, a facility operated by the Department of Health Services of the County of Los Angeles. Operating under the earlier court's refusal to grant an injunction, the hospital staff inserted a nasogastric tube against Ms. Bouvia's express written refusal. At this point she again sought an injunction from the Court of Appeal of the State of California. The Court of Appeal gave a forceful defense of the right of self-determination for a competent patient. It ordered that the hospital staff be directed to remove the nasogastric tube and prohibited from replacing it without her consent.

At no point did the Court of Appeal actually say that the hospital had to keep Ms. Bouvia as a patient on her own terms. It was simply ordered to remove the tube that had been inserted against her will. We do not know what would have happened if the hospital had refused to let her stay once the tube was removed. It is conceivable that the two opinions are actually compatible. The 1983 court made clear that it felt that the hospital staff did not have to comply with Ms. Bouvia's plan against their will. The 1986 court made clear that she has the right to refuse the nasogastric feeding.

Presumably, competent patients do have the right to insist on getting some kinds of treatment in a public facility, but they cannot have the right to get, literally, anything they ask for. Whether they have the right to get palliative nursing care and pain medication while refusing nasogastric feeding was not actually decided by either of these opinions. What was decided was Ms. Bouvia's right to refuse medical treatment, including nasogastric feeding.

The Legal Right of Refusal

The principle of self-determination, especially in matters as critical as life and death, is fundamental in our legal system. This was affirmed as early as 1914 when Justice Cardoza declared that "every human being of adult years and sound mind has a right to determine what shall be done with his own body."[3] He explicitly made clear that medical procedures cannot be done without the patient's consent. In the crucial legal decision that set the standards for informed consent in the 1960s, Kansas Supreme Court Justice Alfred Schroeder declared:

Anglo-American law starts with the premise of thorough-going self-determination. It follows that each man is considered master of his own body, and he may, if he be of sound mind, expressly prohibit the performance of life-saving surgery, or other medical treatment. A doctor might well believe that an operation or form of treatment is desirable or necessary but the law does not permit him to substitute his own judgement for that of the patient by any form of artifice or deception.[4]

The fact is that no competent patients have ever been forced to undergo any medical treatment for their own good no matter how misguided their refusal may have appeared.[5] There are persistent rumors of lower court cases involving competent patients ordered to undergo treatment for their own good, but, in two decades of checking hundreds of cases, I have failed to identify a single exception to the rule. Much of the early case law dealt with the refusal of blood transfusions—often by Jehovah's Witnesses acting on their interpretation of a Biblical injunction against eating blood.[6] If one grants their assumption that the penalty for such blood eating is eternal damnation, the refusal, which merely results in the loss of a few earthly years, seems very plausible indeed.

Although the First Amendment guarantees free exercise of religion, "grave abuses" threatening "paramount state interests" have been held to justify infringement of religious liberty—to require vaccination, forbid polygamy, or require school attendance, for instance.[7] In this light, it is understandable that the court cases regarding the attempt of a competent adult to refuse a blood transfusion included no explicit argument based upon religious freedom.[8] In 1962, for example, Jacob Dilgard, Sr., was admitted to

County Hospital in Nassau County, New York, with upper gastrointestinal bleeding. Dr. George D. Erickson, who later brought the case to court, claimed that an operation was necessary to halt the bleeding and that "in order to offer the best chance of recovery a transfusion of blood was necessary, and that there was a very great chance that the patient would have little opportunity to recover without the blood." Mr. Dilgard was willing to submit to the operation, but refused the transfusion. His son also refused to give permission for the transfusion.

In the court debate there was never any doubt that the patient was completely competent and capable of making decisions on his own behalf. According to the judge, Mr. Dilgard understood the risks and was making a calculated decision. Judge Meyer acknowledged that a court will step in as guardian of an infant or an incompetent, but in this case he refused to intervene, arguing, "It is the individual who is the subject of a medical decision who has the final say and . . . this must necessarily be so in a system of government which gives the greatest possible protection to the individual in the furtherance of his own desires." The court's decision may well have been influenced by the fact that it did not consider the patient's life to be in immediate danger. Still, it acted on the basic premise that a doctor who performs an operation without the consent of a competent, conscious adult patient commits an assault.[9]

There are scores of these cases on the books, but almost all of them involve a special quirk: the patient is comatose, a child, a mental patient, or a prisoner. Usually the issue of the right of the competent patient to refuse treatment is not taken to court—it is assumed. The issue is usually whether the patient really is competent.

One such case was that of Mrs. Delores Phelps.[10] Suffering from gastritis and gastroenteritis, which had caused microcytic anemia because of the loss of blood, Mrs. Phelps needed a transfusion. But she explicitly refused on the grounds that she was a Jehovah's Witness. On July 8, 1972, she signed a "release for refusal to permit procedure." Her husband and adult son had discussed the refusal with her and agreed to support her decision. By July 11, she was comatose and her nephew, Michael Bratcher, petitioned the court to appoint him as her temporary guardian. The judge, Michael T. Sullivan, whose concern for the issues has since led him to write an article on the subject,[11] held a bedside hearing attended by Mrs. Phelps, the attending physician, two nurses, and eleven members of the Jehovah's Witness sect. The physician testified that he did not believe Mrs. Phelps had "the mental capacity to make her own decision at the present time." The two nurses testified that they had spoken to Mrs. Phelps and that she had told them she wanted no blood transfusion. Judge Sullivan said that he would prefer to order the transfusion, but concluded that there was no evidence of mental illness and that Mrs. Phelps was sincere in her religious belief. He then ruled that the court could not "use the guardian device in order to foist its own personal opinions upon an adult competent citizen."[12] Mrs. Phelps died the next day. Again, the issue was whether the patient was really competent to make her decision and whether her decision should be respected after she became comatose. The court's decision indicates that grounds for declaring incompetency are shrinking—an important development to be taken up in the next chapter.

There also seems to be a clear consensus that the competent adult has the legal right to refuse treatment on apparently foolish or misguided grounds, even when the treatments may be as commonly and clearly lifesaving as a blood transfusion.

The Moral Arguments Against Refusal

In these legal cases several moral arguments against honoring competent patients' wishes about refusing treatment have been confronted. In none of them has the argument rooted in the individual's autonomy been overcome.

THE WELFARE OF THE PATIENT

The most straightforward argument is that it does not serve the welfare of persons to permit them to make decisions about refusing treatment, especially decisions where the result is likely to be the person's death. Sometimes if the patient is terminally ill an exception is made on the grounds that the life cannot be saved, that only the time of death is affected by refusing treatment.

The cases of Elizabeth Bouvia, Jacob Dilgard, Delores Phelps, and others like them have shown that even when people are not terminally ill, there will not be a legally supported effort to override a competent patient's wishes. Two kinds of reasons are given. First, as is especially clear in Ms. Bouvia's case, it is not obvious that the patient's welfare will be served by inflicting treatment against the patient's wishes. Here is a case where the agony is severe, intractable, and prolonged. At least in the case where she herself has concluded that the benefits of treatment do not exceed the detriments, no one is in a position to mount a case that her welfare will really be served by forcing unwanted interventions on her.

The Jehovah's Witnesses calculation of benefits and harms is less obvious to us because most of us do not share the beliefs upon which it is based. Nevertheless, unless their beliefs about the facts are to be overturned (beliefs that are rooted in religious ways of knowing that are challenged in a liberal society only with fear and trepidation), we have to acknowledge that it would be difficult to argue that more good would be done for them by forcing treatment against their wishes. Even if we challenge their beliefs about the facts, if we take into account the tremendous psychological and social consequences of forcing blood on the Jehovah's Witness patient against his or her will, the defense of coercion based on the welfare of the patient seems tenuous.

The second counterargument to this defense of forced treatment on competent patients goes further. Refusal of even life-saving treatment, it is argued, rests not merely on considerations of consequences, but rather on a matter of rights. Ours is a society that values autonomy, and the right to refuse treatment is grounded in that autonomy. Hence, critics argue that autonomy should take absolute precedence over consideration of consequences that affect the individual alone.

Privacy vs. Self-Determination

Sometimes in the legal and philosophical literature this claim of the priority of rights over benefits has been made under the rubric of the patient's right of privacy. Ms. Bouvia, for example, originally claimed a right of privacy as well as of self-determination.[13] Many other cases, including those of Karen Quinlan[14] and Brother Joseph Fox,[15] have been argued on the grounds of privacy. The result, though, has often been to create conceptual confusion. W. A. Parent, for instance, defines privacy as "the condition of not having undocumented personal knowledge about one possessed by others."[16] By "undocumented" he means knowledge that is not "in the public record."[17] If that is the case, it is hard to see why refusing to honor a person's refusal of treatment is a violation of privacy. It is rather a violation of autonomy or self-determination, which is quite a different matter.

The reason why privacy has become a key concept in treatment refusal is largely a matter of law and history. Beginning in the 1960s the U.S. Supreme Court began constructing a constitutional right of privacy. Although privacy is not a specific right in the Constitution, it has been taken as implied in various portions including the First, Third, Fourth, Fifth, Ninth, and Fourteenth Amendments.[18] In 1965, the United States Supreme Court ruled in *Griswold v. Connecticut* that a state law prohibiting the use of contraceptives by married couples was a violation of privacy and therefore unconstitutional.[19] This made sense because enforcement would have required "a policeman under every bed," a real invasion of privacy.

In 1973, the right of women to obtain abortions was argued before the Supreme Court on the grounds of privacy.[20] It was probably at this point that privacy and autonomy began to be confused in cases involving the freedom to make medical decisions. Soon thereafter, whenever a lawyer wanted to argue for patient freedom, he or she would include a reference to the right of privacy, even when absolutely no such issue was involved. What was at stake was the autonomy of the individual to act. The confusion between the two concepts would eventually be questioned by at least one court, but for the most part the right of patients to forgo treatment has been referred to as a privacy right even though it is more a question of autonomy.[21]

Regardless of the terminology, many commentators, including spokespersons for the American liberal legal system, have given autonomy priority over the concern for promoting the welfare of competent individuals. In this regard, the American liberal tradition is in direct conflict with the more paternalistic Hippocratic ethical tradition of physicians, which commits the physician to doing what he *thinks* will benefit the patient even in cases where the patient thinks otherwise.

Limits on Self-Determination

The priority of autonomy does not necessarily pertain in cases where the welfare of others is at stake. Later in this chapter I shall examine cases involving efforts to coerce treatment on competent patients for the welfare of others. Now, however, I am concerned with cases that involve, at most, consideration of the welfare of a marginal third party.

If autonomy takes precedence over welfare of the competent individual, then such refusals of treatment by competent patients must be honored. This applies whether or not the patient is terminally ill, at least according to several legal and philosophical commentators. The Bouvia court, for example, maintains that "there is no practical or logical reason to limit the exercise of this right to 'terminal' patients."[22] In fact, those who oppose allowing competent patients to refuse treatment on the grounds that they are not terminally ill probably have in mind one of the other counterarguments to the right to forgo treatment.

THE PROHIBITION ON SUICIDE

The belief that there is an important distinction between terminal and nonterminal patients may well rest on the idea that persons do not have the right to commit suicide. In several cases, the proponents of forced treatment have argued that nontreatment would be suicide and that cooperation in the nontreatment would be assisting suicide.

This position requires several assumptions. First, it requires the conclusion that stopping treatment while one is inevitably terminally ill should not be considered suicide, whereas stopping when an individual is not inevitably dying is. Setting aside the possibility that even forgoing treatment when one is inevitably dying could be thought of as a suicide, I shall consider whether refusing treatment when it could prolong life indefinitely should be considered suicide, and, if so, whether that makes it wrong, legally or ethically.

In cases where the patient acknowledges that forgoing treatment is likely to result in death, then the debate rests on the issues raised in the discussion in the preceding chapter. Those who accept the doctrine of double effect would maintain that forgoing life-sustaining treatment should be distinguished from suicide in that, in some decisions to forgo treatment, the intention is to avoid a disproportionate burden, not to produce death. Holders of this view acknowledge that it would be possible to commit suicide by omission of treatment, that is to purposely forgo a life-saving intervention because one desired to be dead. But the normal case, they maintain, involves only the intention of forgoing useless or burdensome interventions, with the indirect result being death. For them, omission of treatment, even something as basic as nutrition and hydration, would not be tantamount to suicide.

Others do not accept this approach. They maintain that an action that has a fore-known evil consequence is evil unless it is justified on some other grounds. They might still hold that omissions that result in death are not necessarily evil on balance. Someone who maintains that there is a prima facie duty to avoid active killing could nevertheless accept omissions that result in death for the reasons that were discussed in the previous chapter. Thus it is possible, on grounds other than the doctrine of double effect, to hold that active killings resulting in death are prima facie wrong, but that there is no necessary wrong in omissions that lead to death. That in fact seems to be the most plausible position.

Even for those who do not accept the moral conclusion that omissions can be different from both active killings and suicide, the role of autonomy must be assessed. Even if one concludes that decisions by patients to forgo treatment constitute morally unacceptable suicides, it is still possible that individuals have the moral and legal right to refuse. In fact, there is no legal prohibition on suicide.[23] Thus, even if Elizabeth Bouvia's or a Jehovah's Witness's refusal constituted suicide, there is no reason why a court should find that to be grounds for opposing it.

THIRD PARTY INTERESTS

A third counterargument to the right of competent patients to refuse treatment is potentially more powerful. If the right to forgo treatment is grounded in the principle of autonomy, then whatever limits exist on that principle apply to refusal decisions.

The Harm Principle

The most important constraint on autonomy is the "harm principle," the notion that an act is wrong insofar as it does harm to others. Clearly, not all autonomous actions are moral on balance. If they do harm to others, a conflict of principles exists. Even defenders of liberty concede this.[24]

Some claim that *any* third party interest overcomes the claim to liberty of action. That would lead to intolerable tyranny, however, and some absurd restraints on individual freedom would result. For example, consider the refusal of treatment by a victim of a terrible assault that left him in intractable pain and would lead to a slow and certain death. Surely, that person has as good a claim as anyone to refuse life-prolonging treatment. Yet his refusal could have directly bad consequences for whoever committed the assault. The interests of the perpetrator cannot possibly count in deciding whether harm to others justifies overriding a right. If Elizabeth Bouvia's refusal of treatment were to lead to mild anxiety or psychological distress for a citizen totally unrelated to the case, that also would seem not to be a relevant consideration in deciding to honor Ms. Bouvia's claim.

Some third party consequences, nevertheless, are morally relevant. Refusers of treatment for infectious disease probably do not have the right to leave the hospital and expose third parties to severe risks. What is needed is a moral theory explaining what to do when two moral principles (in this case, autonomy and the harm principle) come into conflict.

Utilitarians would hold that rights give way whenever the net benefits to others of overriding the refusal are greater than the net benefits that will accrue from honoring it. Sophisticated utilitarians would take into account subtle and long-term consequences. If they are rule utilitarians, they would opt for the rule that would do more good than any other rule. That might even lead to a rule that always honored refusals. More likely, it would honor refusals except in a specified set of special circumstances.

Still, the ultimate result of this approach is that the rights of individuals can be overridden whenever the aggregate net consequences of overriding exceed the benefits of respecting the refuser's rights regardless of the moral legitimacy of the ones who would benefit. This has the potential of justifying overriding the rights of individuals to refuse treatment in cases where the one benefiting (such as an assailant) has no claim, or when the benefits, though large in the aggregate, are distributed among a very large number of people who are already well off. An ethic that contains within it an independent theory of justice is not likely to accept these implications.

Nonconsequentialist Principles

Another, more plausible, approach is to give principles that are not oriented merely to maximizing consequences absolute priority over so-called consequentialist principles, while permitting a "trade-off" or "balancing" among these nonconsequentialist principles. That would preclude overriding autonomy merely for the benefit of society, although it would still allow certain, limited societal justification for overriding treatment refusal. First, if persons stand in special relation to others because of promises made or bonds created, they cannot autonomously surrender those obligations. In past centuries in England, suicide was prohibited because it meant abandoning one's duty to the king. While that can not justify decisions on treatment refusal today, perhaps special duties to one's dependents would.

Justice. Another principle that does not rely on the maximizing of aggregate consequences is the principle of justice. While merely being detrimental to a third party cannot justify overriding a patient's refusal, perhaps the interest of a third party who has a claim of justice can. If, for example, there is an independent duty of justice calling for welfare to be distributed fairly. This could permit violating the autonomy of individuals in special cases where the person already has such an unusually great amount of welfare in comparison to others that it can be said to be unfair. If justice requires giving people an opportunity to be as well off as others, insofar as possible, then justice is a prima facie principle that is not simply a matter of maximizing the aggregate amount of good. In fact, defenders of a principle of justice routinely accept the possibility that a fair distribution may not be the one that does the greatest good.

If autonomy and justice are prima facie principles that are equal in priority, that must be balanced against each other, then justice could provide counterclaims to autonomy that are morally quite different from the harm principle. Where the harm principle sets any good over against the autonomous action of the individual, this more guarded, more deontological, moral theory permits only certain, carefully constrained counterclaims—those grounded in some other deontological principle, such as fidelity. Patients attempting to refuse treatment normally will not confront a situation where their refusal will harm others who have fairness claims against them (because persons sick enough to refuse life-prolonging treatment are usually quite poor in comparison to others in society). Such a situation would have to require a refusal that generates burdens on others who will be made worse off than the patient who is attempting to refuse treatment. It is hard to imagine who Elizabeth Bouvia could harm to this extent by her refusal of a nasogastric tube.

Fidelity. This leaves the more likely case where refusals could do harm to persons with whom the patient stands in a special obligation of fidelity, in particular dependents of the patient. The most frequent occurrence is a refusal by a competent patient who has dependent children. Once again Jehovah's Witnesses provided the early examples.

Mrs. Jesse E. Jones was brought to the hospital by her husband for emergency care, having lost two-thirds of her blood from a ruptured ulcer.[25] At twenty-five, she was the mother of a seven-month-old child. Having no personal physician, she was under the direct care of the hospital staff. When death became imminent, the hospital sought permission to administer blood. After an initial denial, the request was appealed to Judge J. Skelly Wright of the United States Court of Appeals. In a hurriedly arranged bedside hearing, all he could understand her to say was, "Against my will." In ordering the transfusion, he offered five reasons, some of which are perplexing and will be discussed below. One reason cited, however, was that the state, as *parens patriae*, will not allow a parent to abandon a child.[26] According to Judge Wright, Mrs. Jones "had a responsibility to the community of care for her infant" and the "people have an interest in preserving the life of this mother."[27] Thus one ground for ordering a competent adult to undergo medical treatment is that it is in the interest of a dependent.

That dependent may be an unborn child. In 1964 in New Jersey, a pregnant woman "quick with child" (that is, in the late stages of pregnancy) attempted to refuse a blood transfusion that was necessary to save her life. The trial court ruled, following the usual pattern, that it could not order treatment for a competent adult. On appeal, the court unanimously reversed the decision and ruled that the unborn child is entitled to the law's protection. The authority to transfuse was given.[28]

This denial of the right to refuse treatment when there are dependents is not unlimited, however. Charles P. Osborne, a thirty-four-year-old Jehovah's Witness, desperately needed whole blood if he was to survive internal bleeding caused when a tree fell on him. In bedside hearings, the court first determined that the patient was conscious, understood the consequences of his decision, and "had with full understanding executed a statement refusing the recommended transfusion and releasing the hospital from liability."[29] The court also considered the possibility that Mr. Osborne might consider himself blameless if forced to undergo the blood transfusion, a court-honored special case discussed below. Mr. Osborne, however, expressed the belief that "he was accountable to God, in the sense of a loss of everlasting life, if he unwillingly received whole blood throughout transfusion." His blunt response: "It is between me and Jehovah; not the courts. . . . I'm willing to take my chances. My faith is strong. . . . I wish to live, but with no blood transfusions. Now, get that straight." As his grandfather put it, "He wants to live in the Bible's promised new world where life will never end. A few hours here would nowhere compare to everlasting life." Mr. Osborne made a prudent choice, given the assumptions on which he worked.

The judge raised the possibility of the state's overriding interest because the patient had two young children.[30] Here, however, the result was different form that in the Jones case. The patient's wife made this statement:

My husband has a business and it will be turned over to me. And his brothers work for him, so it will be carried on. That is no problem. In fact, they are working on it right now. Business goes on.

As far as money-wise, everybody is all right. We have money saved up. Everything will be all right. If anything ever happens, I have a big enough family and the family is prepared to care for the children.[31]

The court was persuaded and did not intervene.[32] It was faced with a man who "did not wish to live if to do so required a blood transfusion, and who had, through material provision and family and spiritual bonds, provided for the future well-being of his two children." The strength of that religious conviction may be reflected in a footnote added later: "We are also advised that the patient has recovered though his chances were very slim and that he has been discharged from the hospital."

It is important that these cases involving forced treatments for the benefit of dependents are not simply cases where good will be done for other people. They are not even cases where the crucial factor is that the good to other parties exceeds the harm done to the patient by forced treatment. Rather they involve special obligations on the part of patients. Parents have a special duty to provide for their children. Death would mean failing in that duty.

PROFESSIONAL INTEGRITY

There is a final argument made by those defending forced treatment of competents. It arises in the Bouvia case[33] and others going back to the case of Karen Quinlan.[34] Here it is said that physicians, as professionals, belong to a group that imposes certain moral duties on its members. As such they have not only a right, but a duty to engage in certain behaviors called for by their profession.

The argument raises both empirical and philosophical problems. Empirically, it is probably false to say that the profession of medicine imposes the duty to treat against the wishes of the patient. It is not called for in the Hippocratic Oath (except indirectly in the duty to benefit the patient according to the physician's judgment).[35] In contemporary medicine the evidence is overwhelming that physicians do not believe they have a duty to treat competent patients against their wishes. The position of the American Medical Association (AMA) is more equivocal. It says:

A competent adult patient may, in advance, formulate and provide a valid consent to the withholding or withdrawal of life-support systems in the event that injury or illness renders that individual incompetent to make such a decision. The preference of the individual should prevail when determining whether extraordinary life-prolonging measures should be undertaken in the event of terminal illness. Unless it is clearly established that the patient is terminally ill or irreversibly comatose, a physician should not be deterred from appropriately aggressive treatment of a patient.[36]

The AMA makes clear that even nutrition and hydration can be deemed life-prolonging medical treatment, but it appears to limit its endorsement of withholding life-prolonging medical treatment to cases where death is imminent or coma is irreversible.[37] This means that, at least in cases where death is imminent or the patient is in irreversible coma, there should be no conflict between the professional ethical position and the wishes of a patient refusing treatment, but does not completely resolve the issue. In another situation, the profession might adopt a moral position that was in conflict with the wishes of a competent patient. Elizabeth Bouvia's refusal of a nasogastric tube, for example, could be understood as conflicting with the current view of organized American medicine in that she is neither terminally ill nor comatose. The philosophical problem is whether the moral stance of a private professional group has any bearing on the rights of persons who are not members of that group. Is there any reason why a patient's refusal should be constrained by public agencies such as courts simply because another group of private citizens holds a view contrary to that patient?

It is crucial to emphasize that here I am dealing with rights derived from the principle of automony (also called liberty rights or "negative" rights). This principle holds that autonomous persons are free to act according to their own plans, at least to the extent that those actions do not conflict with other moral principles. And insofar as the patient is simply claiming the right to be left alone, these rights appear to be absolute in the American legal system as well as in most moral commentaries outside of the medical profession. It cannot be that the moral beliefs of one individual or group, no matter how sincerely or carefully thought out, can justify infringing upon the automony of someone outside of that group who in no way has agreed to that moral view.

Because, however, Elizabeth Bouvia is also asking for the right to remain in the hospital and receive care under her own plan, the philosophical problem is more complex. She is no longer merely acting on the principle of automony and the derivative moral right to be left alone. Instead, she is claiming a different kind of right, one often called a "positive" right or an entitlement right. It would force on others not the duty to leave her alone, but rather the duty to engage in certain positive actions, such as providing morphine and nursing care, under circumstances they find objectionable. There is a widespread consensus that health care professionals should have the right to withdraw from cases where to continue would grievously violate their own consciences. Physicians and nurses are routinely permitted to withdraw from abortion services, for example.

In these situations, a problem arises if no other health care professionals are willing to provide the service requested by the patient. Then, a claim to welfare on the part of the patient is in conflict with the autonomy of the professional. If the patient's claim is merely rooted in the principle of beneficence, that is if the patient is merely arguing that he (or others) would be better off if he receives the disputed care, it is plausible that the autonomy of the professional would take precedence. When one takes into account the harm that will come to professionals who are forced to provide care in violation of their consciences, the net result of forcing them to participate in such care is likely to be negative. In addition, the fact that such a policy would also violate the principle of autonomy ought to settle the matter in favor of the professional's right of withdrawal—even for utilitarians, who are not persuaded by the autonomy claim alone.

Patients may rest their case on a different moral argument, however: the principle of justice that requires fairness in the way welfare is distributed in a social system. This principle would permit us to distinguish between a large number of claims to actions that would be beneficial and the much smaller number that are claims of justice. I have suggested that justice and autonomy are to be treated on a par and balanced off against each other while those claims based on mere beneficence are subordinated to either justice or autonomy. That would mean that autonomy can never be subordinated to beneficence, but that it might be balanced against claims of justice.

Determining who is among the "worst off" is an extremely complex task that cannot be pursued in detail here. It requires decisions about whether we are speaking of representative groups of people or of individuals. It also requires determining whether we are speaking of who is worst off at a particular moment in time or who is worst off over a lifetime. Elsewhere I have argued that for many problems of social justice the over-a-lifetime perspective is the appropriate one, but that for certain care, including basic palliative care, the moment-in-time perspective is the correct one.[38]

Surely, from either perspective, Elizabeth Bouvia is among those who are least well off in our society, in which case, she could have not only the right to leave the hospital, based on autonomy, but also a right to receive certain services from a public hospital based on justice. It is possible that in the balancing of competing claims her justice-based right to care while she refuses nasogastric feeding could outweigh the important autonomy-based right of professionals to refuse to participate in her care. That seems to be what the California Court of Appeal has decided. It should not be taken to imply, however, that persons have the right to get from public hospitals whatever will benefit them regardless of the objections of providers of care.

Some Special Cases of Competent Patients

Everything said thus far about the right of refusal applies to the mentally competent patient, to the patient presumed or judged by law to be capable of making a substantially autonomous choice about the medical care in question. If, however, patients refusing treatment could simply be declared incompetent, they would lose their rights to refuse treatment.

Some attempts at this maneuver have been made. In a circular fashion, it has been argued that, although competent persons have the right to refuse treatment, refusing treatment that is life-prolonging is crazy, and crazy people are not competent. This is an effort to have people excluded from decision making on the basis of the substance of their decisions. In this regard, it is important to note that with the movement for rights of the mentally ill it has become increasingly difficult to have someone declared incompetent.

Now even those who are involuntarily committed to a mental hospital may be competent, at least in some jurisdictions, to make financial commitments, marry, execute a will, or refuse medical treatment. In July 1972, a court found that Paula Stein suffered from chronic schizophrenia with acute flare-ups and committed her to Bellevue Hospital in New York City where the psychiatrists decided that electroshock therapy was necessary.[39] This treatment involves passing a current of 70 to 130 volts through the subject's brain, which causes a convulsion similar to an epileptic seizure. It is effective in treating some forms of depression; however, it is traumatic and has been known to cause bone fractures, pulmonary edema, and, in rare instances, even death. Mrs. Stein's mother consented to the shock treatments; in fact she had "consented to the doctors doing whatever they believe might help. . . ." Mrs. Stein, however, refused. The court testimony was conflicting, but the independent psychiatrists permitted by the court to examine Mrs. Stein concluded, "she has the mental competence to consent or withhold consent for her treatment modalities." On the basis of this advice, the judge concluded that Mrs. Stein could indeed refuse the treatment. This did not mean that she was free to leave the hospital. She was still, according to the court determination, "sufficiently mentally ill to require further retention"—in spite of her capacity to consent or refuse the electroshock therapy.[40] The judge concluded by saying, "It does not matter whether this Court would agree with her judgment; it is enough that she is capable of making a decision, however unfortunate that decision may prove to be."

In Mrs. Stein's case, the treatment was not a matter of life and death. In Maida Yetter's case, a Pennsylvania court was willing to find a committed mental patient competent to refuse a treatment even though refusal could very well jeopardize life.[41] Mrs. Yetter was committed to Allentown State Hospital in June 1971, diagnosed as have chronic, undifferentiated schizophrenia. Late in 1972, in connection with a routine physical examination, she was discovered to have a breast discharge, which indicated the possibility of breast cancer. The doctor recommended a surgical biopsy. Mrs. Yetter refused to consent, saying that "she was afraid because of the death of her aunt which followed such surgery." In response to courtroom questions she also said she was afraid that "the operation would interfere with her genital system, affecting her ability to have babies, and would prohibit a movie career." Mrs. Yetter was sixty years old and without children. Her brother finally asked to be appointed her guardian for the purpose of consenting to the biopsy. A caseworker said that Mrs. Yetter was "lucid, rational and appeared to understand that the possible consequences of her refusal included death." The judge concluded:

It is clear that mere commitment to a state hospital for treatment of mental illness does not destroy a person's competency or require the appointment of a guardian. . . .

In our opinion the constitutional right of privacy includes the right of a mature competent adult to refuse to accept medical recommendations that may prolong one's life and which, to a third person at least, appear to be in his best interests; in short, that the right of privacy includes a right to die with which the State should not interfere where there are no minor or unborn children and no clear and present danger to public health, welfare or morals. If the person was competent while being presented with the decision and in making the decision which she did, the Court should not interfere even though her decision might be considered unwise, foolish or ridiculous.

The court would not let her brother consent on her behalf. Thus a person can be competent to refuse treatment even if committed to a mental hospital.

COMPETENCY IN OLDER MINORS

Other people gaining the right to be considered competent are older minors. There is general confusion about the proper age of majority for making critical decisions. "If we are old enough to be drafted, we are old enough to vote," one slogan goes. Perhaps older minors are old enough to consent or refuse consent to some things even before they are old enough either to vote or be drafted (venereal disease treatment and contraceptive services, for example, are available in many states without parental consent).[42] But there are real dangers in a general move to lower the age at which one can choose medical treatment without parental consent. For example, do laws legalizing minors' access to contraceptives also include the right for a fourteen-year-old to be sterilized? The age for competency to refuse lifesaving treatment may not in fact be the same as the age for refusing trivial, experimental, or death-prolonging treatments.

The courts are beginning to grant that older minors can, in some cases, refuse death-prolonging treatments. One case involved a sixteen-year-old-girl suffering from an osteogenic sarcoma. Although her chances of surviving, according to an independent surgeon, were 2 to 3 percent without the amputation of a leg and 20 to 30 percent with it, the girl refused to consent to the operation. The mother agreed with her daughter's decision. But Judge Benjamin Schwartz emphasized the girl's own refusal, not that of her mother: "The girl testified in court that she would rather take her chances without the operation. She said if her leg was removed she would be a charity case the rest of her life. . . . She wouldn't be able to enjoy life, get married or even afford an artificial leg." Whether a person should have to refuse treatment because she cannot afford it is a separate question, but in this case the judge ruled, "I am not going to play God." The court would not impose its will on the unwilling girl.[43]

In another case, sixteen-year-old Ricky Green had had two attacks of poliomyelitis, leaving him obese and with paralytic scoliosis with a 94 percent curvature of the spine. The boy was unable to stand or walk. Doctors said that if nothing was done he would become bedridden. They recommended spinal fusion, which would involve moving bone from his pelvis to his spine. Although there was admitted danger in this type of operation, Ricky's mother consented to the surgery, but with the condition that, as a Jehovah's Witness, she would permit no blood transfusion. The director of the State

Hospital for Crippled Children in Elizabethtown, Pennsylvania, sought a declaration that Ricky was a neglected child and the appointment of a guardian. When the case reached the Supreme Court, Chief Justice Jones, writing for the majority, observed that since the operation itself was dangerous, the state did not have sufficient interest to outweigh the parent's religious belief since the child's life was not immediately imperiled. He went beyond this, however, to declare that "the wishes of this sixteen-year-old boy should be ascertained." He concluded, "we believe that Ricky should be heard."[44] The case was sent back to the lower court to determine the boy's wishes.

The cases in which older minors have had their own opinions recognized are special ones in which reasonable people may differ about what is appropriate. In other cases, the court has decided that it is cruel to place the burden of decision on an older minor. The case of Kevin Sampson, aged fifteen, was one in which it was decided that the parents' refusal of a blood transfusion was unreasonable.[45] He was suffering from Von Rechlinghausen's disease, which caused a massive deformity on the right side of his face and neck. He had not attended school since he was nine. Physicians had recommended delay in treatment until the boy was old enough to decide for himself. The family court judge ruled against this and also against letting him participate in the decision. She decided that such a difficult choice should not be placed on the boy, fearing psychological harm if he was forced to choose between his parent's wishes and his own health.

Older minors are not always judged competent in deciding to refuse treatment, but there is clearly an increased willingness to consider them able to make a judgment. Perhaps the reasonable course is to lower the general age of majority, say to eighteen, and then to make specific exceptions. Some exceptions may be made legislatively—for example, for reversible contraceptive aid or venereal disease treatment—when it seems that bypassing parental consent will often be in the minor's best interest. Other cases will have to be decided individually so that courts can determine if the particular minor has sufficient understanding of the situation to make an informed and voluntary judgment. Legally such minors can be judged "mature" for purposes of making medical choices.[46]

THE WILLING TO BE COERCED

Another special case is technically an exception to the rule that competent patients will never be forced by a court to undergo medical treatment for their own good. What is at stake is really only a semantic distinction between consenting and being coerced. Some individuals who object to receiving blood on religious grounds are unwilling to consent, but let it be known that they would not resist an order to be treated. On December 22, 1965, Mrs. Willie Mae Powell lay critically ill in a hospital after a Caesarian section She was, literally, bleeding to death, to be survived by her husband and six children. She needed a blood transfusion, but because of her religious convictions she felt unable to sign a prior written consent, although she would not actively resist the procedure. Because she had signed a release of liability, the hospital took the view that it had fulfilled its obligations. Was she to die through a technicality? Her husband sought an injunction against the hospital to get an order for the blood transfusion.[47]

Judge Jacob Markowitz, in a rare moment of passion in the history of court opinions, condemned the "legalistic minded" society we live in:

> I was reminded of "The Fall" by Camus, and I knew that no release—no legalistic absolution—would absolve me or the court from responsibility if I, speaking for the court, answered "No" to the question "Am I my brother's keeper?" This woman wanted to live. I could not let her die!

Nine months earlier a Connecticut court reached a similar decision. While rational and coherent, Mr. Elishas George, suffering from a bleeding ulcer, signed a release for refusing a blood transfusion on the grounds that he was a Jehovah's Witness. He indicated, however, that he would not resist a court order directing the transfusion, and the court so ordered.[48] Although the patient did indicate he would not resist, it is not clear in this case whether that was the basis of the legal opinion.

PRISONERS

There is one other group of competent adults for whom treatment may be ordered: prisoners. Among the many rights currently denied the incarcerated is apparently the right to refuse medical treatment. In this strange world, some prisoners, like some mental patients, are fighting for their right to get medical treatment,[49] while others are struggling to avoid the physician's meddling medicaments. There are at least six cases where prisoners have demanded the same right to control their medical treatment that their guards have, but in none of these cases has it been granted. The decisions, however, do not seem to be based on a clear case of a reasonable refusal on grounds unrelated to prison confinement. Not one is based upon long-standing religious convictions; not one involves death-prolonging treatments.

One set of cases denies the prisoner's right to refuse tranquilizers and other psychoactive drugs. One prisoner with a confused and chaotic religious history—he had once claimed to be a "messenger of love" with a secret prophecy for the pope, and his attempted conversion to Judaism was rejected by the prison rabbi—was not permitted to refuse Thorzine and Permitil tranquilizers.[50] Another was not permitted to refuse Prolixin (a potent antipsychotic agent) on the grounds that it violated his will as well as his unspecified religious belief.[51] Third court decision found administration of drugs acceptable if it was sanctioned by an substantial, recognized medical authority.[52]

Approaching the issue from another direction, one prisoner claims that certain medical treatment administered to him, without his consent, constitutes corporal punishment. The judge says that the "petitioner argues in effect that he, and he alone, should determine whether he should receive certain medical treatment, and the forced medical treatment is corporal punishment and cannot be legally inflicted upon anyone confined under sentence that calls for less than capital punishment. . . . [an argument that is] obviously without merit."[53] Although this prisoner's attempt to refuse treatment for his diabetes mellitus seems to have resulted from a misunderstanding of what constitutes reasonable treatment for this disease, rather than from religious objection or an attempt to avoid a behavior-controlling drug, the case is of interest because the opinion spells out at great length the constitutional rights of federal prisoners in relation to medical treatment. After affirming the duty of the prisoner's "keeper" to provide medical attention, the argument is advanced that "intentional denial to a prisoner of needed medical treatment is cruel and unusual punishment." Even treatments that are "unusually painful" or cause "unusual mental suffering" may be administered to prisoners without their consent "if it is recognized as appropriate by recognized medical authority or authorities." Obviously the right and duty to consent to medical treatment are not generally recognized principles in the prison setting. In fact, it is striking that the only grounds for argument in the opinions seems to be that the treatment is "cruel and unusual punishment," a rather different case from that of the free, competent adult. The possibility of rejecting treatment because it violates religious or ethical conviction or the right of self-determination, rather than because it is medically wrong, seems not to have been considered in these cases. The religious objector or the morally motivated refuser of death-prolonging treatments in a prison setting may be in for a difficult time.

Thus even though there are some issues involving special cases of competent adults that remain to be settled, the legal right of refusal for competents is basically settled. And although physicians continue to fear that they will face legal difficulties if they honor patients' wishes to refuse treatment, there is simply no legal basis for that fear. On the contrary, there is increasing evidence that physicians who treat against the consent of the patient are potentially guilty of assault. Cases have already been brought against such physicians.[54] The situation, however, is not as clear in cases involving incompetent patients. It is those cases to which I now turn.

5 | Deciding to Refuse Treatment

The Cases of Incompetent Patients

For incompetent patients—children or adults who lack the legal capacity to make decisions—there is no consensus that either a physician or a guardian has the right to reject medical treatments. In chapter 3, I suggested that the debate over the role of guardians and other surrogates in making nontreatment decisions for incompetents has become confused, in part because there are different types of incompetent patients and different types of surrogates. A few of the relatively simple moral principles introduced in chapter 3 go a long way toward explaining the complex case law involving surrogate decision-making in the United States. Although they are not articulated as clear principles, the notions of individual autonomy extended, objective best interest, and familial autonomy that supports the discretion of bonded guardians within the limits of reason are ideas consistently reflected in American case law. Surrogates must be seen as playing quite different roles for the various types of patients.

Determining the Incompetency of the Patient

Patients are incompetent if they lack the legal capacity to make substantially autonomous decisions about their own care. Incompetency is thus a legal category. Persons may be incompetent for some decisions, but competent for others, so incompetency must be determined with regard to a particular set of choices. Someone may be competent to choose a residence or an approach to a medical problem and at the same time be incompetent to handle financial affairs.

People are determined to be incompetent by courts or by belonging to certain status groups who are presumed incompetent (such as infants and children). The courts also can, and have, determined that persons in these special categories of incompetency possess the capacity to make particular medical decisions.[1] Persons not falling into these categories should normally be presumed competent until proven otherwise. Private citizens, even if they happen to be physicians, should not be able to declare incompetency, however. Due process is needed if someone is to be at risk for having autonomy rights constrained.

PROFESSIONAL DETERMINATIONS

At most, those physicians trained in psychiatry and as psychotherapists may serve as consultants in competency decisions. The fact that in interesting borderline cases such experts often disagree among themselves supports the contention that individual practitioners ought not to have the authority to declare incompetency.

Some persons who are not in special status groups nevertheless clearly lack the capacity to consent or refuse consent to treatment, but have never been declared incompetent. They may be in comas, for instance. An important policy question arises about what should be done when a physician, family member, or friend is convinced that the patient lacks decision-making capacity. Some people favor a policy that permits the physician to determine competency, on the grounds that it could be dangerous for patients to be treated as having the capacity to consent or refuse consent when they are clearly deranged or severely incapacitated. The President's Commission recommends that, "except where state law clearly requires judicial intervention or where real dispute persists after intrainstitutional review, determinations of decisional incapacity be made by the attending physician and regulated and reviewed at the institutional level, and that those who make and apply the law be encouraged to recognize the validity of such determinations."[2]

Such a policy has very dangerous implications. A physician, perhaps one whose perspective is atypical, could get together with family or friends and declare a patient incompetent. It is particularly dangerous when one realizes that the "attending physician" may come into a case without the approval of the patient (such as in an emergency or when chosen by the family). At least in jurisdictions that authorize next-of-kin surrogate decisions, once the patient is determined to be incompetent, the physician along with family could actually cease treatment on the patient even against his will.

At the same time I would not want to insist that the deranged or comatose person's instructions are automatically definitive. Persons in a coma could never get any treatment (because they could never consent). Deranged persons could refuse life-saving treatment that was not only safe, simple, and sure, but also treatment that they would later be grateful to have received. There is widespread recognition that the consent of the patient should be presumed in cases of emergency when patients cannot speak for themselves. The law accepts such a presumption.[3] Beyond that relatively simple situation, however, what should be done? It seems unreasonable to expect the hospital to go to court to get every patient declared incompetent, even those who are comatose. On the other hand, it seems equally unreasonable to give physicians unilateral authority to determine that patients lack capacity to consent even when they are sitting up in bed insisting they are competent.

A SPECIAL CASE OF PRESUMPTION OF INCOMPETENCY

Although neither the law nor the public policy discussion is clear on these matters, I suggest the following. In cases where both attending physician and next of kin concur in the judgment that the patient lacks capacity, reasonable effort should be made to tell the patient of that judgment. (If the patient is obviously unconscious, no actual speech would be necessary.) If the patient concurs or fails to respond, that should be sufficient to act on the presumption of lack of capacity. If the patient objects in any manner, even though the physician and surrogate do not concur, the patient should be presumed to have the capacity to consent or refuse consent until declared incompetent by a court.

This scheme would seem to work in virtually all cases. The one area where it would present a problem is in the extremely rare set of circumstances where the patient objects to being considered incompetent and even a phone call to a judge to get authorization to treat would produce a delay critically jeopardizing the welfare of the patient. It should be emphasized that these are extremely rare circumstances. Most blood transfusions can be delayed for the time necessary to make a phone call. Most patients who are this critical are not in a condition where they can object. I have heard of only one case where these conditions obtain: a patient with a history of mental illness (but who had never been declared incompetent) who refused vasodilation medication during a transient severe asthma attack on the grounds that the treatment would kill her.[4] When such cases do occur, we are legally and ethically on new and complex ground. No clear guidelines are available.

In such a circumstance it seems reasonable to support, reluctantly, the intervention necessary to stabilize the patient (and nothing more). The one making the decision should be prepared to defend (under threat of a charge of committing an assault) the judgment that the patient, in fact, lacked the capacity to make a rational decision and that the decision was necessary to stabilize the patient. Although I do not know any legal basis for such interventions, and morally, if the judgment were erroneous, they could involve violations of the individual's autonomy without due process, reason seems to require legitimizing such limited intervention. It is what philosophers have called weak paternalism, in this case very weak paternalism.

PATIENTS WITHOUT SURROGATES

This scheme might work for patients with family members available to function as surrogates and to concur in the judgments. What of patients without family member surrogates, however? In those situations, the presumption of consent for emergency treatment ought to obtain. For the nonemergency situation, we could rely exclusively on the attending physician's judgment, but, in the long run, another course would be better. We could insist that *every* such case be taken to court. These patients are the most vulnerable members of our society. They should have the benefit of maximum protection, including formal judicial review, due process, and appointment of a guardian.

It seems hard to justify either a blanket authorization to treat or a decision to withhold death-delaying treatment without some more formal process. Eventually, case law will reveal certain categories for which a clinician could be allowed to presume incompetency even when no family is available to concur and will also reveal patterns about what the most reasonable course is. For example, patients in a persistent vegetative state surely should be presumed incompetent. Perhaps eventually we could have as societal policy established through case law that such patients are not only incompetent, but that treatment should be withheld in the absence of the patient's previously expressed wishes to the contrary. In other situations, interventions might be authorized by a pattern of case law. Until the time that such patterns develop, I think it is far better that, before forgoing life-sustaining treatment, we seek guardianship for all patients without surrogates who appear to lack the capacity to make decisions about their own care.

Choosing a Surrogate

Once persons have been determined to be incompetent to make particular medical decisions, someone must make a decision on their behalf.

THE PHYSICIAN AS SURROGATE

Some have assumed that the physician should make those choices. But just as there are problems in relying on the physician to determine incompetency, there are also problems in asking the physician to play the role of surrogate. Both case law and common sense tell us that there is no reason why a physician should have that authority (unless asked to assume that role by the patient while competent to do so). That, in effect, was what the case of Karen Quinlan was all about.

Karen Quinlan, whose case will be discussed in more detail below, was taken unconscious to a hospital where she came under the care of a physician through a random process and not through a choice made by herself or her parents. It turns out that that physician, Robert Joseph Morse, had particular views about the morality of preserving respiratory support of permanently vegetative patients, a view clearly not shared by many lay people, including Karen Quinlan's family and, as far as one can tell, Karen Quinlan herself.

There is no reason why the randomly chosen moral or religious views of that physician should have any bearing on her care. The absurdity of such a policy is made particularly vivid when one realizes that many, apparently most, other physicians did not share those moral views. Even if all physicians had shared them, however, it would not make it any more appropriate for them to be used as a basis for her care. It should by now be clear why the attending physician should not assume that role. He or she has no basis for imposing his or her personal moral and religious views on the patient. Since all medical treatment decisions, including accepting or refusing terminal illness treatments, require some evaluative choices, these should not be made by clinicians.

Deciding who should assume the surrogate decision-making role and on what basis they should act is more complex. Different moral standards ought to be used in different kinds of cases.

THE PHYSICIAN AS SURROGATE SELECTOR

There is some movement to have the clinician pick from among available family and friends the most appropriate surrogate.[5] Support for this is based on the recognition that the legal next of kin is not always the person closest to the patient and best able to make choices for the patient. And this solution can work in those cases where all parties recognize the appropriateness of a relative or friend other than the next of kin acting as surrogate. In more controversial cases where different potential surrogates disagree about a course of action, however, it seems odd to have the physician pick among the candidates. That physician may have his or her own peculiar views and may be aligned with one potential surrogate or another. In cases involving intractable disputes, probably only formal court review provides adequate protection of all interests involved.

A HIERARCHY OF PRESUMED SURROGATES

For more routine cases it seems better to follow a hierarchy of presumed surrogates. We should give first authority for surrogacy to someone formally appointed by the courts. In the absence of such a surrogate, a person designated by the patient should be presumed to have the role, including someone other than the next of kin. In special circumstances this could be the physician although there are good reasons why patients ought not to name physicians for this task, since he or she is not usually the person who best knows the patient's moral and other evaluative patterns. The best role for the physician is as a check against the surrogate, a position that is lost if the physician doubles as surrogate.

If there is neither court-designated nor patient-designated surrogate, the next of kin should be presumed to have the role. The standard state-determined hierarchies of kinship can be used. If there is more than one person of equal degree of kinship, a majority would be appropriate. In those cases it will often be appropriate for those of equal degree of kinship to designate one as the person with surrogacy. The courts have the authority to review surrogates to establish that they are not acting foolishly or maliciously. They have the power to remove a surrogate who is. Only when the courts have reviewed the removed surrogate or when there is no relative available to assume the surrogate role, should the court appoint someone else as surrogate.

THE SIGNIFICANT OTHER PROBLEM

Some people argue that often today there is a "significant other" who is much closer to the patient than the legal next of kin. It sometimes seems appropriate for the significant other to function as surrogate, but there are real problems in making that a formal policy. It would require a consensus on just which significant others have this role. Does it apply automatically to all live-in roommates or only those living in special relationships? Does it apply to those who are anticipating separating, to those who are in homosexual liaisons? Determining exactly which friends should be surrogates would be next to impossible, and certainly physicians would not be in a good position to do so. When we realize that individuals can designate surrogates to cover such cases and that courts have the authority to deal with special circumstances, it is far better to presume the next of kin to be the surrogate until that person yields to someone more appropriate or until the court removes him or her from that role. Determining exactly what the mandate of this surrogate should be will require distinguishing two types of incompetent patients and two types of potential surrogates.

Types of Incompetents

FORMERLY COMPETENT PATIENTS WHO HAVE EXPRESSED THEIR WISHES ABOUT CARE

Some patients who are deemed incompetent by courts (or, potentially, by agreement of clinician and family) were once competent to make choices for themselves. If, during their competency, they developed clear views on medical treatment and the refusal of life-prolonging treatment, their wishes ought to be the basis for choices about their care and should continue to prevail. In effect, their previous autonomy should be extended into the period of incompetency. That is the moral basis of the duty to honor wills that dispose of property after death, a duty that extends even beyond the person's death.

It is conceivable that someone may have expressed wishes so clearly and precisely that all involved including the surrogate know exactly what is to be done for the patient. That is unlikely, however. No one can anticipate all of the complexity and subtlety of the choices that will have to be made. Technology may have changed between the expression of one's wishes and the moment of critical decision. Patients who have said they do not want "heroic" or "artificial" measures may not have prepared lists of exactly which measures they consider heroic or artificial and under which circumstances. Someone will have to determine exactly how the patient's expressed wishes should be applied to the specific circumstances.

The standard that has emerged to deal with such choices is called the *substituted judgment* standard. The terminology is somewhat vague because it can be taken to mean substituting the surrogate's judgment about what is beneficial for the patient, but that is clearly not what is appropriate in these cases. The decision maker should decide what the patient would have chosen under the circumstances based on the patient's beliefs, values, and moral commitments. That is as close as we can come to preserving the autonomy of the patient.

The clearest example we have in the legal literature of a substituted judgment is probably the case of Brother Joseph Fox.[6] In late 1979, Brother Fox, a devout Catholic since the age of 16, sustained an inguinal hernia while moving large tubs of flowers. He was advised by his physician to undergo corrective surgery. The operation was scheduled for October 2, 1979. Prior to that time, Brother Fox was in good health, and the prognosis for a successful operation and recovery period was excellent. The operation proceeded normally until, near its conclusion, Brother Fox suffered cardiac arrest. Emergency procedures were initiated immediately and were ultimately successful in restoring cardiac functioning. Because of the interruption of the flow of oxygen, however, Brother Fox suffered severe brain damage. He was placed on a respirator and moved to the intensive care unit. As time passed, Brother Fox's condition worsened and he soon slipped into a coma, showing little signs of ever regaining consciousness or sapience.

A fellow priest and dear friend of Brother Fox, Father Phillip K. Eichner, brought proceedings to obtain judicial approval for the withdrawal of life-sustaining treatment. The New York Supreme Court (Special Term) appointed Father Eichner "committee of person" and authorized him to terminate treatment under specified conditions; the county district attorney appealed. The Court of Appeals added to the confusion by stating that substituted judgment is not acceptable in such cases.[7] Apparently this court had in mind distinguishing between cases where we know exactly what the patient would have wanted and others where we can only surmise. The latter would be substituted judgments. Upon reflection, however, every such case involves some extension of the patient's wishes to the particular case. We cannot say, for sure, exactly what Brother Fox would have wanted; his surrogate must interpolate. In spite of the court's objection, that is reasonably called a substituted judgment.

The courts have routinely accepted the wishes of the patient expressed while competent as a basis for making decisions about critical medical care. As in the Brother Fox case, these wishes need not be expressed in writing or according to some state-authorized form. From the moral point of view, the critical factor is that we can be confident that we know the patient's wishes. Some cases have involved formal, written "living wills," but often these wishes have merely been expressed orally.[8]

NEVER COMPETENT PATIENTS

Other patients have never been competent. They are infants or children; they are severely retarded; or they simply never let anyone know that they had a particular position while they were competent. In these cases, the idea of extending autonomy to the period of incompetency makes little sense. Some other standard will have to be applied. It seems clear that once a person has stepped into the surrogacy role, his or her task is to serve the best interests of the patient. This has come to be called the "best interest" standard. The surrogate should choose what seems to be in the best interest of the incompetent one.

Two additional court cases bear upon the use of the substituted judgment and best interest standards. In 1976, Joseph Saikewicz was a sixty-seven-year-old mental incompetent who was dying of leukemia at Belchertown State Hospital in Massachusetts. He was unable to communicate verbally and often resorted to grunting to make his wishes known. The Superintendent of Belchertown State School and the staff attorney at the school petitioned the court to appoint a guardian for Mr. Saikewicz to make necessary decisions regarding his health care. Two of his sisters, the only members of his family who could be located, declined to take this responsibility. After reviewing Mr. Saikewicz's case, a court-appointed guardian recommended nontreatment.[9]

The Massachusetts Supreme Judicial Court concurred, but in doing so claimed that it was basing its decision on "substituted judgment."[10] Substituted judgment, however, is the term normally reserved for cases to be decided on the basis of the patient's own beliefs and values, and applied, in the best way possible, by the surrogate. It would work when Father Eichner made decisions on behalf of Brother Fox, who had a well-developed position regarding terminal care, but how could substituted judgment take place for Joseph Saikewicz?

The court said that the guardian ad litem's task was to "ascertain the incompetent person's actual interests and preferences." In short, the decision in cases such as his should be "that which would be made by the incompetent person, if that person were competent, but taking into account the present and future incompetency of the individual as one of the factors which would necessarily enter into the decision-making process of the competent person."[11]

The puzzle is how to determine the "actual" rather than the hypothetical wishes of a severely retarded man who had never expressed his philosophy of terminal care. If we have some limited hint of a unique view of the patient, as we might from a less severely retarded person, we have a basis upon which to construct a substituted judgment, but as the data from the patient diminish all we can do is "fill in" by assuming that the patient would have wanted what we take to be in his best interest. In the limiting case, which Saikewicz approaches, we have no data from the patient. In such a situation the substituted judgment standard collapses into the best interest standard. In spite of its language, the Massachusetts court must have had in mind the patient's best interest and nothing more. In fact, at one point the court refers to pursuit of the patient's "best interests," implying that that is the appropriate criterion.[12]

The second case involved a man named John Storar. At the age of fifty-two, Mr. Storar was profoundly retarded with a mental age of about eighteen months. He had been a resident of the Newark Development Center since age five. In 1979, physicians at the center observed blood in his urine. Permission to conduct diagnostic tests was sought from his mother. Initially she refused, but after consultation with the center's staff she gave her consent. The tests were conducted and revealed that Mr. Storar had cancer of the bladder. Radiation therapy was recommended, and treatment was administered after Mr. Storar's mother, who had been appointed legal guardian by the courts, had given her consent.

After six weeks of treatment, Mr. Storar's disease went into remission. Several months later, however, blood was again observed in his urine and efforts to stop the bleeding were unsuccessful. His cancer was then diagnosed as terminal. Although there was no chance of curing the disease, Mr. Storar's physicians determined that periodic blood transfusions would prolong his life. The physicians at the center asked permission from Storar's mother to give him a transfusion, but she refused. Then, the following day she withdrew her initial objection, and, for several months, blood transfusions were administered to Mr. Storar. On June 19, Mrs. Storar requested the transfusions be discontinued. The director of the center refused her request and petitioned the court for permission to continue treatment. At the same time, Mrs. Storar submitted a request to the court to have her son's treatment discontinued. The court denied the center's request and granted Mrs. Storar's.

The Storars had the misfortune of having their case heard by the New York Court of Appeals at the same time it dealt with the case of Brother Fox, and soon after the Massachusetts courts made the mistake of claiming that Joseph Saikewicz's decision involved substituted judgment. The New York court wanted to make clear that substituted judgment made no sense in the case of a severely retarded person who had not developed his or her own views on terminal care. It said Mr. Storar was "always totally incapable of understanding or making a reasoned decision about medical treatment. Thus it is unrealistic to attempt to determine whether he would want to continue potentially life prolonging treatment if he were competent."[13]

The court went on to hold that the state's obligation in such cases where the patient's own wishes cannot be determined is to "protect the health and welfare of the child [the term used by the court to refer to Mr. Storar, who, though an adult, was incompetent]."[14] The court seems clearly to be using a best interest standard, although it does not use those words. Where it goes seriously wrong is in assuming that the best interest of incompetent persons who have never stated their own views is always to prolong life.

We have seen that judgments about medical treatment for never competent patients ought to be based on what will promote the patient's best interests. But there is now an overwhelming consensus that there are some interventions that are either useless or gravely burdensome, that is, they offer burdens disproportionate to benefits. The New York court must have concluded that there is never a case when life-prolonging treatment offers burdens that are disproportionate to benefits—there is never a case when doing nothing is in the never-competent patient's best interest. In that position, the New York court is seriously out of agreement with the consensus of reasonable opinion. If they had acknowledged that the best interest standard sometimes is open to nontreatment decisions by guardians, their handling of the case would have been far better. Nevertheless, the New York court, like the others, seems committed, in substance if not in specifics, to the view that guardians should do what the patient would have wanted to the extent it can be determined and do what is in the patient's best interests when the patient's wishes cannot be determined.

These cases pose a newer, less carefully analyzed question. Let us assume that in cases where the formerly competent patient's wishes are known the surrogate ought to attempt to determine what the patient would have wanted (substituted judgment) and in other cases the surrogate should strive to do what is in the incompetent one's best interest. In either case, the surrogate's judgments may be questioned. What should be done when others looking on—the physician, nurse, hospital ethics committee, or judge—believe that the choice made by the surrogate was not the one that most reasonably satisfies the standard being used? Most of the confusion remaining in the current public debate over terminal illness decisions stems from a failure to distinguish between two types of surrogates and the different standards that apply to each.

Types of Surrogates
NONBONDED OR STRANGER SURROGATES

Some persons will have surrogates with whom they have had no previous acquaintance: those without families who have guardians appointed by the courts. These people will be strangers to the patient; there will have been no previous bonding. I shall refer to them as *nonbonded surrogates*.

For nonbonded surrogates the moral obligation seems quite obvious. They must do their best to choose what the patient would have wanted (in the case of substituted judgment) or what is in the best interest of the patient (in the case of never competent patients and those whose wishes are not known). They must not permit any personal, idiosyncratic beliefs and values to enter their decision.

This requires a notion of an "objectively best answer" to which the nonbonded surrogate must conform. As a practical matter, judges, juries, clinicians deciding whether to initiate judicial review, and others reviewing the nonbonded surrogate's decision must compare the decision to what they consider to be the most reasonable answer to the question posed. In jury cases this presumably would be established by using a "reasonable person standard." A judge would have to work with a similar notion. Whatever the judge or jury considers to be the single best answer to the question of what the patient would have wanted or what is in the patient's interest is what the standard of reference would be for the nonbonded surrogate. Any deviation based on the surrogate's personal beliefs and values, no matter how much it is offered in good faith, is unacceptable.

FAMILIAL AND OTHER BONDED SURROGATES

The matter is more complicated when there is a preexisting relationship between the surrogate and the incompetent patient. Surrogates may be chosen in advance by the patient while competent, or may, at least in some jurisdictions, be assumed to be the surrogate by state law. It is routine to assume that parents are the surrogate medical decision makers in the case of minor children. These surrogates I refer to as *bonded* to the patient. At first it seems that these bonded surrogates should conform to the same objective, best interest standard as nonbonded surrogates. If we insist on anything less, we run the risk that the surrogate will be permitted to make less than the best choice from a more objective point of view.

Nevertheless, on reflection a very different standard must be used for bonded surrogates. If surrogates are chosen by the patient while competent or if they are family members, we can insist that they attempt to choose what they think is the best answer to the question posed. We should not strive to enforce the more objective determination to assure that they actually make what most reasonable people would consider the best choice of what the patient would have wanted or what is in the patient's best interest.

Even if we anticipated one such decision per surrogate, enforcing the more objective standard would require millions of evaluations of surrogate choices. It would clutter even informal review mechanisms and lead to endless disputes between surrogates and those in positions to review surrogate choices. Clinicians would constantly have to assess the surrogate's choices to determine whether they really were the best possible choice and, if there was doubt, court review would be required.

In fact, parents make critical choices for their children all the time. No one insists that those decisions be reviewed to determine whether they are the best possible choices. Some parental decisions are probably as important to the welfare of the child as a decision about the refusal of life-sustaining treatment for a terminally ill child. Parents choose school systems, religious teachings, strategies for discipline, and many other crucial patterns that have enormous importance for their children. Many of these could have a more significant effect on the life expectancy of a child than would a refusal of treatment for terminal illness. Yet no one seriously expects public review to determine that these are the best possible choices.

All that is expected is that the surrogates are (a) acting in good faith and (b) making choices that are within the limits of reason. If the parents' choice of a minority school system—say military school or a left-wing avant-garde school—for a child seems within reason, no one would propose to have child welfare authorities review that decision for purposes of insisting that the "best possible choice be made."

What exists is a standard that could be called the *standard of reasonableness*.[15] As long as bonded guardians make an effort in good faith to determine the best choice from their point of view, and the choice they make is within reason—is tolerable from a more objective point of view— the surrogate's decision should not be overturned. At the same time there must be limits to which this bonded surrogate discretion can be taken. The parent who chooses no schooling at all for his or her child will be success-fully challenged as exceeding the limits of reason.[16] Similarly, the surrogate whose estimate of what the patient would have wanted or what is in the patient's best interest is totally unreasonable must be removed from the surrogate role and replaced, either by other bonded surrogates or, if necessary, by nonbonded surrogates.

Justifying Bonded Surrogate Discretion

The moral justification for this discretion is hard to establish in spite of its intuitive common sense. It probably depends in part on the nature of the bond between the surrogate and the patient. In some cases, especially those involving formerly competent patients, the bond will permit the surrogate to assess the patient's real interests, because he or she may better understand the fears and concerns of the patient. In this case, the rule to yield to bonded surrogates when they are within reason could simply be a way of assuring that the patient's wishes or best interests are served.

We seem to accept limited familial discretion even when the patient is an infant who may not have developed any special interests or agenda. The family is permitted to choose religious instruction not because it serves the child's interest, but because we believe it is the prerogative of the family to make such choices.

It has been argued that this is society's way of "compensating" parents for socializing the child, for doing a job that is important to society. There is a better explanation, however. The family is a fundamental unit within our society. Just as individuals are believed to have rights grounded in personal autonomy, families also appear appropriately to be given some limited autonomy in shaping their interactions and establishing beliefs, values, and commitments. The extent of this familial autonomy is not as great as individual autonomy. While the competent individual may refuse any medical treatment whatsoever (excluding those required by the overriding interests of others) based on autonomy rights, family members cannot have such unlimited autonomy in making choices for incompetent members. Provided, however, they are within the limits of reason, their limited autonomy should prevail.

If that is the foundation for discretion of familial bonded surrogates, then the same logic cannot justify a similar discretion for nonfamilial bonded guardians, yet they plausibly have such discretion. If the nonfamilial bonded guardian is one chosen by the patient while competent, the grounding of the discretion would appear to come from the decision of the patient that the surrogate should be vested with authority to make such choices. The patient is saying that the discretion of the surrogate should be given precedent over any other possible decision maker. Then, only if the designated surrogate is wildly unreasonable in deciding what the patient would have wanted should that surrogate's choice be reviewed and overturned. A similar justification for other nonfamilial, bonded surrogates would be in order.

Recent Judicial Examples

Only the distinction between bonded and nonbonded surrogates makes sense out of the full range of court judgments involving surrogates. Several courts seem to have accepted familial decisions to withhold or withdraw treatment, for example in Brophy,[17] Jobes,[18] Conroy,[19] Dinnerstein,[20] and Herbert.[21] Those courts were not ruling that the decision by the family members to forgo treatment was the definitive best course. The courts would not have taken custody of the patient for purposes of overriding the family member had the surrogate insisted that treatment continue. The same conclusion seems to apply even when the surrogate is not a family member, but rather a trusted friend appointed by the court for the surrogate role as in the case of Brother Fox.[22]

QUINLAN

Karen Quinlan was a twenty-one-year-old woman in a permanent vegetative state. In 1975 when she suffered a respiratory arrest, apparently the result of a combination of alcohol and tranquilizers, she was left on a respirator. She could breathe spontaneously for only short periods. After six months, her father petitioned the court to be appointed her guardian for the purpose of authorizing the discontinuance of "all extraordinary means of sustaining the vital processes of his daughter."[23]

The Role of the Physician

The lawyers for the physicians and the hospital argued that there was a compelling state interest to preserve human life.[24] Judge Robert Muir concluded, erroneously, "There is a duty to continue the life assisting apparatus, if within the treating physician's opinion it should be done."[25] Judge Muir directed that "the determination whether or not Karen Ann Quinlan be removed from the respirator is to be left to the treating physician. It is a medical decision, not a judicial one."[26] He added, "there is no constitutional right to die that can be asserted by a parent for his incompetent adult child."[27]

The opinion written by Judge Muir, undoubtedly with an agonized and dedicated conscience, was a tragically faulty analysis. In the first place, Mr. Quinlan did not ask that his daughter have the right to die; he asked for the right to refuse medical treatment. The difference between the two has a long legal and moral history.[28] Second, the opinion simply misunderstands the nature of the decision the court was asked to make. It takes the question as one that the medical professional ought to decide on the basis of professional standards and skills. This confuses the technical question, which the physician clearly ought to have a special competence in deciding, with the policy question. It is one thing to ask the physician or the medical community what Karen Quinlan's prognosis was. It is quite another to ask what ought to be done in her case, given that prognosis. The former question is one that physicians should be able to answer; the latter is one in which they have no special skills.

The opinion was self-contradictory. While at some points the decision is to be left to the individual physician, at other points Judge Muir made the standard to be used that of the practice of the medical profession as a whole.[29] At the least, we were left with the unresolved question of what should be done when individual physicians disagree with their colleagues.

A more fundamental question is why the secular courts should be bound at all to the standard values of the medical profession. What if a guardian wanted the treatment to continue while the physician, with or without the support of colleagues, wanted it to be stopped? What if a competent patient were sitting up in bed demanding that the treatment continue, and the physician were maintaining that in his opinion it was in the best interest of the patient to stop treatment so the patient could go ahead and die? If a single physician (or physicians as a whole) favors continuing or stopping treatment, that is certainly relevant—just as any other moral views are relevant—but such a narrow opinion should not be decisive in a court of law. The burden of deciding whether it was reasonable for Karen Quinlan's father to refuse further respirator treatment for her is one that the court ought not to have shirked. It was the court's job to decide whether he was being reasonable. It would have been understandable—wrong, I believe, but understandable—had Judge Muir decided that Karen Quinlan's father was proposing an unreasonable course of action. The judge did not do that, however; he held that the question was for the physicians to decide. In that he must be wrong.

On March 31, 1976, the New Jersey Supreme Court in effect rejected Judge Muir's logic. The higher court found that neither the physician's best judgment nor the tradition of the medical profession were sufficient reasons for the state to cede responsibility.[30]

The opinion contains language in which the court says that "the medical obligation is related to standards and practice prevailing in the profession."[31] This is confusing in two ways. First, it seems amply clear that stopping treatment in Karen Quinlan's condition was not contrary to the prevailing practice of the profession. Second, and more critically, it ought not to matter what the consensus of the profession is, once the guardian decides it is in the patient's interest to have the treatment stopped and the court finds it can accept such a decision. In spite of the language the court opinion goes on to make just this point:

> We are required to reevaluate the applicability of the medical standards. The question is whether there is such internal consistency and rationality in the application of such standards as should warrant their constituting an ineluctable bar to the effectuation of substantive relief for the plaintiff at the hands of the court. We have concluded not.[32]

In other words, the standards of the profession are not sufficiently consistent and rational that the court felt obliged to apply them to Mr. Quinlan's request—a great victory for patients and public responsibility.

It built its new decision primarily on the constitutional right of privacy.[33] The court began by saying:

> We have no doubt, in these unhappy circumstances, that if Karen were herself miraculously lucid for an interval (not altering the existing prognosis of the condition to which she would soon return) and perceptive of her irreversible condition, she could effectively decide upon discontinuance of the life-support apparatus even if it meant the prospect of a natural death.[34]

The court goes on to argue in that case "no external compelling interest of the State could compel Karen to endure the unendurable, only to vegetate a few measurable months with no realistic possibility of returning to any semblance of cognitive or sapient life."[35] The state has a legitimate interest, according to the court, in the preservation and sanctity of human life and in the defense of the right of the physician to administer medical treatment according to his best judgment,[36] but it also recognizes that "the State's interest *contra* weakens and the individual's right to privacy grows as the degree of bodily invasion increases and the prognosis dims."[37]

Thus far the court has followed a line of argument emphasizing privacy and self-determination of the competent patient much like the argument earlier in this volume. The court moved on, however, to more controversial, virgin territory. It begins by recognizing that "the sad truth, however, is that she is grossly incompetent."[38] Then comes the key sentence: "Nevertheless we have concluded that Karen's right of privacy may be asserted on her behalf by her guardian under the peculiar circumstances here present."[39]

This recognition of the right—I would say the responsibility—of the guardian to act on behalf of the incompetent patient is the key insight for the future resolution of similar cases of incompetent patients.

The Role of Privacy

In chapter 4, I showed that there is a real problem in trying to imagine how this could be construed as honoring a right of privacy. Privacy is the state of not having personal information about oneself disclosed to others. A right of privacy would be the right of an individual not to have such information disclosed. Whatever was involved, neither Karen Quinlan nor her parents were exercising any such right. In fact, extensive, intimate details about Karen Quinlan and her family were disclosed during the course of the court proceedings. Moreover, if privacy is a right belonging to an individual, it is hard to imagine how that right could be exercised by someone else on the individual's behalf. The New York Court of Appeals raised these concerns in sidestepping the privacy grounds for honoring Brother Fox's wishes about refusal of treatment.[40]

The duty of the surrogate is something other than protecting the incompetent's privacy. What that duty is will depend on whether the patient had expressed wishes about terminal and critical care while competent. If so, then the surrogate's duty is to assure that the patient's self-determination is honored by exercising a substituted judgment. If not, then the surrogate's duty is to assure that the best interests of the patient are served. If my arguments are correct, these judgments need to be made to the best of the surrogate's ability and need to be within reason.

Substituted Judgment vs. Best Interest

It is very difficult to determine whether the New Jersey Supreme Court considered Karen Quinlan's case to be one in which her parents were to act on Ms. Quinlan's own wishes or to use their judgment about what they considered to be in her interest. The court pointed out that Ms. Quinlan had made prior statements "while competent as to her distaste for continuance of life by extraordinary medical procedures, under circumstances not unlike those of the present case."[41]

The court held, however, that these "lacked significant probative weight" because they were "remote and impersonal." It observed that were she competent she could decide whether she would want treatment to continue. Since Ms. Quinlan could not exercise her own judgment, the court, therefore, turned to Mr. Quinlan, asking that he, in his role as guardian, and the family "render their best judgment . . . as to whether she would exercise it in these circumstances."[42]

There are two possible interpretations of this opinion. The court could be saying that since we do not know Ms. Quinlan's wishes the family should determine what they think is in her best interest, that is, they should apply the best interest standard. Alternatively, it could be saying that even though the court could not determine what Ms. Quinlan's wishes were, the family might be able to since they know her values and beliefs more intimately. In that case they would be expected to conform to the substituted judgment standard.

The two might amount to the same thing. Insofar as the patient's wishes can be surmised, they should be used in determining what she would have chosen. In the discussion of the Saikewicz case, however, it was clear that to the extent that knowledge of the patient's views is lacking, we can only fill in the gaps by assuming that the patient would have chosen what is in his or her best interest. Thus, if we have partial or unconfirmed knowledge, we can use it, supplementing it as necessary by judgments about the patient's best interest. In making these assessments, the bonded guardians should try to make their best judgments, which will be honored to the extent that they are within reason. Thus it is not clear that the court ever asked Mr. Quinlan or his wife to make a substituted judgment as we now understand the term.

Ten years later, in another case, the same court reassessed its exclusion of Ms. Quinlan's own expressions of her views, when it said, "We now believe that we were in error in Quinlan . . . to disregard evidence of statements that Ms. Quinlan made to friends concerning artificial prolongation of the lives of others who were terminally ill. . . . Such evidence is certainly relevant to shed light on whether the patient would have consented to the treatment if competent to make the decision."[43] If that is the case, it seems that the guardian should have been guided by such expressions and, thus, have made a substituted judgment. The court, in my view, should overturn that substituted judgment only if the guardian's conclusion about what the patient would have wanted is beyond reason.

Two Problems in Quinlan

With two possible exceptions, the New Jersey high court in this opinion has consistently recognized the right and responsibilities of patients and their agents to make decisions to refuse treatment. The exceptions are seen in the declaratory judgment where the court says that, after Mr. Quinlan has selected a physician, and with the guardian's and the family's concurrence,

> should the responsible attending physicians conclude there is no reasonable possibility of Karen's ever returning to a cognitive, sapient state and that the life-support apparatus now being administered to Karen should be discontinued, they shall consult with the hospital "Ethics Committee" or like body of the institution in which Karen is then hospitalized. If that consultative body agree that there is no reasonable possibility of Karen's ever emerging from her present comatose condition to a cognitive, sapient state, the present life-support system may be withdrawn.[44]

In order to see the potential problems it is necessary to isolate precisely the tasks given the physician and the so-called ethics committee. The physician is given two tasks. First, he is to determine if there is any reasonable possibility of Karen's ever emerging from her comatose condition to a cognitive, sapient state. That is entirely plausible. Her prognosis should be confirmed before the final decision is made, and a physician is clearly the one with the expertise to do it.

But the court then adds a second task for the physician. It says that he should also decide "that the life-support apparatus now being administered to Karen should be discontinued." That seems to be a mistake. Once the prognosis has been determined, once Mr. Quinlan has been given the right to exercise judgment on her behalf, and once the court has recognized in general that a refusal of treatment by a guardian for such a patient is acceptable, why should the physician then have the second task of determining whether life-support apparatus should be discontinued?

As a practical matter, this mistake may not make much difference. Presumably if things developed to the point where the selected physician determined that there was not only no reasonable hope of recovery but also that life-support apparatus should not be discontinued, Mr. Quinlan would select a new physician. But as a matter of clear thinking, there is no reason why the physician should be given that second task. There should be an understanding between guardian and physician ahead of time to avoid the possibility that the physician would have to participate in treatment decisions that violate his conscience, but the decision to stop must remain with the guardian under the supervision of the court.

The second difficulty is in the ethics committee proposal. In fact, the so-called ethics committee is given one and only one job: to confirm that there is no reasonable possibility of Karen's ever emerging from her comatose condition to a cognitive, sapient state. In other words, its single job is entirely a technical, neurological one requiring no significant ethical judgment. There is no provision for the committee to confirm the ethical judgment of the guardian and no veto power should its members disagree with his decision. In part because of this court opinion, there has been a proliferation of committees and confusion over their task. The dangers of the use of committees to make ethical rather than neurological and other technical judgments will be discussed in the next chapter.

SAIKEWICZ AND DINNERSTEIN

Saikewicz

The Saikewicz court in Massachusetts appears to have taken issue with the New Jersey Supreme Court Quinlan decision. It says:

> We take a dim view of any attempt to shift the ultimate decision-making responsibility away from the duly established courts of proper jurisdiction to any committee, panel or group, ad hoc or permanent. Thus, we reject the approach adopted by the New Jersey Supreme Court in the *Quinlan* case of entrusting the decision whether to continue artificial life support to the patient's guardian, family, attending doctors, and hospital "ethics committee."[45]

However, the two courts really are not in as much disagreement as it would appear. It should be apparent that the Quinlan court never gave the decision about whether to continue artificial life support to an ethics committee. In effect it gave no such authority to the physician, either, since Mr. Quinlan has the authority to choose the physician and presumably can dismiss him if he makes the wrong choice.

The real issue is where the two courts stand on the role of the guardian and family. Although the New Jersey court did not explicitly say so, it seems obvious that the

Quinlan family did not have ultimate decision-making responsibility. Should Mr. Quinlan have chosen a bizarre course, surely the court would retain authority to review. What New Jersey did do, however, was give the guardian initial responsibility to determine what Ms. Quinlan would have wanted or what was in her interest. Does the Massachusetts court really reject the notion that a family acting within reason and in good faith should have no authority whatsoever?

In the Saikewicz case they well might have. Mr. Saikewicz had two sisters who could be located. Apparently, they had not had contact with Mr. Saikewicz for decades, and when contacted they said they would prefer not to become involved.[46] Certainly, the presumption of familial surrogacy should not be sustained in such a case. Thus, Mr. Saikewicz was, in effect, a patient who had never been competent and who had no bonded guardian. In that circumstance, it is reasonable, especially if the professionals responsible for his care cannot agree on the appropriate course, that the court take full and active responsibility. There is no one who ought to have any discretion in deviating from the most reasonable course for serving Mr. Saikewicz's best interest. The only problem is that, having retained active authority for the decision, as we have seen, the court then said that the standard that should be used is the substituted judgment standard.[47]

Still, it should be clear that what is in the interests of a severely retarded person and what is in the interests of someone who can understand the treatment plan may be different. Mr. Saikewicz, if treated, would get something different from a competent patient with a similar disease prognosis. The question is one of whether it is in the interests of a leukemia patient with Mr. Saikewicz's prognosis to get painful treatment he cannot comprehend. The courts found that it was reasonable to conclude that inflicting such pain was not in his interest.

This means that the role of his mental retardation is quite complex. If he is to be treated as an equal to other human beings, we should judge his best interest as we would judge that of others. That means, however, that the same benefit-to-harm ratios that justify nontreatment of a mentally normal person would justify nontreatment of the retarded person. It does not mean that the retarded person should get exactly the same treatment (because the burdens of the treatment are different for one who cannot understand it). This means that although we do not take the retardation into account when we judge what benefit-harm ratio justifies nontreatment, we do take it into account when assessing what the burdens of the treatment are. In this case a simple treatment (injection) has a more severe burden to one who cannot understand why the injections are being given. Only by considering his retardation can we reach such a conclusion. Only by considering his retardation can we treat him as equal to others. This will be critical when we assess in the next chapter the Baby Doe regulations that proposed to prohibit discrimination against the handicapped.

There is one remaining problem posed by Saikewicz. The court seems to preclude the shifting of ultimate decision-making authority not only to the physicians and ethics committee, but also to guardians and family. Moreover, it sounded as though this applied not only in cases where families did not want to become involved (such as

Saikewicz), but also in cases where the family was acting within reason and in good faith. Should families really have no discretion in borderline cases such as the ones we are considering? Must the court actually determine the definitive, most reasonable course, granting no discretion to such families?

Dinnerstein

Soon after the Saikewicz opinion, another case arose in Massachusetts. It was heard by the Appeals Court, directly under the jurisdiction of the Supreme Judicial Court that had heard the Saikewicz case.[48] Mrs. Shirley Dinnerstein was a sixty-seven-year-old woman who had suffered from Alzheimer's disease to the point that she was completely disoriented and had frequent psychotic outbursts and a deteriorating ability to control elementary bodily functions. She then suffered a stroke that left her totally paralyzed on her left side and immobile, speechless, unable to swallow without choking, and barely able to cough. She was fed through a nasogastric tube that was probably causing her discomfort as well as ulceration and infection.

Her attending physician, with the concurrence of her adult son and daughter who were her only relatives, wanted to write an instruction that she not be resuscitated in the event of a cardiac arrest. The son was a practicing physician, and the daughter had provided nursing care for her mother prior to her admission to a nursing home. It seems a straightforward case where resuscitation need not be provided. But the Massachusetts court had just ruled that these matters should not be left to physician or family. In order to accept the decision without court review some explanation was necessary. That is what the court attempted to provide.

The Failure of the Prognosis Distinction. The court tried to distinguish between Saikewicz and Dinnerstein on the basis of prognosis. It pointed out that in Saikewicz the higher court was dealing with "life-prolonging" treatments administered "for the purpose, and with some reasonable expectation, of effecting a permanent or temporary cure of or relief from the illness or condition being treated."[49] It claimed that, by contrast, Mrs. Dinnerstein was in the terminal stages of an unremitting, incurable, mortal illness. Its position was that court review is not necessary in such cases. It even made the terrible error of claiming that in such cases the decision about what measures are appropriate to ease the imminent passing of an irreversible comatose patient are ones "for the attending physician, in keeping with the highest traditions of his profession."

There are two serious problems here. First, even accepting the difference based on prognosis, deciding what is appropriate to ease the dying process is clearly not something medical training can determine. For some terminal patients, struggling for extra hours is worth it based on religious or philosophical convictions. Some Orthodox Jews would presumably want to be resuscitated in such situations. On the other hand, other patients (Catholics, for example) would not find the burdens resulting from the resuscitation worth it. Medical knowledge counts for nothing in making that choice.

More perplexing in this case, the facts do not support the distinction based on Mrs. Dinnerstein being dying imminently while Mr. Saikewicz was not. Mr. Saikewicz had a 30–50 percent chance of remission if treated and would live from two to thirteen months if the remission occurred. He would die in weeks without treatment. The court concluded that it was difficult to predict exactly when Mrs. Dinnerstein would die, but said she had a life expectancy of no more than a year. It seems that the Court of Appeal rested its case on the difference between a life expectancy of no more than a year and a 30–50 percent chance of living two to thirteen months. It is simply wrong to say that one is dying imminently while the other could live indefinitely.

The Availability of a Bonded Guardian. The Appeals Court missed the most important difference between the two patients. Mr. Saikewicz had no bonded surrogate prepared to assume the guardian role. He was particularly vulnerable and deserved the full protection of the court, especially on a controverted decision. On the other hand, Mrs. Dinnerstein had devoted, knowledgeable, responsible relatives ready, willing, and able to assume the surrogacy, and the proposed decision was not in controversy. Mr. Saikewicz needed every protection available to him, to meet the standard of the most reasonable determination of what is objectively in his interest. Mrs. Dinnerstein's children should be her presumed surrogates and need only be questioned in court if their decision appears beyond reason, which it clearly was not. The real difference was the presence of the bonded surrogate, not the difference in prognosis.

CHAD GREEN

The notion of discretion within the limits of reason for bonded guardians can be seen most clearly in two rather famous cases, those of Chad Green and Phillip Becker. Chad Green was a two-year-old boy from Nebraska diagnosed as having acute myocytic leukemia of the null cell type.[50] His family moved to Massachusetts, where he was eventually treated at the Massachusetts General Hospital. Orthodox chemotherapy was prescribed, but the parents objected to the potentially severe side effects, preferring instead "nutritional therapy" that reportedly would consist of laetrile and a macrobiotic diet.

It seems clear that most people would not consider the proposed nutritional therapy to be most objectively in the best interest of the child. Nevertheless, if the concepts developed in this chapter are applied to the case, the critical question is not whether it is the best possible therapy, but rather whether it is within reason. This is a decision that a judge was eventually called upon to make. He ruled that the parents were not within reason and ordered the orthodox chemotherapy.

When the parents continued to protest (and for a time removed Chad from the state in order to pursue their interpretation of what was best for their son), further options emerged. It is reported that shortly before Chad's death, an agreement was reached in which both orthodox chemotherapy and nutritional therapy (laetrile) would be used.[51] While nutritional therapy alone seemed to many observers to be beyond reason, the new compromise probably was not. Here we need not insist that parents acting in good faith do the most reasonable thing; only that they be within reason. Probably the combination of laetrile and orthodox chemotherapy was not the most reasonable course, but it was within reason.

PHILLIP BECKER

The ultimate test of a theory of guardian decision making may be whether it can make sense of the Becker case. When the case first emerged, Phillip Becker was a twelve-year-old boy with Down's syndrome and a serious cardiac defect. When physicians proposed a cardiac catheterization to explore the feasibility of surgery to correct his heart problem, his parents refused, precipitating a court hearing that led to a decision upholding the parental refusal.[52] In early 1981, the Heaths, a couple known to favor the recommended procedure, were appointed to serve as Phillip's guardians.[53]

This case has been widely interpreted by lay people, some lawyers, philosophers, and physicians as one in which a youngster's parents prohibited him from having potentially lifesaving surgery, an operation deemed to be the most reasonable course for his condition. The shift of custody from the natural parents to the Heaths, who made clear their commitment to the surgery, could be interpreted as a rejection of the Beckers' refusal of surgery. There is a more complex explanation, however, one relying on the notion of limited discretion for the bonded surrogate.

Since the Beckers were Phillip's natural parents, they would be presumed to be the proper authority to make medical treatment decisions on behalf of Phillip until such time as they were shown to be foolish, malicious, or otherwise disqualified for this role. The original judicial proceeding focused on whether the Beckers were negligent in their parental duty by refusing the surgery; the court devoted little attention to the more basic question of whether they were the most appropriate individuals to function as Phillip's guardians. Instead, the critical question was the acceptability of the parental decision to refuse intervention.

The Beckers' position was that the high risk of mortality and the pain of the surgery rendered the operation "extraordinary"—that is, gravely burdensome when measured against the expected benefits. The critical question facing the original court was not what the single best possible course for Phillip was, but rather—presuming that the Beckers were acting in good faith and presuming for the moment that they were the most appropriate ones to play the guardian role—whether the course the Beckers chose was among the reasonable courses that were available.

The appeals court, upholding the trial court, invoked the principle of "parental autonomy,"[54] a notion very close to the one of limited familial autonomy developed here. "Inherent in the preference for parental autonomy," the court said, "is a commitment to diverse lifestyles, including the right of parents to raise their children as they think best."[55] The court acknowledged that "[u]nder the doctrine of parens patriae, the state has a right, indeed, a duty to protect children," but it went on to state that "it has a serious burden of justification before abridging parental autonomy by substituting its judgment for that of the parents."[56] Implicit in the court's decision is the conclusion that the Beckers' decisions fell within the realm of reason.

How, then, can the more recent court decision designating the Heaths as guardians of Phillip be reconciled with the earlier decision? One interpretation is that the court simply favored the Heaths' desire to proceed with surgery. But this would be pure speculation; there is no evidence to that effect. Alternatively, one might say that the subsequent decision was an award of custody, irrespective of the substantive choice of treatment favored by each of the potential guardians. In his Memorandum of Decision, the judge said that "this is not a hearing to determine surgery for Phillip. . . . This is a hearing for the purpose of giving Phillip Becker another parenting choice."[57] On appeal of the guardianship decision, the court found that the Heaths had become Phillip's "de facto" or "psychological" parents.[58]

Although it was not emphasized at the time, the Beckers had, apparently on professional advice respectable at the time, institutionalized Phillip soon after birth and had had relatively little contact with him since.[59] Phillip had for many years resided in a facility in which Mrs. Heath served as a volunteer. Gradually, a close bond emerged between Phillip and the Heaths; eventually he spent weekends and holidays with them and began to view them as his parents.[60] Using the novel concept of psychological parent, the court ruled that the Heaths were in the guardian role. They properly were given reasonable discretion with regard to treatment. They chose surgery, and the court did not object. By implication, the Heaths' decision favoring surgery was also within the realm of reason, just as the Beckers' decision against it had been.

What Counts as Reasonable Surrogate Refusal?

If competent persons have an unlimited right to refuse treatment offered for their own good, and if bonded surrogates have the right to refuse within the limits of reason, the only remaining question is what those limits are. The moral argument and the cases I have examined thus far make clear that these judgments must be made on the basis of what is fitting for the patient based on the patient's wishes expressed while competent or, when those wishes are not known, what is in the best interest of the patient. This must be assessed based on the potential benefits and harms of alternative courses of action. What is clear at this point is that adding extra moments or days or even weeks of life is not necessarily a net benefit regardless of the burdens to the patient. Moreover, the patient need not be "terminal" in order for refusal of treatment to be reasonable. Also, there will be occasions where even simple interventions (IVs, nasogastric tubes, antibiotics, and even nursing interventions such as turning the patient) will not offer proportional benefit.

As a society we have not yet completely finished the debate over exactly when treatment refusals pass beyond the limits of reason. We do have an increasing consensus on certain parameters, however. Only some particularly difficult cases remain to be settled. Some preliminary rules for structuring the judgments are now apparent.

SAFE, SIMPLE, AND SURE LIFESAVING REMEDIES

First, when an intervention will, with a high degree of certainty, restore the incompetent one to health safely and simply, and where, without the intervention, the patient will be virtually certain to die, then surrogate refusal, no matter how benevolent and sincere, is beyond reason.

Children

In 1952, two similar cases occurred in Illinois and Missouri. In both, infants were suffering from erythroblastosis fetalis (Rh incompatibility). They needed transfusions to save their lives. The courts appointed guardians to authorize the administration of blood.[61] In 1962, in New Jersey, the parents of a baby with a congenital malformation objected to a transfusion on religious grounds, but the Supreme Court held that freedom of religion did not give parents the right to risk the life of their children.[62] According to the judge's ruling, the First Amendment embraces two concepts—freedom of religion and freedom to act. The first, he held, was absolute while the second could not possibly be.

It is not only Jehovah's Witnesses who have chosen religious faith over faith in modern medicine. As far back as 1903 a father was convicted for allowing his infant daughter to die of pneumonia after he refused on religious grounds to obtain medical services.[63]

In 1972 the *New York Times* reported that an eight-year-old girl, Kalete Tole, suffering from systematic lupus erythematosus, an autoimmune failure where the connective tissue becomes allergic to itself,[64] was rushed to the intensive care unit of Long Island Jewish Hospital. She needed massive doses of phenobarbitol and steroids as well as blood transfusions to combat the disease. The doctor said immediate treatment was essential. Her father, Bendriis Tole, a member of an African sect, the Gheez Nation, refused treatment, saying, "The medication may change her life . . . I lean on divine healing more than on drugs. Once they start drugs, the body relies on them. God will intercede on my behalf." Justice B. Thomas Pantano apparently had more faith in man's medicine than God's intervention. He ordered the transfusions and medications for the girl, on the grounds that the court had an "obligation to protect the interests of the infant child who was a ward of the court and it is our obligation to see to it that whatever steps can be taken to save the child's life be taken."

Incompetent Adults

The long record of cases involving children may be of some guidance in deciding when guardians should be able to refuse treatments for incompetent adults. The case of a twenty-two-year-old Jehovah's Witness for whom blood was ordered resulted in conflicting interpretations in medical journals. A "Doctor and the Law" column headlined "Court-Ordered Blood Transfusion Upon An Adult Patient" implied a break with precedent established for other adult patients.[65] Another column implied that the court decision contradicted the earlier cases where adults have been able to refuse even lifesaving blood.[66] The confusion can be traced to a less-than-clear decision written by Judge Weintraub, then Chief Justice of the New Jersey Supreme Court, when he confirmed the order to administer blood to the young woman, but the facts are quite consistent with the pattern we have already seen.

Dolores Heston was unmarried and twenty-two when severely injured in an automobile accident.[67] She was rushed to John F. Kennedy Memorial Hospital in Stratford, New Jersey, with a ruptured spleen. Her mother, a Jehovah's Witness, signed a release of liability for the hospital and medical personnel. According to Chief Justice Weintraub, the patient was in shock on admittance to the hospital and "in the judgment of the attending physicians and nurses was then or soon became disoriented and incoherent." At 1:30 in the morning the hospital applied to a judge of the superior court for the appointment of a guardian. The court complied "for the preservation of the life of Dolores Heston." At 4 a.m. surgery was performed. Blood was administered. Dolores Heston was saved. There are confusing elements in the judicial opinion, but the result really is not surprising. A mother does not have the right to refuse lifesaving blood for her daughter when she is acting as guardian. That her daughter is twenty-two is irrelevant, at least if the young woman has not expressed her own views in a manner the court can accept.[68]

CASES DETERMINED TO BE HOPELESS

There is agreement that safe, simple, and sure remedies that are deemed lifesaving cannot be reasonably refused. There is similar consensus at the other end of the continuum. In cases that are determined to be hopeless, that is, where intervention offers no significant benefit, surrogate refusals will be honored. As I have argued, the judgement of hopelessness is not a scientific or value-free determination. Thus some latitude is in order based on the beliefs and values of the bonded surrogate.

Terminally Ill Patients

Two kinds of cases arise. In the first, the patient is terminally ill. That determination itself is a judgment, one about which people with different world views will disagree. For many, a period of a few weeks is considered critical. For others, such as some Orthodox Jews, the period is much shorter, about 72 hours when the patient becomes *goses*. Courts are now beginning to question the relevance of requiring that death be imminent.[69] In any case, once the patient is reasonably determined to be dying, it is now generally conceded that treatments designed only to prolong life are expendable if the surrogate so chooses. Of course, any treatment that is palliative continues to offer benefit to the patient and cannot be refused.

Comatose, Vegetative, and Other Permanently Unconscious Patients

The second group of patients about which there is substantial consensus in support of honoring refusals by surrogates is that of patients who are not necessarily terminally ill, but who are comatose, permanently vegetative, or otherwise permanently unconscious. In chapter 1, I examined the increasingly convincing case that such patients are, in fact, dead. Since there is at present no public policy supporting pronouncement of death in such patients, they must be treated as still living. Even though they are living, however, it seems plausible to conclude that they receive no benefit from continuing to be treated with life-supporting measures. Once they have been diagnosed as irreversibly unconscious, their surrogate should determine what they would have wanted based on their beliefs and values. If those are inaccessible, then the surrogate should determine what is in the patient's interest. If the conclusion is reached that no further life-support is appropriate, there is no good reason for society to oppose forgoing further life-saving treatment. This, in fact, is the conclusion that has been reached in Fox, Herbert, Saikewicz, and arguably in Quinlan (assuming that the family was making a best interest determination).[70]

As with the determination that the patient is terminal, so the decision that the patient will not benefit is inherently subjective. Were someone to argue that there is "benefit" in preserving even permanently vegetative life, there is no scientific argument in opposition. It simply violates the insights of most religious and secular systems of morals and values. While not everyone must agree, there is plausibility to the position that society ought not to override the surrogate who reaches such a conclusion in good faith.

JUDGMENT CALLS

In between the cases where safe, simple, and sure treatments restore persons to health and those where lifesaving treatment seems to offer no benefit are cases where the judgments are much more problematic. These may be either life and death matters or cases involving other significant benefits and harms. Since they are inherently subjective, border-drawing decisions, it is understandable that there will be some disagreement in the society. What is at stake, however, when bonded surrogates are the decision makers is not what is the most reasonable course, but rather whether the course chosen by the surrogate is sufficiently plausible that it can be tolerated. In Phillip Becker's case the courts apparently found both acceptance and refusal of the diagnostic tests within the realm of reason.

In cases involving significant choices by surrogates, the courts have found some refusals within reason and others not. This does not mean that legal opinion is simply in a state of chaos, however. Although in common law the state is generally not permitted to take custody of children to provide medical care, modern statutes throughout the United States do permit the court to take custody based on either explicit statutes or general statutes providing for custody of a child who is "neglected" or "dependent," or for whom the parent has failed to provide the "necessaries."[71] Even so, in every case the presumption is that the parents have the right to refuse until the court determines that the refusal is so unreasonable that it constitutes neglect. The reasonableness of the refusal on the part of the guardian is the key point.

Cases Where Courts Overrode

In some cases the court intervened to order treatment, overriding parental judgments apparently made in good faith, but based on aberrant religious or quasi-religious views. A father lost custody of two children, aged five and eight, to their maternal grandmother after his wife and his three other children had died of diptheria within a few months of each other. He had treated them all himself by the "Bannscheidt system," not calling a doctor until "death was at the door." His system "consisted of pricking the skin of the patient on different parts of the body with an instrument composed of about 30 needles, and operated by a spring, and then rubbing the parts thus pricked with an irritating oil." The father explained his failure to call the doctor by stating that he "had not entire faith in the infallibility of the old school of physicians."[72]

A mother was not permitted to rely solely on home remedies and faith healing to treat a twelve-year-old boy with pain and impaired movement from arthritis and complications following rheumatic fever.[73] Another mother was able to get a court to charge a father with neglect for refusing to permit an operation for their ten-year-old to correct and prevent extension of a leg deformity induced by poliomyelitis.[74] A woman who objected only to a blood transfusion was charged with neglect when she refused to permit surgery for her fifteen-year-old son suffering from neurofibromatosis. The disease had caused a deformity on one side of his face and neck so severe that he had not attended school since he was nine. Tests showed that with surgery the boy had a reasonable chance of being educated and becoming partly self-sufficient, but without it he had little chance of living a normal, useful life.[75]

Cases Where Surrogate Refusal Was Honored

In these cases, the refusals seem beyond reason, but in other cases, the refusals are much more plausible. There seem to be three acceptable grounds for refusing treatment.

Substantial Risk. The earliest case of which I am aware illustrates the principle that a refusal is reasonable if the proposed treatment itself carries substantial risk. A seven-year-old boy suffering from rickets was destined to remain crippled for life unless he had an operation. It was conceded, however, that "there was some probability that the child could die from the operation." The parents, who had already lost seven of their ten children, were supported in their judgment that they did not want to risk the boy's life.[76]

Lack of Need. A second basis for finding refusals reasonable is the lack of a clear need for treatment. Certainly an excessively paternalistic physician who attempted to get a court order for minor treatment of a child against the parents' wishes—say to get a boy to take his vitamins—could find little sympathy in the courts. If the court has a responsibility to exercise a parental role (as parens patriae), it may still in some cases reach the decision that the proposed treatment is too trivial or too controversial to be necessary. Perhaps that was a contributing factor in a case where a parent was permitted to refuse treatment for his child. The father was charged with neglecting to get proper care for a speech impediment in the child. The maternal grandmother sought and was given custody, but the judgment was reversed in appeal on the ground that the father had no obligation to furnish medical assistance in this case.[77]

Nonemergency Cases. A third basis for a reasonable refusal is that nonemergency cases, particularly those involving older minors, the treatment can wait until the minor becomes competent to be consulted. A nineteen-year-old with a massive harelip and cleft palate probably should have had surgery when he was an infant, but his father had refused because of his belief in "mental healing." The boy had been influenced by his father to the point that he also opposed the surgery. The court ruled that if the case had been brought to it before the boy had formed his own convictions, it would have no hesitation in ordering the treatment, but now, since the boy's cooperation would be necessary in postoperative rehabilitation and no further harm would result from waiting, it would not intervene.[78] The appellate court reversed the decision against intervening, only to be reversed in turn by the Supreme Court of the State of New York on a split decision, four to three.

This disagreement among the judges suggests that reasonable people may well disagree about the state's right to intrude on the family relationship. If the criterion for justifying a guardian's refusal is that it be reasonable at the time the decision is to be made, then there will naturally be borderline cases and split opinions. Nevertheless, the right of the parent or guardian to refuse will depend upon the reasonableness of the refusal.

LIFESAVING BURDENSOME TREATMENTS

I now return to the most difficult of all the problems, the situation where a dying child's life could be saved, but with a burden that some would consider too great. It is not an accident that the "Baby Doe" cases have become the most controversial of all the treatment refusal cases in the contemporary debate. They are cases on the frontiers of the ethical theory and public policy. The treatments are certainly not safe, simple, and sure. On the other hand, the infants are not inevitably terminally ill or comatose either. The cases involve substantial, but probably not unbearable, burdens. They also involve some disagreement over the facts regarding life expectancy. The cases are well known.

Bloomington Baby Doe

In Bloomington, Indiana, on April 9, 1972, a baby boy was born with a tracheo-esophageal fistula and possibly other abnormalities. He also had Down's syndrome. Surgical intervention to correct the fistula was considered. Nothing could be done to correct the Down's syndrome. Nontreatment was recommended by the medical staff. It was called the "medically recommended" course, but we now recognize that to be meaningless unless it means that it was the course that the medically trained person proposed based on personally held beliefs and values.

The parents chose to refuse the surgery and intravenous nutrition. The hospital attorney, concerned with the legal ramifications of this decision, contacted a circuit court judge who arranged for an emergency hearing. The circuit court sustained the decision, and the Indiana Supreme Court did not take the appeal. Appeal to the United States Supreme Court was made moot by the death of the infant on April 16.[79]

The interpretation of the case is made difficult by the fact that the court records were sealed so that the public does not have the facts considered by the court. One version of the story has it that the esophageal problem was easily correctable. If the boy's mental retardation is excluded, as I have argued that it should be in such cases, the case, by this set of facts, also approaches the criterion of safe, simple, and sure cure.

Another version of the story, however, has it that the tracheoesophageal fistula had, by the time the court heard the case, caused irreparable damage to the lungs as a result of gastric acid regurgitation. Stories appeared in the press describing with great pathos the agony of a supposedly similar child who was treated and suffered constant, severe pain. It was also reported that cardiac anomalies and other anatomical defects made the case much more complex. One report had it that the child, if treated, had no more than a 50 percent chance of survival, a statistic incompatible with a simple tracheo-esophageal fistula. This version of the story makes it sound as though it is a case where the child has a poor survival possibility if treated, and, even if he were treated, he could live a life in perpetual agony.

Thus two different sets of data present what amount to two different cases. In the first, the parents seem to be beyond the limits of reasonable refusal. In the second, grounds of both uselessness of the treatment and grave burden might be brought forward to defend the parents as being within reason. The truth may well be somewhere in between these two pictures of the boy's prognosis. That would put it in the range where the most difficult judgments would have to be made and, quite possibly, in the range where parental discretion should be honored. In any case, that is the conclusion reached by the judge, the only one who had access to the facts.

Long Island Baby Doe

The second Baby Doe case involved an infant born at St. Charles Hospital in Port Jefferson, New York, on October 11, 1983. She had a myelomeningocele, micro-cephaly, hydrocephalus, and other serious disorders.[80] She was transferred to Stony Brook Hospital where surgery to correct the back lesion was proposed. When the parents refused to consent to the surgery, a court order was obtained appointing a guardian to consent on the infant's behalf.

That decision was overturned by the appellate division. It argued that "careful examination of the testimony at Special Term [the original trial court] reveals that there is no support for its finding that the infant is being deprived of adequate medical care or that her life is in 'imminent danger' without performance of the proposed surgery."[81] The appellate court concluded that the parents' choice was "well within accepted medical standards and there was no medical reason to disturb the parents' decision."[82]

The court specifically mentioned the types of considerations that I have found to justify nontreatment of being within reason: lack of immediate danger, the availability of alternative therapy (antibiotic therapy), and the great risk of the surgery. The court concluded, rightly or wrongly, that

> this is not a case where an infant is being deprived of medical treatment to achieve a quick and supposedly merciful death. Rather, it is a situation where the parents have chosen one course of appropriate medical treatment over another. These concededly concerned and loving parents have made an informed, intelligent, and reasonable determination based upon and supported by responsible medical authority. On this record, and in light of all the surrounding circumstances, we find the parents' determination to be in the best interest of the infant. Accordingly, there is no basis for judicial intervention.[83]

This opinion has remained controversial. The structure of the argument is what is of interest here. On the face of it, the judges were not exactly following the logic set forward in this book. They seem to go so far as to hold that the parental judgment was the "best interest" of the child, not merely one among reasonable courses of action. Moreover, they cite as evidence for this conclusion the fact that the parents were "supported by responsible medical authority."

Once again we need to read between the judges' lines. It seems quite irrelevant that the medically trained people these parents happened to encounter hold moral or religious positions that consider conservative treatment reasonable. It is even irrelevant if the entire corps of medical professionals consider the conservative course the best. What is critical is whether the reasonable person would consider these parents within reason.

The judges perhaps really did not need to say that the parents were pursuing the course that was in the baby's *best* interest. The general tone of the opinion is one that emphasizes that the parents were within reason—they chose one reasonable course from among those available. Even that is a controversial conclusion, but it is certainly easier to defend than the conclusion that the course they chose was the best for the baby. Without having a great deal more information than we have about these two babies, it is extremely difficult to determine whether we agree that the parents were within reason.

The most severely afflicted myelomeningocele infants have an abnormality high in the spinal cord that protrudes from the baby's back. In such cases, there is certainty of paralysis, at least below the waist, lack of control of bladder and bowels, and serious risk of blocked flow of cerebrospinal fluid. This produces hydrocephalus, a condition in which fluid trapped in the ventricles of the brain produces swelling and eventual mental retardation. Hydrocephalus can be corrected by a shunt providing passageway for the cerebrospinal fluid from the ventricles of the brain. A tube is placed below the skin from the skull, down the neck, draining into the heart or the peritoneal cavity around the intestines.[84] If these operations are not performed, the severely affected baby will almost certainly die. If the cord abnormality is corrected surgically, the baby in many cases will live, but with possibly serious physical and mental handicaps that predictably can be severe. In some cases, many operations may be necessary to correct problems with the shunt, and other difficulties may arise.

What, then, is the position of the parents who wish to refuse the initial surgery to repair the spinal abnormality?[85] Robertson argues that the "parental decision to refuse consent to a medical or surgical procedure necessary to maintain the life of a defective infant quite clearly falls within the bounds of homicide by omission."[86] He believes, "Parents undoubtedly have a legal duty to provide necessary medical assistance to a helpless minor child."[87]

I am convinced that the legal evidence at the present time simply does not support this conclusion. While it is clear that the courts would require lifesaving treatment that would restore or improve the child's health to a relatively normal state, it is not yet clear about cases where treatment would save the life of the child, but leave it with severe mental and physical burdens.[88] Especially where repeated surgery for shunt correction is anticipated, I am convinced that parents who decide against such treatment are within the limits of reason. What is important is to realize that we were not being asked to determine that what they chose was the best course—only that it was within reason. Considerably more public discussion will be required before we know exactly where the limits are on such guardian discretion. It is to the public policy alternatives that I now turn.

6 | Dying Morally

The Formation of a Workable Public Policy

Although the laws permitting refusal of treatment are much clearer than many realize, there is still confusion in the practical day-to-day decisions about the care of the seriously ill and dying. What steps are needed to resolve this confusion and bring about a workable policy? What are the options of individuals who know they, too, will someday be among the dying? What choices can and should be made by family members, friends, clergy, lawyers, and medical professionals?

In this chapter I address these practical questions. I survey the public policy options now being debated in hospital halls, congressional caucus rooms, research institutions, and bedrooms throughout the nation. Before looking at four major public policy alternatives, I think it is important to see what any policy would have to do—what variables are critical—and how policy must deal with the theoretical ethical distinctions discussed in chapter 3. Should a policy include active killing of the dying or only the withdrawal of treatment? Should it permit any treatment to be withdrawn, or only "extraordinary" or "unreasonable" treatments? Should the policy apply to those who are severely afflicted but not dying, or only to those whose dying process is out of human hands?

In particular, a policy will have to come to terms with the remaining legal ambiguities discussed in chapter 5. How is the decision to be made whether the individual is personally competent to decide a treatment, and should refusal of treatment be a ground for declaring incompetency? Does it clarify decision making for those who are incompetent or only for competents? For incompetents, does it distinguish between those formerly competent persons for whom substituted judgment is appropriate and those who have never expressed their wishes about critical care for whom a best interest standard is appropriate? Does it distinguish between bonded and nonbonded guardians and give bonded guardians a reasonable range of discretion? Does it provide the presumption of guardianship for those with bonded surrogates available and provide for those who do not?

Issues in the Public Policy Debate

In addition to these questions about what is ethical and what should be legal, other variables arise, primarily at the policy level rather than in the context of the earlier discussions. Three such variables are of special significance.

VAGUENESS AND SPECIFICITY

Some years ago, one distinguished physician drafted an informal letter that he, or someone in his position, might write to his own physician. It includes this sentence: "I find it hard to think of any circumstances in which I would regard it as sound practice to employ artificial respiration to prolong my life if I had lost the ability to breathe for more than two or three (not five or six) minutes."[1]

The specification to the minute is an illustration of how precise instructions can be in defining when one wants to be allowed to die. At the other extreme, an early bill introduced into a state legislature merely provided that any person may "execute a document directing that he shall have the right to death with dignity and that his life shall not be prolonged beyond the point of a meaningful existence."[2] Very few people, even physicians, can specify their desires as precisely as indicating the number of minutes of anoxia before treatment should be forgone. Moreover, even if one could so specify desires at a particular time, they may change over the years or technology may change sufficiently so that the details may no longer be appropriate. On the other hand, if one is so vague that terms like "meaningful existence" or "extraordinary means" are used, someone will have to interpret exactly what is meant.

ANTICIPATORY OR AD HOC DECISION

In addition to how specific a policy proposal is, there is the related matter of whether it requires individuals to act before the onset of a terminal condition or whether it can be applied in crisis situations. In both the proposals above, individuals are expected to contemplate their fate calmly in advance and initiate some action that presumably would guide others at some future time to decide that they should be allowed to die.

On the other hand, some proposals being offered can be called, for lack of a better label, "ad hoc." They do not require signing any formal document or writing any letter in advance. The vagueness of the legislative proposal just cited stems in part from the requirement that lay people write an understandable document that can apply to all possible conditions when life might become "no longer meaningful," and that would not lead to unacceptable actions should future technology provide remedies not yet contemplated.

Ad hoc proposals eliminate these problems. They simply provide ways in which decisions can be made on the spot about whether treatment is morally appropriate at a particular time, with a particular patient, in a particular condition. A policy whereby the individual physician considers each case and then makes a decision day-by-day whether to go on is an ad hoc type of policy. To be sure, any plan-ahead policy will require supporting ad hoc decisions. If a physician is authorized to cease treatment when the patient cannot regain consciousness, then the physician will have to decide at some point that the time has come. The real distinction is between policies where the initial directive is given ahead of time (with some subsequent decision making required to determine when the specified conditions have been met) and those where the initial directive is given on the spot.

One of the major functions of any public policy will be to clarify the lines of authority about who makes the decisions to allow the dying to die. In an earlier day, there was a working assumption that physicians had the authority to make such decisions. Some espoused the extreme view that it is the "medicine man's burden" to assume this responsibility and that it cannot be abandoned. There are other candidates for the decisive role, however, including: the potentially deceased person; a court-appointed guardian; the person's agent; the members of the family; the courts or other government agency; some hospital authority (committee or board, for example). Any policy will have to distribute authority among such possible candidates or others.

As important as who exercises the authority is the kind of mandate given to them. Will the agents be permitted discretion within certain limits or will they be obligated to carry out particular directions? In the most obvious case, patients may have written documents granting their physician leave to cease treatment or not initiate it at the physician's discretion. Alternatively, if a patient, while competent, orders that treatment cease, physicians and other health care personnel are placed under a specific obligation, removing all physician discretion. It is apparent that when one agent is given discretion, other agents in the list may, and in many cases will, have their freedom in decision making restricted. If the physician has discretion, the patient and family will not. One of the major differences among policy proposals is the permissive tone of some and the obligatory terms of others.

Policy Alternatives

With these theoretical and policy distinctions spelled out, I am finally ready to review some of the major alternatives for developing a more explicit and consciously formulated public policy to deal with the problems of the dying patient. Some of the policies will also permit decisions that will terminate the living of a living patient as well as the dying of the patient. Here, I shall deal with four basic groups of proposals. The first is the unacknowledged status quo—permissive, ad hoc decision making by personal physicians.

Some will say that we should have no policy at all to facilitate dying. The fact is that we have always had a public policy—not one that has been thought out, but a policy, nevertheless. Before it was recognized that these choices cannot be made on the basis of medical expertise, that policy was that individual physicians should, using their knowledge of their patients and the patients' conditions, consider the alternatives carefully and then, perhaps after consultation with others, based on their view of the best interests of the dying, decide when certain treatments would no longer be attempted.

The Traditional De Facto Policy

Still today there are a small number of physicians and an even smaller proportion of the lay public who hold, at least in principle, that the physician should never decide to omit or stop a treatment that is at all relevant to the patient's condition because the physician's duty is to preserve life at all costs. Historian of medicine Darrel Amundsen claims that there are no roots in ancient medicine for this notion.[3] It does not appear in any modern professional codes of medical ethics. The AMA, for example, has never taken that to be the duty of the physician. Nevertheless, some physicians, perhaps influenced by personal fears of death or feelings of messianic obligation, have assumed this to be not only their duty but their right.

Similarly, there are minority religious and philosophical positions that commit lay persons to similar views. Some Orthodox Jews consistently maintain that life is to be preserved, at least until the patient is moribund. Some people who hold a view they call a "right-to-life" position also adopt this stance, although, at least with regard to competent patients, their position is really more one of a "duty-to-life."

Most people would recognize that there are some conditions for which some possible treatments are not morally obligatory, even though they might conceivably be life-prolonging. I shall assume that some such omissions may at least occasionally be justified, for example, when a terminal, deeply comatose patient could be the subject of some new experimental procedure that would require flying the patient, the medical staff, and perhaps the family, around the country or around the world.

The injunction "preserve life at all costs" exists primarily within the professional fraternity of physicians: it does not derive, at least in its stark form, from a universally legitimated source. It is possible that a commitment to preserve life can be derived from an ethic committed to maximizing good consequences on the presumption that life is always a good thing regardless of its burden. It might also be derived from a Kantian ethic of treating the person always as an end, never only as a means. Neither position would support a claim that life should be preserved at all costs.

If, in fact, all physicians have occasionally omitted some theoretically relevant treatments for individual patients, we have not judged them in all cases to be morally culpable. Thus there has always been a public policy regarding allowing the dying patient to die. It has for the most part been limited to omitting means that are thought useless or that would impose grave hardship on the patient, or to hastening death indirectly by giving drugs to relieve suffering. The policy was extremely vague; it was ad hoc; it was certainly permissive rather than mandatory (with the complicating exception that sometimes the patient had the right to withdraw from treatment and therefore from the responsibility of the physician involved); and it placed the physician first in the line of authority.

Problems with Physician Decision Making

I am now convinced that the minority that hold that physicians should never decide to omit or stop treatment are, in a certain sense, morally correct. It is not realistic to hold that no one should ever decide to forgo treatment on critically ill or dying patients, but physicians need not be the ones who make these decisions. There are two good reasons why the society should adopt the policy that physicians, in the role of physician, should never decide to forgo life-sustaining medical treatments.

Judging Patients' Interest. The first reason is the difficulty of judging patients' interests. The traditional practice placed decision making in the hands of one who knew the patient's medical condition and one who, at least in principle and by tradition, was committed to caring for the patient. In the Hippocratic Oath, the physician pledged to work "for the benefit of the sick according to my ability and judgment." Of course not all physicians do, in fact, always work for the benefit of the sick, even according to their ability and judgment. This is a real problem, but not one raising ethical complexities. In fact, the vast majority of physicians seem profoundly dedicated to promoting their patients' welfare. That, in itself, may sometimes be the problem.

One reason that dying patients should be concerned about this norm is precisely that it calls for physicians to work for the benefit of the sick according to the physician's own judgment. There are serious deviations between what physicians see as being in their patients' interests and what patients see as being in their own interests. The explanation of the discrepancy in judgments about patient interest may be that physicians judge what they think would be in their own interests if they were in the patient's condition. This is a dangerous moral principle, sometimes called "the Golden Rule," particularly when there are systematic differences between what two groups (for example, physicians and laypeople) might want in a specific situation. Feifel,[4] Kübler-Ross,[5] and others have suggested that physicians as a group have unusually high anxiety in the face of death. This may be in part because individuals with a high fear of death choose to enter a death-conquering profession and in part because of socialization after entering the profession. If physicians do tend to have a greater than normal desire to conquer death, they may then tend to misjudge what is in the patient's best interests.

In any event, it cannot be denied that there are random variations in physicians' judgments on the subject. Under the traditional policy of ad hoc decision making by physicians, whether a treatment was forgone was to a large extent a matter of luck, depending on which physician happened to be assigned to a patient who happened to be in a potentially death-producing condition. If a patient is fortunate enough to be under the care of his or her personal physician, this randomness might be reduced somewhat, but even then most patients do not pick their physicians primarily on the basis of their attitudes about termination of treatment.

The Use of Special Norms. The second problem with ad hoc decision making by physicians is that physicians may use special ethical norms. As well as having a different attitude toward death, physicians may feel they have a special moral duty that is codified in the medico-moral folk tradition already discussed, "Life is to be prolonged at all costs." Although this ethical norm is not incorporated into any more formal code of medical ethics, some physicians are committed to it. If physicians feel bound by such a special ethical norm in their professional roles, then it is quite possible that they will systematically reach different conclusions about what is ethically required of them even if they overcome the social and psychological problems involved in calculating how to advance their patients' interests.

Lord Brock, in a particularly blatant example of ethical special pleading, has argued:

> As an ordinary citizen I must accept that the killing of the unwanted could be legalized by an Act of Parliament, but as a doctor I must know that there are certain things which are part of the ethics of our profession that an Act of Parliament cannot justify or make acceptable.[6]

He concludes, "We may accept the need for euthanasia on social grounds but we cannot accept that doctors should implement it."[7] Lord Brock's position is that the morality of euthanasia is an open question in a more general or universal moral perspective, but that "as a doctor" he knows, as only doctors can, that they have a special moral norm: never deliberately kill a patient.

Let me bracket this conclusion and examine his ethical argument. His claim is that physicians as a class have special moral norms that can only be known by and relevant to physicians. This claim is a strong reason why the decision to allow patients to die or actively bring about their deaths should never be left to the individual physician. This mode of special ethical reasoning is particularistic. It cannot be made universal in the Kantian sense. There is no claim that all reasonable persons should agree that anyone in the physician's position should act as physicians claim they do. Knowledge and applicability of special norms is limited to one social group.

If physicians make judgments based on a set of moral norms that is different from those their clients hold appropriate for physicians and, in fact, those norms cannot even be known by their clients, predictably what is done will reflect a different perception of what is morally required. Thus, if it is widely held within the medical profession that special moral norms apply to physicians, and I think it is, it will be very dangerous if individuals—patients or healthy lay people—cede moral decision making to their physicians. The physician may misjudge what patients would consider to be their best interest, and he or she may be operating with a special set of moral norms that leads to systematic differences in judgment about what is morally required.

But let us assume that the problems of the physicians' special outlook and particular professional code can be overcome so that medical personnel reach exactly the same decision that the patients personally would have reached if they had made the decision. Better still, say the physician reaches the "morally right" decision even if the patient would not have. The pragmatic arguments are thereby ruled out, but the moral problem still remains. Even when exactly the same decision would be reached (which I believe would not happen often), patients' freedom to control their own bodies and to make decisions that affect them personally is violated.

Dying with dignity may be inherently impossible. It certainly will be if the critical decisions surrounding one's own dying are taken away. Too often, the patient is treated as a thing, or at least as a child in need of careful "management." The parent-child metaphor for the physician-patient relationship is a favorite of establishment medical sociologists. Such an assault on patient freedom and dignity is dehumanizing. It is probably also illegal in the United States. The Declaration of Independence proclaims the inalienable rights not only of liberty and the pursuit of happiness, but life as well. These rights are protected in the Constitution and in specific laws granting individuals the right to self-determination, including self-determination in the treatment and control of medical interventions into their bodies. A decision by another individual to continue or terminate treatment without consent of patients or their legal agents would appear to violate this right rather explicitly. Thus even if physicians should, by chance, reach the same decision (or even a morally superior one) that patients would have reached, they are assaulting their patients' humanity, freedom, and dignity in the process. It is always wrong for clinicians, in their role of clinicians, to decide to provide or forgo any medical treatment.

HOSPITAL ETHICS COMMITTEE DECISION MAKING

In choosing a public policy to facilitate decisions about critical or terminal care, an alternative proposal would have a hospital committee of medical personnel reach the decision to omit or cease treatment. This could turn out to be even worse than the individual physician model. Such committees were used in early experimental programs to decide who would have access to scarce medical resources such as artificial kidney machines. When Ernie Crowfeather walked away from the dialysis program at the Northwest Kidney Center in Seattle, for example, a committee had already decided that he could not continue in treatment under that institution's auspices and financing.[8]

The presumed advantage of committees is that they will not be subject to random and inevitable variations among physicians, thus avoiding imposing on patients bizarre beliefs of clinicians from either extreme. It is assumed that there is greater probability of knowledge of relevant data and greater likelihood of impartiality.

Quinlan and Ethics Committees

Support for the use of committees in making such decisions was first stimulated by the case of Karen Quinlan. The opinion of the New Jersey Supreme Court explicitly calls for an "ethics committee."[9] Great danger and serious confusion have resulted, even though the court opinion, if taken literally, poses no real problem. It says that if Karen Quinlan's father (acting as guardian) and the physician he selects agree that the treatment is to be discontinued on the grounds that there is no reasonable possibility of her ever emerging from her present condition to a cognitive, sapient state, then the ethics committee should be consulted. The court opinion clearly says that the committee has one and only one function: to confirm that there is no reasonable possibility of Karen's ever emerging from her present comatose condition to a cognitive, sapient state. In other words, the committee called an ethics committee is given only a technical neurological task of confirming prognosis, not that of approving or disapproving of the ethical decision that the life-support apparatus should be disconnected. The committee should really be called a prognosis neurology committee and be made up only of neurological experts. In fact, a prestigious group made up of the New Jersey Commissioner of Health, the state Attorney General, the President of the Board of Medical Examiners, and representatives of the state medical society, the Association of Osteopathic Physicians and Surgeons, and the New Jersey Hospital Association insisted on calling this committee a prognosis committee.[10] It carefully distinguished technical medical tasks from moral decisions about what care should be rendered and when it should cease.

The court, nevertheless, seemed somewhat confused. It may not have realized the importance of the difference between asking a committee to determine prognosis and to decide when treatment should cease. It took the idea for a committee from one of several articles proposing that ethics committees make or share in the actual ethical decisions, rather than merely confirm prognosis. Karen Teel, a pediatrician and director of Pediatric Education at Brackenridge Hospital and Central Texas Medical Foundation, proposed rather casually in a law review article appearing shortly before the court acted that such a committee might be an appropriate forum for reviewing ethical dilemmas in order to provide assistance and safeguards for patients and their medical caretakers.[11]

Even in her offhanded proposal she recognized some of the problems I have mentioned with using such committees to make or even advise about decisions to stop treatment: problems of logistics and imposition on the freedom of patients or their agents. She does not pursue the analysis at a very deep level, however. She does not take up the difference between confirming a medical prognosis, which is a task for medical experts, and making ethical judgments about the prognosis, which is not properly a task of medical experts at all. It is simply illogical to give such authority to privately constituted committees, even if those committees happen to include lay people, as she proposed. If anyone is to override the patient or the guardian in making the ethical judgment, it must be a public agency such as the court. On the other hand, it is also illogical to give a committee that includes lay people the task of making a purely neurological judgment.

The New Jersey court, in giving a committee a purely technical task, specified the correct job for a neurological committee, but in calling it an ethics committee and connecting its instructions to a not very carefully analyzed proposal for committees to perform a different task, the court led us to confusion.

Post-Quinlan Developments

After the Quinlan decision many of us expected hospital ethics committees to become a social phenomenon. At the Hastings Center we held a meeting with many of the principals soon after the decision to begin exploring the roles, functions, and potential problems with ethics committees.[12] In fact, except in New Jersey, almost nothing happened. It was not until the early 1980s that the idea of institutional ethics committees began to take off. Several events stimulated this renewed interest. The President's Commission for the Study of Ethical Problems in Medicine and Biomedical and Behavioral Research gave prominent attention to the use of ethics committees.[13] It also commissioned a national study, which revealed that only one percent of hospitals had ethics committees actively reviewing case decisions involving decisions to forgo treatment.[14] It found no hospitals with fewer than two hundred beds that had committees. Nevertheless, the work of the commission, including the study it commissioned, stimulated considerable interest in the use of committees.

At about the same time, the Baby Doe regulations gave specific endorsement to the use of committees.[15] There were also national meetings giving favorable attention to the help that committees could provide in resolving difficult terminal illness treatment decisions,[16] and several scholarly articles focused on the utility of hospital ethics committees.[17] The striking thing about all of this enthusiasm for ethics committees is that, with the exception of some of the individually written articles, no one paid much attention to what the ethics committees were supposed to do. The President's Commission and the Baby Doe regulations never supported giving these committees decision-making authority.

Several tasks have been envisioned, including staff and patient education, guideline writing, case consultation, and review of decisions for the purpose of initiating judicial review or for reduction of future problems.[18] Some commentators seem to imply that these committees should have the authority to overturn decisions by parents, surrogates, or even competent patients. These committees, however, are essentially private groups, appointed through private channels—by hospital administrators, by chairpersons of medical staffs, or even self-appointed. It would be a serious violation of the principle of autonomy if such groups of private citizens had the authority to overrule a competent patient. It would raise similar problems if they had the authority to override surrogate decisions. Such private groups have no publicly authorized operating rules. They lack what political scientists call "legitimation," an authority bestowed by the public to make decisions.[19] There would be no formal due process or similar legal protections, which would seem necessary even in cases where surrogates are evaluated under the limits of reasonableness concept developed in chapter three.

Problems with Committee Decision Making

No carefully thought-out justification has been proposed for giving committees the power to decide for or against a treatment. In fact, a number of serious problems arise with such proposals. First, if there is any merit in ad hoc, permissive decision making by the individual physician, it is that the individual physician may know the patient personally, may be committed to giving personal attention, and may even have discussed the alternatives with the patient. The committee mechanism makes death bureaucratic, destroying the one possible advantage of individual physician decision making.

Second, while the committee may reduce the random biases of individual physicians, it in no way eliminates the systematic biases of the medical community as a whole. If health professionals as a group tend to exhibit peculiar psychological responses to death or to operate on moral norms unique to them, and if the committee is made up predominantly of health professionals, then the committee would still reflect these biases. The assumption that a collection of expert opinions will eliminate bias could be called the fallacy of consensus of expert opinion.

Third, even if both random and systematic bias were eliminated, the committee approach would still depend upon and reinforce the misconception that health professionals as a group have expertise in making moral decisions about when, if ever, treatment should be omitted or stopped. Even if the committee is expanded to include other health care professionals—nurses, chaplains, social workers, and administrators—these problems would remain. Adding lay people, especially patients who have previously been hospitalized with serious illnesses, would help, but it would still not eliminate these problems.

This assumption of moral expertise assaults patient freedom and dignity perhaps to an even greater degree than the ceding of decision-making authority to individual physicians. If a committee with authority to override is to be used at all, it would be preferable to have the committee analogous to a jury made up of randomly picked citizens, peers of the patient, rather than of members of a group with a particular type of technical knowledge. I see no reason why any person or group, including a hospital ethics committee, should ever have the authority to override a competent patient who is refusing medical treatment.

The matter of review of decisions by surrogates for incompetent patients is more complex. Certainly, groups of private citizens should not have that responsibility. Since court review is cumbersome and time consuming, it would be helpful if a local group could take on this responsibility. It would have to be a group with public legitimation, however. It would be functioning as an adjunct to the civic officials who have the authority to take custody of the patient from parents and other surrogates suspected of abuse of incompetents. If society were to create committees with careful rules of due process and guidelines to assure that the standards used were rigorously consistent with the laws pertaining to taking custody, I would support such a mechanism. It would have to be a public committee, that is, one appointed by public mechanisms rather than by a private hospital, and one that operated under publicly endorsed rules and procedures. No ethics committee comes close to meeting these standards at the present time.

This does not mean, however, that ethics committees at the local hospital level have no use at all. They have been extremely helpful in educating staff and patients; but the guidelines they have generated have been of uneven quality. Many contain provisions that could be dangerous—some, for example, authorizing nontreatment without the consent of the patient.[20] Others even authorize decisions against resuscitation without the approval of the family of the patient.[21] Good procedural guidelines, however, have been very helpful in dealing with decisions about resuscitation, declaring death based on brain criteria, and a wide range of other difficult decisions. Local hospital committees that adapt model guidelines such as those prepared by the Hastings Center

Research Group on Guidelines for Terminal Illness can provide a very valuable service to patients and staff.[22]

Committees can also play an active role in reviewing cases, either retrospectively to assure that mistakes do not happen in the future, or prospectively to provide assistance to patients and their surrogates in making difficult decisions. When they do so, though, their role should be one of assisting the primary decision maker (that is, the patient or the surrogate) in reaching a choice that is consistent with the principles appropriate for such decisions. That means the goal should be to further patient autonomy where possible and to help surrogates make appropriate substituted judgments or best interest judgments within the limits of reasonableness when patients are not competent.

There is one other possible role for ethics committees. While committees have no business overriding patients or their surrogates, they might be formally charged with the responsibility within the health care institution for making a decision to seek judicial review to determine whether surrogates are acting within the limits of reason.

The Problem of Confidentiality

This suggestion is more complex than it may appear. One of the most important traditional principles of medical ethics is that of confidentiality. Patients are presumed to have the right to have information they disclose kept confidential. A decision by a clinician or other health care professional to take a case to an ethics committee would appear to violate that confidentiality unless the patient or surrogate has approved. A patient or surrogate who is genuinely seeking moral assistance in making a difficult choice might welcome the assistance and readily give permission to have the case discussed. Others, however, who have made up their minds really may not welcome the ethics committee review. In fact, they may have a great deal to lose. The committee might go to public authorities in an attempt to have the decision overturned. Even if the surrogate eventually is sustained, a great deal of emotional difficulty would have been encountered. I have reached the conclusion that no case should go to an ethics committee unless the patient or surrogate has approved. Otherwise there is a violation of confidentiality.

Some opponents of this position point out that it is routine for clinicians to discuss cases in the hospital before other committees such as tissue committees. There is an important difference, however. Confidentiality is a requirement that can be overcome on two grounds: if patients grant permission to disclose or if disclosure is required by law. In consulting with colleagues or the normal hospital committee, the interests of the patient are clearly the goal. The patient or surrogate's consent to disclose information is plausibly presumed even if it is not given explicitly. In other committee consultations, such as quality assurance committees, either patient permission is given for disclosure (through consent connected with insurance reimbursement requirements) or is required by law (in the case of certain public insurance mechanisms). Neither the presumption of patient consent nor the requirement of law is present in decisions by clinicians to seek consultation with ethics committees, however. This forces me to the conclusion that normally no committee should meet to discuss a specific active case unless it has the explicit permission of the patient or surrogate.

Furthermore, if the goal is to provide assistance to the patient or the surrogate, the primary decision maker, usually the patient or surrogate, ought to be present when the committee meets to discuss the case. It is by hearing the range of arguments about treatment options that the decision maker stands to learn. Any effort to meet to assist the attending physician or other health care professionals may imply that the patient is playing a less than central role. Meetings of the ethics committee at the request of the clinician without the permission of the patient or surrogate ought to be prohibited. The use of the committee, therefore, to decide to seek judicial review of a surrogate's problematic decision is itself problematic.

PERSONAL LETTERS AND DOCUMENTS

To correct the difficulties arising when health care professionals attempt to make the decision to omit or cease treatment on their own or in committee, several mechanisms have been proposed to provide guidance. These attempt to shift the locus of decision making to patients themselves so that they have control over what happens to them. The initial approach was to encourage persons with concern about terminal care to write informal letters. Often these were prepared not as legally binding instructions, but as personal communications to family, friends, physician, clergy, and others who might be responsible for the writer's care should he or she become incompetent. Later it was realized that there was a need to have instructions binding on caregivers. Several kinds of legislation have emerged to give legal force to expressions of personal wishes. I shall look first at the issues in the preparing of documented personal wishes, now termed *advanced directives*. Then I shall turn to the legislative proposals.

Early Physician-generated Letters

Some of the early advanced directives were prepared by physicians who had become aware through personal experience of the dangers of being subjected to aggressive treatment during a terminal illness.[23] They were limited to withholding or withdrawing treatments, rather than to addressing the issues of active killing. They were written by people who had the knowledge to be quite specific about what they wanted (cessation of ventilators after three minutes of anoxia rather than after five minutes, for example). Still these are anticipatory documents. They are written while the authors are healthy and competent. As such they may miss dimensions that cannot be anticipated: new technological developments or new subtleties in the decision making. Many authors of documents in the 1970s, for example, did not anticipate making specific decisions about withholding medically administered nutrition and hydration. Thus no matter how specific one's instructions, someone will have to interpret and to translate the patient's wishes into specific decisions at the moment of crisis.

The Original Living Will

The group that did the most to encourage the writing of such advance directives went through several name changes. During its developmental period in the 1970s, it was called the Euthanasia Educational Council. (It has since split into two separate groups, one focusing on legal interventions calling itself the Society for the Right to Die, and the other, focusing on more educational activities, calling itself Concern for Dying.) As the Euthanasia Educational Council, it drafted and circulated millions of copies of a model letter that it called the *living will*, which contained explicit language stating that it was not a legally binding document, but that the signer hoped that caregivers would feel "morally bound" to follow the instructions given. The model centered on the operative request: "If there is no reasonable expectation of my recovery from physical or mental disability, I, _____, request that I be allowed to die and not be kept alive by artificial or heroic measures."

It is thus anticipatory, as were the letters drafted by physicians. It was, however, much more vague. It made use of the then standard language of "artificial and heroic measures," leaving to others the interpretation of exactly what treatments were to be excluded. When one realizes that many clinicians tended to classify treatments as artificial or heroic on the basis of how unusual or how technologically complex they were, rather than on the basis of whether benefits exceeded burdens, one realizes how dangerous such vague wording can be.

As with the physician-written letters, and in spite of the troublesome word euthanasia in the title of the sponsoring society, authorization was limited to omission and cessation of treatment. The Living Will, however, specifically distinguished between direct and indirect hastening of death by condoning the use of drugs. It stated, "I ask that drugs be mercifully administered to me for terminal suffering even if they hasten the moment of death."

As with the earlier prospective proposals, a secondary decision-making process was generated. Who was to decide when there was no longer reasonable expectation of recovery and what criteria of reasonable expectation and recovery are to be used? Since the letter is addressed to a number of parties, the answer is vague, but the physician seems to be implied. If this is the case, then authority is once again handed to an individual who has no special competence for this kind of decision making.

Legally Binding Instruction

All the early informal letters and instructions lacked the power to relieve those who feared they might not do their dying in the care of a physician they could trust. It may be possible under present legal authority to create a more forceful instrument. Although the early Living Will did not attempt to be legally binding, it is possible to draft such an instruction that is intended to be. Two approaches are possible, both relying, in part, on already existing legal mechanisms. First, one could attempt to make substantive treatment instructions legally binding by deleting any wording that says they are not. Once could rely on existing common law rights of self-determination or constitutional rights to communicate substantive wishes about what treatments are desired or refused. The result would be a substantive advance directive, the intention of which is to be legally binding. Both Concern for Dying and the Society for the Right to Die have prepared model substantive directives. Second, one could supplement this with what is now termed a *proxy directive* to designate someone (a spouse, adult offspring, or friend) as an agent for the purpose of making decisions about medical care should the individual become incompetent to make those decisions.

In 1976, in the first edition of this book, I first proposed a legally binding directive that included both substantive and proxy provisions. At the time, I suggested giving the agent power of attorney for the purpose of making such medical decisions. It is now clear that in all jurisdictions there are laws that permit a power of attorney to remain in effect when a person lapses into incompetency. Called *durable powers of attorney*, these provisions seem perfectly suited to solve the problem of who should have authority should the patient become incapable of expressing or interpreting wishes. By 1983, the President's Commission recognized the importance of this strategy, endorsing it as a decision-making mechanism.[24] At that time, a few states had not specifically authorized durable powers of attorney, but by 1987, with the passage of such a law in the District of Columbia, all fifty states and the District have such a device available.[25]

Such a power of attorney could begin with a general statement about the importance of receiving medical care that would preserve social, psychological, and spiritual wholeness rather than merely physical, vitalistic signs of life. Instead of acknowledging that the document has no legal weight, it could designate the individual who should be responsible for medical decisions should the writer become incompetent. By clearly indicating that it is the responsible agent of the patient whose judgment is decisive, the specific decisions can be made in an ad hoc fashion when necessary. The vagueness of the anticipatory letter is thus overcome.

The most important recent development in the debate over preparation of advance directives is the realization that there are virtually infinite variations in the plans that individuals might put forward. Thus *any* substantive model letter would have to be open to modification. In fact, the variation is so great that model forms such as those from death education groups or those appearing in state laws are of less and less value.

In the 1970s the standard pattern was one where physicians were committed to continuing treatment to the last gasp, and lay people were desperately trying to make sure that they could get treatment stopped once it no longer offered what for them was proportional benefit. In the 1980s, however, medical professionals have become increasingly realistic about the limits of care. Some, in fact, have been so taken with the reasonableness of stopping treatment that they are quite prepared to make such decisions. In doing so, though, they are violating the patient's autonomy just as much as if they were forcing decisions to continue treatment without consulting with the patient. For this reason, today one of the most important reasons why a person might want to write a substantive advance directive is to spell out the conditions under which he or she would want treatment to continue as well as when treatment should be stopped. The existing model letters and living wills provide little help.

Increasingly the discussion should focus on the elements of a complete advance directive and alternative sample wording rather than on single, standard forms that are put forward for everyone to accept. With this in mind, a complete directive might include the following considerations.

Elements of an Advance Directive

1. *A Statement of Underlying Principles.* An advance directive might open with a general statement of the basic principles or system of thought that underlies the author's position. A Roman Catholic might, for example, adopt the wording of the "Christian Affirmation of Life," the statement of the Catholic Health Association of the United States.[26] It expresses the philosophy that dying is a natural part of life and that patients have a legal and moral right to choose what will be done to care for them. It rests its position on the "Christian belief in the dignity of the human person and my eternal destiny in God." Protestants and Jews may prefer to draw on theological premises from their own traditions, while secular persons may turn to their own sources for the foundations of their directives.

2. *A Statement About Being Informed.* No one can make decisions about terminal care unless he or she is adequately informed. Nonetheless, some people might prefer not to receive certain information or might prefer that their proxy receive it. The problem of disclosure of terminal illness is the subject of the next chapter, but suffice it to say here that any advance directive ought to contain some general expression of the author's desires about information. For example, the Catholic Health Association's model says, "I ask that if I become terminally ill I be fully informed of the fact so that I can prepare myself emotionally and spiritually to die." Others who might want the option of making medical treatment decisions when there is no terminal illness might wish to broaden this statement to include being informed about serious or critical illness that is not terminal.

3. *When the Directive Takes Effect.* One of the most important elements of an advance directive is a clear statement of when it is to be put into effect. Many documents say that treatment is to cease if the patient is terminally ill and death is imminent. Terminal illness is a very ambiguous term, however. If the patient is terminal and death is imminent regardless of treatment, then the importance of ceasing treatment diminishes. On the other hand, may state living will statutes apply only under these conditions. To avoid confusion, the author might want to spell out what treatments should cease if his or her condition is inevitably terminal and also what should happen when treatment is disproportionately burdensome even though the condition is not inevitably terminal. If this is done in different paragraphs then there is some reason to hope that the paragraph referring to terminal illness that is in accord with state law will be valid even if the other, more problematic paragraphs are not.

In spelling out conditions where death is not inevitable, it is important to avoid accidentally covering conditions not intended by the author. The early model for the Euthanasia Council asked for withholding treatment when there is no reasonable expectation of recovery from physical or mental disability. Taken literally, that could include persons with amputated limbs or chronic mild mental impairment such as neurosis or mild retardation. Surely, that is not what is intended. It is now clear that persons can be permanently comatose or in a permanent vegetative state and not be terminally ill in the sense that they are inevitably declining toward death. To make matters clear, writers of advance directives might spell out treatments to be rendered or withheld when they are inevitably dying, permanently unconscious, and neither dying nor permanently unconscious.

4. *What Treatments Should Be Rendered.* Probably the most important provision is a careful spelling out of which treatment should be rendered and which should not. The early statements that refer to withholding extraordinary or heroic measures are no longer adequate because they do not communicate the same thing to all readers.

The appropriate specification will be a function of personally held beliefs and values. One approach is to attempt to list all the treatments that one wants or does not want. The list could include ventilators; dialysis machines; organ transplants; burn treatments; surgery of various kinds; cardiopulmonary resuscitation; or medically supplied nutrition and hydration. The difficulty with such an approach is that it is inevitable that items will be left off the list. Depending on whether one is making a list of items to be provided or omitted, the result will be undertreatment or overtreatment. Moreover, even if one is dying, it is possible that one might want a particular intervention under some conditions but not others. One might want a ventilator necessary to provide comfort, but not merely to prolong life.

A second strategy is simply to specify that no treatment should be rendered merely to prolong life. Treatments should be provided to provide comfort. Even if one is dying, however, one might want life prolonged under some circumstances: to see a distant relative or to see a child graduate from school or be married, for example.

A third strategy is to spell out the criteria for desired treatment, but to leave the specifics up to the patient or, if the patient cannot speak for himself or herself, a proxy. People might say, for example, that they want no treatment when the benefits do not exceed the burdens. Others might say they want no treatment if it will not extend life more than a minimal time, but they want treatment even if it is burdensome provided it will extend life beyond the minimal time specified.

This strategy will necessarily depend on having someone designated who can interpret whether the benefits exceed the burdens or whether the minimal time period will be exceeded.

5. *The Designation of a Proxy or Surrogate.* A designated proxy or surrogate should be the person who best knows the patient's own beliefs and values, who can most be trusted to find out what they are in a time of crisis, or whose own views are most acceptable to the patient. Often this will be the patient's spouse or next of kin. It could also be a friend, a member of the clergy, or an associate. It might be a physician, but only in the case where the patient picks the physician because the physician best knows the patient's beliefs and values pertaining to terminal care or where the patient has reason to know that the beliefs and values held by the physician are those upon which

the patient would most want treatment decisions to be made. Almost always a physician would not meet these criteria as well as a relative, friend, or member of the clergy.

6. *The Designation of an Attending Physician.* Even though physicians are not normally the appropriate persons to act as surrogates, they do play important roles in terminal care decisions. They provide information about diagnosis and about the reasonable options for treatment. Some clinicians may exclude certain options that would be reasonable for the patient on the grounds that the clinician does not even consider them plausible enough to present. All persons writing advance directives ought to consider specifying which physician should be the attending one with whom the proxy should work. This would normally be the patient's primary caregiver. This is particularly important if the patient has negotiated with a primary caregiver a treatment plan that would be considered unusual by most clinicians.

7. *The Hospital or Jurisdiction.* In addition to specifying the attending physician, it may be important to specify the hospital or jurisdiction in which care should be rendered in cases of controversy. The Jewish patient may specify a Jewish hospital, for example. For persons who travel frequently or who live near the borders of states where laws pertaining to treatment decisions vary, it could be important to specify the jurisdiction. If one happens to commute to work across state lines and happens to have an accident in the jurisdiction that has less favorable state laws regarding terminal care decisions, specifying that one wishes to be transferred to the preferred jurisdiction might avoid considerable controversy.

8. *Specifying Advisers.* Some people may be in a position to specify advisers of various kinds so that the designated proxy could turn to them for assistance in cases of particularly difficult decisions. Advisers would not be actual decision makers but persons whose views the author of the directive has grown to respect. These might be medical, legal, or ethical advisers. They could be persons known personally to the author of the directive or persons known only through writings.

9. *Common Law vs. Statutory Law.* In jurisdictions that have natural death or living will statutes that are quite narrowly formulated, persons might wish to specify that they are refusing treatment based on common law and constitutional law as well as state statute. This could cover the refusal of nutrition and hydration in states that exclude these refusals in statutes.[27] It could also cover refusal of treatment if one is in a permanent (but not terminal) vegetative state in a jurisdiction where the statute only permits withholding treatment in terminal cases.

10. *Special Provisions.* Individuals may have other special requests not covered by this list. For example, even if one has specified that treatment should not be accepted unless it offers benefits that exceed burdens, in the current climate it may not be clear whether the writer means to omit nutrition, hydration, medication, or other simple interventions. One might state specifically that a proxy should refuse even these treatments when they are not judged to have benefits that exceed burdens.

Other special provisions may refer to positions previously stated by the writer. Someone who has written or made other public expressions may refer to these writings. In my own case, I have often defended the right of persons to have certain aggressive treatment even if they are dying. This is based on the principle of respect for personal autonomy. I am somewhat concerned that this defense of the autonomy of others could be mistaken for my own judgment that it is desirable to have aggressive treatment under such conditions. I thus include a statement in my directive that these defenses of the rights of others should not be taken to be my own views.

A *Model Advance Directive*

An advance directive that covers all of these points will not necessarily be complete and unambiguous, but it is likely to be more complete than some of the early model directives. Since the variations are almost infinite, no single model can be definitive. Nevertheless, one such sample, based on one currently signed by the author, will help show how these elements can be combined into a single statement:

DECLARATION made this ____day of _____, 19 ___. I, _____, being of sound mind, willingly and voluntarily make known my desires that my dying shall not be artificially or in any other way prolonged under the circumstances set forth below, do declare:

If at any time I should have an incurable injury, disease, or illness certified to be a terminal condition by two (2) physicians who have personally examined me, one (1) of whom shall be my attending physician, and the physicians have determined that my death will occur if life-sustaining procedures are not utilized and where the application of life-sustaining procedures would serve only to prolong the dying process, and when such withholding or withdrawal has been approved by _____, I direct that such procedures be withheld or withdrawn, and that I be permitted to die naturally with only the administration of medication or the performance of any medical procedure deemed necessary to provide me with comfort care or to alleviate pain.

Furthermore, if at any time I should have a condition (whether incurable or not) which, in the opinion of _____ (regardless of the opinion of any physician), involves treatment which is either itself directly gravely burdensome to me or will sustain life in such a way that it is gravely burdensome to me or others, I direct that any procedures being used to sustain my life or prolong my dying be withheld or withdrawn and that I be permitted to die with only the administration of medication or the performance of any medical procedure deemed necessary to provide me with comfort care or to alleviate pain.

In either circumstance, that is, when continued treatment merely prolongs a terminal condition or is directly or indirectly responsible for grave burden to myself or others, I explicitly instruct that _____be my agent for the purposes of all medical decisions. I urge him (or her) to refuse any medical procedures which (s)he believes would be useless or gravely burdensome based on my values as (s)he can discern them or based on his (her) own values if (s)he cannot deduce what my position would be. I explicitly instruct him (her) to refuse not only complex procedures such as respirators and dialysis machines, but also simple treatments such as IV's, antibiotics, nasogastric tubes, hyper-alimentation, or even oral feeding, if they are no longer appropriate in his (her) judgment. Furthermore, I give him (her) all authority to engage or dismiss the two physicians referred to above (including my attending physician), should I be unable to do so. I expect him (her) to dismiss immediately any physician who fails to comply with his (her) decisions.

Should (s)he want guidance in interpreting what I would have wanted in any particular circumstance, I urge him (her) to consult my own writing. (In doing so, [s]he should note that recently I have expressed concern that some patients who may not want to have treatment stopped, will have it stopped by physicians who are paternalistically trying to do what they think is best. [S]He should be aware that I have expressed this solely out of concern for the rights of those who want treatment continued. This should not be interpreted to imply that I am one of those people.) Should (s)he want futher guidance, I urge him (her) to consult _____, _____, and _____all of whom hold positions on these subjects which I respect. Should (s)he need medical guidance, I urge him (her) to consult Dr. _____and Dr. _____whose medical skills and ethical positions I respect. I urge him (her) to transfer me to the medical care of Dr. _____should that become necessary to have my wishes or his (hers) respected. I also urge him (her) to move me from one state to another, if necessary, in order to have my wishes respected. Should (s)he need legal guidance, I urge him (her) to consult _____.

It is my intention that this document be legally binding as a declaration of my wishes under the law of _____and all other states having living will or natural death act legislation and that it be seen as expressing my wishes under common law and constitutional law as well as conveying a durable power of attorney in all states.

It is by belief, after studying the matter for many years, that the wishes expressed here are consistent with and based upon principles of Judeo-Christian ethics. In particular, I affirm that while life is precious, it is not the ultimate good. When medical treatments are no longer fitting, when they are useless given the patient's own beliefs and values, or when they are gravely burdensome to the patient or others, then humans should step aside and let nature take its course.

In the absence of my ability to give directions regarding the use of life-sustaining procedures, it is my intention that this declaration shall be honored by my family and physician(s) as the final expression of my legal right to refuse medical or surgical treatment and accept the consequences from such refusal.

I understand the full import of this declaration and I am emotionally and mentally competent to make this declaration.

_____

NAME

The declarant is personally known to me and I believe him (her) to be of sound mind. I did not sign the declarant's signature above for or at the direction of the declarant. I am at least eighteen (18) years of age and am not related to the declarant by blood or by marriage, entitled to any portion of the estate of the declarant according to the laws of interstate succession of _____or under any will of the declarant or codicil thereto, or directly financially responsible for declarant's medical care. I am not the declarant's attending physician, an employee of the attending physician, or an employee of the health facility in which the declarant is a patient.

_____

WITNESS

_____

WITNESS

Although several lawyers who have examined this form believe that it would give legal force to a treatment refusal, there are many unsettled legal questions pertaining to advance directives. No one should assume, at least without the advice of an attorney, that a power of attorney would necessarily stand up and be legally binding. Nevertheless, the power of attorney may be one way of moving beyond the clearly nonbinding living will and of relieving some of the anxiety of those who fear they will not be able to die in accordance with their own ethical convictions.

Legislation

Although the personally written advance directive provides the best guidance available for critical and terminal care decisions, it cannot solve all the policy questions in this area. Many people will never write directives. Others will never be in a position to because they are children, severely retarded, or otherwise not competent to form legally binding instructions. Other policy problems will arise because it is not clear that personal advance directives can give sufficient authority for a decision maker to act. The most obvious example would be a directive that authorized active killing for mercy. Present law clearly does not permit killing for mercy upon request. Other instances where there is now no clear legal authority to act include decisions by competent patients to refuse life-sustaining nutrition and hydration and decisions by next of kin or other surrogates on behalf of incompetents. In each of these situations, legislation has been proposed to clarify the authority of various persons to make treatment decisions.

Legalizing Active Killing for Mercy

As early as 1936 the British House of Lords considered legislation to permit "voluntary euthanasia" under certain conditions. In 1947 the General Assembly of the State of New York considered a bill with similar intentions. It would have permitted sane persons over twenty-one who were "suffering from painful and fatal disease" to petition a court for "euthanasia." The court would have appointed a commission of three, two of them physicians, to investigate the case and determine whether the patient understood what he or she was doing and whether the case came under the provisions of the act. If the court accepted the report, then a physician or other person chosen by the patient or commission could have "administered euthanasia."

The bill failed, and the legislatures were dormant on the issue until the late 1960s when a new flurry of activity began. The Euthanasia Society of England prepared a draft bill which was considered in Parliament in 1969. A similar bill was introduced into the Idaho legislature in 1969. This bill unambiguously included actively assisting the dying process. It defined euthanasia as the painless inducement of death and stated, "euthanasia shall be administered to a patient in accordance with the terms of his declaration." Once the all-inclusive nature of the bill was made clear, there was no need to explore the distinction between ordinary vs. extraordinary means.

Some effort was made to specify the nature of illnesses and afflictions under which persons could have been killed for mercy. This is particularly important since the bill included action which could cause the death of the not otherwise dying. The conditions were general enough to include virtually all conceivable legitimate reasons for ending the dying process and, at the same time, specific enough to exclude trivial, nonterminal cases.

The bill was basically anticipatory in character. The document was to be executed ahead of time. But patients might still be involved in the ad hoc decision to cease treatment or hasten death actively. They requested euthanasia "at a time or in circumstances to be indicated or specified by me . . ." or, if they suffered from a condition of physical brain damage, "as soon as it is apparent that I have become incapable of leading a rational existence." One would prefer that the last clause read "permanently incapable," but otherwise the bill seems to permit a maximum of ad hoc decision making by the patient.

The primary line of authority was that the patient retained decision-making authority as long as possible, and then it passed to the physician. There is no provision for relatives to be involved, even though, as individuals with special knowledge of the patient's values and special responsibility for family members' welfare, relatives are often more plausible decision makers than the physician.

The bill was clearly permissive in places rather than mandatory. The patient "requests" euthanasia and presumably the physician decides if and when "it is apparent that I have become incapable of expressing wishes," so that the decision is made "at the discretion of the physician in charge." More significantly, the document concludes, "I ask and authorize the physician in charge of my case to bear these statements in mind when considering what my wishes would be in any uncertain situation." After the resounding defeat of the Idaho proposal and the more publicized defeat of the British version, there was a slackening of activity. Then in 1973 two more states, Montana and Oregon, considered bills on the British model to permit active hastening of death. There were slight differences in wording.[28] Neither came close to passing.

In part because of the ethical and political problems discussed in chapter 3, the likelihood of these active killing statutes becoming law seems very small. Since the early 1970s no serious legislative effort has been made to legalize active killing for mercy. This is in part because in order to make such an approach at all plausible, the proposals limited their concern to mentally competent persons who authorized in writing the active hastening of death. But it has become increasingly clear that a large portion of the cases where it is plausible to make terminal care decisions involve persons who are not capable mentally of giving such instructions. Instead, attention has focused on a second kind of legislative effort, one directed at making it clearly legal to write advance directives expressing personal wishes about withholding and withdrawing of treatment.

Bills to Permit Instructions on Terminal Care

Early Proposals. Walter Sackett, a state representative and a physician long concerned with terminal care, made several attempts to have the Florida state legislature act on the subject—at various times with a constitutional amendment, a bill, or the establishment of a committee to investigate the matter. He introduced legislation in 1970 that would have been the first to legitimate advance directives. In the early 1970s several other states, including Wisconsin, Oregon, and Delaware, considered bills closely following the Florida model.

The 1976 California Natural Death Act. The legislative breakthrough came in 1976 when California became the first state to pass a statute clarifying the rights of persons to write instructions about their terminal care.[29] The passage was largely the result of the efforts of Assemblyman Barry Keene. Debated at a time when even decisions of clearly terminal patients to withhold life-sustaining treatment were controversial, the political process leading to the passage of the bill was hotly contested and led to many compromises.

It began with several paragraphs of preliminary philosophical foundations: The legislature found that "adult persons have the fundamental right to control decisions relating to the rendering of their own medical care, including the decision to have life-sustaining procedures withheld or withdrawn in instances of a terminal condition." The legislature, claiming it was interested in protecting individual autonomy, expressed concern about the "loss of patient dignity and unnecessary pain and suffering, while providing nothing medically necessary or beneficial to the patient."

Already the notion that some medical treatments might be deemed "medically necessary" had begun to creep into the discourse, a problem that was to plague the debate over the next decade. No one then, or even today, seems to grasp how deceptive the term is, how meaningless it is to refer to a treatment as "medically necessary" or "medically indicated." Presumably those who use the term must believe that "medicine" or "medical people" can make some group of treatments required in some sense. Of course, medicine can do no such thing. Some treatments may be morally necessary based on some system of philosophical or religious belief. The personal beliefs of medical professionals may lead them to hold that some treatments are necessary, but that is a personal ethical judgment not based on medical science.

The legislature goes on to hold that, because of concern for "dignity and privacy . . . any adult person may execute a directive directing the withholding or withdrawal of life-sustaining procedures in a terminal condition." It must be signed in the presence of two witnesses not related to the declarant or entitled to any portion of the estate of the declarant, not the attending physician or an employee of the attending physician. The statute provides a specific form to be signed in which the individual signing declares that he or she is of sound mind and does not want his or her life to be artificially prolonged "in the event of incurable injury, disease, or illness certified to be a terminal condition by two physicians, and where the application of life-sustaining procedures would serve only to artificially prolong the moment of my death and where my physician determines that my death is imminent whether or not life-sustaining procedures are utilized." This legislation became the model for much of the debate in the decade that followed, so its provisions should be analyzed carefully.

1. *The Patient Must Be Terminal When Treatment Is Stopped.* Most patients who contemplate living wills anticipate that treatment will be stopped after they have a terminal condition. The California law defines terminal as "an incurable condition caused by injury, disease, or illness, which, regardless of the application of life-sustaining procedures, would, within reasonable medical judgment, produce death, and where the application of life-sustaining procedures serve only to postpone the moment of death of the patient."

While many people envision their advance directives to be used when they are terminal, this is probably the most controversial and potentially dangerous provision of this type of legislation. In fact, many people, such as Karen Quinlan, are not terminal by this definition. Persons in a permanent vegetative state (or what used to be called coma) are not necessarily suffering from a condition that would produce death. Persons suffering from Alzheimer's disease and strokes, from chronic kidney failure, or from certain malignancies may not be terminal but nevertheless consider aggressive, life-sustaining medical interventions to produce a disproportionate burden. For these reasons prominent spokespersons within Catholic moral theology and many secular perspectives support the moral legitimacy of refusing medical interventions on the grounds of grave burden even though the patient is not terminal.

2. *To Be Binding the Directive Must Be Signed Fourteen Days After Being Notified of Having a Terminal Condition.* Not only must the patient be terminal, but even then, if the declaration is made prior to being so diagnosed or within the first fourteen days after being so diagnosed, it is not binding. "The attending physician may give weight to the directive as evidence of the patient's directions regarding the withholding or withdrawal of life-sustaining procedures and may consider other factors, such as information from the affected family or the nature of the patient's illness, injury, or disease, in determining whether the totality of circumstances known to the attending physician justify [*sic*] effectuating the directive."

Remarkable as it may seem, the attending physician, however he or she comes into that role, apparently has the authority to ignore explicit directions from the patient if the directive is not reaffirmed fourteen days after the terminal diagnosis. That physician may even take into account the wishes of the family and "the nature of the patient's illness." Many people who are defenders of patient's rights opposed the entire legislative initiative on the grounds that it takes away already existing rights of patients to refuse treatment under common law right of consent. In California there was, for the first time, in the name of patient dignity and privacy, legislation condoning a physician's treatment of a patient in violation of that patient's expressed wishes to the contrary.

3. *Treatment Is to Be Stopped Only When Death Is Imminent.* Even if the person signing the directive has a terminal condition and has signed the directive fourteen days after being informed of the diagnosis, still treatment can only be stopped when death is imminent. *Imminent* is never defined in the law, but, if death is imminent it seems

that most of the potential advantage that might be gained by forgoing life-sustaining treatment would have been lost. Remembering that many commentators support the legitimacy of refusing treatment even when the individual's condition is not terminal, it seems even more plausible that terminally ill patients might want to refuse treatment because of grave burden when death is not imminent, whatever that means.

4. *The Directive Shall Have No Force or Effect Five Years from the Date It Is Executed.* Many people are concerned that, once executed, directives might remain in existence for many years, perhaps after the persons executing them have changed their minds. To remedy this concern the bill's authors were forced to make the directives completely without effect after five years. Keep in mind, however, that if they were executed prior to a diagnosis of terminal illness, they were only advisory in any case. Apparently, the attending physician is not even required to take into account, let alone follow, the wishes of the patient expressed more than five years previously.

5. *The Directive Has No Force If the Person Is Pregnant.* The right of pregnant women to refuse medical treatment is a controversial issue. It has generated recent debate over the right of women to refuse intrauterine surgery, for example. Still, keeping in mind that the pregnant woman has broad legal rights to abort her fetus, it seems odd that the legislature could conclude so quickly that an advance directive is void while a woman is pregnant. It could lead to forcing a terminally ill pregnant woman to have an abortion in order to exercise her right to refuse treatment, an odd implication in legislation designed to promote autonomy and dignity.

6. *The Directive Shall Have No Force If the Declarant Is a Patient in a Skilled Nursing Facility Unless It Is Witnessed by a Patient Advocate.* This provision was included out of concern that nursing home patients were particularly vulnerable and lacking in protection. To circumvent this problem, the legislation provided that a state-certified patient advocate or ombudsman had to be a witness to the directive. Whether all nursing home patients need this protection and whether any have had the rights of refusal constrained by this requirement are open to question. It also raises the question of whether there are other categories of patients needing such special protection.

7. *The Directive May Be Revoked at Any Time.* The signer can negate the directive by canceling, defacing, obliterating, burning, tearing, or otherwise destroying the document, by writing a revocation, or by verbal expression.

8. *Immunity Is Granted.* No physician or health facility acting in accordance with the directive will be subject to civil liability, or be guilty of any criminal act or professional misconduct.

9. *The Forgoing of Treatment Shall Not Constitute Suicide.* For legal purposes, such as insurance claims, the legislature simply declares that forgoing treatment is not suicide.

10. *Penalties Are Provided.* The legislation makes an important distinction between two kinds of potential violations. Any person who willfully conceals, cancels, defaces, obliterates, or damages the directive is guilty of a misdemeanor. Anyone who falsifies or forges a directive to make it look as though a person was authorizing withholding of treatment is subject to prosecution for unlawful homicide. This distinction between

ignoring a directive to stop treatment and acting as if there were a directive is often not followed in some other proposed legislation that otherwise followed the California bill.

11. *No Legal Right or Responsibility Is Superseded.* One of the most important provisions of the legislation provides that no other right that person has to effect withholding or withdrawal of life-sustaining procedures is in any way impaired or superseded. This means that common law rights of refusal remain effective, even in the face of a law that states that a physician need only "take into account" a directive executed prior to the time the patient has been terminal for fourteen days. This leaves some nonterminal patients in the very confusing situation in which they cannot make legally binding refusals under the California Natural Death Act while they can under common law.

In fact, one of the most forceful arguments against legislation of this type is that all the rights provided in the statute and other rights of refusal as well already exist under common law. In response, however, the defenders of the legislation point out that, in actual practice, many clinicians believed that they had the right to force treatment even on terminally ill patients whose deaths were imminent even in the face of written living wills. In cases where all the provisions of the statute were met, this legislation at least made clear certain refusal rights and, in fact, changed the perception of physicians about their role in terminal illness treatment decisions. However, it left some patients who had not executed such a directive in an ambiguous position in which clinicians might believe they had the right to treat without or against consent.

Post-California Developments. The passage of the California Natural Death Act seemed to open the floodgates for legislation in other jurisdictions. Within one year, six states (Arkansas, Idaho, Nevada, North Carolina, Oregon, and Texas) had passed similar laws. Within eleven years, thirty-nine states and the District of Columbia had acted.[30] In many cases the most implausible features of the California legislation were modified.

No other jurisdiction retains an automatic expiration such as California's five-year time limit. Only Hawaii and Oklahoma retain the provision that the directive be executed after the diagnosis of terminal illness in order for it to be binding. Several states have dropped the provision that the directive is not valid during pregnancy (Arkansas, Idaho, Louisiana, Maine, New Mexico, North Carolina, Oklahoma, Tennessee, Vermont, Virginia, and West Virginia, as well as the District of Columbia). Others have modified the provision so that pregnancy only invalidates the directive if the fetus could develop to the point of live birth (Alaska, Arizona, Colorado, Iowa, and Montana).

While some of the problems with the California legislation have been corrected, one new area of concern has emerged. In the early 1980s people began to be aware that simple treatments such as nutrition and hydration, as well as more complex medical technologies, could be withheld. Beginning in 1983, court cases established the legal possibility. Some of the state laws passed in 1984 (Florida, Georgia, Illinois, Missouri, and Wyoming) and all except Montana of those passed in 1985 (Arizona, Colorado, Connecticut, Indiana, Iowa, Maine, Maryland, New Hampshire, Oklahoma, Tennessee, Utah, and Wisconsin) exclude forgoing of nutrition and hydration. In 1986 the pattern was partially reversed. Alaska and Hawaii do not exclude nutrition and hydration from the treatments that may be refused while South Carolina does. Indiana's law prohibits withholding of "appropriate" nutrition and hydration, leaving open the argument that nutrition and hydration that are disproportionately burdensome or are serving no purpose are expendable as inappropriate. Oregon's law permits withholding when the declarant specifically authorizes it (a reason why advance directives should refer to the writer's wishes about specific treatments in controversy).

By far the biggest problem with the original California Natural Death Act was the fact that it provided no guidance for decision making for patients who had never been competent to execute a directive or had not done so while competent. Most states have not been able to face this most difficult of questions in decision making. Still, especially since it is now generally recognized that common law rights of refusal support written advance directives regardless of whether specific state statutes endorse their use, the most important action a state legislature can take at the present time is to clarify who should be making decisions for incompetents and how much discretion they should have.

Legislation Dealing with Decisions for Incompetents

Early Bills. Even before the passage of the California law, some states were exploring legal provisions to designate the next of kin as the decision maker for incompetents who had not expressed their wishes about terminal care while competent. The bill introduced into the Florida legislature in 1970 by Walter Sackett contained a provision that, in the event the patient was unable to make the decision, the spouse or closest relative would have the authority. While that bill never passed, it provided a model for future debate.

In March 1977, Arkansas enacted a law that permits relatives to execute a directive requesting or refusing medical and surgical procedures calculated to prolong life.[31] If the individual is physically or mentally unable to execute the document, an order of priority is established among relatives. The order specified is the parent of a minor, a spouse, a child aged eighteen or over, a parent, the nearest living relative, and the legally appointed guardian.

The following month, New Mexico passed similar legislation with the curious provision that a spouse, parent, or guardian could execute documents only for minors.[32] While this provided a mechanism for disproportionately burdensome treatments to be stopped for terminally ill minors, it left the incompetent adult without any voice. In 1984 this limitation was modified somewhat with the passage of an amendment providing that treatment can be stopped for an incompetent patient when "all family members who can be contacted through reasonable diligence agree in good faith that the patient, if competent, would choose to forgo that treatment." "Family" is defined as spouse and children over the age of eighteen. If the person has no spouse and no children over the age of eighteen, then the parents or, if neither parent is alive, the incompetent person's adult siblings are defined as the family.[33]

In 1983 North Carolina and Oregon amended their 1977 statutes to provide for next-of-kin decisions for incompetents. The Oregon law limits such decisions to cases of terminally ill, comatose patients. The North Carolina amendment is further limited to refusal of "extraordinary means" for patients who are terminal, incurable, and irreversible as well as comatose.[34] They both make the controversial move of adding the attending physician to the bottom of the list of persons who may make decisions for incompetents. Thus, if there is no relative available to make the critical decisions, the attending physician, acting on his or her own, has the authority to withhold life-sustaining treatment. This is a potential conflict with the role of the clinician as advocate for the patient who provides a check on the surrogate for the patient. It also creates the possibility that the clinician will draw on personal values. In the previous chapter I argued that while there is good moral reason why family members might have limited autonomy to draw on their personal values in making treatment decisions, there seems to be no reason why a clinician should be permitted to do so (unless appointed as a surrogate through a durable power of attorney device).

Fuller Family Surrogacy Statutes. Beginning in 1983 a group of states began passing family surrogacy statutes granting to family members decision-making authority that is not limited in the manner of the early New Mexico law or the laws limiting decision making to comatose patients. As of 1987, Florida, Georgia, Iowa, Louisiana, Maine, Maryland, Mississippi, Texas, Utah, and Virginia have passed such statutes.

The Virginia statute is one of the best. Entitled *The Natural Death Act*, the Virginia law is based on a fundamental right of competent adults to "control decisions relating to their own medical care, including the decision to have medical or surgical means or procedures calculated to prolong their lives provided, withheld or withdrawn."[35] The law provides for executing a declaration stating when treatment is to be withheld or withdrawn. It provides a standard wording with some of the limits discussed earlier. The standard wording is limited to terminal conditions when death is imminent. The law further states, however, that the declaration need not be in the form provided, holding open the possibility that persons might expand their directive to conditions that are not terminal or when death is not imminent. Individuals might also include specific provisions such as refusal of nutrition, hydration, and medication, as well as other medical interventions, when they are disproportionately burdensome in the eyes of the patient or a designated surrogate. While the statute is limited to terminal conditions, it also specifies that the "provisions of this Act are cumulative with existing law regarding an individual's right to consent or refuse to consent to medical treatment and shall not impair any existing rights or responsibilities which a health care provider, a patient, including a minor or incompetent patient, or a patient's family may have in regard to the withholding or withdrawing of life-prolonging medical procedures under the common law or statutes of the Commonwealth." It also states that "should any specific directions be held to be invalid, such invalidity shall not affect the declaration." This seems to give as much room as possible for persons to add provisions reflecting their specific ethical views about accepting and refusing treatment.

The Virginia law provides a specific authorization for surrogate decision making for patients who are comatose, incompetent, or otherwise physically or mentally incapable of communication in cases where the patient has not executed an advance directive. The order of priority is one that makes sense:

1. The judicially appointed guardian or committee of the person of the patient if one has been appointed. This paragraph shall not be construed to require such appointment in order that a treatment decision can be made under this section.
2. The person or persons designated by the patient in writing to make the treatment decision for him should he be diagnosed as suffering from a terminal condition; or
3. The patient's spouse; or
4. An adult child of the patient or, if the patient has more than one adult child, by a majority of the children who are reasonably available for consultation; or
5. The parents of the patient; or
6 The nearest living relative of the patient.[36]

While there is no specific endorsement of a durable power of attorney for purposes of making critical medical decisions, Virginia has a general durable power of attorney statute, and there is no reason why adding a designation of a proxy could not be one of the provisions individuals would add on their own. All in all the Virginia law is as good as any that have been drafted thus far.

An Ideal Life-Sustaining Treatment Act. None of the existing statutes is perfect, but we have come a long way in the past decade toward creating statutes that clarify the rights of persons to have or refuse life-sustaining medical treatment. In 1981 a project sponsored by the Society for the Right to Die drafted a model *Medical Treatment Decision Act.* It has provided the framework for recent decisions about legislation, including the Virginia law, and has much to recommend it. It was published as part of an appendix (though not endorsed explicitly) by the President's Commission for the Study of Ethical Problems in Medicine and Biomedical and Behavioral Research.[37] The Virginia statute is an improvement primarily in the inclusion of the much needed surrogacy for decision making for incompetents. Even so there are changes that could well be contemplated in any future legislation. In particular:

1. The decision should be cast in terms of the right to have access to or to refuse medical treatments generally, not just treatment for patients who have terminal illnesses and who are dying imminently. The competent patient or the surrogate for the incompetent patient should have the right and responsibility to determine whether proposed treatments are useless or disproportionately burdensome.

2. Persons executing documents while competent should have the right to refuse any treatment that they determine, based on their own beliefs and values, to be useless or burdensome.

3. Surrogates should be expected to determine, within the limits of reason, what the patient would have wanted. When it cannot be determined what the patient would have wanted (because the patient was never competent to develop such a position or never expressed wishes while competent), then the surrogate should determine, again within reason, what is in the patient's best interest. As long as the surrogate is within reason, no further question should be raised. If the surrogate appears to be beyond reason, then judicial review should be required.

4. The presumed surrogate for all incompetents should be a court-appointed guardian. If no guardian has been appointed it should be someone designated as proxy by the person while competent. If no one has been so designated, the surrogate should be the next of kin according to normal orders of degree of kinship existing in the state.

5. No private person or persons (such as an attending physician or ethics committee) outside this framework of bonded surrogates should ever be given authority to make life and death decisions for persons. In cases of persons without bonded surrogates, judicial appointment of guardians should be routine until such time as categories can be established for which nontreatment is routinely acceptable.

6. Persons should be permitted to refuse all disproportionately burdensome and useless treatments regardless of how simple or common they are. There should be no automatic exclusion of nutrition and hydration.

7. State laws should explicitly recognize documents of essentially similar nature written in other jurisdictions.

8. An explicit provision should be made for the naming of a proxy (a durable power of attorney).

9. Any model declarations included in legislation should be prepared with awareness of the fact that persons' views on life-sustaining treatment have nuances and that no form will ever serve the purposes of all citizens of any given state. Alternative model forms should be provided. A model form that asks for provisions of all reasonable life-sustaining treatment should be provided, as should forms offering various options for refusing treatment.

10. Explicit provision should be made to assure that persons are adequately informed of their medical conditions in order to make choices based on their personally held beliefs and values.

It is to the problem of truthful disclosure to patients that I now turn.

7 | She'll Be Happier If She Never Knows

The Patient's Right and Obligation to Have the Truth

It was the first time the fifty-four-year-old patient had been hospitalized. She was born in Puerto Rico and had lived in Spanish Harlem for the past ten years. She had come to the emergency room two weeks earlier with a severe pain and a mass in her right lower abdomen. The previous December she had had a severe attack in the same area. Her history revealed that she was past menopause. She had worked in a nursing home and so was familiar with medical procedure. A third-year medical student obtained the pertinent material in her medical history and talked with her briefly. She told him that she was afraid that she had cancer. When the student assured her that she would have a complete work-up, she replied sadly, "If it was cancer you doctors wouldn't tell me." The student did not comment on the patient's statement, but said that the lab tests and examinations would tell them much more about the possible causes of the pain and mass. Two days later, after the patient had been examined by the medical students, the resident, the chief resident, and the attending physician, the woman was diagnosed as having a degenerating fibroid, which would explain the severe pain and the mass. It was pointed out, however, that after menopause the most common cause of a painful mass was cancer. The patient went to surgery the next morning. The same day, the medical student spoke to the resident, who reported that she had stage IV cancer of the cervix. They had cleaned out all the tumor they could see, but since it had spread to pelvic wall, the only alternative was to try chemotherapy and radiation. The five-year survival rate of stage IV cancer at the time was not more than 20 percent.

When the patient awoke from the surgery, the medical student's first reaction was to go to her and explain the findings. He felt he should speak frankly with her, attempt to share her grief, and be there to support her. However, since he had not had much experience with cancer and this was his first patient "who had been given a death notice," he decided to speak first to the chief resident about how best to approach telling this woman. The medical student explained that he wanted to tell the patient that she had cancer, and that he felt close enough to her to share some of the process. The chief resident's reaction was agitated. "Never use the word 'cancer' with a patient," he said, "because then they give up hope." He suggested using other words or medical jargon.

The student was in turmoil. He felt it was important to convey to the patient what he knew himself: that, according to the best medical understanding of her condition, she had a limited time to live; that new biomedical technology and medical discoveries meant that there were possible treatments, which would be tried; that new discoveries are continually being made. But he wanted to convey to her that the chances were that she would not live out her normal life span—in fact, she would not survive more than a few years.

The discussion got more heated. The resident angrily asked, "I'd like to know how you'll feel when the patient jumps out the window." The student's response was that he felt he had to evaluate the patient's desire to know and that this woman had given a clear message that she wished to know.

The resident told the young student a story about a distinguished internist, the senior attending physician on their service and internationally known as author of a major medical textbook, who while on grand rounds asked if there was anyone present who would tell the patient they had just seen that he had cancer. When one medical student raised his hand, the internist said, "You march down to Dean's office and tell him that I said you are to be kicked out of medical school." Since an authoritarian and often hostile relation between master and student still exists in the clinical teaching setting, the student took him very seriously and turned toward the door. At that point the internist said, "Now you know what it's like to be told you have cancer. Tell a patient that, and it will destroy the last years of his life."

The student left the meeting with the resident wondering what the patient should be told and who should do the telling. He had a good idea what would be said by the senior attending physician, by the resident, and by himself.

The Consequentialist Case for Withholding the Truth

Physicians are strongly committed, in the ideal at least, to protecting patients from potential harm, both physical and mental. Traditionally, this has often manifested itself in a paternalism that has led to decisions by clinicians to withhold disturbing information from patients. According to one, now dated, study, 88 percent of physicians responding reported that they usually follow a policy of not telling patients that they have cancer.[1] Some of these physicians may have decided not to tell for irresponsible reasons: to tell someone he is about to die is not a pleasant task and can be time consuming. But, until recently, physicians for the most part have been dedicated morally to the principle of judiciously withholding information that they feel would do serious harm to the patient. Bernard Meyer, a physician who wrote in the 1960s on the ethics of what should be told to the terminal patient, says, "Ours is a profession which traditionally has been guided by a precept that transcends the virtue of uttering truth for truth's sake; that is, 'So far as possible, do not harm.'"[2]

The medical student who wondered what to tell the woman who had cancer of the cervix faced the same argument. This kind of moral argument is a type well known to those familiar with ethical theory. It is situational, individualistic, consequentialist, and it may give harm a special priority.

MEDICAL CONSEQUENTIALISM

The argument of the physician is consequentialistic, that is, it looks to the consequences of the act of telling or not telling. The primary or sole concern is the potential benefit or harm in a course of action. The ethics of calculating the benefits and harms of alternative courses of action is the subject of a very long and confusing debate.[3] Consequentialists worth their salt will extend harms and benefits well beyond the economic consequence to include physical factors of pain and suffering and even psychological factors such as happiness, anxiety, depression, and fear. In the ethical debate over whether to keep a terminal patient alive by using marginal or heroic means, the economic factor may be a consideration in a consequentialist argument, although many using this mode of reasoning would claim that the noneconomic factors so outweigh the economic ones as to make the monetary considerations practically irrelevant even in those cases. In the case of what to tell the dying patient, a calculation of utility will have to give weight to happiness, anxiety, and hope.

There is a special twist to the consequentialist ethics of the traditional physician, particularly in the notion that the physician's moral duty is "Above all preserve life." One understanding of this principle is that life has such ultimate value and is to be so heavily weighted in the consequentialist calculus that other goods are trivial by comparison. The resident in the case under consideration is arguing that if the patient is told, she might commit suicide. This is an often made claim, but, to my knowledge, one without documentation. Nevertheless, the resident may be saying that he thinks that if the patient is told, she will commit suicide, and that is the ultimate bad consequence—at least for those in the practice of medicine. If this is his argument, he is a special kind of consequentialist who not only considers suicide a harm, but also considers it the ultimate harm. The possibility of provoking suicide throws the scales completely off balance in favor of not telling.

Others using the consequentialist mode of ethical reasoning do not consider it the physician's primary duty to preserve life at all. Rather it is, more generally, to prevent harm, in particular psychological harm such as suffering, fear, and especially anxiety. This has been the dominant, normative ethical theory operating in medicine. Yet this theory deviates from the simple consequentialism of Mill and Moore. First, at least according to some physicians, there is a greater imperative to prevent harm than there is to produce good. This is often quite a conservative moral principle—one that would lead ultimately never to do anything for any patient—but one that has played an extremely important role in medical ethics. W. D. Ross makes a similar sort of argu-

ment with similar anti-interventionist results.[4] For Ross, this deviation is morally required, because there is a special imperative to eliminate harms. Other contemporary
analysts have reached the same conclusion.[5] Thus the arguments that the physicians
presented to the medical student were utilitarian, but of a special sort.

MEDICAL SITUATIONALISM

Second, the physician's mode of ethical reasoning is situational.[6] It focuses on the
individual case as a unique moral entity. Any overarching rule such as "always tell the
truth" or "truth for truth's sake" is unacceptable. This is certainly Meyer's position and
probably that of the resident in our case although he says never use the word cancer.
The attending physician seems to be less of a situationalist in saying, "Don't ever tell
a patient if he has cancer. It will always destroy the last years of his life."

MEDICAL INDIVIDUALISM

Finally, the physician's mode of ethical reasoning is individualistic. The Hippocratic
Oath says that the physician's duty is to act for the benefit of the patient, not for the
relatives, for patients as a whole, or for society. This then is still another modification
of classical consequentialism. For Mill[7] or Bentham[8] the morally required act is the
one that produces the greatest total amount of good—"the greatest good for the greatest
number." The Hippocratic physician, ideally, if not in practice, is committed to producing the greatest good for one individual—the patient. In the case of the dying
patient, the physician believes the primary moral consideration should be to prevent
anxiety, to stave off death, prevent suicide, or maintain the patient's hope. Under this
kind of moral system, most physicians, until the 1970s, concluded that they would
tend not to tell patients of a terminal cancer diagnosis.

The Formalist's Case for the Principle of Telling the Truth

The physician's plan is to avoid harm by not telling the patient of a terminal diagnosis. The first and most obvious countervailing principle is the common moral principle that there is a duty to tell the truth—at least under certain conditions. According
to those who follow this principle, even if withholding information from the dying
patient would prevent harm or preserve life, one would still have to ask whether withholding or deceiving the patient is right. Separating the rightness of withholding information from the good consequences produced (or the bad consequences prevented) is
fundamental to the ethical instincts of many. Kant is perhaps this position's most famous
defender. He puts it bluntly: "The moral worth of an action does not depend on the
result expected from it."[9] Kant applies this to the defense of the inherent rightness of
telling the truth in his essay "On the Supposed Right to Lie from Altruistic Motives,"
where he claims:

If, then, we define a lie merely as an intentionally false declaration towards another man, we need not add that it must injure another. . . . To be *truthful* (honest) in all declarations is therefore a sacred command of reason, and not to be limited by any expediency. . . . Although by a certain lie I in fact do no wrong to any person, yet I infringe the principle of justice in regard to all indispensably necessary statements *generally* (I do wrong formally, though not materially); and this is much worse than to commit an injustice to any individual. . . .[10]

The inherent rightness of telling the patient the truth is a simple notion, one which may be retained or rejected by individuals according to their normative ethical positions. Although views on the subject appear never to have been tested empirically, it seems that physicians, being committed (theoretically) to the consequentialist principle of working for the benefit of the patient, have traditionally been particularly skeptical of the moral relevancy of the "truth for truth's sake" principle. On the other hand, many lay people are not so willing to discard it, especially in relation to matters so fundamental as life and death. If patients and their physicians evaluate the validity of the truth-telling principle differently, it is only logical that they may differ on what a patient with a cancer diagnosis should be told.

Even those who would not want to discard the principle that telling the truth is justified on grounds of inherent obligation might not be willing to go as far as Kant. It may be that both inherent right-making characteristics and consequences are relevant in determining rightness and wrongness. The technical name for this plausible resolution of the debate is *mixed deontologism*. As used by W. D. Ross and others, it is simply the view that there are many factors determining moral rightness. Some characteristics are prima facie right making, such as justice in distribution, keeping promises, making restoration for previous wrongs done to another, and, most significant for our purposes, telling the truth. Yet also included in Ross's list of prima facie right-making characteristics is the production of good (beneficence) and prevention of harm (nonmaleficence).[11]

If we accept this position, we at least include the requirement to tell the truth as one of the relevant factors, but we also examine the consequences. To the extent that physicians have tended to abandon the ethic grounded in Hippocrates that gives exclusive place to consequences for the patient, they have tended to adopt this mixed deontologism, the position that both consequences and the truth-telling principle are morally relevant considerations. Any holders of this position, however, must have some basis for relating these two considerations. If they are intuitively balanced, then different people may give different weights. A clinician, steeped in the tradition of pure Hippocratic consequentialism, may give greater weight to consequences than a patient who is oriented to the principle of honesty.

I have argued that nonconsequentialist principles such as telling the truth, justice, and the avoidance of killing should have absolute priority over concern about producing good consequences. For our purposes, what is important is that different theories for relating the principles of honesty and beneficence lead to different conclusions about whether there is a moral duty to reveal a diagnosis that may provoke anxiety. If the physician and patient differ, it is not necessarily because one has greater knowledge of the consequences of disclosure than the other. They may simply hold different moral positions.

Although the primary moral dimensions of the debate are the bad consequences of telling the patient about the malignancy and the principle of telling the truth, it is possible that there could also be bad consequences from nondisclosure. There may even be nonconsequentialistic reasons why there is a duty not to disclose.

The Consequentialist Cases for Telling the Truth
SHORT RANGE PERSONAL UTILITY

In the earlier discussion of possible consequences from the action of telling the truth, we considered the harms that might result. Both the utilitarian and the mixed deontologist, however, would also be required to examine the possible bad consequences of not telling. The most obvious consequence is the general malaise that comes from not knowing one's condition. Lack of knowledge about whether the lump in the chest means death or means nothing can generate oppressive anxiety. Psychological variables like happiness and anxiety are difficult, if not impossible, to measure. Most of the anecdotal reporting of the severe harm or great benefits of telling patients seems to be only intuition. Fitts and Ravdin, in a study of physicians' views on what to tell cancer patients, reported the comments of several. One declared:

> I feel strongly against letting the patient know he has cancer! To all people, intelligent or not, the word cancer means a death sentence, and, even if you meet an occasional patient who insists on knowing the worst and says that it will not affect him one way or another, he will be mentally affected by knowing the worst.[12]

But another seemed to have a different experience:

> I always tell the patient he has cancer. In forty years I have had only two instances where the full truth was not well received. . . . All patients can bravely face even death if they know the truth and trust the honesty of the one they have selected to aid. They condemn their physician or even their close family if they discover they have been deceived and will not even trust a favorable prognosis should such be possible. To deceive a patient or even evade a real fact of certain death, is to torture the intelligence of those who will know, even if it be at the very last, that they could trust no one.[13]

Either these two physicians see very different patient populations or they are reading the psychological data very differently. The latter is more likely. To many patients, the anxiety from not knowing their diagnoses accurately must be at least as great as that from knowing the terrible truth—at least if the truth is revealed in a humane manner.

The psychological factors of happiness and anxiety are not the only consequences to consider. What of the physical ones? I have already suggested that the fear of provoking suicide may be exaggerated, often existing more in the mind of the death-fearing physician than in the patient. But if many potentially terminal illnesses are treatable to the extent that even several years of happy, productive life can be expected, it seems essential that patients know their real diagnoses and prognoses. Patients whose denials are reinforced by overly protective physicians are denied the opportunity of knowing the seriousness of their conditions. This may, in some instances, lead to a lack of rigorous cooperation in treatment.

Without emphasizing monetary factors, there are cases where lack of knowledge can do serious economic harm to a patient's interests. This is true not only in those cases where patients might refuse an expensive and protracted death-prolonging treatment and thus preserve their savings for their families, but in more straightforward cases where economic decisions might be made differently if patients knew their real fates. If, for instance, a patient is deciding whether to undertake speculative ventures for long-term gain, a decision made under the assumption that a lump is merely an innocent cyst may be totally different from a decision made in the knowledge that this capital would be the family's sole means of support six months later. At least in some cases very bad decisions will be made when patients lack the knowledge of their conditions.

Of course, not all decisions of the dying are of an economic nature. Practicing Roman Catholics, for example, have a duty, not merely a right, to prepare for death. Many choices ought to be made to fulfill their religious obligations. Many other people also believe that they should prepare for imminent death. While this will not include last sacraments, it does mean preparing or reviewing wills, clarifying business arrangements, and perhaps making a final reconciliation with family members.

Finally, there is another noneconomic good—an ultimate value in many individuals' minds: freedom to control one's life at least to the extent that it does not impinge on the freedom of others. This is fundamental to human nature and applies no less to the dying. To deprive people of information is to deprive them of freedom to make a responsible choice, which, for some, is an ultimate harm—a moral outrage. And it is quite probably a violation of constitutionally protected liberties.

All of these consequences of telling and not telling must be added to the calculus of the consequentialist or mixed deontologist to determine the total balance of good and harm. Even with the normative ethical theory of individualistic consequentialism—of deciding what to do on the basis of what will benefit patients and protect them from harm—all of these factors must be weighed.

LONG RANGE UTILITY

The consequences of telling or withholding the terminal diagnosis do not stop here. The patient we have been discussing was reported to have said, "If it was cancer you doctors wouldn't tell me." Where did she develop this apprehension that she will be told a lie? If it is true that at one time in our recent past 88 percent of physicians tended not to tell a patient of such a diagnosis, her fears were well founded. Each act of lying or withholding of information from the patient contributes to the general mistrust. To the physician who is committed to benefiting only the isolated patient dying in the hospital bed at a particular moment, the significance of the long-range impact of an act is obscured. Nevertheless, any good utilitarian will be quite aware that there is indeed a cumulative impact from individual deceptions. That is common sense to ordinary persons, who are concerned to protect their good word even if a little white lie would be quite harmless in an individual case. To many physicians, however, long-range consequences have been either imperceptible or irrelevant because they fall outside the scope of benefit to the present patient.

One patient, a woman near retirement age, became concerned about a lump in her breast and came to the tumor clinic with some fear. After extensive tests the chief physician called her in for a conference. "We have good news," he said. "The lump is nothing to worry about. You can expect a long and happy life." She immediately began preparing for her funeral. "If it was cancer, you doctors wouldn't tell me." The medical profession, which has built its ethics on trust and confidence in the personal physician, has, under the traditional Hippocratic ethic, been in danger not only of undermining confidence in medicine but of destroying any workable relationship by perpetuating the image that patients can be lied to whenever it may benefit them. From the childhood innoculations ("This won't hurt a bit") to the published statements of world-famous kidney transplant surgeons that when they encountered potential donors whom they feel would have psychological difficulties, they tell them they have a "tissue incompatibility," the patient has learned, and often learned correctly, that the medical profession can not always be trusted.

Henry Sidgwick, one of the great philosophical ethicists of the turn of the century, was a strong defender of the physicians' principle that right and wrong are to be determined solely on the basis of consequence. But Sidgwick recognized that even where "benevolent deception" was thought to be beneficial to the individual patient, it still had to be weighed against the total impact of the individual act of deception. His argument is one which, at least until recently, the medical profession has not dealt with adequately. It is summarized in his *Methods of Ethics:*

> The quality denoted by our term [veracity] is admittedly only praiseworthy in so far as it promotes individual or general welfare and becomes blameworthy—though remaining in other respects the same—when it operates adversely to these ends.
>
> It does not seem clearly agreed whether Veracity is an absolute and independent duty, or a special application of some higher principle. We find (e.g.) that Kant regards it as a duty owed to oneself to speak the truth, because "a lie is an abandonment or, as it were, the annihilation of the dignity of man." And this seems to be the view in which lying is prohibited by the code of honor, except that it is not thought (by men of honor as such) that the dignity of man is impaired by any lying: but only that lying for selfish ends, especially under the influence of fear, is mean and base. . . .
>
> Where deception is designed to benefit the person deceived, Common Sense seems to concede that it may sometimes be right: for example, most persons would not hesitate to speak falsely to an invalid, if this seemed the only way of concealing facts that might produce a dangerous shock. But if the lawfulness of benevolent deception in any case be admitted, I do not see how we can decide when and how far it is admissible, except by considerations of expediency; that is, by weighing the gain of any particular deception against the imperilment of mutual confidence involved in all violations of truth.[14]

RULE UTILITY

Even now, with the long-range implications of the individual act taken into account, we have not placed all of the weights on the scales. There is still another type of utility to consider. Over the past two decades there has been an extensive debate over the position known as "rule utilitarianism."[15] According to this view, it is not individual acts that are to be justified by appealing to their consequences, but general rules or practices.[16] To decide each individual act on the basis of a thorough examination of the benefits and the harms it may bring is likely to be impossible. It would require endless calculation and is cumbersome at best. More than likely it would lead to confusion and lack of predictability in the actions of others because we could never know how they would calculate the benefits in each individual case. To avoid this chaos, or for more theoretical reasons, one opts instead for the general practices (rules) that will maximize the good.

How does rule utility apply to the decision about what to tell the dying patient? If it is true that, at one point, physicians would tend not to tell and 90 percent or more of patients said they wanted to be told, this suggests that if physicians used their own judgment about what is in the patient's interests, they would have made many mistakes. Physicians, at least physicians other than psychiatrists, are not trained in determining what is in the patient's interests. In the public realm, people are subjected to the rule of law even in those cases where they think their own judgment is better. This is in part because there is value in order and predictability in life and in part because we know from experience that in many cases when individuals try to decide each case situationally they will make mistakes.

Physicians are often individualists and inveterate situationalists. They pride themselves on their commitment to examine each case individually. Piatt, for instance, offers the classical, if dangerous, medical ethical platitude in response to his question "What shall the cancer patient be told?": "Each case is an individual one and what is to be told the patient depends on the personal temperament of the individual."[17] Even Oken, who provided the dramatic early data on the differences between physicians and patients on what should be told, offered the situationalist attenuator, "Intuitive understanding of what the patient experiences is a time proven and essential guide for the physician," although he does temper this with the warning, "instinctive judgments, however, can be terribly misleading."[18] The consequences might be better on the average if the general rule of telling the truth is followed than if fallible physicians tried to decide each case individually by what they think will benefit the patient. This would be the case especially when patients say explicitly that they want information or even if they refrain from an explicit request that their diagnosis be withheld. The potential goods produced by following a rule that sets up a bias in favor of telling the truth must also be added to the scales in the consequentialist weighing. Thus the short-range utility for the individual patient, the long-range impact on the patient-physician relationship, and the extra utility of following a rule even when it may not appear to be the benefit-maximizing solution all provide consequential reasons why the terminal patient should be told. These should be added to the formalist reasons.

The Contract Theory Cases for and against Telling the Truth

There is still another moral dimension in the decision whether to reveal potentially meaningful information to the patient whose diagnosis is terminal. This is an inherent prima facie moral obligation arising from the relationship between medical professionals and lay people. There are several models for this relationship. Some see the physician as a priest. According to one establishment medical sociologist, the doctor's office has "somewhat the aura of a sanctuary"; he claims that "the patient must view his doctor in a manner far removed from the prosaic and the mundane."[19] Closely related to the priestly analogy is the view of the physician as parent. According to one senior physician presenting a case in which the medical team was trying to decide what to tell a dying middle-aged woman, "Every patient is a dependent child who demands of his physician that he be a good parent." (For some reason the dying patient who is viewed as a child is very often female, and the dominating physician's conclusion is, "She'll be happier if she never knows.") In the priestly or parental model of the patient-physician relationship, the physician assumes the role of moral and decision-making authority.

Some offer a second model, a radical critique of the authoritarian pattern. They make the physician a plumber, an engineer plugging in tubes and cleaning out clogged pipes to meet the owner's specifications with no questions asked. This is a dangerous move, laying the groundwork for absolving the medical professional of any moral responsibility.

A third model tries to equalize the status and authority relationship by seeing the patient and physician as engaged in a common task—restoring or maintaining the patient's health. This model is pleasant but a bit utopian. Equality cannot be established by decree. The fact is that, for the most part, the patient and physician do not share a common status, knowledge, or social background to justify any assumption of a collegial relationship.

The fourth model is one that tries to maintain the shared authority and responsibility in the medical relationship, but without the unwarranted assumptions of the collegial model. The professional and the lay person enter into a partnership in a common enterprise, but one in which each has a certain role to play. The patient and physician are seen as entering into something like a contract, often an implied contract, but the more explicit the better. The relationship between contracting parties is one where there will always be differences in abilities, resources, and needs. It is a limited relationship in which each party is committed to certain specific obligations and obtains in return certain goods or rights. Until the day when there can be a more natural sharing of perspectives, the more or less formal contract should be the model for specifying the relationship between patient and physician and for protecting each party from potential abuses by the other.

THE CONTRACT CASE FOR WITHHOLDING INFORMATION

The strongest case against telling dying patients their prognosis may be based on the limited rights and obligations of the contractual relationship between patient and health professional. No matter what the purpose of the medical relationship, patients approach the professional with some idea of what they hope to gain. They do not turn to the physician for general wisdom on all areas of life. It can be argued that under certain circumstances the physician's advice is being sought about a particular limited condition. The physician has no business meddling in other, more general problems that the patient has not raised. If, for instance, a man came to a physician for the sole purpose of obtaining a physical examination for an insurance form, he might rightfully resent the physician's advice that he needs psychiatric counseling.

Would this same contractual limitation ever apply to the case of patients with terminal diagnoses? It seems that in most cases the relationship between such patients and their physicians would be much more involved. Physicians are dealing with the total process of the disease, and only under very limited circumstances would the diagnosis and prognosis be irrelevant. One such case, which I shall take up later in this chapter, might be where patients specifically request that they not be informed. A second, more obvious case where the contractual relationship might justifiably limit the disclosure of a known prognosis is that of a consultation. The physician who sees the patient casually for a neurology consultation or radiation therapy is probably limited by the "contract" from disclosing much that would be appropriate or even obligatory for the primary physician to disclose. If, however, the consulting physician feels that the primary physician is not fulfilling the obligation to discuss some condition with the patient, then the moral right and obligation to disclose may become much greater.

A similar contractual argument to justify nondisclosure of a terminal illness might apply to other health professionals who are not the primary caregivers. Nurses, pharmacists, and social workers, when they are not in the primary caregiving role, might well feel as obliged as a consulting physician to withhold sensitive information from a patient even though they believe that the patient has a right to it and that it would be helpful.

THE CONTRACT CASE AGAINST WITHHOLDING INFORMATION

Of course, the same contract may require that the diagnosis and prognosis of a terminal illness be disclosed to the patient (with the obvious qualification that it be done in a sensitive and meaningful way). A contract is a set of mutual promises, that rests upon the trust and confidence that those promises will be fulfilled. If a patient approaches a medical professional with a problem and there is a finding that is in any way potentially useful and meaningful to the patient, it seems clear that there is an implied understanding in the contract that the patient will receive the information. Barring a communication that a given area is excluded from the contract, certainly the health professional must assume that, if the information can be expected to be of significant use or meaning to the patient, it should be disclosed. Certainly a terminal prognosis must fall under the category of potentially significant information. To do other than communicate with the patient is a violation of the trust and confidence upon which the contract is based. According to this line of argument, the contract model of the medical relationship provides a strong prima facie case against withholding any potentially significant information.

Five Rationalizations for Lying

I have now examined a number of arguments both for and against telling patients of their cancerous conditions and prognoses. Obviously, there will be differences on the proper conclusion in each case. The individual decision about what is right will depend upon how one fills in the data, the extent to which different moral factors are present in a given case, and one's implicit weighing and balancing of competing claims. One first has to decide how much good and how much harm will be done by each alternative and then how significant those goods and harms are for the moral conclusion.

Before discussing the different ways physicians and lay people carry out the process of evaluation, I will give attention to a serious problem, a kind of lying that far exceeds any deception of the patient: the physician's own self-deception. I call this the "big lie," a lie so big that it even fools the liar. The big lie can take many forms.

JARGON: THE TRUTHFUL LIE.

The truthful lie seems to fool many physicians. One of the best ways to avoid the guilt of lying and at the same time avoid the discomfort (to physician or patient) of disclosing anything is simply to tell the truth—in fact, to tell it in a very complete and scientific way. One physician discussing what to tell a patient after abdominal surgery said he would have no problem if the patient insisted on knowing. He would tell him he had a neoplasm with the characteristics of a leiomyosarcoma with possible secondary metastatic growth. Nothing could be more true and yet communicate less truth to the patient. Simply to tell the patient he had a cancer in a kind and gentle way would be less precise but perhaps more honest. Unfortunately many physicians are able to fool even themselves into thinking that rapid spewing of jargon, preferably with polysyllabic words, fulfills their obligation to their patients and to themselves. It seems far preferable to tell the bold-faced lie to the patient and at least know yourself what you are doing.

WE'LL NEVER KNOW FOR SURE.

A physician was discussing the case of a fourteen-year-old boy with leukemia. He introduced the case with the remark that there was not a chance that this boy would live another six months. He then commented that no one would think of telling him the horrible truth because the boy was still happy, was involved with his school work, and was planning to be a doctor—an ambition that must have been seen in a very positive light by the physician. When asked what he was telling the boy and why he felt that the prognosis should not be disclosed, he remarked rather defensively that it would be bad science and bad medicine to say that he had a 100 percent chance of dying soon. "After all, we have seen stretcher cases who we thought did not have a chance, and they walked out of the hospital six months later. Miracles happen sometimes, you know."

Of course miracles happen, that is to say our best scientific prognoses are sometimes still in error. It is wrong to tell a patient that there is 100 percent chance of dying soon if there is not. But that does not explain why the physician did not have the obligation to communicate the real picture to the patient in the best and most gentle way he could. It is indeed bad science and bad medicine to tell a patient he has virtually no chance of surviving six months and it would take a miracle to save him. In fact one would wonder about the initial comment of a physician who confidently said, "He doesn't have a chance." It does not justify, however, failure to convey in a sympathetic and meaningful way what the picture is to the best of the physician's knowledge with all of the proper qualifications including the possibility that a miracle will happen.

A more perverse form of this type of self-deception is the overoptimistic hope for the best. At times, it becomes so clearly untruthful that it borders on a lie of the plain, ordinary type but, in some cases, the expression of hope in the face of a cancer diagnosis can be a "big lie," that particularly malicious form which seems to fool even the physician. This pattern still occurs today in subtle forms, although it was much more common and more blatant in an earlier era. Physician Charles C. Lund, writing advice to the physician in the 1940s, provided a striking example of the kinds of self-deception that physicians once experienced. He began with a case of what I have called "the truthful lie." He parlayed this into what is more probably overoptimistic hope for the best:

> Certainly at the start of the interview he should avoid the words carcinoma or cancer. He should use cyst, nodule, tumor, lesion, or some loosely descriptive word that has not so many frightening connotations. He should then suggest that the operation is indicated and give some rough idea of the extent of the operation. If the consent is given at this stage, this is enough. But he should inform the most interested relative that there is only a 50 percent chance of a successful outcome. [If the patient fails to consent], however, no bridges have been crossed and many resources are still open to the doctor to secure consent for proper treatment. In one case the matter may be presented to the family and the family doctor who can take over at this point and who can frequently present the situation in such a light that the patient will consent. . . . It seems clear that the doctor can only fully meet his obligations to the patient if she makes her final decision after being put in possession of as close an approximation to the truth as can fairly be conveyed to her. One should, at least, state that the lesion is in imminent danger of becoming a cancer and that a good chance of a cure still remains if action is immediate. If the patient asks directly, "Is this cancer?" the doctor is forced to answer, "Yes," but can always go on to explain in the same sentence, "but it probably is not as serious you fear because you have a good chance or cure."[20]

This rather clever playing with the truth begins with a compulsive avoidance of language meaningful to the patient and a recognition of a 50 percent chance of survival, yet ends with an optimism that can hardly be called "as fair an approximation of the truth as can be conveyed." This kind of open and cavalier manipulation of the truth and of consent can only destroy what trust and confidence remain in the patient-physician relationship.

Meyer writing in the 1960s cited, with apparent approval, a case of planned over-optimism of a similar sort. He called it "a carefully modulated formulation that neither overtaxes human credulity nor invites despair":

> A doctor's wife was found to have ovarian carcinoma with wide-spread metastases. Although the surgeon was convinced she would not survive for more than three or four months, he wished to try the effects of radiotherapy and chemotherapy. After some discussion of the problem with a psychiatrist, he addressed himself to the patient as follows: to his surprise, when examined under the microscope the tumor in her abdomen proved to be cancerous; he fully believed he had removed it entirely; to feel perfectly safe, however, he intended to give her radiation and chemical therapies over an indeterminate period of time. [21]

While he may not have overtaxed the patient's credulity, he certainly overstretched the truth in the case. The fact that his prognosis was unduly pessimistic and the patient lived longer than he had predicted does not seem to justify deceiving the patient and probably himself as well.

"YOU CAN'T TELL A PATIENT EVERYTHING"

The third way in which some physicians seem to deceive themselves is by arguing that the facts about a patient's case are literally infinite and extremely complicated. The exact nature of the illness and prognosis would be impossible for a patient to understand and literally impossible for a physician to disclose. This fact is used by clinicians and researchers who belittle the notion of "fully informed consent." They argue that it is impossible even for the physician to be "fully informed." Of course this is true, but no one, or at least no one who has thought about the situation at all, ever claims that the physician's duty is to tell the patient "everything." This fact, however, does not affect the obligation to give information that may be meaningful or useful to the patient. The infinite range of possible facts about a patient's case will mean that the physician must do some selecting. There is no way around that, and some borderline pieces of information may be difficult to evaluate, but certainly the impending death of the patient can never be confused with such trivia.

LYING AND WITHHOLDING INFORMATION

In discussing the decision to end the prolongation of dying, I examined the difference between active killing and the mere omission or withdrawal of treatment which, provided there is an underlying terminal morbidity, leads to death. This difference between an action and an omission is also important in the truth-telling debate. Physicians discussing the disclosure of information to the dying patient will, on occasion, say they could never lie to the patient, but they sometimes fail to tell all that they know.

In discussing the action of killing for mercy and comparing it with forgoing of treatment, I found the relationship to be extremely complex. From a consequentialist point of view the results are often essentially the same. From the point of view of deontological ethics, however, I found some grounds for holding on to the often intuited distinction between actions and omissions. Active killing, I suggested, could be a violation of the prima facie principle of avoiding killing. Omitting treatment, on the other hand, might be nothing more than honoring the autonomy of the patient who is refusing treatment. Furthermore, I showed that there were some strong pragmatic reasons to hold on to the action-omission distinction. How do these conclusions compare with the distinction between the action of lying and the omission of information that might be meaningful to a patient?

Again, from the consequentialist point of view, there is little difference. If a patient would find a diagnosis meaningful in planning for the future, omitting to disclose it (because the patient did not think to ask) has about the same consequences as deliberately lying should the patient happen to ask if he is dying.

From the point of view of nonconsequentialist ethical principles, the parallel stands. Many nonconsequentialists hold, with good reason, that there is a prima facie principle of veracity. Other things being equal, it is a wrong-making characteristic of an action that it is a knowing communication of a falsehood. But just as the principle of avoiding killing cannot possibly entail a duty to preserve all life whenever possible, so the principle of veracity cannot possibly entail communicating all the truth that one knows in all circumstances. Just as there are countless lives that could be saved, so there are countless truths that could be spoken. In some cases persons have no business speaking them. They are too trivial, too time consuming, or too far outside the sphere of one's responsibility.

In the case of the action-omission distinction with regard to preserving life, I found that the relationship of the one who might omit treatment (such as a physician) and the one who might die as a result of the omission (the patient) was critical. In many cases, the physician has no right to act because he or she has not been authorized to do so by the patient. Even in cases where the one omitting treatment is a responsible surrogate for the patient (through a power of attorney, for example), that person is only obligated to act insofar as the action does more good than harm or insofar as a promise has been made to engage in the action.

With the problem of truthful disclosure of a terminal diagnosis, the relationship is slightly different. Some persons may be outside the nexus of responsibility. They may have no duty to disclose information because they are not in a special fiduciary relationship. Normally, however, even strangers have the right to intervene in another's affairs to the extent of speaking a truthful piece of information. The absence of a duty to speak does not, in itself, imply a duty not to speak. Only in special circumstances would there be a duty not to disclose. One such example might be where the patient has waived his or her right to knowledge, and the physician has agreed with a patient that the physician should retain all critical knowledge and decision making. It is debatable whether that is a morally noble way for a patient to live even during a terminal illness. But should a physician have made a promise to a patient not to disclose information, there is at least a prima facie duty not to do so. The physician or family member has seldom made such a promise and usually has not been authorized by the patient to withhold information. In such cases, the duty to disclose information will depend on the moral obligations of the relationship.

If the patient sees a physician for diagnosis, prognosis, and treatment of an illness the physician believes to be terminal, a contractual relationship is established. Unless some other arrangement is agreed to, an obligation is implied in that contract on the part of each party to disclose what is meaningful or useful to the other party in the performance of his or her responsibilities. This means that the patient has an obligation to be open with the clinician, but the clinician also has a similar obligation to disclose what is meaningful and useful to the patient in making decisions about his or her care and in order to consent or refuse consent to treatments recommended by the clinician.

In this sense, withholding meaningful information differs significantly from withholding treatment a patient has refused. Withholding information is an omission for which one is responsible—because the patient has the right to expect such information to be transmitted. The relationship of physician to patient in the case of transmitting information is therefore one where omissions routinely produce culpability. In the case of omitting treatment, there would be a similar culpability if providing care were part of the agreement and it was omitted, but there surely is no culpability if the patient has excluded such care from the contract. To the contrary, there is a duty not to provide it. In the case of omitting information that the patient would potentially find meaningful or useful, the moral wrong is not the violation of the principle of veracity. It is rather the failure to fulfill the expectations of the relationship.

The duty of one in such a relationship seems as stringent as the duty not to tell an outright lie. The physician may want to argue that either a lie or an omission is justified, but the action-omission distinction cannot be used to soften the moral implications of the omission. Physicians are deceiving themselves if they think they have avoided moral culpability simply because they have engaged in an omission instead of a positive lie.

INDIRECT COMMUNICATION

Once a physician recognizes some moral obligation to tell the truth, the second line of defense is a claim that communication takes place, but is "indirect." This is a platitude that may or may not be justified. Information is sometimes communicated more effectively in a less blunt and more indirect manner. Lund, for instance, says, "This must always be done gently, and perhaps, indirectly."[22] William May has suggested that there are at least four types of discourse available: (1) direct, immediate, blunt talk; (2) circumlocution or double-talk; (3) silence (which he points out can be a mode of sharing, but often is a way of evading); and (4) discourse that proceeds by way of indirection. He claims that we often assume that "direct, immediate, blunt talk is the only alternative to evasive silence and circumlocution." He gives as an example the perceptive recognition that the questions "Should I marry or buy a house?" may really be an indirect search for a clue from patients about their diagnosis. A simple "No" he claims would make discussion impossible, but saying that one recognizes the importance of the question leads to further discussion of uncertainties, anxieties, and fears. The language of indirection, he says, is appropriate because death is a sacred event, one which requires a special language.[23]

When does the language of indirection become the language of avoidance and self-deception? Often one hears the excuse that the patient seems to know anyway as justification for avoiding the difficult subject. But the language of indirection is a dangerous language to speak, perhaps more dangerous than simple, direct communication.

It often leads to rationalization of what one wants to hear. In the case with which I opened this chapter, for instance, the patient is quoted as saying, "If it was cancer you doctors wouldn't tell me." Clinicians, scholars, and students debating that sentence have had markedly different interpretations of its meaning. Some, inclined toward justifying nondisclosure, have insisted that the patient is pleading with the physician not to disclose. Others, prone to defending disclosure, hear the patient complaining about physicians who do not tell, implying that she really would like to be told. Some attempts at "reading" patients' indirect communications are even more obscure. The patient who crosses her legs is signaling that she is closed to communication. The patient who looks at his watch is saying that he wants the conversation to end. Indirect communication is easily subject to misunderstanding and to the desires of the one who is "hearing" it. It is not an adequate substitute. The real alternative is not "direct, immediate, blunt talk," but direct talk that is gentle, considerate, and open. Even this is no guarantee that the patient has received that truth, but it at least provides some assurance that the physician is not self-deceived into feeling justified in failing to communicate.

Although it may be justifiable to lie to a patient or withhold the truth in some cases, the big lie, the lie in which physicians fool themselves as much or more than their patients, cannot be justified under any circumstances. Before taking up those rare cases where deception may be justified, I shall first examine the traditional gap between professional and lay perceptions of the moral justification of lying or withholding information from the dying patient, and recent changes in that pattern.

Changes in Physician Disclosure Patterns

Before the mid-1970s these forms of self-deception simply reinforced a deeply held moral conviction on the part of physicians that their duty was to protect patients from harm by withholding distressing information. During the late 1970s, however, a dramatic change seems to have taken place in physician views about disclosure of bad news. What the changes were and what accounts for differences between those who oppose disclosure and those who favor it is important to consider.

Two early studies, one from 1953, the other from 1961, provide overwhelming evidence that physicians of the period were inclined not to disclose diagnosis of malignancy. In 1953 Fitts and Ravdin asked 444 Philadelphia physicians whether they tell their patients that they have been diagnosed as having cancer; 89 percent of the physicians responded.[24] They found that 3 percent always tell their patients and 28 percent usually do, while 57 percent usually do not tell and 12 percent never do. A serious shortcoming of the study was the undersampling of nonspecialists, who were less likely than average to tell patients, and the oversampling of dermatologists, who were most likely to tell. Thus the percentage of physicians who disclosed such information may actually have been even lower.

The second study showed even fewer physicians willing to disclose information. Oken asked 219 physicians affiliated with a major hospital in Chicago to indicate their "usual" policy and the frequency of exceptions to this policy.[25] Only 12 percent usually told their cancer patients of the diagnosis.

During this same period, several other studies found patients consistently reporting that they would like to be told. In the earliest published study (1950), Kelly and Friesen reported on two groups of 100 outpatients: the first, known cancer patients; the second, patients without known cancer. In the first group, 89 indicated they preferred knowing that they had cancer, 6 said they would rather not, and the remaining 5 were indefinite. In the second group, 82 said they would want to be told, 14 said they would not, and 4 were indefinite. In another study, when the researchers asked the same question of a group of 760 patients being examined at the cancer detection center of a university hospital, 729 or 98.5 percent wanted to be told, 7 (0.9 percent) did not, and 4 (0.5 percent) were indefinite.[26] Although it is difficult to ascertain whether patients are expressing their real desires, the data are very strong and consistent.

In a study published in 1957, Samp and Curreri asked patients and visitors in a waiting room of a tumor clinic: "If a patient has cancer, should he or she be told this fact?" Of 517 responding to the question with a yes or no answer, 451, or 87 percent, said yes.[27] Branch found that 48 of 54 cancer-free patients (88 percent) reported that they would prefer to be told about their condition.[28]

Later studies continued to find the same desire on the part of lay people to know a terminal diagnosis. In 1962 Daniel Cappon found that 91 percent of nonpatients wished to know if a serious illness was terminal.[29] In a study reported in 1970, nearly 80 percent of patients (50 to 86 years of age) in a gerontology center said they wanted to be told if they had an incurable illness.[30] By 1979 a Gallup poll found that between 82 percent and 92 percent of adults, depending on sex, race, education, age, income, and occupation, would want to be told.[31] The pattern is clear and persistent. During this period there were dramatic differences between physicians and lay persons on the ethics of disclosure of cancer diagnosis.

In the early 1970s, however, something equally dramatic began happening to reports by physicians of their views about disclosure. In 1970 Henry J. Friedman got responses from 180 physicians on the staff of the Faulkner Hospital in Boston; he had asked them whether they inform their patients of any diagnosis of a malignancy. Unfortunately, he gave his respondents three choices: always, sometimes, and never. Sixty-six percent opted for sometimes, leaving unclear whether that is their usual pattern or only an exceptional instance. Still 25 percent said they always tell and only 9 percent said they never do, clearly a shift in pattern from the earlier data.[32]

Two studies published in 1974 showed further evidence of this shift. Mount, Jones, and Patterson found that 13 percent of the physicians they studied at the Royal Victoria Hospital in Montreal said that the patient with a critical illness should always be told the nature of his disease, and about 80 percent said that the patient should usually be told. Still, physicians differed from patients. In the same study, 78 percent of the patients said they should always be told, and almost all of the rest said they usually should be told.[33] The same year Travis, Noyes, and Brightwell reported that 53 percent of the Iowa physicians they studied said they always or frequently told terminal patients of their prognosis.[34] The following year, Rea, Greenspoon, and Spilka reported that though 39 percent of the physicians they studied acknowledged some negative feelings about informing dying patients of their condition, the remainder felt the patient must be told.[35] All in all, the data show a clear, if gradual, shift in the direction of disclosure.

Four years later the transition was virtually complete. A group of researchers led by Dennis H. Novack asked physicians almost identical questions to those asked by Oken in 1961. Now, 98 percent of physicians reported that their usual policy was to tell the cancer patient. Seven percent of the sample never made exceptions to this policy. This is in contrast with Oken's finding that only 12 percent usually told their patients.[36] Other studies published since 1979 report that between 79 percent and 90 percent of physicians favor disclosure.[37]

We are thus left with a pattern that is much different from that of a decade earlier. While the earlier pattern was one of substantial difference in consensus between physicians and lay persons, by the 1980s the majority of physicians and lay people report on surveys that they favor disclosure. There is, nonetheless, the potential for important moral differences.

First, the survey data seem to show that physicians are not quite as uniform as patients in their support of disclosure. Second, even for Novack's physicians, apparently most made exceptions to their usual policy of disclosing information. Third, there is beginning to be evidence that the earlier Hippocratic reservations that physicians showed regarding disclosure of bad news are now manifesting themselves in the timing, pattern, and completeness of the disclosure. Michael Blumenfield and his colleagues reported in 1979 that 90 percent of medical residents held that patients have a right to be told, but only 47 percent of those same residents thought that the patient should be informed "as soon as possible."[38] There is evidence that physicians are distinguishing between telling the truth and telling the "complete truth" and between the right to know for patients who ask and for those who do not ask.[39] Thus, although a general consensus has emerged that patients should be told, there may be more subtle disagreement about how much, how soon, and how clearly. It is quite possible that some physicians who say they support disclosure are relying on some of the techniques discussed above (such as indirect communication) to satisfy their commitment to disclose information.

Finally, the patient surveys have made clear all along that, even though the vast majority of patients want to be told, not every patient does. The minority who would prefer not knowing may just get paired up with the ever-increasing group of physicians who are committed to disclosure. For all of these reasons, it is important to explore the reasons behind the possible differences in moral judgments about disclosure.

Reasons for Disagreement on Disclosure
DIFFERING DATA

One critical difference between those favoring and those opposing disclosure may be that they are using different data in their decision making. The surveys ask patients and other lay people to report what they want or would want; while the responses are probably reasonably honest, normal subjects who are not facing the immediate prospect of a terminal illness may not really know what they would want at that distant and threatening moment. On the other hand, those patients who already know they have a fatal illness might feel compelled to say that they are happier knowing. In surveys asking parents if their children were "wanted," ex post facto reports of what was desired at a previous time are not particularly reliable. For a dying man to report he would be happier not knowing the truth would at least be a blow to his ego. But Kelly and Friesen also questioned patients being examined in a cancer detection center, finding that a dramatic 98.5 percent said they wanted to be told.[40] It is hard to account for this result by the explanations given for the other groups of lay people.

It may be more plausible, however, to claim that data may be skewed by a widespread and significant psychological factor operating at the unconscious level—patient denial. By its very nature, denial is not a type of datum available to the lay people responding to the survey. Traditionally, most physicians have considered patient denial of illness and death to be an extremely important phenomenon. It is safe to say that it is an important element in the thoughts of those physicians who judge that they should not tell the usual patient of a terminal diagnosis.

W. A. Crammond, in an article "Psychotherapy of the Dying Patient," warns that "common defensive manoeuvers are denial, withdrawal, and counterphobia."[41] Freud goes so far as to say that at the bottom, nobody believes in his own death, and his influence on modern psychiatry has been considerable. Meyer warns, "There is the naive notion, for example, that when the patient asserts that what he is seeking is the plain truth he means just that. But as more than one observer has noted, this is sometimes the last thing the patient really wants."[42]

Aldrich claims that the appropriate way to handle denial is to provide patients with an opportunity to select either acceptance or denial of the truth.[43] Meyer exemplifies the physician's resistance to generalization about telling the truth and fascination with the uniqueness of the individual case mentioned earlier when I considered the rule-utilitarian basis for telling the truth:

> From the foregoing it should be self-evident that what is imparted to a patient about his illness should be planned with the same care and executed with the same skill that are demanded by any potentially therapeutic measure. Like the transfusion of blood, the dispensing of certain information must be distinctly indicated, the amount given consonant with the needs of the recipient, and the type chosen with the view of avoiding untoward reactions.[44]

This extreme situationalism can be both dangerous and insulting to the patient. In the first place, the physician is frequently conditioned to look for subconscious cues from the patient. Yet the reliability of the reading of those data is open to serious question. On the other hand, the traditional argument used by physicians in which they claim that patients are denying their inability to deal with death is now being questioned. The increasing majority of physicians, including those trained psychiatrically who now favor disclosure, presumably have access to these data about patient denial, and they are no longer dissuaded from disclosure.

A psychiatrist in the United States who has gained much attention for her warm and sensitive dealings with the terminal patient is Elisabeth Kübler-Ross. Dr. Kübler-Ross recognizes denial of death as the first major step in the psychology of dying.[45] She certainly gives denial a much more significant place than most medical lay people would. She reports one case where a twenty-eight-year-old Roman Catholic woman dying of a terminal liver disease, when confronted with her diagnosis before her hospitalization, "fell apart" until a neighbor assured her that there was always hope. Dr. Kübler-Ross claimed that in this case the patient "made it quite clear from the very beginning that denial was essential in order for her to remain sane."[46] Yet, even with her extensive discussion of the need for denial in some patients at a certain stage of their illness, Dr. Kübler-Ross still raises serious problems about the ability of physicians to read denial in their patients:

> I am convinced from the many patients with whom I have spoken about this matter, that those doctors who need denial themselves will find it in their patients and that those who can talk about the terminal illness will find their patients better able to face and acknowledge it. The need of denial is in direct proportion with the doctor's need for denial.[47]

DIFFERENT WEIGHTING OF DIFFERENT KINDS OF GOOD

Recognizing that physicians may include denial in the moral calculation raises the more general question of the different kinds of goods considered in deciding the course that will be most likely to benefit the patient. People differ on the weight they give to various goods. Many surgeons and other nonpsychiatric physicians seem to place a unique emphasis on physical health and sheer survival. Perhaps they would not have become physicians if they did not.

There are other goods, however, and others, including lay persons, may be more willing to balance health and even survival itself against some of them. Cigarettes, sweets, and excess weight may be definitively demonstrated to be harmful to your health, but many knowing this still would prefer their psychological or other benefits and would be willing to trade health for them. It is reasonable to compromise ideal medical care for a kind of care that costs less. A surgeon may justify a deception in order to get the patient to consent to a procedure by saying, "We have all seen miracles." Yet the patient might give relatively little weight to that one-in-a-thousand chance of survival and prefer to save his rapidly dwindling estate for his children. Psychiatrists join other physicians in placing great emphasis on mental suffering, depression, and anxiety as crucial factors in deciding whether to withhold the truth from a patient. But in order for that argument to work, these psychological harms must be given enough weight to offset goods that come from disclosure. The more one is distressed at dealing with death, the more weight one will give the harm done by discussing it.

Part of the explanation of the traditional pattern of physicians withholding information about terminal diagnosis might be that physicians had unusually high fear of death. In a brief but provocative study published in 1967 by Herman Feifel and his colleagues,[48] physicians' fear of death was measured in depth using a forty-item questionnaire with open-ended questions such as "What does death mean to you personally?" The answers were coded independently by two of the investigators, all of whom had diplomas in clinical psychology and psychiatry. A group of eighty-one physicians was compared with a group of seriously ill and terminally ill patients and another group of ninety-five normally healthy individuals. The physicians were significantly more afraid of death than either the healthy or sick lay people. This was the case even though 63 percent of the physicians said they were less afraid of death now than they had been heretofore.

Speculating on the origin of this difference, the authors noted that physicians reported that they first became afraid of death at a significantly earlier age than the lay people. The major reasons for this were personal accident, threat of death, or personal illness. They speculated that this above-average fear of death might be a factor in physicians' selection of medicine as a career. However, they also compared their findings from physicians with those from a group of medical students and found that the students were more fearful of death than the lay people, but less so than the experienced physicians. This seems to suggest that in spite of the physicians' reports, part of the abnormally high fear may be learned through years of daily contact with death and the inability to conquer it. It is not surprising, then, that this study, like the others, found that the physicians were significantly less willing than the patients to inform others of incurable disease.

There has been no comparable recent study to determine whether physicians of the 1970s and 1980s who are more willing to disclose have fewer fears of death. In a study published in 1983, Hatfield and his colleagues found that, compared to other groups, physicians responded more conservatively to statements about terminal care.[49] In 1982 Howells and Field published a study of British medical students in which they found no significant difference in the fear of death when comparing British medical students and students in the social sciences.[50] That is a hint that, if British and American experience is comparable, the difference in fear of death between those who choose medicine as a career and those who do not may be narrowing.

Data on the psychological condition of patients who have been given terminal diagnoses are harder to come by. Most of the studies are quite dated. The results reported by Kelly and Friesen in 1950, however, implied that these patients had adjusted to the knowledge.[51] These are also the findings of a British study by Aitken-Swan and Easson. They found that only 7 percent of 231 patients could be classified as disapproving of the disclosure.[52] Another 19 percent denied having been told, which might be taken as evidence of some patient denial, but it is not clear from the published study whether some of this is attributable to faulty, incomplete, or indirect communication by the physicians.

The physician discussing the case of the Puerto Rican woman cited at the beginning of this chapter expressed the extensively rumored fear that the patient would jump out the window if told. Stories of suicide following disclosure run rampant in medical school corridors, but when the perpetrators are pressed for documentation, the evidence turns out to be remote hearsay. A director of a major suicide prevention center has said that there is no evidence of abnormally high suicide rate after the revelation of cancer or other terminal diagnosis, and I have been able to find no such evidence. Peck found that no patient in a group of fifty cancer outpatients admitted an attempted suicide and only four had suicidal thoughts, ranging from one patient with firm suicidal intent to others who placed such thoughts completely in the past.[53] For patients in such condition, that rate of suicidal thinking seems remarkably low.

Data measuring patient anxiety and suicidal risk are difficult to interpret. Physicians are quick to point out that patients may not report accurately their true feelings on emotionally charged subjects such as death. It is also possible, however, that those physicians who are concerned about the psychological harms of disclosure are letting their own unique psychological profiles influence the weighting of the data.

In order to examine the various ways that data can be weighted, it is interesting to compare the attitudes of physicians in different specialties. In particular, those in psychiatry can be compared to those in specialties without special psychiatric skills. Unfortunately, the more recent studies do not adequately differentiate between psychiatric and nonpsychiatric specialties.[54]

In the early study by Fitts and Ravdin (1953) when most physicians were opposed to disclosure, they were able to find differences among specialties. The pattern was intriguing, however. They found that only 60 percent of the Philadelphia psychiatrists and neurologists in their study preferred disclosure, in contrast to the 90 percent of lay people who would want to be told. At first this suggests that professional judgment about psychological harms inclined experts of the day to be less willing than lay people to reveal terminal diagnosis. Yet the low percentage of psychiatrists and neurologists who preferred disclosure may have a more subtle explanation. Psychiatrists' views may be seen as being made up of at least two components: professional judgment about psychological risks and general psychosociological characteristics of physicians of the day. Psychiatrists were more willing to disclose than physicians in other specialties, indicating that if we were to eliminate the general psychosociological characteristics of physicians, there would still remain some factor that makes psychiatrists more willing to tell than other physicians. The physicians who were in a position to know the data best were more inclined to disclose than were their colleagues.[55]

The discussion of suicidal risk and prevention of anxiety presupposes a heavy weighting of physical and psychological harm in the utilitarian calculus in contrast with other social, cultural, religious, and economic goods and harms that would be given relatively greater weight by others. This suggests that when physicians began the radical reassessment of the morality of disclosure of terminal diagnoses, they may simply have reassessed the amount of harm that comes from disclosure. This could have taken place because as the discussion over death and dying became more public, and as physicians developed more skill in discussing death with their patients, disclosure itself became less traumatic. Or it could simply have been that physicians changed their assessment of the impact of disclosure—either because they learned more about the differences between their own attitudes and those of their patients or because their own psychological profiles had changed significantly. There is, however, one other possibility to account for the differences between those who support disclosure and those who oppose it. Holders of the two positions may be operating on different normative ethical principles.

DIFFERING NORMATIVE ETHICAL PRINCIPLES

All of this discussion assumes that the proper way to make a moral judgment about what should be done is to estimate as accurately as possible benefits and harms and then to choose the course most likely to benefit the patient. For the traditional Hippocratic physician, whether the patient will benefit, physically or psychologically, is the definitive factor. But if patients have different underlying moral principles, they may find a different factor of the highest importance. Patients may plausibly hold that they have a right or even a duty to know their medical condition even if they will be less well off in knowing. They may feel a duty to their spouses or children to make proper arrangements. They may feel a religious obligation to set things in order. They may simply feel a right and duty to exercise self-determination knowledgeably in consenting to their medical treatment in a responsible manner.

Even in a more liberal era when most physicians have adopted an ethic that is more committed to the inherent rightness of open disclosure, disagreement over ethical principle can still account for disagreements about what to tell patients. The more recent survey data still show a minority of physicians unwilling to disclose information. The surveys do not make clear whether they are using different data, weighting consequences differently, or using different ethical principles than their colleagues more willing to disclose. There is evidence, for example, that increasingly physicians accept the deontological ethic of autonomy, self-determination, and telling the truth more generally accepted in a liberal society. For instance, the 1980 revision of the AMA's Principles of Ethics states bluntly, "A physician shall deal honestly with patients,"[56] a radical departure from the traditional ethic of determining whether patients should be told solely on the basis of the physician's estimates of the consequences.

Nevertheless, even though the majority of physicians have adopted a stance more supportive of disclosure and, in many cases, have shifted to an ethic that accepts an independent principle of telling the truth, still differences between physicians and patients can occur. Just as a minority of physicians remain Hippocratic and conclude that disclosure would be harmful, so a minority of patients apparently would prefer that their physicians keep silent in cases where the physician believes that disclosure would be harmful. In some cases patients and physicians may be able to reach a special understanding authorizing physicians to withhold diagnoses when they think it is in the patient's interest. Often, however, this will not be done. In some cases, physicians may be so committed to the moral necessity of patient responsibility for decisions that such a waiver on the patient's part would violate the conscience of the clinician.

Whenever there is a mismatch in the ethics of the parties in the patient-physician relationship, moral disagreements can be expected. Where one party is reasoning consequentially and the other deontologically, it is not surprising if the two reach different moral conclusions. There should be, then, a conscious effort to pair patients and health care professionals on the basis of the moral principles they hold. If one holds that the decision is to be made on the basis of what the physician thinks will benefit the patient and is willing to let the physician use his or her own selection of data and his or her own weighting of the amount of psychological harm to be done by telling the patient, then the decision to withhold critical information about fatal illness may be justified. If the patient is to be respected, however, the paternalism of the Hippocratic ethic will have to be abandoned and the right of patients to have the information necessary for them to make crucial decisions about their own care must be recognized, even if, in some cases, there is a risk of increasing their level of anxiety or driving them into deeper depression. Indeed, disclosure may be required by the need to respect the patient and the individual's right to determine his or her own medical treatment, as well as by the inherent duty to tell the truth, the contractual obligations of the professional, and the utilitarian considerations that require disclosure of potentially meaningful and useful information.

The Exceptional Cases

Even if the dominant view of both health professionals and lay people has emerged in favor of disclosure of terminal illness, there are so-called exceptional cases in which some people are inclined to waiver in their commitment to openness between physicians and patients. Three special situations deserve attention.

WHEN THE FAMILY REQUESTS WITHHOLDING

A somewhat senile gentleman with a history of cardiac disease has exploratory surgery for a mass thought to be a cyst. After laboratory analysis, the mass is found to be cancerous. Surrounded by wife, children, in-laws, and grandchildren of various ages, he has received much loving attention. After leaving the patient, the surgeon turns to his wife and children and asks for advice about what to tell him. There is concern about the patient's health, fear that the shock might trigger another coronary, and perhaps a general aversion to having to discuss death. The wife asks the physician, "Doctor, what do you think is best?" Together they agree with the concurrence of the children that it would be better to let the gentleman continue to believe that the "cyst" was removed so that he can spend his last days in peace.

This scenario has been so common that it would not be worth discussing if it did not happen to violate both the most fundamental principles of medical ethics and the laws of many jurisdictions. No one ever seems to ask on what basis the family members are told about a diagnosis of which the patient himself is still ignorant. The World Medical Association's Code of Medical Ethics is blunt in its condemnation of unauthorized disclosure of information: "A doctor shall preserve absolute secrecy on all he knows about his patient because of the confidence entrusted in him."[57] The 1980 version of the AMA's Principles of Medical Ethics also contains a blunt commitment to confidentiality, saying, "a physician shall respect the rights of patients, of colleagues, and of other health professionals, and shall safeguard patient confidences within the constraints of the law."[58] Of course, these are only positions adopted by professional organizations and are not binding on either professionals or lay people outside those organizations. Still, the opinions expressed are quite consistent with broader ethical frameworks, including mainstream secular and religious medical ethical traditions. In light of this substantial consensus in favor of the right of patients to have information about them held in confidence, it is hard to see how a physician can give relatives enough information for them to make an informed decision about whether to tell the gentleman of his cancer.

Of course, the traditional physician who is still committed to the ethic of the Hippocratic Oath would be more open to violating confidentiality in such circumstances. The Hippocratic Oath is worded so evasively on the question of confidentiality that it offers no help on any difficult question, such as whether to tell the patient's family first. It simply says, "Whatever, in connection with my professional practice, or not in connection with it, I see or hear, in the life of men, which ought not to be spoken abroad, I will not divulge, as reckoning that all such be kept secret."[59] Therefore, that which should not be disclosed should not be, and presumably that which should be should be. In the context of the overarching Hippocratic benefit-the-patient principle, this may be taken to justify violating patient confidentiality by disclosing diagnoses to relatives first. The Declaration of Geneva, however, which is a revision of the Hippocratic Oath for modern times, is much more blunt. It has the physician pledge: "I will respect the secrets which are confided in me."[60]

The violation of patient confidentiality may not only infringe the principles of professional medical ethics; it may also violate more universally held moral principles. And in some jurisdictions it may be illegal. The laws on patient-physician confidentiality are extremely complex. In common law, the right to privileged communication exists between husband and wife, priest and penitent, and attorney and client, but not between physician and patient. In 1828 the state of New York enacted the first statute to forbid a physician to disclose any information acquired while attending a patient. Now, two-thirds of the states in the United States have such laws. That within the medical profession they are called "laws of privilege" indicates their primary objective: protecting physicians from disclosing against their will information about their patients in legal proceedings. The legal statutes and case law make clear, however, that if privacy is a privilege, that privilege is the patient's.

Patients have both a right and a duty to consent to their medical treatment based upon reasonable knowledge of their medical conditions. This right and duty cannot be waived on behalf of a mentally competent patient by a spouse, children, or relatives. This, of course, would not apply to the legally incompetent patient. But in the case of the legally competent—even one who happens to be a bit senile or mentally unstable—paternalism, even by one's spouse or children, is still paternalism. When requirements of patient consent for surgery or other medical treatment are waived by relatives, it may be illegal as well as immoral.

WHEN THE PATIENT REQUESTS WITHHOLDING

The principle of patient autonomy must be confronted in a more challenging way when the patient is the one who personally says, "Doctor, if it's cancer I don't want to know." Based on the now somewhat dated surveys, even among patients in a cancer detection center, perhaps 1.5 percent say they would rather not know if the news is bad. Although that is a small percentage, it represents a large number of patients. Physicians hear (or think they hear) such requests frequently. But does even the patient's own request justify withholding information?

In the first place, it is not clear whether patients are always saying they do not want to be told in all cases where physicians feel they hear that message. If it is true that physicians find denial when they need to or want to, the argument by physicians against telling the truth based on receiving indirect communication or nonverbal cues from the patient must be taken as very suspect. If, however, we limit consideration only to those cases where the patient has made a blunt request to the physician, saying, "Doctor, you do what you think is best and don't bother me with the details," there still may be problems.

Here the principle of autonomy, which has led us to reject the paternalistic withholding of information by physician or family, cuts in exactly the opposite direction. Most would accept that it is reasonable at some point to say that further information is not worth having. Consent for further treatment under these conditions may not be informed but it will be free, and it can be informed to the extent that one knows that there is relevant information that one chooses not to have. This can hardly violate the principle of autonomy.

This may end the debate if one is concerned only about the duty of physicians to tell patients their diagnoses. Virtually no physician would want to tell a patient a diagnosis when the patient actively requests not to be told. Both the fallibility of the physician in knowing what is in the patient's interest and the overriding importance of patient freedom would create strong barriers against the physician imposing the truth upon the patient. But that is not the end of the matter. We still must face the question: is it morally acceptable for the patient to make such a request in the first place?

There are two kinds of countervailing claims. First, consider the case of the thirty-eight-year-old married man with three children, aged seven through thirteen. He owns a real estate firm and speculates in housing development projects and similar ventures. He has just initiated negotiations for a large shopping development when he goes to the local physician for his first checkup in nine years. He has had persistent cold symptoms and skin rashes for some time, but he is unconcerned. He is a busy man with little time for health matters. As he begins his physical exam he tells the physician that he is sure he is in good health. The physician will not find anything significant, and he does not want to hear any sermons about watching his diet and getting plenty of exercise. He also adds firmly that if the physician really does find something, he doesn't want to be troubled by being told. The physician should do what he thinks best.

After discovery of nodular lesions in the respiratory tract and repeated examinations, the physician's eventual diagnosis of Wegener's granulomatosis leads to a moral dilemma. The disease involves the breakdown of normal immune mechanisms and is usually relentlessly progressive. It is usually fatal in six to eight months, although occasionally the condition does not become acute for years. Very little treatment is possible, but steroid injections are recommended. The physician feels there is little he can do. Faced with the patient's plea to be left alone, what is the morally appropriate response?

In avoiding the burden of a fatal diagnosis, the patient has jeopardized the welfare of his family, since he is considering risking his savings in a speculative shopping center which may pay off but not for many years. The physician, committed to narrow patient-centered concern, may not be moved by the potential harm to the family, but fortunately the moral obligations to the lay person are not so constraining. Most would grant that, in this case when the welfare of others is at stake, there is a moral obligation not to avoid the trouble of getting the medical facts. When others stand to be harmed, especially those in a relationship of special obligation, there is a duty to have information that is potentially meaningful and useful.

A similar problem arises in the diagnosis of AIDS. Patients may reasonably conclude that they are better off not knowing if they have AIDS. The psychological impact could be devastating, and the social and economic impact can be as well. Yet third parties have a clear stake in having the patient informed.

Suppose, however, that this same thirty-eight-year-old man with Wegener's granulomatosis was a bachelor without dependents. If the welfare of others is not at issue, is there any obligation to have potentially meaningful information disclosed about one's condition? The case is finally forced to the most difficult extreme. There seem to be virtually no utilitarian reasons for the disclosure. Presumably the patient who has instructed that he not be given the details is as good a judge of his own desires as anyone else involved in the case. There is virtually no treatment to which the patient could be motivated by knowing his condition. Others will not benefit in any measurable way from his knowing. Aside from the rule-utilitarian concern with maintaining a trustworthy image for the profession, there would seem to be no harmful consequences from withholding the information. If the physician could act on the rule "Always tell the truth except in those cases where the patient has clearly requested not to know and where others would not suffer for the withholding," there would be little risk even to the image of the profession.

The case against the patient's position, if there is one, must rest on the most fundamental moral obligations growing out of the nature of a person's interaction with others. It is possible to grant that the principle of autonomy would be sufficient to restrain a physician from imposing unwanted bad news upon such a patient and yet hold that human dignity requires responsible decision making by individuals, especially about matters of such ultimate significance as life and death. A desire to avoid the extreme psychological stress of dealing with a diagnosis of dying can certainly be understood and perhaps even excused, but that is not to say it is a responsible way of dealing with one's life. Even in this extreme case, where the patient has freely chosen to avoid knowledge of his condition and no one else will suffer directly from his refusal, there may still be a moral duty to know one's self and one's fate.

OVERWHELMINGLY NEGATIVE CONSEQUENCES

If there are moral arguments in favor of a patient knowing his condition when the family requests that information be withheld and even when the patient requests that information be withheld, is there a case for a hard and fast rule upholding telling the truth in all circumstances? The argument has been made against the danger of situationalism—that mistakes made in violating moral rules in the name of the good can be serious. But, in the end, ethical decision making is a trade off among competing norms and values. The principles of truth-telling and contract-keeping may not always lead to the same moral conclusions as the principles of benefiting and not harming.

There are extreme cases when some would hold that the truth-telling principle must be compromised. Should a captured soldier tell the truth when asked for information by an enemy if doing so will expose the position of and risk the lives of comrades? Of course not. The reason why disclosure is not required is less obvious. Some would retreat to the calculation of consequences, at least for this extreme circumstance. They would conclude that the consequences of honesty are so serious in comparison with lying that they override the normal rule of telling the truth. There is, however, a more subtle explanation of why the soldier need not respond factually. One possibility is that the principle of truth-telling contains within it exceptions in cases where malicious use will be made of the information honestly provided. In effect, the social contract generates a principle of truth-telling containing the proviso that truth must only be told when the person to whom it is told will use the information responsibly. While this notion that there are people to whom the truth is not owed provides an easy out, it may also be too easy. It would seem to permit a broad utilitarian overriding of the principle of veracity, one so broad that it might easily be overridden in virtually any situation where one wanted to avoid the truth.

However, there may also be a more limited explanation to the duty to tell the truth. It rests on what should happen when two ethical principles come into conflict. There are other principles potentially at stake in the example of the soldier. If there is a principle that says that killing is wrong and honesty will necessarily lead to killing, then the two more deontological principles will necessarily be in conflict and, even for nonconsequentialists, some trade off among ethical principles will be necessary. Also, it is possible to invoke the principle of justice. The principle of justice, as I interpret it, holds that an action is right (prima facie) when it betters the condition of the person who will otherwise be among the worst off (or when it makes the otherwise worst off person more equal). If the soldier's comrades were, in the case of disclosure, the worst off group, then any action that betters their lot would be prima facie right. Justice might legitimately be traded off against the principle of honesty even if a more general consequentialist principle cannot be.

Are there similar conditions in the care of the dying patient where the overwhelmingly bad consequences of telling the patient would justify withholding potentially meaningful information? There may be, but simply arguing that there will be some bad consequences in the eyes of someone such as the physician is not sufficient cause for breaking a rule designed to promote the general good and protect the dignity of the responsible patient as well as to maintain minimal conditions for human interaction.

It seems very unlikely that the withholding of a terminal diagnosis would prevent a homicide. It may prevent a suicide, but even there the relative moral importance of violating the veracity principle and the principle of avoiding killing would have to be weighed. It is not obvious, even in the case where it is believed that withholding information would prevent the suicide of a terminally ill patient, that the principle of avoiding killing would outweigh the prima facie requirement of veracity. It is conceivable that the disclosure of a terminal diagnosis would make the patient among the worst off and therefore trigger concerns of justice that could be balanced against the veracity principle. Even here, however, justice would not automatically outweigh the requirements of veracity.

On occasion the prospect of overwhelmingly negative consequences may justify, not total withholding of information, but moderating what is told for the time being. For example, in the case of a patient known to have a history of infrequent, brief intermittent suicidal depressions who was in such a period of crisis when a terminal diagnosis was made, complete information might be withheld until the crisis period had passed and psychiatric help could be arranged. Postponement of disclosure to a patient whose malignancy was discovered during a physical examination in conjunction with a commitment proceeding might well be justified until competence had been determined by a court in order to decide whether the decision to disclose should be placed in the hands of a guardian.

Withholding information rightfully the patient's, like positive killing of the terminally ill, suffering patient, may best be handled under the rubric of civil disobedience. The term may be more metaphoric here, although treatment of the patient without consent would certainly violate the law. Rather, I mean violating the general moral law, a suspension of the normal requirement of personal relationships, justified by the conviction that in some cases the other right-making characteristics of actions override the normal moral obligation to disclose.

This might lead to abuses. Physicians, prone to take civil and moral law into their own hands under the paternalistic Hippocratic patient-benefiting principle, could use this license to excuse antinomian situationalism. We would then have to retrench into the legalism of a flat rule mandating telling the truth. Perhaps, in the end, society must stand by this rule. Only in extremely rare, exceptional cases—whose moral complexity extends well beyond the ordinary sort where the physician feels that harm would justify withholding the bad news—can withholding information potentially useful or meaningful to the patient be condoned.

8 | The Newly Dead

Mortal Remains or Organ Bank?

On October 26, 1984, cardiac surgeon Leonard L. Bailey opened the chest of a fourteen-day-old infant, removed the baby's heart, and replaced it with the heart of a seven-month-old baboon.[1] Baby Fae, as she quickly became known to the world, was suffering from hypoplastic left heart syndrome, from which she was going to die. She survived twenty days. The world's moral sensitivities were once again aroused, just as they had been some seventeen years earlier when Christiaan Barnard had, in December 1967, cut out Louis Washkansky's heart with the faith that he could put a new one in its place. In these events the biological revolution has its symbol. Here was an all-out war on the mortal flaws of the human body. There had been preliminary skirmishes: the seventeenth-century ventures in blood transfusion, the great debates about dissection of the corpse, the discovery of penicillin, the first transplant in 1954 of a kidney to a patient whose kidneys had been destroyed.[2] But these were really only border forays into the new territory. The vision of a surgeon purposefully cutting the heart from the human breast has symbolized the new era of the biological revolution as much as Sputnik has that of the physical sciences.

The Remarkable Newly Dead

Baby Fae became, for the 1980s, a new symbol of heretofore unimagined horizons to which the biological revolution might go. Much of the early transplant work, however, was done with kidneys. By 1986 over 60,000 people in the United States had received kidneys from other human beings.[3] In 1975, 2,756 transplants were performed;[4] by 1986 the number was 8,800.[5] Both patient and graft survival rates have improved substantially so that by 1980 the one-year survival of patients receiving grafts from living, related donors was 97 percent. For patients receiving cadaveric transplants it was 90 percent, and this figure has improved since then.[6] Graft survivals are now up to 88 percent for living, related donors and have reached 71 percent for cadaveric organs.[7] The major reason for the significant improvement in survival rates has been the development of better techniques of immunosuppression, especially the use of cyclosporine.[8]

197

By contrast, the heart transplant, the flashy standard of the revolution, has much less tactical significance. By the end of 1985 there had been 1,898 hearts transplanted in the United States.[9] The pattern appears to be changing rapidly, however, as heart transplant is again apparently at a critical developmental stage. In 1986 alone, there were 1,386 heart transplants, almost as many as in all previous years combined.[10] From a lifesaving potential, the possibilities are startling. About a million people a year die of cardiovascular diseases. It is estimated that as many as 14,000 could benefit from a heart transplant.[11] Since living donors are obviously not available, and the artificial heart is not yet as available as the artificial kidney, the main potential lifesaving device is heart transplant from corpses.[12]

Other technical problems remain. Rejection by the body's own immunological system is a well-known problem with transplants—especially with hearts from unrelated donors. With the use of cyclosporine, there is renewed optimism about solving this problem. One-year survivals have increased from about 65 percent to between 75 percent and 85 percent.[13] Still, it is clear that the rejection problem has not been solved. It is now recognized by sociologists of medicine that new technological innovations produce cycles where pessimism leads to periods of caution.[14] There was a virtually complete moratorium on heart transplantation in the 1970s after rejection problems were first encountered. There appears to be a similar moratorium on implantation of the permanent artificial heart following severe problems with strokes in the first implant patients. The results with heart transplantation are now sufficiently encouraging that a renewal of a moratorium seems unlikely. This means there is likely to be a continuing problem of supply of organs. The supply problem is particularly acute for neonatal and pediatric hearts, which has led to the special interest in cross-species (xenograft) transplants, such as that of Baby Fae. Estimates even for the United States are very difficult to acquire, but the potential for cadaveric donors annually available in the United States has been estimated by the national Organ Transplant Task Force to be between 17,000 and 26,000 kidneys, primarily from persons suffering subarachnoid hemorrhage and violent or accidental brain injury.[15] That would probably supply more than enough kidneys to meet the demand and possibly enough hearts as well as lungs and other organs. We are presently recovering only a fraction of those organs, however. In 1984 approximately 3,290 cadaveric donors were available. This means that there is likely to be demand for organs for transplantation that exceeds the supply for the foreseeable future. It is clear that potentially thousands of lives could be extended by heart transplantation if the technical difficulties were solved. That would lead to even greater problems of supply.

Hearts and kidneys are not the only transplantable organs, of course. As many as twenty-five different kinds of organs and tissues have now been transplanted in human beings with varying degrees of success, including livers, lungs, pancreas, spleen, bone marrow, and skin, as well as eye corneas, bone, cartilage, fascia, and teeth.[16] Even an ovary transplant has been reported.

Liver transplants have become increasingly successful and are now widely considered accepted therapy for pediatric biliary atresia as well as some liver diseases in adults. As of 1986, 2,365 liver transplants had been attempted.[17] The advent of cyclosporine has increased five-year survival rates from 18 percent to 68 percent.[18] The same problem of supply of cadaveric organs from infants and children affects pediatric liver transplantation as pediatric heart transplantation. In addition, some adult liver transplants are necessitated by alcohol and other drug abuse, which raises questions about the effectiveness of liver replacement as well as the justice of using scarce resources (time and money as well as organs) for these adult transplant candidates. At the present, pediatric, but not adult, liver transplantation is classified as nonexperimental and therefore funded under many state and federal insurance programs.[19]

Pancreas and heart-lung transplantation is less well developed.[20] As of 1986, 511 pancreas transplants and 129 heart-lung transplants had been attempted.[21] We have clearly entered the era when transplantation is more than an exotic experiment. Until such time as artificial organs are perfected, the use of cadaveric organs will be an important part of the care of the critically ill, raising serious ethical questions about the intrinsic moral limits on grafting organs, about allocating organs that are in short supply, and about procuring organs so that the supply is more adequate.

When one signs a donor card according to the Uniform Anatomical Gift Act, one does not simply agree to make body parts available for needed transplants. Unless the donation is restricted, then it is "for the purposes of transplantation, therapy, medical research or education." Since transplantation is either therapy or medical research, it is not clear why it is even necessary to mention it separately. The new corpse is amazing not only for its transplantable parts but also for its other uses for the living. The use in the anatomy laboratory comes readily to mind. Other medical uses are not so apparent. Medical research can use body tissues and organs for physiological and biochemical tests. The placenta, for example, is now used routinely, often without the new mother's permission. Tissues from a fresh corpse are a major new source of human tissue for research. Dangerous new drugs could be tested on some fresh cadavers, as could experimental surgical or other procedures. The thought of therapeutic uses of the corpse other than transplantation is rather bizarre, but certainly the blood might be used; in fact a transfusion is really a tissue transplant.

But what of a "respiring cadaver"—a human body pronounced dead according to brain-oriented criteria of death for which respirator and other maintenance systems have not been stopped? Suppose that the respiring corpse is producing a rare blood factor, enzyme, or other therapeutically valued substance. If it were "worth it," it might be possible to maintain such a cadaver for a long period in order to obtain the valued substance. It has been proposed that new cadavers be used for educational purposes not only in anatomy labs, but also in order to practice surgical and difficult diagnostic procedures including pelvic exams. The body of the newly dead pregnant woman can, as we have seen, be used as an incubator for her fetus. The dead body has unlimited use for the imaginative living.[22] These valuable contributions of the dead to the living are not, however, the only or even the most significant reasons that the new corpse is so remarkable.

Occasionally a distinction will be made between the body and the self, suggesting a gnostic view of humanness where the personal essence is set apart from the body which is its temporary captor. But even the Platonic view of the human separates not the self but the soul from the body, suggesting that the self is essentially more than either of these components taken alone. In the Judeo-Christian tradition, however, the individual is inseparable from the body. William May, one of the few who has specifically addressed our attitudes toward the newly dead, puts it more forcefully: "A man not only has a body, he is his body."[23]

Paul's great exhortation to the Romans begins, "I appeal to you, therefore, brethren . . . to present your bodies a living sacrifice."[24] Some knowledgeable interpreters say this is a conscious maneuver on Paul's part to shock the Roman spiritualizers and confront those who would find repulsive the thought of a body being a spiritual sacrifice worthy of being called "holy and acceptable."

But Judeo-Christianity is the religion of the resurrection of the body. For those who interpret this doctrine literally, the significance of the corpse is obvious. It has led to reluctance to approve of removal of organs for transplantation. Most Christians, however, are not troubled by this. Indeed, Christians have had to deal with this problem in contemplating bodily resurrection of burn and other accident victims where the body is not buried intact. Even among those who believe in a literal bodily resurrection, it is widely held that the body will be a new, more perfect one, not the one with all the imperfections that one had at the time of death. For many contemporary Christians the resurrection story is taken more as a metaphorical affirmation of the importance of the body rather than as something that creates a problem for organ procurement.

Another example of respect for the body is seen in Orthodox Judaism's grave reservations about autopsy, generally forbidding it unless the living will benefit (for example, one accused of murder might be acquitted if the cause of death were determined).[25] Even then there is great concern that all organs be returned for burial.

As in Christianity, the point is not that resurrection would have to depend upon the intact corpse. Should victims of fire, explosions and other violent accidents be deprived of eternal life by the sovereign God? Even those who demythologize the doctrine still place great emphasis on the body.

At least for the newly dead, intact corpse there is still an aura of sacredness felt by even the most secular of us. The medical student's experience of the anatomy lab is one of highly charged emotion, in fact a training ground for the physician in dealing with death.[26] The carefully controlled access to the lab, the draping of the corpse, and gallows humor are all ways of coping with the trespass of the sacred that is anatomical dissection. I personally recall the great impact of the intact cadaver, especially in the autopsy room, but also in the anatomy lab. Preserved specimens of internal organs in glass jars can be displayed for the uninitiated in hospital corridors; even isolated external body parts which are available in the anatomy lab for students to study do not inspire the same quality of awe. But the intact body, recognizable as the "mortal remains" of a human individual—not simply the shell in which the individual was once encased— still retains a quality of the sacred that gives it special significance.

If the philosophical concern that modern persons have with death is uniquely focused on the experiences of the living before death, this intraworldliness does not mean that the modern concern stops at the moment of death. This intraworldliness still generates great ethical and policy issues after the moment of death. It is to these that I now turn.

The Newly Dead and the Ethics of Transplantation

A discussion of the ethical issues in the care of the newly dead is not the same as a full survey of the ethics of transplantation. This is a book on the ethical and policy questions related to death and dying. There are crucial medical ethical issues outside the scope of this discussion: kidney donation by a child to an identical twin, rejection on psychological grounds of living donors who are given the excuses of "tissue incompatibility," and the gift of an organ by a nonrelated living donor. These are dealt with in many more general discussions of transplantation.[27] I shall limit my attention very narrowly to questions of the treatment of the newly dead.

Three major ethical problems emerge in dealing with transplantation in the context of the newly dead: the ethics of the use of the cadaver body part itself, the ethics of allocating scarce organs, and the ethics of procuring organs.

THE ETHICS OF TRANSPLANTING BODY PARTS

When Christiaan Barnard transplanted the first human heart, the first and most fundamental question that arose was whether there was something intrinsically immoral about taking the heart out of a corpse of one person and sustaining the life of another with it.

Intraspecies Transplants (Allografts)

One potential basis for concern would be the implication for the deceased whose heart (or other organs) is removed. The most obvious concern would be among those who believe in a literal, physical resurrection of the body. I have already shown, however, that this question has been faced and surmounted by both Jews and Christians who had to deal with religious questions arising from persons whose bodies were seriously maimed at death.

At a more subtle level, though, there might be some lingering doubt that a person is "really dead" if parts of the body continue functioning in someone else. It is striking that these questions arose in a much more serious way when hearts were transplanted than they did for other organs such as kidneys. No one really asked whether Joe Smith was still alive when his kidney functioned in another, but the question did arise when it was his heart.

This forces us back to the questions raised in the first chapter about what organs and what functions are essential to considering an individual alive. If one holds that the heart and its functions are what are essential to the human, then it is reasonable to ask whether a person really has died if his or her heart continues to beat. For those who reject the heart's function as critical, however, this should not be a problem.

To test the relevance of these considerations, imagine the possibility of a brain transplant. Many people would consider such a procedure intrinsically immoral even if, technically, it could be done safely. They probably do so because there would be mingling of the essential characteristics of two persons in such a way that it really would be difficult to determine which one was living. If embodied capacity for consciousness and social interaction, that is, both mental functions and bodily forms, is what is critical, as I argued in the first chapter, then combining one person's mental capacities with another's body does raise fundamental moral questions. If, however, all that is being transplanted is some sustaining body part, the problem is not a critical one even if it means that the recipient will survive with some living tissues that are not genetically his or her own.

This position requires the conclusion that there is nothing inherently wrong with sustaining a life with material that is not genetically entirely that person's own. Any other conclusion would rule out not only heart and kidney transplants, but also blood transfusions and skin allografts.

Interspecies Transplants (Xenografts)

If the mixing of genetic material from two humans raises potential problems, the possibility of interspecies transplantation (normally called xenografting) is even more ethically charged. That is surely part of the reason why the Baby Fae case with which I opened this chapter, was so controversial. Just as some people for religious or other reasons may question the mixing of genetic material within the same species, there are those who find the mixing of genetic material from two different species an even more serious violation of the natural processes. To use religious language, are we violating God's plan for creation when we mix genetic material from two different species?

The Intrinsic Morality of Xenografts. Even though some people are intuitively repulsed by interspecies transplants, especially when they involve humans, it is important to realize that there are no objections in principle to xenografts among the major Western religious traditions. Catholic theologian Richard McCormick, who as a member of the NIH panel reviewing the Baby Fae case, refers to a "special concern" about xenografts, but focuses mainly on the psychological problems they could cause both for the individual receiving the graft and for others who might stigmatize the recipient in some way. He sees no reasons in Catholic natural law ethics to oppose xenografts in principle. While the problem deserves special concern, it is not "insuperable."[28]

Orthodox Jews go even further in their support of xenografts. Fred Rosner, a Talmudic scholar and physician, applies the principle that "the preservation of human life is of infinite and supreme value."[29] He, of course, insists that the normal rules of the ethics of human experimentation and of respectful treatment of animals be followed, but assuming they are complied with, he finds no Jewish objection to supporting human life with organs transplanted from other species. This argument, of course, would not work if human organs were transplanted to other species of animals. Secular commentators on the ethics of xenografts have found nothing, in principle, to object to, although they warn of the dangers of taking advantage of patients and families and of the potential problem of abuse of animals.[30]

Unfair Subject Recruitment. Some critics have raised the question of whether there was a seduction of distraught patients and families into what is essentially an experimental attempt to learn more about cross-species transplants without realistic hope of benefit to the patient.[31] They suggested that Baby Fae was, in effect, the unconsenting subject of a painful experiment that had no therapeutic justification. Baby Fae was dying. Her parents would reasonably be vulnerable to suggestions for an experimental effort, no matter how implausible it was. There was the potential for them to be unfairly recruited to approve of the procedure for their infant.

On the other hand, I have argued that parents have the right and the responsibility to use their own judgment, as long as it is within reason, in deciding how to serve the interests of their wards. A case can be made that the choice made by Baby Fae's parents was within reason. Two alternatives were considered: a largely palliative procedure called the Norwood procedure and obtaining an infant human heart for transplantation. According to the NIH committee that reviewed the case, the mother was told that it was unlikely that a human heart would be available for transplant that was properly matched for size and also histocompatible.[32] The parents ruled out the Norwood procedure. There had been very poor results with it when it had been tried elsewhere.

There was considerable controversy over the quality of the consent. The NIH committee that reviewed the case concluded that there were three shortcomings: compensation for injury was not explained in the consent document, the benefits of the procedure were overstated, and there was no provision for searching for a human heart.[33] Nevertheless, the committee concluded that "the parents of Baby Fae fully understood the alternatives available as well as the risks and reasonably expected benefits."[34]

It goes without saying that the consent for xenografts must be adequate. If there were shortcomings, they need to be corrected; that is true for all medical interventions, whether for research or not. The real issues raised, however, are whether it is possible for the parents to have made a free choice under the extremely tense circumstances and whether there was enough of a possibility of benefit to accept a parental choice in favor of the xenograft. There are many circumstances, medical and otherwise, where parents have to make choices under tension. I see no reason to rule out the possibility of their making a reasonably informed and free choice in this situation. And, while many people might have concluded that the possibility for benefits to the infant were too small to justify the surgery, there was some possibility of helping. Since the other alternatives were extremely unattractive, I see no reason to conclude that the parents were beyond reason.

The Welfare of Animals. Concern over the welfare of the animals in a xenograft is another ethical issue. Tom Regan, for example, refers to the baboon in the Baby Fae case as "the other victim."[35] It is true that the use of animal tissues to support humans implies a priority for humans in the moral calculus. It is also true that, historically, animals have not been treated as well as they could have been. That having been said, whether the moral concern for baboons and other animals who are the potential source of organs for xenografts is sufficient to justify prohibiting such transplants will depend on where one stands on the more general question of our moral obligation to nonhuman animals.

If any use of animals for human ends can be justified, it would be the situation where sacrificing one animal provides a chance for a human to live. That is much easier to defend than more general laboratory use of animals where hundreds may be sacrificed. It is also easier to defend than use of animals for food, where human life is not as directly at stake. If any use of animals is acceptable, and most people conclude that it is, it would seem that their use as a source of organs for lifesaving transplants falls into this category.

The matter may get more complicated, however. One of the reasons why Dr. Bailey turned to animals was that human organs were in extremely short supply. With regard to infant hearts, the shortage is likely to continue even if current inefficiencies in recovering cadaver organs are overcome. Even if an infant heart were available, the chances of histocompatibility are small. With xenografts, however, there is the possibility of breeding large colonies of baboons or other animals for purposes of harvesting organs. We could potentially have a "grocery store" where a surgeon could "go to the shelf" of thousands of tissue-types and take the baboon that matches best. On the other hand, the more crass breeding aspect could turn some originally sympathetic people against xenografts.

Just Allocation of Resources. The only other question raised by xenografts in the early stages is whether scarce resources would be consumed in unacceptable ways. Not only animals, but surgeons' time and talent and hospital resources would be used. It is possible that if society determines that the possibilities of success are sufficiently remote, then such procedures could be banned on social resource allocation grounds even if surgeons and patients (or their surrogates) are willing to proceed. That strikes me as an unfortunate outcome. From the utilitarian perspective, it is extremely hard to determine how much good eventually will come from the use of xenografts. For those of us who are more concerned about autonomy and fairness than about maximizing utility, such a prohibition would be even harder to justify. Competent patients are autonomous agents. It is hard to justify prohibition of free agreements entered into by them. If the patients are minors or incompetents, we have argued that their bonded surrogates ought to retain a broad range of discretion in determining what is in their ward's interest. There is thus a substantial autonomy claim that would have to be overcome. I have argued throughout this book that mere production of aggregate good cannot justify overriding autonomy; only justice or some other deontological principle can. Justice would be in conflict with autonomy if there were some other persons who were less well off who could use the resources contemplated for an experimental infant xenograft.

On a number of occasions I have defended a theory of justice that considers well-being over a lifetime as the basis for allocating resources.[36] Fairness requires, according to this perspective, that persons be given an opportunity to have well-being over a lifetime equal to that of others. This means that infants, who have had no opportunity for well-being, would get a higher priority than older persons who have had many good years of life. It is hard to imagine anyone who would have a higher priority in terms of this justice-based argument than an infant dying of a malformed heart. That has led me to the conclusion that (assuming parental approval) such an infant has a very high claim on our resources, even if that means tolerating some inefficient use of resources and some long-shot surgical procedures such as xenografts.

THE ETHICS OF ALLOCATING ORGANS

Once we have concluded that, in principle, organs can be used from the newly dead or from other sources for the benefit of the living, a second ethical concern arises. It is estimated that at any one time there are between 6,000 and 14,000 people in the United States awaiting organs for transplant.[37] Since cadaver organs are going to be in short supply for the foreseeable future, decisions will have to be made about allocation.

Allocation by the Deceased

One possibility is to view cadaver organs as the property of the deceased to be disposed of by the will of the deceased or by those who inherit from the deceased. That, in fact, approximates the policy today with regard to living donors. They are permitted to give kidneys to relatives or, potentially, to unrelated recipients of their own choosing. The only limit is that, in the United States according to federal law, organs cannot be sold.[38] In the next section I shall examine arguments pertaining to treating body parts as property. It is conceivable that the allocation of cadaver organs could be left to the individual himself or herself to specify while alive or, in the case where no specification was made, relatives could have such authority.

There are practical and moral reasons why this is unlikely to be the primary basis for allocation of organs, however. There is increasing sentiment for routine salvaging or "opting out" schemes that will be discussed below. These reject the premise that individuals are the owners of organs and have allocational authority over them. Moreover, many people will die having no idea who should receive their organs. Given the constraint of the short life expectancy of many people needing organs, the unpredictability of deaths that make organ donation possible, and the requirements of tissue typing, most cadaveric organs are likely to go to persons unknown to the deceased. Some more systematic allocational system seems necessary both to be practical and to be fair.

Increasing attention is being given to regional and national systems that attempt to maximize the rationality of organ allocation. The national Organ Transplantation Act provides federal assistance for qualified private procurement organizations.[39] Two national systems, the United Network for Organ Sharing (UNOS) and the North American Transplant Coordinators Organization (NATCO) assist in such coordination. No matter how sophisticated these systems are, however, some policy must be formulated to determine who among the available candidates should get priority for an available organ. It could be on the basis of social utility, medical benefit, medical need, length of waiting time, utterly random, or some combination of these.

Social Utility

The most obvious policy directive to give to those responsible for allocating organs is to put the organs where they will do the most good. This, of course, is the moral maxim of utilitarianism: the greatest good for the greatest number.

There are both utilitarian and nonconsequentialist reasons to reject this policy, however. Early allocations of scarce medical resources (dialysis machines as well as organs for transplant) were often attempted on this basis. An interdisciplinary committee was used, for example, by Belding Scribner's group in Seattle in the 1960s to decide who should receive dialysis machines. The committee was to take into account how the machines could do the most good. They considered such factors as whether one was a productive citizen, a parent responsible for young children, and career potential.[40] The committee quickly discovered that it was not obvious who should be chosen in order to maximize the benefits. It could require deciding whether saving the life of a business executive or a poet would do more good; or choosing between a homemaker responsible for small children and a soldier. In fact, the dissension generated by merely asking the question could be seen as a disutility of such an allocation system. A rule utilitarian might even end up choosing a rule that allocates in a manner which excludes such social utility judgments on a case-by-case basis.

There are also more fundamental, nonutilitarian reasons to question allocation on the basis of social utility. Even if a society could figure out how to allocate organs in a way that maximizes the good, such a system might be terribly unfair to some. Utility-based allocation is likely to single out the young, physically fit, intellectually superior—that is, those with great potential for social contribution. A deontological ethic, which bases morality on right-making characteristics other than aggregate consequences, has been cited a number of times in this book as offering a moral basis for terminal care decisions that is superior to consequentialism. A principle of justice, as part of such an ethic, might hold that an allocation is right insofar as it gives people an equal chance for well-being over a lifetime *even if that allocation does not maximize aggregate benefit*. Applied to problems of organ allocation, this principle suggests that people in equal need of an organ ought to have an equal shot at it even if one potential recipient would be more likely to make a socially worthwhile contribution. A number of analysts of the organ allocation problem have concluded that medical criteria and then random allocation among those medically qualified would eliminate the unfairness that accompanies social utility allocations.[41]

Medical Criteria

It is remarkable how many people believe that they can eliminate subjectivity and unfairness by using medical criteria as the primary basis of organ allocation. For example, the national Organ Transplant Task Force recommends that "given the scarcity of organs and the cost of transplants, we believe that the most ethical means of organ distribution is to use medical criteria."[42]

Medical Benefit. First, at points the Task Force takes "medical benefit" as the medical criterion. Its criteria, it says, "are designed to use organs to maximize graft and patient survival and quality of life."[43] Even assuming that benefits are limited to "the medical" and that it is these benefits that are taken as the criterion, the problem of subjectivity is not eliminated. For instance, the patient survival criterion could be taken to mean reducing the possibility that the patient will die from failure of the organ to be transplanted, in which case considerations such as tissue compatibility and cause of original organ failure would dominate. On the other hand, patient survival could be taken to mean survival from all causes, in which case the patient's age might be relevant. An older patient might be excluded on the grounds that, even if the organ in question does not fail, other systems will. The patient's style of living might be taken into account, so that an active alcoholic in kidney failure might be excluded on the grounds he has poor life expectancy even if his new kidneys did not fail.

The subjectivity of the medical benefit criterion becomes even more blatant when quality of life is taken into account. Sometimes quality of life has become a code word for nonmedical considerations. A wealthy intellectual might be said to have a better quality of life than a mechanic. In other cases, however, quality of life is limited to "medical quality," meaning such factors as absence of pain and suffering and good mobility. Even if quality of life is limited to these more narrow medical considerations, inevitably subjective judgments must be made. Allocation of an organ between a person with long life expectancy at low medical quality and one with a short life expectancy at higher medical quality inevitably would have to be made. We would eventually have to determine whether mental anguish or physical suffering counted as worse medical quality. In principle, medical facts alone cannot determine which of these candidates medically benefits more by a transplant. "Medical benefit" is inherently a subjective notion that will require value judgments by the one allocating the organ.

Even if we could figure out which candidate had the best chance to benefit medically, it is not at all clear that that person ought to receive the organ. Medical benefit is essentially a utilitarian criterion, with the proviso that benefits for some reason are limited to the medical sphere. But maximizing medical benefit also has the potential to be unfair.

It is now known that histocompatibility increases the probability of a successful graft. For this reason it seems commonsensical to give priority for transplant to the recipient with the best match. For this reason, the Task Force on Organ Transplantation gave priority in organ sharing to recipients with a six HLA antigen match and zero mismatches.[44] That is, in fact, what a medical benefit criterion would dictate.

There is a fascinating problem with maximizing medical benefit, however. For technical and statistical reasons, it is harder to get six antigen matches in certain racial and ethnic groups (because identification of HLA phenotypes is less complete, and these phenotypes are different from the donor pool).[45] This means that a policy that gives priority to the best tissue matches will be a policy that gives priority to whites. This is not because of any overt racial judgment, but because statistically whites are easier to tissue type and match. If a policy is grounded in justice, and justice requires an equal opportunity for well-being, then some correction will have to be made in the allocation to give persons who are hard to tissue type a fair chance at an organ. This will, of course, reduce the overall benefit (measured in aggregate number of years of life given by the organs transplanted).

It is not only the racial correlate of tissue typing that creates this injustice. It is harder to locate organs for blood group O recipients.[46] A policy that maximizes blood-group matching will provide fewer organs for O blood group recipients. In fact, hypothetically, it might be shown that any number of social measures predict successful graft. Men might do better than women, younger persons better than older ones, rural people better than urban dwellers. A pure utilitarian would nevertheless insist that those who have the best chance of success get priority. Those committed to justice would be willing to sacrifice overall efficiency in order to be fair. A medical benefits criterion that fails to deal with these claims of justice is open to criticism from holders of justice-based ethics. That includes the mainstream of Judeo-Christianity as well as modern secular liberalism.

There is a third problem with a medical benefit criterion. The case of Baby Jesse illustrates the problem. After the publicity surrounding the Baby Fae xenograft, Loma Linda surgeon Leonard Bailey received many requests for assistance for infants with severe cardiac problems. One such infant was a potential human heart transplant candidate.

Baby Jesse met the preliminary criteria for transplant, but was in a social environment that raised serious questions. The parents were unmarried adolescents with a history of legal and drug problems, and there was other evidence that they would not be able to provide the support necessary following cardiac transplant (rigorous follow-up including return visits to the hospital and careful administration of immunosuppression medications would be required).[47]

The case generated substantial public controversy because it was widely reported that the clinicians rejected the baby because of the social circumstances of the parents. Rejection linked to the lack of maturity and responsibility of the parents sounds like social criteria—the sort of criteria rejected early in the allocation discussion. Yet clinicians argued that they were, in fact, using medical criteria. Their judgment could be based solely on their prediction of the likelihood of success of the transplant. Assuming their assessment was accurate, their argument seems sound. If rigorous follow-up is necessary for success and these parents could not provide the follow-up, then the baby would not benefit medically from the procedure. He could be rejected on medical grounds; not social grounds.

The medical grounds, however, were, in turn, dependent on social circumstances. In fact, it seems likely that the same reasoning could be applied to every imaginable social condition. Parents with low intelligence or lack of a permanent residence or employment could probably be predicted statistically to provide a less supportive environment for a transplant patient. Studies could be done that would show that probability of successful transplant correlates with the recipient's socioeconomic status. Thus any of these apparently social criteria could be turned into medical criteria if they predicted the chance of a successful graft. The neat line between social and medical benefit collapses. Any allocation system that incorporates medical benefit could, in fact, be bootlegging social criteria.

Medical Need. All of these problems emerge if only medical benefit is the criterion. An even more complex difficulty arises in using the medical criterion when one realizes that the term can sometimes refer to medical need rather than medical benefit. It seems equally intuitive to allocate organs to the patients who have the greatest need. Yet this can often lead to a distribution of organs that conflicts with allocation on the basis of potential medical benefit.

The Task Force on Organ Transplantation recognizes the implications of racial and blood group differences and recommended selection of patients without consideration of race or sex or ability to pay, but it never told us exactly what should happen when ignoring such considerations reduces the expected medical benefit. The fact is that medical need and medical benefit are sometimes in tension.

What ought a transplant center coordinator do when she must choose between the following two potential recipients? One recipient is relatively healthy so that he has a 60 percent chance of one year survival without a heart transplant graft and a 95 percent chance with one, in part because of the benefits of other medical support. A second patient is much sicker. He has only a 5 percent chance of surviving one year without a transplant, but a 35 percent chance with one. In terms of predicted benefits, the first patient should be chosen, but in terms of need the second seems to be the candidate.

Medical need may also be affected by age. A young patient may do well on the medical benefit criterion. This will especially be true if expected years-of-life added is the measure of medical benefit. Older patients will predictably get fewer years of life from a transplant, both because older patients can be expected to have more medical complications and because, even if the graft is successful, the patient is more likely to die of other causes. An older patient may have greater immediate need, but be expected to get less benefit than a younger patient. To say that medical criteria should be used without differentiating benefit and need provides little guidance.

There is another complicating factor. Medical need might be measured in terms of immediate need "at a moment in time" or in terms of well-being over a lifetime. An eighty-year-old with a two year life expectancy may be worse off than a forty-year-old with a five year life expectancy at a moment in time but from the over-a-lifetime perspective may be much better off. If justice requires giving people an equal opportunity to have needs met, then it will make a difference whether we are speaking of a need at a moment in time or over a lifetime.[48] This argument from justice for giving priority to younger patients may explain the decision to fund pediatric liver transplants, but not adult transplants. (There are, of course, other reasons why adults might be excluded. The chance of success might not be as great or the causes of adult liver failure might be more voluntary or less amenable to control.)

Combined Criteria

The Task Force on Organ Transplantation is not the only group trying to combine medical benefit and medical need criteria. A more formal scheme has recently been proposed by Thomas Starzl and his colleagues at the University of Pittsburgh.[49] Starzl's group uses a point system that takes into account antigen matching, antibody analysis, and logistic practicality as well as medical urgency and waiting time. Their criteria grouped separately persons with different blood types and persons less than ten years of age or twenty-seven kilograms in weight. The proposal seems to have met with acceptance.[50]

It may be as good a formula as has yet been proposed, but it is not value-free. Some of the factors seem to relate closely to predicted medical benefit (such as antigen matching and probably logistic factors). Others relate to need (medical urgency). Apparently, the panel reactive antibody score (a measure of the percentage of the population against which the recipient possesses antibodies) is used as a measure of need, since antibody sensitized individuals will have a much more difficult time finding another suitable transplant, but using the score also relates to efforts to maximize medical benefit.

Starzl and his colleagues offer no reasons why the weights for the various factors should be what they are. In fact, they do not even reveal whether they realize that they are taking a position on the controversial moral issue of balancing medical benefit against medical need. Someone with a much stronger commitment to medical benefit might give a higher weight to antigen matching and less weight to medical urgency, while someone committed to justice in giving persons an equal opportunity to be healthy might give greater weight to medical urgency or to waiting time.

The point is not that Starzl's weights are wrong. Rather it is that choosing the criteria and picking the weights are inherently moral projects. They have nothing to do with medical knowledge. Others in the community might opt for a different formula that gave a different priority to benefit or need. They might include factors excluded by Starzl and his colleagues, for example, whether the need for the transplant was a result of voluntary behavior. They might have excluded logistic considerations. The Starzl group gives an example in which there were five potential recipients. In the example, the person getting the highest total score had the lowest score on medical urgency and had had the shortest waiting time. That person scored highest in part because of having a full six antigen match and in part because of a high panel reactive antibody number. That means that the chance of success was high and that it would be difficult to find another suitable donor against whom the recipient did not have antibodies.

Clinicians are historically trained to emphasize medical benefit rather than justice. Someone more committed to justice and less worried about maximizing overall benefit might assign weights differently. In their example, a patient who had been waiting a relatively long time and who had the greatest medical urgency had the lowest total score because none of the antigens matched and the panel reactive antibody number was low. If antigen matching were considered half as important, urgency considered twice as important as in Starzl's scheme, and scores for waiting time were proportional to the length of wait, that patient would have scored highest instead of lowest. A justice-based allocation would not require giving an organ to a person who had no chance of benefiting. It would demand that highest priority be given to medical need and length of time the patient has been in need.

The main moral objection would seem to be that a purely justice-based scheme could mean giving an organ to a person who has an infinitesimal chance of benefiting, provided that person was the neediest, rather than giving the organ to someone who is healthier, but who had a much better chance of benefiting. Once again we encounter the infinite demand or bottomless pit problem faced by all proponents of egalitarian justice. If the person on the bottom could benefit slightly by having all the available resources devoted to his or her welfare, egalitarian justice would seem to demand it.

Since that is counterintuitive, egalitarians need to respond. There are, in fact, several available responses. I cannot develop them fully here. That has been done elsewhere.[51] Nonconsequentialist considerations do place some limits on the demands generated by such a theory of justice. For example, justice itself places some limits. If all resources were devoted to the least well-off person, others in the society would become even worse off and have claims of justice. Other nonconsequentialist considerations would also place limits. The candidate with the greatest medical need might exercise his autonomy-based right to refuse treatment. (This seems likely in the case of a transplant which would bring substantial burdens, but which had only a remote chance of success.) Promises may have been made to others that could also set limits on the allocation scheme. Finally, if none of these nonconsequentialist considerations offset the implausible conclusion that the worst-off person with only the slightest chance of benefit has priority over the healthier person with a much greater chance of benefiting, policy-makers might incorporate consideration of aggregate benefit to justify giving the organ to the better-off candidate. Generally, however, I believe that is both dangerous and unnecessary. I would give much greater weight to medical need.

THE ETHICS OF PROCUREMENT

The discussion of the allocation of organs from cadavers is based on the premise that there are far from enough organs to meet the existing need. That, in turn, is based on current procurement policy and practice. In the United States each year approximately 3,000 deceased individuals serve as sources for transplantable organs.[52] Currently, about 10,000 persons are waiting for kidney transplants, but the potential has been estimated to be as high as 25,000 if suitable donors were found. About 100 individuals are estimated to be awaiting heart transplants, with a potential of 14,000 if suitable donors were found.[53] The shortage is real.

Yet it is also estimated that between 12,000 and 27,000 persons die each year in the United States from brain injury, brain tumor, stroke, or other conditions that would permit cadaver organ recovery.[54] Even though not all of these organs would be matched suitably in timing, location, and tissue compatibility with potential recipients, it is clear that a more efficient procurement system would go a long way toward solving the supply problem in the United States. Moreover, the time has come to begin viewing organ procurement and transplantation as a worldwide problem. Unfortunately, adequate data do not exist on either the potential supply or the need for cadaver organs on this scale.

In the late 1960s, after extended debate, the United States decided on a procurement system that relies on the gift model. The Uniform Anatomical Gift Act provides that organs can only be procured when an individual, while alive, has signed a donor card or, if the individual has not expressed wishes to the contrary, when the next of kin agrees to the donation after the death of the individual.[55] The most obvious alternative is to view human cadaver organs as a public resource to be used for lifesaving purposes without any explicit consent from the individual or relatives.

Routine Salvaging of Cadaver Organs

In 1968 lawyer Jesse Dukeminier and physician David Sanders proposed the routine salvaging of cadaver organs for purposes of transplantation. Declaring that the "need for cadaver organs to save human life is so great that the law should be changed to satisfy this need," they propose four principles as a basis for organ salvaging:

1. Making removal of useful cadaver organs routine.
2. Removing organs in a way which does not burden the bereaved.
3. Honoring objection by the "donor" made during his lifetime but also honoring his express wishes even if next of kin objects.
4. If donor neither objects nor expressly assents, honoring kin's objection to organ removal.[56]

Since their scheme permits individuals (or relatives, in the absence of any stated wish of the individual to the contrary) to veto the use of their organs, it has since been referred to as routine salvaging with "opting out."

Dukeminier and Sanders defined their proposal as a way of saving life, a goal they called "the first and most important principle of medical ethics." Once this is accepted as the most important principle, it is hard to deny that routine salvaging might be a logical outcome, but I have shown that there is reason to doubt that preserving life is always the totally dominant concern in medical ethics, even among physicians, let alone lay people. In fact, if preserving life were the only consideration, logically we would not permit opting out.

Another of their controversial arguments for routine salvaging is that it would "minimize the traumatic effect of the practice upon bereaved relatives," to whom, they argued, such a request might seem "a ghoulish request."[57] Empirically, however, it is not really clear that routine organ salvaging without informing relatives would always minimize the trauma. What would the response be of a relative who independently approached the medical staff to volunteer a donation of organs only to discover that the vital "gifts" were already on their way to several primed recipients?

With the years of experience with the donation model, there has recently been a renewed interest in routine salvaging. Usually these proposals carry with them a possibility of opting out.[58] Sometimes the proposals even suggest calling the arrangement "presumed consent."[59] The assumption is that by the passage of the law authorizing salvaging there has been a societal "consent" and that those who have not opted out are giving their actual consent. That assumption is simply false. Surveys indicate that between 40 and 70 percent of persons are willing to donate cadaver organs,[60] yet only

17 percent have signed donor cards.[61] It is thus clear that a substantial number who have not signed cards would refuse to do so. It seems likely that under a salvaging law with a clause for opting out a significant number of people who had not opted out in writing would, in fact, object to having their organs used. It is simply wrong to claim that consent can be presumed in the face of data showing that a significant number of people disapprove.

Nevertheless, it may still be ethically acceptable to salvage (with or without an opting out provision). A number of countries have salvaging laws although they tend to be countries without a long history of respect for human rights.[62] Other countries follow the American pattern of requiring actual donation by the individual while he or she is living, or by family in cases where the deceased has not expressed wishes to the contrary.[63] Most of these countries permit a hospital official or a coroner to give permission when the family is not available.[64] A similar provision exists in the model Uniform Anatomical Gift Act in the United States. (In fact, in twelve jurisdictions, coroners may routinely authorize removal of corneas without even a requirement that next-of-kin permission be sought.[65]) The most serious problem with these provisions for access to organs when family cannot be reached is that they may encourage less than rigorous efforts to locate the family. In some laws a wise provision is included that requires the person making the authorization to document for the record the efforts that were made to reach family.

What many of the routine salvaging proposals fail to address is the moral basis of the donation model. Only by examining the reasons why the donation model was adopted in the first place and evaluating newer sophisticated schemes for encouraging donation is it possible to assess the wisdom of salvaging.

The Giving of Cadaver Organs

The strongest objection to proposals for routine salvaging is really a moral one. Do we want to be a society that conceives of body parts as essentially property of the state to be taken by eminent domain or is that a dangerous misordering of moral priorities? If the state can assume that human bodies are its for the taking (unless contested by the individuals or the relatives as in the Dukeminier and Sanders proposal), what will be the implication for less ultimate, less sacred possessions? If the body is essential to the individual's identity, in a society that values personal integrity and freedom, it must be the individual's first of all to control, not only over a lifetime, but within reasonable limits after that life is gone as well. If the body is to be made available to others for personal or societal research, it must be a gift. This is what stands behind proposals for the giving rather than the taking of bodies and body parts.[66] A committee under the chairmanship of E. Blythe Stason approved a model Uniform Anatomical Gift Act designed to bring order to the confusion of differing state policies. The model act's basic provisions are:

1. Any individual over eighteen may give all or part of his body for educational, research, therapeutic, or transplantation purposes.

2. If the individual has not made a donation before his death, the next of kin can make it unless there was a known objection by the deceased.
3. If the individual has made such a gift, it cannot be revoked by the relatives.
4. If there is more than one person of the same degree of kinship, the gift from relatives shall not be accepted if there is known objection by one of them.
5. The gift can be authorized by a card carried by the individual or by written or recorded verbal communication from a relative.
6. The gift can be amended or revoked at any time before the death of the donor.
7. The time of death must be determined by a physician who is not involved in any transplantation.

The procedure is made simple by providing that the donation can be made by a card, signed before witnesses and suitable for carrying on the person. The National Kidney Foundation designed a model card and most states now have incorporated the information onto driver's licenses.

Although there has been widespread acceptance of the Uniform Anatomical Gift Act in the medical and legal community, as well as by the general public, there are still problems. The first is pragmatic. While most know about the program and as many as 70 percent of the public approve it in principle, only a tiny fraction of those who approve have actually signed up to be organ donors. Since only the very rare death provides organs suitable for donation, there is a desperate need for a massive pool of potential donors.

There are also some ethical problems remaining in the Uniform Anatomical Gift Act. For one, although individuals can object to particular or even any uses of their bodies, they must make their objections known by an actual notice of contrary indications. If few willing donors actually fill out a card, it may also be that many with reservations (for instance, to the use of their bodies for practice surgery or prolonged medical experiments) may not be fully aware that their bodies may be subjected to such use after their death by blanket permission from the next of kin.

Furthermore, the act provides that if no relatives are available at the time of death, the decision to donate may be made by "any other person authorized or under obligation to dispose of the body." There are cases on record where accident victims have had organs removed by authorization of the medical examiner without notifying the relatives. When there is more than one relative equally close to the deceased, any one of them who is available at the time of the death may donate the organs. When the closest relatives are not available, someone less close may authorize the organ removal.

All of these provisions leave loopholes where the personal wishes of the individual or the next of kin might not be honored, either because in the rush to get authorization the wishes are not discovered or because there is an attempt to hide those wishes. It would clearly be preferable if actual donation were on the basis of a responsible personal judgment of the individual. It is the individual's last chance to make a responsible ethical choice, and that freedom and responsibility should be honored if at all possible.

Required Request Proposals

The tension between the donation model and the salvaging model has led to a number of compromise proposals. In fact, the incorporation of opting out provisions into the salvaging schemes implies that even those who are most eager to obtain organs acknowledge the legitimacy (or at least the political expediency) of conscientious objection to organ procurement.

A compromise between salvaging and donation would be to give people the opportunity to "opt out" or "opt in." This could be done by institutionalizing arrangements whereby people are asked in such a manner that they must provide some response to the organ donation question. Such an arrangement would eliminate the possibility of falsely presuming consent and would, as a bonus, retain the donation model. Even if the state does not have a right to one's organs, it may well have a right to an answer to the organ donation question, even if one of the possible answers is "I don't know whether I agree to the use of my organs." I first proposed the routine and organized solicitation of donation in 1976 in the first edition of this book. Since then a number of schemes have emerged based on the required request notion.

Postmortem Familial Requests. Although it was not anticipated a decade ago, it is now clear that there are two very different types of required request policies. One is based on postmortem requests of relatives, the other on forced questioning of individuals who are alive and healthy about their willingness to have their organs used after their deaths. At least seven states have now passed postmortem familial request laws.[67] Calling them "routine inquiry" laws, the Task Force of Organ Transplantation has recommended that all states enact them.[68]

Postmortem familial requests nevertheless raise a serious problem. The entire organ procurement scheme in donation model countries is based on the moral premise that individuals themselves have the right and the responsibility to decide about the use of cadaver organs and tissues. Familial request, as originally incorporated into the Uniform Anatomical Gift Act, was clearly meant to be a backup in those cases where the autonomously expressed will of the individual could not be determined. Although the language was not available, families were presumably being expected to make a substituted judgment as a second best alternative to individual self-determination. In cases where the individual's own will could not be determined, presumably the family would express familial beliefs and values. (The best interest of the deceased seems not to be a meaningful concept.)

Now, however, postmortem familial request is becoming the centerpiece of procurement policy. What was clearly a second-best, decision-making mechanism has become the dominant one. It is even possible that as postmortem familial requests begin to generate more organs, more traditional efforts to get individuals to express their own wishes will disappear. If that happens, the original moral cornerstone of organ procurement, individual autonomous choice, will have been replaced by familial second-guessing.

This suggests that the current practice of requesting permission from families for the use of organs even in cases where the deceased has executed a donation card needs to be reassessed. Clinicians often ask family for permission even though a valid donation already exists from the deceased. The relatives, however, have no legal or moral authority to veto the deceased's donation. A better course would be to inform the relatives in a diplomatic way that the donation has been made.[69]

There may be a more serious moral problem. There is evidence that some advocates of postmortem required familial request laws have chosen this device precisely because they believe it will lead to obtaining some organs from persons who would not, themselves, be willing to donate. The numbers are striking. Surveys have attempted to determine what percentage of Americans would be willing to agree to the use of their own organs after their deaths and what percentage would be willing to donate deceased relatives' organs. The numbers vary tremendously, but always more people are willing to donate their relatives' organs than their own. In a Gallup poll commissioned by the American Council on Transplantation, 45 percent of respondents said they were very or somewhat likely to donate their own organs, but 85 percent said they were very or somewhat likely to donate a relative's organs.[70] In private, promoters of organ procurement have admitted to advocating requiring postmortem familial requests because they realize it will produce a greater yield than asking individuals themselves to sign anatomical gift act cards or drivers' licenses. If that is the case, it is a conscious scheme to obtain organs from a group who, statistically, are known to be unwilling to donate. That violates the very core of the morality of donation. A routine salvaging scheme—even one that prohibited opting out—would surely be preferable.

Required Request of Competent Persons. There is an obvious alternative: required request of persons while alive and competent. People could (and should) be required to answer the question of organ donation during any of a number of actions they take during their lives. The most obvious is that they could be *required* to answer the question during each renewal of their driver's licenses. Alternatively, they could be so required as part of completing their income tax returns. In both cases, responses could be stored in state computers. To assure maximum freedom, persons could be given three possible answers: yes, no, and "I don't know." For organ procurement purposes, an "I don't know" would be treated as no response and familial permission would be required.

Similarly, there could be a required request of living persons during all admissions to hospitals and as part of all medical histories.[71] A report of the Project on Organ Transplantation of the Hastings Center makes the distinction between required requests postmortem and of the living (confusingly calling them weak and strong requests), but, for some reason, it endorses the postmortem request policy rather than the one that more obviously promotes autonomy.[72] But facilitating free choice of competent persons is surely superior to asking family members who are in the midst of a major crisis and do not necessarily know the patient's wishes anyway. Postmortem familial requests should be reserved for procuring organs from minors and other incompetents and from those whose wishes are not a matter of record.

Marketing Organs

There is one final possibility that might well increase the supply of cadaver organs. If organs are to be viewed in the donation model in which autonomous choice of the individual while living is the preferred mode of decision making, this seems to imply that organs belong to the individual rather than to the state. If they do, why not encourage "donation" by providing enticements for people to agree to the use of their organs? Persons who agree in advance to the use of their organs could be rewarded with an insurance policy that would pay burial expenses if organs are used therapeutically, or some other inducement. Alternatively, relatives who agree to the postmortem use of an individual's organs could be paid. There could be a market in human organs that would reward individuals who agree, at the same time serving the important social purpose of increasing the supply of organs.

In fact, such a scheme has been proposed. In 1983 physician Barry Jacobs proposed becoming a broker of organs on a profit-making, commercial basis. He even went beyond these devices to procure cadaver organs by proposing that he obtain organs from living persons willing to sell them for a fee. He suggested that $10,000 might be appropriate for a kidney, but, in true free-market fashion, he pointed out that the market would set the price.[73] Other defenders of free markets have applied their ideology to the organ procurement problem.[74]

The Arguments Against. The proposal to permit a free market in either living or cadaver organs has met with almost universal cries of horror from both medical-professional and lay communities. Medical professionals have been particularly distressed.[75] During the 1983 hearings of the Subcommittee on Investigations and Oversight of the Committee on Science and Technology of the U.S. House of Representatives, two of the most outspoken critics of the marketing of organs were Ira Greifer, Medical Director of the National Kidney Foundation, and Oscar Salvatierra, President of the American Society of Transplant Surgeons.[76]

However, the fact that the professional medical community opposes marketing cannot, in itself, be sufficient reason to conclude that it is wrong. Barry Jacobs, himself a physician, took the opportunity to point out that transplant surgeons already profit handsomely from transplants. Referring to the members of the American Society of Transplant Surgeons, he said he had not seen them "give up the Cadillacs and Mercedes for the poor in this country. I haven't seen them drop their fees to 10 percent of what they are ripping off the public for. I haven't seen them drop down their office charges for the indigents."[77]

If there are arguments against marketing the organs of the newly dead, they must be derived from basic moral premises to which lay people as well as medical professionals have access. The core arguments against marketing have come from secular and religious ethical systems and have been quite similar.[78] First, there are some practical considerations. With regard to markets for procuring organs from living donors, the risks to the donor of a paired organ such as a kidney may be greater than we have believed.[79] It has been argued that patients cannot really consent to the removal of an organ when the long-term risks are so uncertain. That argument is really no different, however, than attempts to oppose consent for any medical procedure on the grounds that "we cannot know all the risks." In a liberal society, persons are routinely permitted to take risks. The only requirement in the medical context is that they be informed of the degree of uncertainty.

Also at the practical level, it has been argued that a market in organs (either cadaver or live-donor) would undercut the existing altruistic donation system. This is a more serious objection. Would people really be willing to sign donor cards and relatives willing to donate organs of the deceased if they knew they could get paid for the organs if they would only hold out? At the least, it seems that we would end up paying for some organs that we now get as gifts. It is even possible that some people would be sufficiently repulsed by the market system that they would refuse entirely to make organs available for transplant. It is even conceivable that the increase in supply of organs, which has been the primary goal of the advocacy of free markets, would not appear at all.

Third, it has been argued that if there were a free market, the quality of organs procured might decrease. Under the donation system, people have no reason to hide medical problems that would make organs unsuitable. We know from commercial markets in blood that if persons are paid for their blood, they sometimes will hide the fact that they have had hepatitis or other diseases that make them unsuitable suppliers. Quite possibly the same would happen with solid organs purchased in a free market system.

The most fundamental argument about free markets in organs has nothing to do with these practical considerations. It has been widely argued by critics that a market in a fundamental life-saving good such as a human organ is morally wrong in principle. It makes the poor the suppliers of life-saving human tissue at some risk, or at least pain, suffering, and inconvenience. The organs procured primarily from the poor would go to the highest bidder, presumably the wealthy. This would make life and death a matter of who could pay the highest price.

The Radical Implications of Opposing Markets. This argument really has two components: first, that the poor could be forced into selling their organs; and, second, that the wealthy could be the ones who would get the life-saving benefits. The defenders of the free-market scheme are quick to point out that those who are poor are paid to take life-threatening risks all the time in other areas. They are paid premium wages to do unusually dangerous work. They are "offered" expensive medical insurance policies that provide the potential of life-saving medical treatment and must turn them down for lack of resources. The defenders of free markets for organs claim that the risk of selling a kidney is much less than other choices routinely given persons for money. Why, they ask, should a person whose children are starving be prohibited from selling a kidney (either pre- or postmortem) in order to earn enough money to feed them when that person is permitted to walk scaffoldings or tightropes for less money and much less important good?

Similarly, the wealthy are routinely permitted to use their discretionary income to buy lifesaving opportunities. They can buy special, premium-quality health insurance, safer automobiles, and the best surgeons. They can even travel to other parts of the world if they believe they can find a medical provider who has a better record. Is there anything morally different between permitting a wealthy person to buy cadaver kidneys that are well matched and permitting those persons to buy the surgeons who have the best record in an operative procedure or the special insurance coverage that will give them extra lifesaving opportunities?

Quite a number of the critics of markets in organs have concluded that it is wrong to make life and death a matter of economics.[80] This is a sound conclusion, one that is consistent with some of our most cherished values, especially those within the Judeo-Christian tradition that underlies our contemporary secular morality. This, in fact, is the basis for a law that was passed in 1984 making it illegal in the United States to profit commercially from the procurement of human organs and tissues.[81]

The implications are far more radical, however, than many of the critics of free markets for organs realize. If life and death ought to be beyond monetary considerations, then it is not only human organs that should be beyond commercialization; it is all matters of a decent minimum of health care. In fact, it goes beyond health care. All matters having to do with decent minimums in employment, housing, education, and travel ought to be excluded from commercial considerations. At the very least, a policy that prohibits the poor from selling their organs in order to provide food for their starving children ought to assure that those children have enough food to eat. It is the height of unfairness to prohibit the one course that is available for saving the lives of one's children without providing the basic necessities of life. The same arguments that make it immoral to sell human organs seem also to make it immoral to fail to provide the necessities of life when they can be provided. That means that a prohibition on marketing organs should carry with it a right of universal access to a decent minimum of health care as well as the other necessities of life. If that cannot be provided—as it should be—then perhaps it would be better to accept the free-market ideology with all its implications, including the right to market organs either before or after death.

An Ethic of Responsibility

This leaves the newly dead body in a delicate intermediary position. It is not the property of the state to use as it sees fit, but it is not the property of the individual or the living beneficiaries of that individual.

Quasi-Property Rights in the Body. The relationship of the living to the newly dead has had a confusing history. Originally in English common law, there was no clear guidance because the ecclesiastical courts had jurisdiction over matters involving dead bodies.[82] When the common law began to take jurisdiction in the seventeenth century, no "property rights" to the dead body existed for the survivors. From an advertisement offering $3,000 for a kidney to full-blown markets in organs from living persons, we can see the potential dangers. Presumably, the early courts feared undesirable commercialization of the care of the corpse. Nevertheless, the courts began to recognize that the kin should have some role in determining the mode of burial. The unfortunate notion of *quasi-property right* emerged, implying some authority to dispose of the remains.

From the beginning society had been uncomfortable with this concept. Even the opinion in Pierce v. Swan Point Cemetery, which was important in the development of the concept, seethes with ambiguity:

> That there is no property right in a dead body, using the word in the ordinary sense, may well be admitted. Yet, the burial of the dead is a subject which interests the feelings of mankind to a much greater degree than many matters of actual property. There is a duty imposed by the universal feelings of mankind to be discharged by someone towards the dead; a duty, and we may also say a right, to protect from violation; and a duty on the parts of others to abstain from violation; it may therefore be considered a sort of quasi-property.

Duties vs. Rights in Caring for the Body. This is really not so much a specification of a quasi-right as a set of duties—or, at minimum, a set of rights derived from a set of duties. The "rights" of the survivors are those of treating the newly dead body properly: obtaining proper burial, bringing damages for harm done to the corpse, and otherwise fulfilling responsibilities. It is strange that these ethical relations should be labeled *rights*. The critical ethical relation is really one of duties and obligations—of responsibility—rather than one of rights. It makes no sense to talk of the kin having a right to protect the corpse from violation. To do so implies that such protection would be offered merely at the survivor's discretion. Clearly the so-called right to bury a corpse is in fact a duty. The liability for costs for interment is placed upon a surviving spouse.[83]

Throughout this book I have explored the notion that the ethics of death and dying is not simply an ethics of rights. It is also one of duties, obligations, and responsibilities. To confuse a corpse maintained in irreversible coma with the living human who was once that body is not simply a wasteful luxury, it may be an ethical affront. The decision by the patient or the patient's agent to stop a particular, no longer appropriate medical treatment is not simply a right to be enjoyed; it may, at the appropriate time and place, be affirmed as the morally more acceptable course and even a duty. Dying patients have not only the right to knowledge of their condition, but a duty to have the information necessary to make decisions about their care. Of course there may be circumstances modifying the duty to act responsibly, but in all of these ethical dilemmas generated by the biological revolution, we are first and foremost dealing with an ethic of human responsibility.

One might be puzzled how there can be a duty to the deceased. There might be a duty to his or her memory, some would argue, or to the living who retain a respect for the deceased, but can there be a duty to nonliving creatures? The complementary relationship between rights and duties has often been noted. Yet where rights often imply specific reciprocal duties for other individuals (the right of patients to reasonably meaningful knowledge of their condition implies a duty of those primarily responsible for the patients' care to disclose that knowledge), it is not clear that all duties have their source directly in other individuals.

Antigone contested Creon's claim that her brother's body was at the disposal of the state. When ordered to leave the rebel's body exposed, she claimed no simple right to bury it. To do so would have been a weak and hollow appeal. Rather she appealed to a duty decreed in the "unwritten laws, eternal in the heavens." That Polynices was now dead in no way affected the obligation to care appropriately for him. At least according to many theories of moral authority, obligation has its origins in universal sources beyond the claims of another person. This is a perspective we are learning once again from those who remind us of our duty to the environment. That man had dominion over nature is not the same as man being the origin of all value and obligation.[84]

If we stand with Antigone in recognizing that duties vis-à-vis the dead take precedence over any rights of the survivors, then who has the obligation to act responsibly to the newly dead? Antigone seemed to claim the duty because it was her brother who had died. William May also argues for the centrality of the familial unit. "The corpse, the deceased, and the family belong, as it were, to a continuum which should enjoy a certain sanctuary against the larger society and the state."[85]

The Responsibility of the Family. I would have to go even further to hold that the family is and should be the central unit of responsibility. The question is similar to that of who should be the incompetent patient's agent to make decisions about appropriate medical treatment or who should ensure that the patient will have information which could reasonably be expected to be meaningful or useful. There are other options, of course: the physician, the hospital staff, a member of the clergy, or the state. Their commitment cannot compare, however, with the strength of the familial bond, with its loyalty and responsibility.

If the responsible treatment of the corpse by the family is not simply a right but a responsibility, what is the content of that responsibility? It must include at least the following obligations:

1. To honor the wishes of the deceased. Instructions by the deceased about how the body is to be treated after death have a strong claim on the family. This is partially a matter of protecting the common good; the living would lead uncomfortable lives if they feared that their wishes would not be respected following death. But the obligation goes beyond that. It is based on respect for the newly dead one.
2. To fulfill commitments to the deceased. The duty of keeping promises, of fulfilling the covenantal relationship, is particularly important.
3. To protect the integrity of the corpse. This is already clear in the legal and moral tradition. The family has not only the right, but the duty to insist that the corpse not be mutilated or exposed to injury or assault without good justification.
4. To provide a fitting removal of the body from society. This is also clearly established within the law. Whether the removal be burial, cremation, or other means, it is both ritualistically and practically important that the separation of the dead from the living be carried out properly.

5. To offer reasonable and responsible service to the living.

Here a new obligation is added to those traditionally recognized. It is not simply that for its own satisfaction the family has the right to help out others. That can hardly be an adequate justification for the familial donation of a body or body parts for the benefit of the living. The exact nature of what would be a reasonable and responsible service to the living will depend greatly on the system of beliefs and values held by the family and by the deceased. But certainly the contribution of the body or body parts must be recognized as significant within many family relationships.

The Jewish tradition holds that an autopsy is normally forbidden but can be justified for the service of the living. At least some interpreters of that tradition believe that if an autopsy can realistically benefit the living, it is not only permitted but required. Immanuel Jakobovits, Great Britain's chief rabbi, is reported to have said that autopsy in the case of saving a life "is not only a matter of permission but of obligation and mitzah."[86]

It would be irresponsible for a family to refuse to aid the living for no reason at all. The obligation is more universal than simple loyalty to the living. We should also be reasonably able to assume the deceased would have assented to it. This is emphatically not to say that the family always has an obligation to provide the body or body organs of the deceased whenever they would be useful. There is certainly no such obligation when it is known that the deceased would have objected, and there may well be other valid reasons. I say simply that there is a prima facie obligation of the family to serve the living, an obligation that may be negated only by good reasons. At least when the family believes that donation of the body or body parts is consistent with its beliefs and values, and particularly with those formerly held by the deceased, the responsibility to serve the living should not be set aside for trivial reasons. It is this ethic of responsibility that must be the moral basis for using the newly dead body for the service of the living.

A Policy for Treating the Newly Dead

This leaves a complex set of conclusions. The donation model seems morally preferable to the assumption that organs belong to the state to be used for whatever good purpose the state concocts. The best arrangement would be one in which people voluntarily executed Uniform Anatomical Gift Act donations except in special cases where they held morally weighty reasons of their own for not doing so. Those people, to protect their beliefs and values, ought to execute a document indicating that they object to specified (or all) uses of cadavers or body parts.

Since there is now evidence of substantial inertia in executing such documents, there ought to be state policies requiring regular requests, such as in conjunction with issuing drivers' licenses, taking medical histories, being admitted to a hospital, or filing state or federal income tax forms. Required request laws should not depend primarily on postmortem requests of relatives. In fact, such laws should not be passed except in jurisdictions that also have made routine the required request from living persons.

Postmortem required request laws should be limited to cases involving the death of children, incompetent adults, and persons who have given an explicit "I don't know" response when asked while competent.

I am convinced that such a policy would, in all likelihood, supply the organs necessary for the need of persons needing transplants and for other important social purposes. If such a policy is not adopted, I would prefer routine salvaging with opting out to a policy of universal routine postmortem inquiry of relatives of the deceased, a policy that fails to give adequate priority to the autonomous choice of the living, and one that, at times, may purposely circumvent the wishes of the individual. Routine salvaging with opting out would at least put objectors on notice that they needed to express their dissent in writing. It is not a good policy, but it is better than a policy that would perpetuate noncommitment on the part of the individual.

If there were a required request law that living, competent persons routinely express their wishes about the use of their bodies, I am convinced that a market in organs would not be necessary to meet the needs of the population. Such a market might still be necessary in a world in which some persons are so poorly off that they have to consider selling body parts in order to meet their own or their family's basic needs. In such a world, even with a required request of the living, we should still not prohibit a free market in organs. We should do everything in our power, however, to make sure that we do not live in such a world.

9 | Natural Death and Public Policy

Thou shalt not kill; but needs not strive
Officially to keep alive.—Arthur Hugh Clough

We have come a long way in exploring what it means for individuals and groups to be responsible in making decisions regarding death and dying in the age of the biological revolution. There is much more openness in discussing the tragic decisions that sometimes must be made if individuals are to be responsible for their own lives. In fact, during the 1970s, "death with dignity" became something of a movement; the "right to die" became an almost faddish slogan.

Although I have been, in some sense, part of that movement, I have always avoided using those particular terms for several reasons. For one thing, even after all the years of philosophical debate and legal adjudication, it is still not clear what the legal status of the right to die is. In 1975 Robert M. Byrn wrote a law review article in which he challenged the idea that there is any such legal right at all.[1] Now, a decade and hundreds of court cases later, some courts have shied away from using the specific language of the right to die. Much more often, the right to die is left an open question, with the courts referring instead to the right to refuse treatment. This right, which in certain circumstances will also lead to the eventual death of the individual refuser, rests on much firmer legal and ethical ground. It is the principle I have emphasized as integral to a theory of responsible medical decision making by individual patients or guardians as well as by society. This distinction, of course, rests on the validity of the omission-commission distinction and the direct-indirect effect distinction—two philosophical distinctions discussed in chapter 3. Both those who accept the importance of these distinctions and those who do not can at least agree on the right of the competent patient to refuse treatment (except in special cases where the interest of third parties are overriding).

There is a more basic reason for avoiding the slogans. Although there may be more or less undignified ways of doing one's dying, I remain uncomfortable with the thought that the death of a person can really be called something of "dignity." One of the remaining philosophical challenges is to reconcile our new willingness to face death and dying responsibly with the more traditional Judeo-Christian notion that death is

224

an evil, a punishment for sinfulness that has cost man immortality. Along with many others,[2] I have been forced to face the implications for our health care policy of this more open acceptance of death.

Strange world this. That a serious argument must be made that death is an evil to be conquered, that, now, when for the first time in human history we have the power to conquer at least some deaths we should begin to romanticize the beauty, the grace, the "right" to a natural death. How strange that, when Arthur Hugh Clough tried, with bitter sarcasm, to chide us for our indifference to the plight of the dying in the "Latest Decalogue," his couplet should be taken a century later as the slogan of a death-with-dignity movement.[3]

The concept of "natural death" has crept up on us. We are not sure what it means for death to be natural and yet are quite certain it is a good thing. The concept has implications for public policy—dangerous implications, it seems to me. If death is not only natural, but good because it is natural, then as a matter of public policy we ought not to combat it. It is past time for a full-blown exploration of the impact of this seductively alluring concept, whose temptress is not without her dangers.

Dylan Thomas has become the straw man of the death-with-dignity movement when he urges us to "Rage, rage against the dying of the light." We poke fun at his patho-logical resistance to that which is clearly natural and inevitable. Certainly, in the case of the Welsh poet, the struggle was not terribly fruitful. He died at thirty-nine. Yet it may be that—in a world where the artificial has become the natural; the heroic, the expected; and the eternal punishment for Adam's sin, a glory to be praised—the time has come to make a case for the goodness of life, even for the ideal of immortality. In this chapter I hope to make that case, or at least to make it prima facie. In the end I shall argue that the concept of natural death is as least dreadfully ambiguous and dangerous and possibly romantically elitist. If prolonging physical life even to the point of immortality is an ideal long cherished by the common person and consistent with the most profound image of the human and the human community, we must face profound policy dilemmas. Realistically, the ideal will never be achieved. Moreover, other policy goals are also crucial for the image of the human individual and of the human community. This means that in the end, the case for immortality is only a modest one, and a task of complex research in economics and philosophy confronts us.

Natural Death: Its Public Policy Impact

In the contemporary world, much more rides on the outcome of the debate over whether death is a good or an evil than it did in the time of Socrates. When the traditional arguments against the physical immortality of the body were made, little more rested on the outcome than the mental satisfaction of an Athenian elite. Indeed, philosophers have always tried to resolve one of life's great philosophical dilemmas: Why is it that man must die?

Even if the struggle over the meaning of death once was rather esoteric, as soon as death was seen as a "natural" phenomenon, it acquired implications for political policy. This thesis is developed by Ivan Illich.[4] He claims that from the first signs in the fifteenth century of the shift in understanding death as a supernatural messenger from God to a natural force, the impact was to keep the doctor away from the deathbed of the peasant. By the eighteenth century, humans had become unequal in death as in life. Death in active old age had become the ideal for elites. The leisure class could live longer because their lives had become less wearing. They refused to retire because an expanding bureaucracy favored the ageless who had been around for a long time. By the nineteenth century, according to Illich, health had become a privilege of living long enough to have a natural death. Industrial workers began demanding the right to medical and retirement insurance. Finally, with the union movement, demands for equality in death produced a proletarian form of natural death. Workers were redefined as health care consumers, a move which first had revolutionary potential, but soon became a means of social control. People now feel obliged to die a natural death. The right to die a natural death has become a duty. The physician now gives the patient "permission to die."[5] Biomedical intervention—a condition for a natural death—becomes compulsory, unless special dispensation is received.

It is clear that making complex biomedical technologies necessary for a natural death was a blatant contradiction that could not survive long. Nor could the radical egalitarianism of the proletarian form of natural death. It is natural that someone would seize upon the ambiguities in the term *natural*, that the death-with-dignity movement would recognize that the artifacts of biomedical technology need not be called natural. Those who no longer need worry about life's necessities—food, shelter, and especially medical care—now seem to have discovered the right to die the new natural death.

If that is the case, then Illich's clever analysis may be open to reinterpretation. He sees the proletariat enslaved by a medical elite and demanding what as "health consumers" they have been taught is the natural death of the intensive care unit. But it could also be that the elite is outflanking the masses, preparing the ground for a new stage in the combat—a stage where a basically healthy group can undermine the newly won right to life-extending medical interventions. The new natural death is the gnosis, accepted willingly by the enlightened and enforced upon the masses.

Whether Illich's interpretation and this reinterpretation of the modern history of natural death are correct, today the question whether death is a good or an evil is argued for much higher stakes. Budgets of the National Institutes of Health depend upon whether conquering arteriosclerosis in old age ought to get more or less priority than death in infancy from some rare genetic disease. They depend on whether it is more important to extend the life span of those already living or to overcome the infertility that affects as many as 10 percent of married couples in society. They depend upon whether natural death or natural weather disasters producing very unnatural death ought to get the greater share of the national resources.

An estimated $191 billion was spent in 1982 by the federal government alone on problems related to aging.[6] Most of this was in support and social services for the elderly.

The Institute of Aging's current budget is $237 million. Of this, a tiny fraction is spent on research on the aging process itself.

IS AGING A DISEASE?

The idea that there is a natural point at which people die is controversial. The underlying conceptual model is one in which people may die "prematurely" of various diseases or from accidents, suicide, or homicide, but that if they are not struck down from one of these then they will simply "die a natural death of old age" at some inherent end point. The exact length of time is debatable, but the figure often used is ninety to one hundred years.

According to this model, deaths can be divided into two groups: those that are "adventitious" or "premature" and those that are at the natural end of life for the species.[7] From this it follows that interventions to overcome (or, more realistically, postpone) death can be of two kinds. One group of interventions attempts to overcome disease, accident, suicide, and homicide. In a society with much premature death, if one diagrams the number of people alive at various years, the graph drops rapidly in early years with the line approaching zero quite rapidly. As interventions to overcome premature death are more and more successful, the graph drops less precipitously so that if all premature death were overcome it would resemble a straight line with 100 percent survival to age ninety or one hundred and then a vertical line dropping to zero at the point at which "natural death" occurs. It is that enterprise that has been called "squaring the longevity curve." These interventions would allow more persons to reach the presumed normal life span.

A second kind of intervention would change the normal life span itself. This might take place independent of squaring the curve. Individuals might continue to die at the same rate from disease and accidents, but survivors might live much longer, say to one hundred twenty or even one hundred fifty years. Conceivably, persons could decline to serious physical and mental disability, as they now do, and then remain in their debilitated states for much longer times. No one finds that kind of change in the life span terribly interesting. It is possible, however, that the life span could be changed so that one remains in the prime of life longer and then declines precipitously to death at a much older age than at present. It is believed by some researchers that extension of the life span itself might be possible if we gain a greater understanding of the mechanisms of aging.

A number of interventions have been contemplated. Drugs such as procaine, vitamin E, butylated hydroxytoluene, and dimethylaminoethyl compounds have been tried in animals and humans.[8] Another intervention involves the attempt to reduce body weight significantly.[9] Many theories attempting to account for a general aging process have emerged over the past decade or two. They involve theories related to deficiencies in the immune and neuroendocrine systems, as well as physiological theories such as the free radical theory, a cross-linkage theory, and a waste product accumulation theory.

Others have focused on somatic mutation, the accumulation of errors in DNA sequences, and a theory that there is a genetic program for aging.[10]

It is conceivable that within fifty years a change of twenty to fifty years in the life span could be brought about.[11] This would not be immortality, but it would extend life well beyond what is now thought to be "natural." It would also produce a radical social, political, and psychological change in society.

It is here that important ethical and policy questions arise. Is it worthwhile to understand and attempt to modify the normal human life span, and, if so, how important is it in comparison with other possible interventions to overcome disease and get more people to reach the normal life span? The answer will depend, in part, on whether the normal aging process is thought of as a disease (to be overcome like other diseases) or is merely "natural."

If a natural death is a good to which all are entitled, then this research is malicious. If we still live after the fall when humans are entitled to three score years and ten and no more, the pharmacologists are trying to bite the fruit of the tree of life. Adam's most recent descendants have gained that knowledge of good and evil which was the fruit of that first fruit. Now they must decide whether drugs being tested for their life-extending properties are an antidote for the apple or merely a synthetic and more flavorful modernization of that first temptation.

The Food and Drug Administration (or the society for which it speaks) must make a choice.[12] Unlike Plato's inquisitive colleagues, the FDA must have an answer. Should they decide that tasting this new fruit is as evil as biting the first, then they must decide how they will regulate it under the present requirements of safety and effectiveness.

In order to present the policy implications of the concept of natural death most starkly, let me sketch two scenarios for the future of the concept over the next decade or two.

NATURAL DEATH: TWO SCENARIOS

The Dignified Death Scenario, or Death Ought to Be Natural

The world of the dignified death is the world of Marya Mannes,[13] the signers of the *Humanist's* "Plea for Beneficent Euthanasia,"[14] and advocates of death-with-dignity legislation.

Over the next decade the remaining jurisdictions will pass natural death acts granting people the right to execute directives requesting that they be allowed to die natural deaths without having their lives prolonged with "heroic" measures. Other states will join the handful that have made clear that families have the duty as well as the right to make such decisions refusing treatment on the part of their incompetent family members so that they, too, can have the benefit of a natural death.

Medical ethics courses will complement clinical instruction in medical schools so that physicians will gradually, if reluctantly, abandon what Francis Bacon called the third and new duty of the physician: the prolongation of life. The grounds will be that in medicine physicians have always believed that every case is so unique that no general rules can apply. Decisions will have to be made about continuing treatment on a case by case basis.

In the death-is-natural world, the aging process will be kept radically distinct from disease. Physicians in gerontology programs will be taught to help the elderly grow old gracefully without complaint. They will be taught to respect the elderly, but not to treat them as having conditions subject to medical correction.

Research on aging will be given low priority because it is not a medical problem, but a natural stage of life. Interventions that prolong the natural life span will not be covered under Medicare or other health insurance because aging is not a disease. Premature death will be challenged aggressively, but death at the fullness of time will not be on the national agenda. In fact, as resource shortages become more acute, it will become harder and harder to justify spending billions of dollars annually to prevent death in those who have lived out their full life spans. They will have earned the right to die with dignity.

The protection of the health of the citizenry will have become a priority of the government, but death at old age will not be unhealthy; it will be natural.[15] Those who attempt the unnatural—to live beyond their years—will be gently persuaded of their duty to make room for others. The right to die a natural death could easily become the duty to die naturally.

The Death Is Evil Scenario, or No Death Is Natural

Natural death may have a rather different future over the next decade or two. We may discover that "natural death" was nothing more than a temporary accident in human history, arriving in the fifteenth century as humans began to discard the accretions of supernaturalism and departing in about 1984 when we realized that no death is a natural death. In this scenario, the pathologist is prophet. For the pathologist today as for the rest of us tomorrow, something always causes death. It never just happens.[16]

If this view dominates, we may be at a transition point in history where some deaths are thought caused by specific disease processes or human acts, while others are just the natural wearing out of the machinery. At the present time the nonpathologists among us still are able to think of some deaths caused by specific diseases and voluntary acts of man as controllable, as potentially conquerable if we are aggressive enough in applying Western ingenuity and modern biomedical technologies, while other deaths are just natural. The goal is to let everyone spend eighty or ninety years wandering the face of the earth so that death may come the way nature intended it.

Research on aging may change that. It begins to suggest that that "natural" limit may be subject to human control. In the No-Death-Is-Natural future, every death will be seen as caused by events potentially subject to human control. Deaths will be of three types, each someone's responsibility.

One large group of deaths will be caused by the deceased's own behavior. Heart attacks are already believed caused in part by bad diet, poor exercise, smoking, and other controllable behaviors. AIDS easily fits the model as well. The first critical development for this view was the germ theory of disease and the recognition that there were things we could do to keep microorganisms out of our bodies. Death resulting from failure to take medicines, have proper immunization before foreign travel, or have safe sex would now be thought to be culpable. Cervical cancer in the woman who had failed to have a pap smear and automobile accident injury for one not wearing a seat belt are now inevitably on their way to being seen as voluntarily induced medical conditions.

Second, there will be those diseases that are the responsibility of one's parents. If Tay-Sachs disease is evil and is predictable, can acceptance of the risk of the disease be anything but voluntary and culpable behavior? Parental culpability is clearly a growth category.

Finally, there will be those deaths for which the medical research community is responsible. To be convinced that a particular death is the result of potentially controllable processes and not make the societal effort to understand and control those processes is a voluntary political choice. It may well come to be seen as a culpable choice, especially if those afflicted are senile, or children, or otherwise incapable of making a rational claim to be happy in their condition.

In any event, the notion that there is no responsibility for getting a disease—a concept which has been the core of the medical model—will be short-lived. Little by little the biochemical and genetic factors contributing to the deterioration of the body will be identified and given names as diseases. The process by which free oxygen radicals that cause cell damage will be named. The development of demonstrated treatments (whether they be vitamin E, vitamin C, or some other intervention) will stimulate the naming process. Or the breakdown in the immune system will, like AIDS, be given a name as the mechanisms responsible for aging become understood. Genetic mutations will be mastered and named. Or the genes responsible for relatively early aging listed in McKusick, the definitive volume describing genetic diseases. Little by little, each of the factors responsible for the countless components of what we now call natural aging will be subsumed into and interpreted according to the disease model. [17] If no death is natural, death, even in old age, will be seen as even more evil than it is now.

While both scenarios are caricatures with unpalatable elements, I think a case can be made that the second view—that death is combatible and ought to be combatted— is the more human course. Much depends on the meaning of the term *natural* and on some distinctions that must be made if we are to be clear in formulating a policy about death. It also depends on our perception of the term *human*.

Distinctions Needing to Be Made
THE MEANING OF NATURAL

The concept of "natural" in relation to death is not the only application of the term *natural* in doing ethics and life sciences. We have a frustratingly rich tradition of natural contraception, natural foods, natural drugs, natural sexual preferences, and natural instincts. Equally frustrating is the closely related concept of *normal*, as in normal behavior, normal intelligence, normal life span, and normal temperature. Standing behind some uses of both terms is an ethical-legal tradition of natural law.[18] Before examining the policy implications of the concept of natural death, a brief linguistic analysis of the term natural is in order. There are at least five distinct conceptions of the natural.

The Statistical

The natural is the "usual," that which is the modal or near the mean. It is "natural" for a couple to prefer that their first child be a male. It is natural for a man to die, so natural that the class of those who do not may be a null class. The opposite of natural in this sense is *unusual*. From this empirical description of the natural, it is clearly impossible to draw any policy conclusions about what we ought to do without an additional evaluative premise. To be ordinary is not necessarily to be right. To be unnatural in the sense of being statistically unusual is not to imply that change is appropriate.

The Biological

The natural is that which occurs "among the animals" or "among the higher animals" or "according to the human's biological nature." It is natural for humans to desire food and sexual activity, to avoid pain, and to die. Most if not all forms of contraception are unnatural in that the animal species do not practice them. Those who seek the normative from the human's biological nature—an Epicurus, a Nietzsche, a Spencer, or a Darwin—are very interested in this sense of the natural. It should be clear, though, from this biological descriptive use as with the statistical use of the term, that another premise is needed to reach policy conclusions. The needed premise, that what occurs in animals is good or right for humans and what does not occur among animals is wrong, seems most implausible.

The Anthropological

The natural is that which occurs in nature, that which is not man-made or processed. Detergents are artificial; soap is natural. Dannon yogurt is 100 percent natural; it contains no artificial ingredients. It all comes straight from the cow and the culture without the addition of any man-made chemicals. The opposite of natural in this sense is cultural, artificial, or artifactual. The distinction between the natural and the man-made seems to be a primitive one. In *The Raw and the Cooked* Lévi-Strauss analyzes myth systems for their symbolic differentiation of the world into the natural and the cultural.[19] Talcott Parsons distinguishes between those deaths that American society conceives to be natural and those caused by disease or accident, which he calls "adventitious."[20] A death by murder or by automobile accident is not natural in the sense that it is caused by human intervention into the natural. In the "back to nature movement" we affirm that if it is natural (not man-made) it is good.[21] Once again the evaluative premise is needed. Stated in its boldest form—that all that is man-made is evil, and all that comes raw from the state of nature is good—it is certainly wrong. Some human interventions must be evil on balance. That is the judgment of those who are repulsed by the tubes and tracheostomy and technicians that keep the corpse respiring in the modern intensive care unit. But, by the same notion, disease caused by the natural invasion of the body by pathological microorganisms would have to be thought of as good, but the antibiotics (or, at least, the synthetic ones) that save the child from pneumonia, as evil. Artificiality, by itself, cannot be sufficient to declare an innovation to be an evil.

The Religious

The natural is that which is part of the creation as opposed to the "supernatural," that is, the events and forces that result from direct divine activity. There is a parallel dualism between the natural-supernatural dichotomy and the nature-artifact dichotomy. Lévi-Strauss's Hegelian dualism is also at home with the natural-supernatural distinction of the Greeks, Thomas Aquinas, and Eastern conceptions of nature. Illich has claimed that the notion that death is a natural rather than a supernatural event is a uniquely modern phenomenon.

The Moral

The reason that the natural and natural death cause us so much trouble at the policy level is that natural can also mean moral. The natural is that which is in accord with the nature of the species and the nature of the universe. Murdering innocent children is unnatural for humans. Lying, making war, and hatred can be unnatural even if they are ubiquitous. Classical natural law tradition—Ulpian's trichotomous theory of law, the Stoics, Thomas, Troeltsch, and modern Roman Catholic moral theologians—all understand the moral to be natural. So does the contemporary naturalist tradition in metaethics.[22]

Problems arise when the conception of the natural is applied in two or more senses simultaneously. This may happen in several ways: A particular object or event may fit more than one conception: "It is natural (statistical and biological) for grass to be green." It may also happen when certain schools of thought hold that one conception of the natural provides the content for another conception: "To determine what is natural (moral) for man, see what is in accord with his (biological) nature. This is Ulpian's *ius naturale* formulation. Finally, the multiple conceptions of the natural may occur as fallacious arguments: "I have demonstrated that homosexuality is unnatural (statistical and maybe biological). Therefore, since it is unnatural (moral), it should not be practiced." "Death is a natural event (statistical, biological, nonsupernatural); therefore, the scientifically trained expert should determine when natural (morally significant) life ceases." Making these leaps is what G. E. Moore called the naturalistic fallacy.[23]

The problem with the concept of natural death is that while death is clearly statistically and biologically natural, and presumably natural in the sense of not being caused by divine spirits, it is not clear whether natural deaths are always to be preferred to man-made ones. Presumably all agree that adventitious deaths by gunshot or rampaging automobiles are not desirable, but there is utter chaos in deciding whether deaths prolonged by technological interventions are better or worse than those brought about in nature's uninterrupted course. Is there any difference between using technological innovations to prolong life when a person would otherwise die prematurely and to prolong a life beyond the normal life span? The critical problem for public policy is whether such deaths are to be evaluated as good or as evil. Are they moral because they are natural, or should they be conquered if possible through the use of the human's rational capacity for technological intervention?

SPECIFIC AND SYSTEMIC CAUSES OF DEATH

The received tradition gives natural death two types of enemies: specific and systemic. Parsons, astute as he was in observing culture, seemed to accept that adventitious deaths can be clearly distinguished from the category of "the inevitable 'natural' deaths of all individuals."[24] Specific causes of death are normally thought to thwart natural death by making death premature. But the death-with-dignity movement has made us aware that the biomedical assault on these specific causes of death can also make us view arteriosclerosis as natural and the struggle against death once one has arteriosclerosis as artificial and evil. Thus specific diseases can hasten natural death, but fighting against death can create a situation where death is unnaturally prolonged. Even Parsons held to the notion that there is a natural, inevitable death that would occur if we only left the body alone and gave it a chance.

The field of gerontology is rapidly emerging as a new science with a rather old set of conceptual tools. Even the leaders in research on aging accept the view that the systemic aging process, "the biological clock," is fundamentally different from specific diseases. Leonard Hayflick speaks of the death of cells and the destruction of tissues and organs to be a "normal part of morphogenic or developmental sequences."[25] Harman views the human being as having a "natural human maximum life span" and the basic aging processes as having diseased states "superimposed and intertwined."[26]

This received view may not stand scrutiny. The generalization often made that conquering specific diseases such as heart disease and cancer would add little to the life span appears to rest on a model of total system collapse after a "natural" life span. This in turn requires two assumptions: one, that other disease systems (respiratory or neurological) will not be mastered, thus leading to further extensions of life expectancy, and, two, that the aging process is not itself a "disease" or set of diseases subject to medical control. Most of the theories of aging, though, appear to lend themselves to medical intervention. Antioxidants may bind free radicals. Autoimmune reactions may be controlled with the emerging techniques of immunology. Genes programmed for aging may be controlled with genetic engineering. Monoamineoxidase inhibitors or appropriate analogues may correct enzyme defects.

The view that aging is somehow different from disease may be wrong. The famous graphs showing life expectancy at birth asymptotically approaching one hundred years and capable of modification with age-span or biological-clock modifiers may simply be a product of a false dichotomy between natural life span and disease-induced shortening of that span. That arteriosclerosis or phenylketonuria are considered diseases but free radical accumulation or synthetase malfunction are considered natural aging may be a temporary accident of history. If distinguishing the natural and the abnormal has policy implications—as seems apparent—then clarifying such distinctions will be crucial for priorities in research and clinical health care.

SOCIOECONOMIC AND PHILOSOPHICAL PROBLEMS OF IMMORTALITY

The billions of dollars spent yearly on aging, primarily for services to the elderly, make clear the enormous social and economic implications of modifying the life span. Several authors have pointed out the phenomenal impact that would be made on our social institutions if we tamper successfully with the aging process.[27] If the number of years in retirement are significantly changed, the social security system will require radical reorganization. The labor force, housing market, family structure, political alliances, and, to some extent, the population size will change. To calculate just the economic impact of extending life span by ten years would be an incredibly large task.

As critical and complex as these social and economic problems would be, there is a separate set of issues that really should be dealt with first. These are the philosophical-ethical considerations of whether such life-extending innovations are good, independent of the social and economic costs. A strong case has been made in the history of philosophy for the goodness of death. If death's defenders are correct and influence policy accordingly, then the social and economic problems will be avoided. In this chapter I am concerned only with these latter problems—whether death at the fullness of life is essentially an evil to be conquered or a good to be welcomed.

EXTENDED MORTAL LIFE AND IMMORTALITY

If it is concluded that life is indeed a good and death an evil, then two alternatives are conceivable: extended mortal life and immortality. It is possible to find either alternative good in theory while judging the other unacceptable. One might conclude, for instance, that immortality would be ideal, but that extended mortal life (which is all that we can realistically hope for) is no better than our present finite existence. If it all must end, then what does it matter when? On the other hand, some might find the prospect of immortality unbearable, but the option of an additional twenty to forty years quite attractive.

Since extended mortal life is accessible to human endeavor as immortality is not, the most difficult problem is presented by the individual for whom immortality is utopia but mere extension of mortal life has no value. The Stoics distinguished two natural laws: one, more absolute, was the law of the utopia; the other was the relative natural law for the real world.[28] Pacifism might be an absolute law of nature, while just-war theory might be appropriate for the real and sinful world. I have always found one of the most perplexing dilemmas in philosophy to be whether one ought to pursue an ideal that probably can never be achieved or should, instead, accommodate to the real world and pursue the relative ideal, which is the best course once one concedes that the ideal cannot be achieved. Building the perfect jail is conceding that crimes will be committed. Establishing peer review committees is conceding that individual researchers will not always make the wisest, most detached judgments.

The idealist holds that one should not deviate from the telos, that approaching the real goal is better than achieving the substitute.[29] We in fact do not abandon the ideals of love, peace, and justice simply because we know they cannot be achieved, but realists do modify their behavior because they cannot be perfectly achieved. For idealists, the prospect that the quest for immortality will only lead to extended mortal life will not dissuade them even if they think that extended mortal life would be no gain. Realists, on the other hand, may have to be convinced that extended mortal life is a good in itself. This desire for extended mortal life appears to be in accord with the normal behavior of most humans and may be a sufficient justification for a policy committed to extending the life span even in the face of the reality of failure to achieve the eschaton. Commitment to life-span-prolonging efforts, then, may have two independent justifications: the idealist's quest for immortality and the realist's desire for extended mortal life. At the policy level it may not be necessary to distinguish the justifications if identical policies result.

The Cases for Life

It seems strange to make a case for life. Like happiness, truth, freedom, or justice, life seems to be an intrinsic good. Yet philosophers have been remarkably ingenious in putting forth arguments why the ending of life is not necessarily an evil. In fact, I believe life is not an intrinsic good in the same way that happiness, truth, freedom, or justice are. On the other hand, it is not simply an instrumental value either. If we are forced to make arguments against death and for life, presumably they must have more substance than the gut level affirmation of the pro-life movement. When pressed, I find two arguments cogent.

THE RATIONALIST CASES FOR LIFE

The first argument is that of the rationalist. Life should be affirmed as good and death as evil if doing so is consistent with promotion of the prudent, personal self-interest of the rational person. This argument is really history's response to Epicurus' frustratingly coherent argument that we should not fear death: "So long as we exist death is not with us; but when death comes, then we do not exist."[30] Epicurus may be comforting about what follows death, but even if he is right about that, he does not convince me that I should not fear the process of dying. More significantly, he does not convince me that I should not anticipate with regret the nonexistence of my self. Since the fear of dying is uniquely horrifying because of the anticipatory regret of nonexistence, it is really the latter that leads to the proposition that my death is an evil for me.

But why this anticipatory regret? There are many future states that I desire. Some have nothing to do with me; they will occur or fail to occur quite independent of my existence. Others involve me in some way or another. Some of those involving me, I desire only on the condition that I am alive. An example is my desire to have my pension.[31] The desired future state in that case in no way makes me desire to continue to live. A second group of future states I desire involve me because I think I am able to promote those states better if I am alive. My desire to see my children receive a college education is an example. Finally, some of the future states I desire involve me because I must be present. My desire to see my research on my favorite subject completed or my desire to see my children graduate from college requires that I be around. These desires differ from my pension in that for the pension I desire that it exist only if I am around, but for the research and the commencement I desire to be around in order to have those experiences. For anyone who has desires about future states requiring his own existence, it is rational that he regret the anticipation of his nonexistence.

That I may desire my existence, of course, does not demonstrate that it is desirable that I continue to exist, much less that the state has a reason to undertake efforts to see that I continue to exist. The common desire of many people for future states that require their existence does, however, create a common interest. To the degree, however, that the state has a legitimate interest in promoting the general welfare, and particularly promoting it when the individual efforts of individual citizens taken separately would not be effective, the state may prudently adopt a policy of supporting research and medical services that will tend to promote the general welfare. Prudent individuals form a contract to achieve together what they cannot achieve separately.

While this may provide an argument that the state can legitimately support death-averting programs, I do not think it is the strongest argument. First, it may confuse the desired and the desirable. That I desire future states requiring my existence does not make my future existence a good and my death an evil. That the vast majority of citizens desire their future existence does not mean it is right that the state should promote their future existence. Second, and I believe more devastating, the case for life and against death based on the prudence of the rational individual contracting with other individuals is, in the end, both too egocentric and too individualistic. A stronger argument for life and against death, I believe, rests in what, for lack of a better label, I will call the social-eschatological case.

THE SOCIAL-ESCHATOLOGICAL CASE FOR LIFE

To argue the evilness of death is to argue the human's place in the cosmos. Persons must come to grips with death through an understanding of their nature and their vision of their place in the telos—the ideal world toward which we strive. Western culture is incessantly teleological. Its members dream of a Kingdom of God that is a social, political reality—kingdom is a very political metaphor. They dream of life immortal (if influenced by the Greeks) or of resurrection of the body (if taught by the Christian vision). In combining the strands of our heritage, the body has won a place for itself from which we need never again feel we must escape. Common to all the significant Western eschatologies is a vision of perpetuation. While the pre-Christian Jewish tradition devoted relatively little attention to the problem of death, it transmitted the belief that death is the wages of sin. At least by the period of the Maccabees, it also had a vision of a messiah who would atone for that sin and create a perpetual kingdom.

The modern Westerner is deeply rooted in this social eschatology. Anticipated in the Johannine realized eschatology, it becomes much more this worldly in the modern era. People pray, "Thy kingdom come on earth," and mean it. They are activists who see it as part of their task to bring into reality that vision of the new world, the world where evil is no more. And one of the evils that they dream about conquering is the evil of death. Their social vision is one that they themselves must play a part in constructing—and one in which life can be prolonged through the use of human ingenuity to master diseases one by one. Life shall be a struggle. But in the end the goodness of life is to be affirmed. Humans shall have dominion over the earth and subdue it. Life shall prevail and death shall be no more.

If this social eschatology is made the basis for a commitment to a governmental policy of prolongation of life, we need not be confined to the individualism of the rationalist. Overcoming death—my own and my fellow man's—is the final step in overcoming evil and building human community.

The Cases for Death and against Immortality

Against this vision stands a long line of argument from Plato and Aristotle through Darwin to Hartshorne, Morison, and Kass. I have identified five arguments as potent counters thrust against the goal of extended mortal life of the ideal of immortality. Let me examine each in turn.

DEATH AS RELIEF FROM SUFFERING

Perhaps the most common case to be made for death is that it is the great liberator. The poet cloys with death's sweetness:

Come lovely and soothing death,
Undulate round the world, serenely, arriving, arriving,
In the day, in the night, to all, to each
Sooner or later, delicate death.
Prais'd be the fathomless universe,
For life and joy, and for objects and knowledge curious,
And for love, sweet love—But praise! praise! praise!
For the sure-enwinding arms of cool-enfolding death. [32]

That death can be the great liberator was clear to Socrates. Plato has Socrates say in the Crito, "When man has reached my age, he ought not to be repining at the approach of death." While in Plato's account escaping the miseries of old age plays a secondary role for Socrates, in Xenophon it becomes the main reason for Socrates' uncompromising position before his judges:

> Do you not know that I would refuse to concede that any man has lived a better life than I have up to now? . . . But now, if my years are prolonged, I know that the frailties of old age will inevitably be realized. . . . Perhaps God in His kindness is taking my part and securing me the opportunity of ending my life not only in season but also in the way that is easiest.[33]

In speaking of ending his life "in season" Socrates is the original advocate of the naturalness of death. Xenophon has Socrates say, "Have you not known all along from the moment of my birth nature has condemned me to death?" But in our day, that condemnation by nature to a natural death is being challenged. The choice need not be as with Socrates between "the frailties of old age" and death, but between death and medical treatments that may prolong the prime of life and conquer at least some of the debilitating diseases from which death was a human release.

DEATH AS RELIEF FROM BOREDOM

A related case for death and against immortality is made by those who fear the unbearable tedium of an endless life. To be condemned to eternal life is seen as a Sartre-esque torture of enormous proportion. Here the distinction between extended mortal life and immortality may be crucial. Those who believe they fear immortality more than death may be quite delighted with a few score more years for completion of their earthly projects. The case for death as a relief from the boredom of immortality does not create a problem for those who advocate only public policy of support for research to extend the life span. If, however, immortality would be boring, it does prevent a formidable challenge to the other principle upon which support for such research is based, that ever-extended life is the ideal toward which we strive.

Does this argument against the ideal work? I think not. I find in it a hollow, sour-grapes quality that might be satisfying to some, but should be rather unconvincing to a broader public. There is a play by Karel Čapek in which a woman named Elina Makropulos was given an elixir of life by her father, a sixteenth-century emperor. At the time of the play she is 342 and lives, apparently physically healthy, but in a state of boredom, indifference, and coldness.

Bernard Williams has examined this situation. His argument, as I understand it, is that it is not an accident of her particular life that she is bored, but that it is essential to human nature that an endless life would be a meaningless one. Elina Makropulos's problem, according to Williams, is that "everything that could happen and make sense to one particular human being . . . had already happened"; he then maintains that the fact that life ceased to have meaning for her, that she "froze up," is essential to human nature and not dependent on her particular contingent character or on the failure of others around her to share her immortal capacities.[34]

In developing his arguments he considers several alternatives: one continuous life, a series of lives connected by a common memory, and theories of an afterlife. The core of the argument, though, focuses on the primary case of one continuous life. Williams argues that two conditions would have to be met for the prospect of living forever to be attractive: (1) it should clearly be me who lives forever, and (2) "the state in which I survive should be one which, to me looking forward, will be adequately related, in the life it presents, to those aims which I now have in wanting to survive at all."[35]

I readily concede the first condition. It poses no problem for the kind of ideal relevant to public policy for research on aging. It would be me who lives forever. The second condition is more difficult. It includes two component arguments: (1) it is irrational to pursue a future desire if it is clearly impossible to achieve it, and (2) it is impossible to have an infinite agenda of categorical desires (desires requiring my presence for their fulfillment).

Williams does not explicitly deal with either of these assumptions. I think both can be challenged. I have already discussed the first. I find the position implausible, especially when holding that ideal would reasonably lead us toward that ideal even though it cannot realistically be achieved and when approaches to the ideal are considered progressively better in and of themselves. The second forces us to deal with the claim that human nature is such that boredom will eventually result from living forever, that Elina Makropulos's plight was not an accident of her personality, but integral to the human condition.

This position requires the presumption that the human necessarily has finite categorical desires or at least a finite capacity to develop new ways of fulfilling all of those desires. If my more eschatological understanding of the human as a community builder is correct, I see no reason why this must be the case. If the human's hopes are infinite, it is possible to have hope of continually fulfilling some categorical desires while at the same time not fulfilling all of them. If the vision is utopian, the possibility of new and fulfilling experiences is infinite. Furthermore, some realistic categorical desires, some of the most important ones, do not depend on the newness of experiences. The desire to live in a loving and happy relationship with one's family does not necessarily require continual novelty for its fulfillment. In fact, such a relationship conceivably might be quite stable without inevitably leading to boredom. While the prospect of death might enrich some such experiences by giving them a timely quality, it certainly also introduces great tragedy.

Finally, Williams appears to argue that for immortality to be attractive boredom must be unthinkable.[36] It could be that he is simply not a gambler and is not willing to take a chance. If, however, continual nonboring existence is really an ideal, it should not be necessary to rule out failure as unthinkable in order to be willing to give it a try. It might not be worth the gamble if the boring immortality were compulsory, but Elina Makropulos's was not. She stopped taking the elixir and died. Certainly any realistic public policy effort to combat death should hold out the same escape. Compulsory immortality is not among the conceivable treatments. As long as continual fulfillment of categorical desires is possible, it would seem both that there is hope that total boredom might be avoided and that it is worth the risk—especially since failures can be aborted. On the contrary, it would seem that the burden of proof is on those who would hold that boredom is inevitable. I do not see that as either plausible or provable.

DEATH AS A SOURCE OF MEANING

Teleologists may make their case for as well as against death. Death, it may be argued, gives life a sense of timeliness and purpose. This is the argument explored by Paul Ramsey, that death gives us reason to "number our days."[37] Were we to believe that we had forever to complete our projects, the sense of urgency and excitement in life would be lost. This is probably one of the most convincing cases for death faced by Judeo-Christians, whose world view is temporally oriented. Were immortality to come at the price of giving up a sense of time and timeliness, the price would be high indeed. But would that in fact be the result? Certainly not, unless the eschatological ideal is achieved, but even then it is not clear why perpetual life would be a timeless life. The test of this objection to immortality as with the previous one rests with the human—the wise and the many. Would, indeed, humans who are not part of Illich's elite seriously consider abandoning the possibility of extending physical life for fear of endless boredom and loss of a sense of time? I think not.

DEATH AS A FORCE OF PROGRESS

For this particularly modern argument for death I cite the poet Morison: "Every human death is ultimately for the good of the group. . . . To rage against death is to rage at the very process which made one a human in the first place."[38]

That evolution has depended upon the death of the weak so that the more fit may thrive is the first law of Darwin. Until now, it has seemed irrefutable. But need the evolutionist's position remain valid? To be sure, were immortality to be achieved, reproduction would have to cease if the population were to remain stable. But if mortal life is extended that reproduction process would at the most merely be slowed. Even if biological evolution ceased completely, it is not clear to me that at this point in history this would necessarily be an evil. For one who believes as firmly in progress as I, that may be heresy, but I wonder whether, for instance, continual evolution in intelligence so that more people have the intellectual capacities to build world-destroying weapons systems is an adaptive environment. If evolution was once only biological, it may now be cultural as well. If continued adaptation is necessary for survival in an ever-changing universe, possibly cultural adaptation may be sufficient or even preferable.

NATURAL DEATH AS A COMFORTING FICTION

We are left with one, last-ditch line of defense by the advocates of death. Natural death, they may concede, is a fiction. Indeed, deaths all do have a cause and that cause is potentially susceptible to description and control. But the fiction is a comforting one.

It is agonizing to realize that every death, and the suffering that accompanies it, is the result of some human choice, that some human individual or group is responsible. Perpetuating the fiction of natural death at least relieves the common person of the burden of responsibility.

Relieve us it does, but at the expense of continuing the suffering of death striking out in random and unregulated viciousness. It is the death of the animal species, but in being so it is subhuman. If our vision of the human is correct, if the human is a responsible agent charged with the task of creating and sustaining life and his or her environment, then such fictions are escapist. Such fictions may give freedom, but the result is a tyranny. To escape from responsibility to the imagined comforts of natural death cannot be a sustainable defense.

Qualifications on a Public Policy of Prolonging Life

If prolonging life and combating "natural" death are goods that are part of the human's responsibility in building human community, problems still remain, problems hinted at in the arguments in favor of death. Socrates' choice of death over the frailties of old age anticipates the first.

DEATH AS A RELATIVE RATHER THAN AN ABSOLUTE EVIL

To maintain that death is fundamentally incompatible with the ideal human community is not to say that death must always be fought. It is possible to maintain that immortality is a desirable goal and still hold that some deaths may be preferred to a painful and dehumanizing struggle toward that goal. If death is an evil, there still may be lives that are worse evils. Both the evil of death and the acceptability of individual deaths may be affirmed. To hold death to be an evil and still feel that individual deaths are acceptable may be a tragic view of death; it may mean that "accidental" deaths and deaths from the culpable choices of individuals or governments may be seen as more traumatic. The ideal, however, is not incompatible with advance directives, legal documents to facilitate refusal of intolerable death prolonging medical treatments, or even legislation to clarify the right of individuals and their guardians to make such refusals. As an active participant in the movement for the right of the dying to refuse treatment, I write this present chapter really as a footnote to correct any mistaken implication that affirming the evil of death and the relative acceptability of particular deaths is incompatible. Until the day of the eschaton, such tragic choices will still have to be made.

THE PRIORITIES PROBLEM

If (and only if) life is worth prolonging and death is worth combating, then the social and economic problems of policy choices become central. To make a case for immortality or extended mortal life is not to say conquering death has the highest priority on the human agenda. This is a question of the allocation of resources. The answer will depend on both economic and social data and on philosophical-ethical choices.

For the utilitarian, the goal is the greatest amount of aggregate good no matter how it is distributed. Deciding whether to strive to extend life will reduce to an empirical question whether it will produce the most net good. With regard to efforts to overcome diseases of the elderly without changing the underlying life span, the answer seems fairly clear. Only simple, inexpensive interventions could be justified even if one believes that continued life is a good. Efforts to overcome life-threatening illnesses in younger persons are likely to have a much greater payoff because they are likely to live a much longer time to experience the good that life can bring.

If one adds to the consideration, the possibility of life-span increase, the utilitarian calculus is harder to make. It is conceivable that some interventions to extend the life span from, say, 100 to 120 could be developed more cost effectively than developing interventions to extend the lives of an equal number of terminally ill infants to age twenty. If that were so, then a consistent utilitarian would opt for the greatest good per unit of cost and would support life-span extension over research and development of treatments of terminally ill infants.

For those whose ethics of distribution is more deontologically inclined, the moral analysis will be quite different. They will not be influenced by the fact that it will often be cheaper (measured in cost per year added) to extend the lives of younger persons than older ones. They would not necessarily consider it morally acceptable to give priority for transplants to younger persons on the grounds that, if successful, the recipients will live longer. An ethic driven by a principle of justice would consider the relative needs of potential recipients and allocate resources on the basis of need rather than who will live the longest if treated.

On the other hand, an ethic of justice may not always support care for the elderly, even elderly who are medically in great need. It may not even support certain research on the medical problems of the elderly who are in great need. I have hinted throughout this book and developed more fully elsewhere the distinction between equality at a moment in time and equality over a lifetime.[39] An egalitarian principle of justice is one that holds that distributions are right prima facie to the extent that they give people opportunities for equality of well-being. Holders of such a principle may split, however, on the issue of whether they strive for equality at a given moment in time or equality over a lifetime.

The distinction is critical when it comes to providing care for the elderly and making policy decisions about research and development of life-span increasing interventions. If the government is contemplating allocation of research budgets and considering allocation between terminally ill infants and terminally ill centenarians who have lived out their normal life spans, from the point of view of the moment in time they may be equally poorly off; they are both terminally ill. However, considering the amount of well-being each group has experienced over a lifetime, certainly the centenarians are much better off than the terminally ill infants. For egalitarians, it will make a tremendous difference whether we are striving for opportunities for equality at the moment or over the lifetimes of the individuals involved.

It is not obvious which perspective is the morally correct one. For certain interventions, the moment in time seems the correct perspective. For example, in deciding to administer analgesics for people in severe pain, they seem rightly given out on the basis of pain at the moment regardless of the fact that the suffering centenarian has had many more good years previously. Similarly, for safe, simple, and sure treatments for acute illness when the treatment is desired by the patient or surrogate, the need at the moment seems the relevant criterion.

On the other hand, for expenditures for more exotic, high-technology, expensive interventions for research and development of new therapies (including the development of life-span increasing interventions), it is not at all clear that the need at the moment is the morally correct perspective. It seems plausible that research on incurable conditions of infants has a higher moral claim on us than research on life-span increase of centenarians. This conclusion might be reached on utilitarian grounds, but it is more plausibly reached on the grounds of the egalitarian principle of justice interpreted to require opportunities for equality of well-being over a lifetime.

If this interpretation of egalitarianism works, then the relatively low priority for research and development of life-span increasing technologies is a result not of the fact that aging is "natural" rather than the result of disease or because a natural death is a good death, but rather because even though death in old age is still an evil, the "diseases" that account for what used to be called natural death have a morally lower priority in a just health care system. This is not because of a utilitarian claim that the centenarian will be less useful than the younger person, but rather because justice requires giving priority to those less well off over a lifetime. Euripides said, "When death approaches, old age is no burden." The modern revision might appropriately be, "The less one has to fear that death is approaching, the less will be the burden of old age."

When God created the human being—so the Judeo-Christian heritage tells us—it was in God's own image. Human beings are creatures to be sure, but they are responsible creatures. They are to have dominion over the earth and subdue it. There are two ways they may have dominion to lessen that fear of death. In some cases it will mean ingeniously using their scientific and technological skills responsibly to challenge particularly evil deaths. In other cases it will mean ingeniously using their intellectual and humanistic skills responsibly to decide that death should no longer be challenged.

The primary purpose of this book has been to explore this second alternative. The human can and must decide what death means; when we may appropriately treat individuals as if they were dead; when, if ever, it is acceptable for patients or their agents to refuse medical treatment; when, if ever, patients should not be given potentially meaningful and useful information about their condition; and when it is reasonable to make use of the mortal remains of the newly dead so that others may live longer or better. The purpose of this last chapter has been rather different: to affirm that deciding in individual cases that the struggle against death need not continue is not incompatible with a more general social commitment to a public policy that sees at least some deaths as evil, that promotes research to overcome them. Affirming simultaneously that death is an evil and that certain deaths ought to be accepted is a difficult task. Individual and social decisions in response to these questions are required. Making such decisions is part of our quest for responsibility in the era of the biological revolution.

Notes

Is Death Moral? An Introduction

1. This case is based in part on Dillon, et al. 1982. Since then several other attempts have been made to treat pregnant women with dead brains in order to save their fetuses.

2. Somers, 1982.

3. Raymond S. Duff and August B. Hollingshead, *Sickness and Society* (New York: Harper and Row, 1968), p. 307, cited in President's Commission 1983, p. 18.

4. In one sense, of course, we are all dying from the moment we are conceived, but that is not of interest in any practical sense. *Dying* is used here to refer to anyone with a specific, progressive, normally irreversible ailment which will eventually end in death and which has become so debilitating that it has seriously disrupted normal life patterns. Cf. Bayer, et al. 1983, p. 1491, where terminal illness is defined as "an illness in which, on the best available diagnostic criteria and in the light of available therapies, a reasonable estimation can be made prospectively and with a high probability that the person will die within a relatively short time."

5. U.S. Department of Health, Education, and Welfare, Public Health Service, *Expenses of Hospital and Institutional Care During the Last Year of Life for Adults Who Died in 1964 or 1965, United States*, Vital and Health Statistics, ser. 22, no. 11 (Washington, D.C.: U.S. Government Printing Office, 1971), p. 14.

6. Scitovsky 1984, p. 599.

7. U.S. Department of Health, Education, and Welfare, Public Health Service, *Episodes and Duration of Hospitalization in the Last Year of Life United States—1961*, Vital and Health Statistics, ser. 22, no. 2 (Washington, D.C.: U.S. Government Printing Office, 1966), p. 3.

8. President's Commission 1983, p. 17.

9. Fletcher 1980; Scitovsky and Capron 1986; Riley, et al. 1986.

10. *Expenses for Hospital and Institutional Care* 1971.

11. Detsky, et al. 1981, p. 669.

12. Lubitz and Prihoda 1984, p. 118.

13. S. H. Long, J. O. Gibbs, J. P. Crozier, et al., "Medical Expenditures of Terminal Cancer Patients During the Last Year of Life," *Inquiry* 21 (1984): 315–27, cited in Scitovsky and Capron 1986.

14. Lubitz and Prihoda 1984, p. 123.

15. Cassel 1973.

16. *In re* Quinlan, 137 N.J. Super. 227, 348 A.2d 801 (Super Ct. Chancery Div., 1975).

17. Oken 1961. A thorough discussion of these data will be undertaken in chap. 7.

18. See Kelly and Friesen 1950, and Branch 1956.

19. Fletcher 1969.

20. Lief and Fox 1963.

21. Robert N. Bellah, "Religious Evolution," *American Sociological Review* 29 (1964): 358–74.

22. See Choron 1963, p. 14.

23. For summaries of death in Eastern thought see Holck 1974; and Reynolds and Waugh, eds., 1976. For a classic document, see *The Tibetan Book of the Dead*, 1973.

24. *The Book of the Dead*, trans. and intro. by E. A. Wallis Budge (New Hyde Park, New York: University Books, 1960).

25. For summaries of death in Western thought, see Aries 1974; Boase 1972; Stendahl 1965; Gatch 1969; also Choron 1963.

26. Choron 1963; Oscar Cullmann, "Immortality of the Soul or Resurrection of the Dead," Stendahl 1965, pp. 9–53.

27. See Thomas W. Furlow, Jr., "A Matter of Life and Death," *The Pharos* (July 1973): 84–90.

28. "As to the exposure and rearing of children, let there be a law that no deformed child shall live. . . ." Aristotle, *Politics* 7, chap. 16.

29. Aristotle, *Nichomachean Ethics 5*, chap. 11.

30. Plato, *The Republic* 3 406 A–B.

31. Ibid., 3, 407 D—E.

32. Seneca, *Ad Lucilium Epistulae Morales* 2, trans. R. M. Gummere (London: William Heinemann, 1920), epis. 70. Cited in Furlow, "A Matter of Life and Death," p. 87.

33. Max Weber, *Sociology of Religion* (Boston: Beacon Press, 1963); Talcott Parsons and Winston White, "The Link Between Character and Society," *Social Structure and Personality*, ed. Talcott Parsons (New York: Free Press, 1964), pp. 183–235; and Talcott Parsons, *The System of Modern Societies* (Englewood Cliffs, N.J.: Prentice- Hall, 1971). For a specific application of this analysis to the American response to death, see Parsons and Lidz 1967, pp. 133–70; and Parsons, Fox, and Lidz 1972.

34. See Veatch 1976.

Chapter 1. Defining Death Anew

1. This account is based on David Sell, "Flyers Goalie Lindbergh Is Declared Brain Dead," *The Washington Post*, Nov. 11, 1985, pp. D1, D13; Alex Yannis, "Lindbergh Is Critically Injured," *The New York Times*, Nov. 11, 1985, pp. C1, C6; David Sell, "Lindbergh Was Legally Drunk," *The Washington Post*, Nov. 12, 1985, pp. D1, D4; Craig Wolff, "Alcohol Level Cited in Lindbergh Crash," *The New York Times*, Nov. 12, 1985, pp. B7, B8; Dave Sell, "Flyers' Lindbergh Is Declared Dead," *The Washington Post*, Nov. 13, 1985, pp. D1, D8; and Robert McG. Thomas, "Flyers' Goalie Dies: Organs Donated," *The New York Times*, Nov. 13, 1985, pp. B7, B8.

2. State v. Watson 191 N.J. Super. 464 (1983). To make matters more confusing, that same court opinion nevertheless ruled that "the 'brain death' suffered by the victim was death in fact and could have been so declared before the respirator was turned off."

3. Ad Hoc Committee of the Harvard Medical School, 1968.

4. Beecher 1970, p. 2.

5. Morison 1971.

6. Kass 1971.

7. Dillon, et al. 1982; Veatch 1982.

8. Frederick 1972. For another review of the case, see Converse 1975.

9. In making this statement I am explicitly holding that the concept of death is a moral concept, that is, to say someone is dead is, by definition, to say that certain behaviors (death behaviors) are appropriate. The alternative view is to hold that we could define the concept of death independent of making any moral claims. We would then have to go on to make independent moral determinations of whether any of these behaviors (the ones I have called death behaviors) are appropriate for all in the category we have defined as dead and only for those in that category. If death is to be defined ontologically rather than morally, it remains an open question whether any of the behaviors traditionally appropriate for dead people is really appropriate. I am explicitly taking the position that death is now nothing more than the term we use to refer to that class of people toward whom these behaviors are appropriate. I take this position because I am convinced that the association between the term *death* and these behaviors is so

strong that it could not be broken without creating chaos in normal conversation, legal proceedings, and social policy. For a provocative early argument to the contrary see Green and Wikler 1980. The most thorough recent treatment of the subject is Gervais 1986.

10. Ramsey 1970, p. 103, chap. 2, "On Updating Procedures for Stating That a Man Has Died."

11. Beecher 1970, p. 1.

12. This is argued most forcefully in Tomlinson 1984.

13. Byrne, O'Reilly, and Quay 1979.

14. Brierley et al. 1971.

15. Beecher 1970, p. 4.

16. Engelhardt 1986, pp. 104–27; Green and Wikler 1980; Michael Tooley, "Abortion and Infanticide," *Philosophy and Public Affairs* 2 (1972): 37–65; Mary Anne Warren, "On the Moral and Legal Status of Abortion," *The Monist* 57 (January 1973): 43–61.

17. Green and Wikler 1980. Their account is made somewhat confusing since they do not always distinguish between "brain death" and "upper brain death." Sometimes they say "brain" when they must mean upper brain. For instance, in two consecutive paragraphs (on p. 131) they say, "We have argued that the death of a person's brain is that person's death" and then, "It is loss of upper brain function which marks the person's death." They make clear that they are referring to what they call upper brain death, but sometimes use the designation "brain death" for the death of the person.

18. President's Commission 1981, pp. 39–40.

19. Green and Wikler 1980, p. 127.

20. Ibid., p. 116.

21. President's Commission 1981, p. 39.

22. Engelhardt 1975a.

23. President's Commission 1981, p. 40.

24. René Descartes, "The Passions of the Soul," in *The Philosophical Works of Descartes,* vol. 1 (Cambridge: Cambridge University Press, 1911), p. 345.

25. Beecher 1970, p. 2.

26. Brierley, et al. 1971.

27. Ad Hoc Committee of the Harvard Medical School 1968, pp. 337–38. See also Mellerio 1971.

28. Mohandas and Chou 1971.

29. Cranford 1978, p. 562.

30. Walker, et al. 1977.

31. President's Commission 1981, pp. 159–66.

32. Mohandas and Chou 1971.

33. Ad Hoc Committee of the Harvard Medical School 1968, pp. 337–40; Cranford, 1978, pp. 561–63; Rosoff and Schwab 1968.

34. German Surgical Society 1968.

35. Toole 1971.

36. Walker 1981, p. 134.

37. Ingvar and Widen 1972; Netherlands Red Cross Society 1971; German Surgical Society 1968.

38. Korein, et al. 1977; Pearson, et al. 1977; Kricheff, et al. 1978.

39. Walker 1981; Kricheff, et al. 1978.

40. Kaste, Hillbom, and Palo 1979.

41. Ingvar and Widen 1972.

42. German Surgical Society 1968.

43. Netherlands Red Cross Society 1971.

44. Ueki, Takeuchi, and Katsurada 1973.

45. Conference of Royal Colleges and Faculties of the United Kingdom 1976.

46. Working Party 1979.

47. Law Reform Commission of Canada 1981.

48. Denmark, Israel, and Japan. Pallis 1983.

49. Belgium, Germany, Great Britain, India, Ireland, The Netherlands, New Zealand, South Africa, South Korea, Switzerland, and Thailand. Pallis 1983.

50. Argentina, Australia, Austria, Canada, Czechoslovakia, Finland, France, Greece, Italy, Norway, Puerto Rico, and Spain. Pallis 1983; President's Commission 1981, p. 71.

51. Task Force on Death and Dying of the Institute of Society, Ethics, and the Life Sciences 1972, pp. 50–51.

52. Silverman, Masland, Saunders, and Schwab 1970.

53. Mohandas and Chou 1971, p. 214.

54. Walker, Diamond, and Moseley 1975. Walker and Molinari 1977.

55. Korein and Maccaria 1971, p. 184 (italics added).

56. "Report of the Medical Consultants on the Diagnosis of Death to the President's Commission for the Study of Ethical Problems in Medicine and Biomedical and Behavioral Research," 1981.

57. Korein and Maccaria 1971.

58. The inclusion of absence of breathing and reflexes in the criteria suggests but does not necessarily lead to this. It might be that, empirically, it is necessary for lower brain reflexes and breathing to be absent for twenty-four hours in order to be sure that the patient not only will never regain these functions but will never regain consciousness.

59. Brierley, et al. 1971.

60. Ibid., p. 560.

61. Ibid.

62. Cranford and Smith 1979, p. 201.

63. President's Commission 1983, pp. 174–75.

64. Berrol 1986.

65. Cranford and Smith 1979, p. 204.

66. President's Commission 1981, pp.89–107.

67. Arts, et al. 1985.

68. Walshe and Leonard 1985.

69. President's Commission 1983, p. 177.

70. Capron and Kass 1972, pp. 105–6.

71. President's Commission 1981, p. 74.

72. Byrne, O'Reilly, and Quay 1979; Nilges 1984.

73. Ad Hoc Committee of the Harvard Medical School 1968.

74. Cranford 1978, pp. 561–63.

75. President's Commission 1981.

Chapter 2. Defining Death Anew: Policy Options

1. Collins 1977, p. 19.

2. World Medical Association, Declaration of Sydney, 1968, in Hendin 1973, p. 36.

3. Warren 1972, p. 3.

4. Pope Pius XII 1958, p. 396.

5. Henry H. Foster, Jr., "Time of Death," *New York State Journal of Medicine* (December 1976): 2189.

6. Cowie 1981, pp. 190–91.

7. High 1972, p. 456.

8. Biorck 1968, p. 542. For a similar position by a lawyer see David W. Meyers, *The Human Body and the Law* (Chicago: Aldine, 1970).

9. Warren, "Developing a New Definition of Death," p. 4.

10. Loren F. Taylor, "A Statutory Definition of Death in Kansas, *Journal of the American Medical Association* 215 (1971): 296.

11. Of course even the most rigid interpretation of the old definition of death would only preclude taking organs from donors not yet dead. The old definition does not even preclude that unless one assumes that organs can be taken only from the corpse. But Dr. Taylor can be granted his hyperbole for the purposes of the political debate.

12. Halley and Harvey 1968, pp. 423–25.

13. 1972. Md. Laws 693. The phrase "in the opinion of a physician" was deleted from the first paragraph, and the phrase "and because of a known disease or condition" was added in the second paragraph following "ordinary standards of medical practice." It is not clear why the irreversible loss of brain function must be caused by a known disease or condition unless this is thought to be a protection against falsely diagnosing irreversibility in cases where a central nervous system depressant is present, but unknown to the medical personnel.

14. Alabama, Alaska, Arkansas, California, Colorado, Connecticut, Florida, Georgia, Hawaii, Idaho, Illinois, Indiana, Iowa, Kansas, Kentucky, Louisiana, Maryland, Maine, Michigan, Mississippi, Missouri, Montana, Nevada, New Hampshire, New Mexico, North Carolina, Ohio, Oklahoma, Oregon, Pennsylvania, Rhode Island, South Carolina, Tennessee, Texas, Vermont, Virginia, West Virginia, Wisconsin, Wyoming.

15. Arizona, Massachusetts, Nebraska, New Jersey, New York, North Dakota, Washington.

16. Kennedy 1971; Capron and Kass 1972; and President's Commission 1981.

17. Kennedy 1971, p. 947.

18. Md. Code Ann. §54F (1980); N.M. Stat. Ann. §12–2–4 (1978); Va. Code §54–325.7 Cum. Supp. (1981).

19. Kennedy 1971.

20. Capron and Kass 1972, p. 94.

21. Ibid., p. 111.

22. 100 A.B.A. Ann. Rprt. 231–232 (1978) [Feb. 1975 Midyear Meeting].

23. 12 *Uniform Laws Ann.* 15 Supp. (1981).

24. President's Commission 1981, p. 2.

25. According to both the Kansas and the Capron-Kass proposals, physicians may pronounce death without actually making measurements of brain activity. The implication of the Kansas wording is that there are really two meanings for death—at the conceptual level something like either irreversible loss of vital fluid flow centering in the heart and lungs or irreversible loss of bodily integrating capacity centered in the whole brain. Capron and Kass seem to lean toward a single concept underlying the statute: the irreversible loss of integrating capacity. It is not shocking that there may be two alternate criteria under different circumstances for accurately predicting the loss of this essential function. Indeed, I find this explanation much more plausible.

26. Halley and Harvey 1968, pp. 23–25.

27. Halley and Harvey 1968. Michael Sullivan, county probate judge in Milwaukee, had to make two critical decisions concerning whether patients have the right to refuse treatment. These cases and the general issue of refusing treatment are the subject of the next three chapters. He has explained the basis of his decisions in the *New England Law Review*. He writes in his article that he does not believe legislation defining death to be advisable "in this context." Since he is discussing whether dying patients have the right to refuse treatment, this attitude is perfectly plausible. But, even though it is irrelevant to his context, he goes on to state his opinion on who should decide what definition of death should be used: "The individual should decide whether he will employ the Harvard criteria, or some other definition for his death." According to Sullivan, it is the individual, not the physician, the medical society, or the state, who should have the "right to prescribe his death style" including the person's own definition of death. See *New England Law Review* 8 (1973): 192–216.

28. Capron and Kass 1972, p. 105n66.
29. President's Commission 1981, pp. 80–81.
30. Capron 1978.
31. Ibid.
32. President's Commission 1981.
33. Capron 1978, p. 357.

Chapter 3. Dying Morally

1. "Man Convicted of Killing Wife Who Begged to Die," *The New York Times*, May 10, 1985, p. A16; "Florida Man, 75, Sentenced to 25 Years in Slaying of Terminally Ill Wife," *The Washington Post*, May 10, 1985, p. A11; Gilbert v. State, 487 So. 2d 1185 (Fla. App. 4 Dist. 1986).
2. For a summary of the earlier cases see Baughman, Bruha, and Gould 1973, pp. 1213–14.
3. Fletcher 1968, p. 148.
4. Pope Pius XII 1958.
5. Ludwig Edelstein, "The Hippocratic Oath: Text, Translation, and Interpretation," in *Ancient Medicine* (Baltimore: Johns Hopkins University Press, 1967), pp. 9–13.
6. Williams 1973, pp. 90–91.
7. Brown, et al. 1970. See also the views of physicians as found by Crane 1973.
8. Immanuel Kant, *Groundwork of the Metaphysics of Morals*, trans. and analyzed by H. Paton (New York: Harper and Row, 1964 [1785]), pp. 61–67 (pages 393–99 of the edition issued by the Royal Prussian Academy in Berlin). Also see W. D. Ross, *The Right and the Good* (Oxford: Oxford University Press, 1939), p. 7; James Rachels correctly makes the point that intention alone does not always separate actions and omissions (1975, p. 79). I shall show, however, that there are problems with his analysis.
9. Rachels 1975, pp. 78–80.
10. Rachels 1979.
11. Ibid., p. 159.
12. Ibid., p. 161.
13. Ibid., pp. 155–56.
14. Twycross 1982.
15. Alexander 1949.
16. See Kohl 1975, p. 137; and Fletcher 1973, p. 114.
17. Compare the discussion in Lucy C. Dawidowicz, *The War Against the Jews 1933–1945* (New York: Holt, Rinehart, and Winston, 1975), pp. 131–34; and also Klaus Dorner, "Nationalsozialismus und Lebensvernichtung," *Vierteljahrshefte für Zeitgeschichte* 15 (1967): 121–52, especially pp. 130–31.
18. Mansson 1972.
19. Lifton 1986, p. 497.
20. Ibid., p. 503.
21. John Rawls, "Two Concepts of Rules," *The Philosophical Review* 44 (1955): 3–32; David Lyons, *Forms and Limits of Utilitarianism* (Oxford: Oxford University Press, 1965); Paul Ramsey, *Deeds and Rules in Christian Ethics* (New York: Charles Scribner's Sons, 1967).
22. Beauchamp 1979, pp. 181–94.
23. Kohl 1975, p. 139. Also see Kohl 1974 for a fuller discussion.
24. Beauchamp 1979, pp. 190–92.
25. A more complex version of this argument appears in Thomson 1976. I leave unaddressed the question of whether the prima facie principle of avoiding killing applies only to the killing of human beings or covers as well other living species, especially sentient beings who are not humans. It may well extend far beyond humans.

26. Here I draw on Ross, *The Right and the Good*.

27. Veatch 1981, p. 25.

28. Ibid., p. 27. In fact, in some cases the bond, whether it is with a lay person or a professional, can be established, especially when the patient is not competent, without consent or acceptance on the patient's part. This is especially true with regard to the duty of parents and other relatives in the case of a child. It is also true in the case of emergency care of incompetents because society has agreed that the consent of the patient can be presumed if the patient is incompetent and there is an emergency. In these cases there is a duty to promote the welfare of the patient. The health care professional, like the family member, is now responsible for the welfare of the individual involved (subject to the limits of the person's concurrence when competent).

29. Veatch 1981, pp. 291–305.

30. Fletcher 1967, p. 1009.

31. Ibid., p. 1012. While I find this portion of Fletcher's analysis sound, he goes on to reach what to me is the totally unacceptable legal and moral judgment that whether it is legally permissible for doctors to turn off respirators, "all depends on what doctors customarily do" (p. 1015). Courts are now, I think correctly, overruling the criterion of customary medical practice in deciding liability for harms which should be evaluated by the "reasonable man" criterion.

32. President's Commission 1983, p. 77.

33. Ibid., p. 74.

34. Ibid., p. 76.

35. United States Catholic Conference, Department of Health Affairs, *Ethical and Religious Directives for Catholic Health Facilities* (Washington, D.C.: United States Catholic Conference, 1971), p. 8.

36. Ramsey 1970, p. 151.

37. Kelly 1958, pp. 13–14.

38. Ibid., p. 13.

39. McCormick and Ramsey, eds. 1978, p. 7.

40. President's Commission 1983, pp. 81–82.

41. Pope Pius XII 1958, pp. 393–98.

42. Healy 1956.

43. Pope Pius XII 1958, p. 397.

44. Pope Pius XII 1958, p. 396.

45. Sullivan 1949, p. 72.

46. Congregation for The Doctrine of The Faith 1980, pp. 8–9.

47. McCormick 1974, p. 174; Paris 1986.

48. President's Commission 1983, pp. 88–89, n. 132.

49. Meilaender 1984; Horan and Grant 1984; Siegler and Weisbard 1985.

50. Meilaender 1984, p. 11.

51. McCormick 1985b, pp. 269–73.

52. Lynn and Childress 1983, pp. 18–19.

53. Callahan 1983.

54. Lynn and Childress 1983; Lynn 1987.

55. Lynn and Childress 1983.

56. President's Commission 1983, p. 132.

57. Ibid., pp. 134–35.

58. These notions were first developed in Veatch 1984a.

59. See Natanson v. Kline, 186 Kan. 393, 350 P.2d 1093 (1960), where Kansas State Supreme Court Justice Alfred Schroeder held that "the physician's choice of plausible courses should not be called into question if it appears, all circumstances considered, that the physician was motivated

only by the patient's best therapeutic interests and he proceeded as competent medical men would have done in a similar situation."

60. Berkey v. Anderson, Cal. App. 3rd 790, 805, 82 Cal. Rptr. 46.

61. For example, in Hunter v. Brown, one of the important cases in this series, Judge James concluded "whether or not Dr. Brown violated his fiduciary duty in withholding information is a question of fact to be judged by reasonable man standards," Hunter v. Brown, 4 Wash. App. 899, 484 P.2d 1162 (1972). For other cases see Dow v. Permanente Medical Group, 90 Cal. Rptr. 747 (Cal. 1970); Cooper v. Roberts, 286 A.2d 647 (Pa. 1971); Cobbs v. Grant 520 P2d 1 (Cal. 1972); and Wilkinson v. Vesey, 295 A.2d 676 (R.I. 1972); Barnette v. Potenza, 359 N.Y. S.2d 432 (1970). Cf. Martin v. Stratton, 515 P 2d 1366 (Okla. 1973); Canterbury v. Spence, 464 F.2d 772 (D.C. Cir.), *cert. denied*, 409 U.S. 1064 (1972). For summary discussions of these developments see David S. Rubsamen, "Changes in Informed Consent," *Medical World News* (February 9, 1973), pp. 66–67; Joseph E. Simonaitis, "Recent Decisions on Informed Consent," *Journal of the American Medical Association* 221 (1972): 441–42; and Joseph E. Simonaitis, "More About Informed Consent, Part 1," *Journal of the American Medical Association* 224 (1973): 1831–32.

Chapter 4. Deciding to Refuse Treatment: Competent Patients

1. This account is based on the court record of Bouvia v. County of Riverside, No. 159780 (Calif. Super Ct. Dec. 16, 1983), and Bouvia v. Superior Court of Los Angeles County, California Court of Appeal, Second District, 1986. 179 Cal. App. 3d 1127, 225 Cal. Rptr. 297.

2. Bouvia v. Superior Court of Los Angeles County.

3. Schloendorff v. New York Hospital (1914). In Jay Katz, *Experimentation with Human Beings: The Authority of the Investigator, Subject, Professions, and State in the Human Experimentation Process* (New York: Russell Sage Foundation, 1972), p. 526.

4. Natanson v. Kline, 186 Kan. 393, 350 P.2d 1093 (1960).

5. The Bouvia court decision affirms this. See also Satz v. Perlmutter, 362 So. 2d 160 (Fla. Dist. Ct. App. 1978), *aff'd*, 379 So. 2d 359 (Fla. Sup. Ct. 1980); Bartling v. Superior Court (Glendale Adventist Medical Center, et al., Real Parties in Interest), 163 Cal. App. 3d 186 (Cal. App. 2d 1984); *in re* Application of Plaza Health and Rehabilitation Center (N.Y. Sup. Ct., Onondaga County Feb. 2, 1984) (Miller, J.); Erickson v. Dilgard, 44 Misc. 2d 27, 252 N.Y.S.2d 705 (Sup. Ct. 1962); *in re* Quackenbush, 156 N.J. Super. 282, 383 A.2d 785 (1978); *in re* Brooks Estate, 32 Ill. 2d 361, 205 N.E.2d 435 (1965); Byrn 1975; Foster v. Tourtellotte, No. CV 81–5046–RMT (C.D. Cal. Nov. 16, 17, 1981), 704 F.2d 1109 (9th Cir. 1983); *in re* Farrell, 212 N.J. Super. 294, 514 A.2d 1342 (N.J. Super. Ct. Ch. Div. 1986), *motion for direct certification granted* (N.J. July 11, 1986); *in re* Guardianship of Grant, No. 52509–5 (Wash. Nov. 20, 1986) (order with opinion to follow); *in re* Requena, 213 N.J. super. 443, 517 A2d 869 (Super. Ct. App. Div. 1986) (per curiam); *in re* Rodas, No. 86PR139 (Colo. Dist. Ct. Mesa County Jan. 22, 1987) (Buss, J.); *in re* Triarsi, No. 86–14241 (N.Y. Sup. Ct. Suffolk County Aug. 21, 1986) (Yachim, J.) N.Y.L.J. Sept. 18, 1986, at 12, col. 5; Leach v. Akron General Medical Center, 68 Ohio Misc. 1, 22 Ohio Op. 3d 49, 426 N.E.2d 809 (Com. Pl. 1980); Cantor v. Weiss, No. 626 163 (Cal. Super. Ct. Los Angeles County Dec. 30, 1986) (Newman, J.); Delio v. Westchester County Medical Center, 134 Misc. 2d 206, 510 N.Y.S.2d 415 (Sup. Ct. Westchester County 1986), 516 N.Y.S.2d 677, *rev'd*, 129 A.D.2d1 516 N.Y.S.2d 677 (1987); Cantor 1973; Solnick 1984; Veatch 1984a; Cantor 1987, pp. 1–30; President's Commission 1983, p. 124; Bates 1982; Sendak 1978; Strand 1976; Clarke 1982–83; Shaub 1980; Davis 1978; Kutner 1979; McGinley 1980; Brant 1981; Moore 1983; Vorys 1981; Harber 1985; Cantor 1985; Hill 1980; Davis 1980. There are three very special classes of exceptions to this flat rule: those who indicate they would not resist being coerced, adults with dependents, and prisoners. These special cases will be taken up later in the chapter.

6. Acts 15:28–29, Deuteronomy 12:33, Genesis 9:3–4, and Leviticus 17:10–14. See Ford 1964; see also *in re* Estate of Brooks, 32 Ill.2d 361, 205 N.E.2d 435 (1965).

7. Cantor 1973, p. 238. For specific cases, see Wisconsin v. Yoder, 406 U.S. 205, 215 (1972) and Prince v. Massachusetts, 321 U.S. 158, 166–167 (1944).

8. Erickson v. Dilgard, 44 Misc. 2d 27, 252 N.Y.S.2d 705 (Sup. Ct. 1962); cf. *in re* Brooks Estate, 32 Ill.2d 361, 205 N.E.2d 435 (1965).

9. Byrn 1975, p. 3.

10. *In re* Phelps, No. 459–207 (Milwaukee County Ct., filed July 11, 1972).

11. Sullivan 1973.

12. Cited in ibid., p. 199.

13. Bouvia v. County of Riverside, No. 159780 (Cal. Super. Ct. Dec. 16, 1983), pp. 1–9.

14. *In re* Quinlan, 70 N.J. 10, 355 A.2d 647 (1976), *cert. denied sub nom.* Garger v. New Jersey, 429 U.S. 922 (1976), *overruled in part, in re* Conroy, 98 N.J. 321, 486 A.2d 1209 (1985).

15. *In re* Eichner, (*in re* Storar), 52 N.Y.2d 363, 420 N.E.2d 64, 438 N.Y.S.2d 266, *cert. denied*, 454 U.S. 858 (1981), p. 530.

16. W. A. Parent, "Privacy, Morality and the Law," *Philosophy and Public Affairs* 12 (1983): 269.

17. Ibid., p. 270. It might be argued that even if the knowledge possessed by others is a matter of public record, one still lacks privacy, but this will not be critical for our purpose.

18. David M. O'Brien, *Privacy, Law and Public Policy* (New York: Praeger, 1979), pp. 178–79.

19. Griswold v. Connecticut, 381 U.S. 479, 85 S. Ct. 1678, 14 L.Ed. 2d 510 (1965).

20. Roe v. Wade, 410 U.S. 113, 93 S.Ct. 705, 1973.

21. This thesis and the related confusion between autonomy and privacy has been analyzed thoroughly by Sara T. Fry, "Protecting Privacy: Judicial Decision-Making in Search of a Principle," Ph.D. diss., Georgetown University, 1984.

22. Bouvia v. Superior Court of Los Angeles County, California Court of Appeal, Second District, 1986, 179 Cal. App. 3d 1127, 225 Cal. Rptr. 297, (Ct. App.), *review denied* (June 5, 1986), p. 302.

23. President's Commission 1983, p. 37.

24. John Stuart Mill, *On Liberty* (New York: The Liberal Arts Press, 1956), pp. 91–92.

25. *In re* President and Directors of Georgetown College, Inc., 333 F.2d 1000 (D.C. Cir.), *cert. denied sub nom.* Jones v. President and Directors of Georgetown College, Inc., 377 U.S. 978 (1964).

26. Another reason was that, because Mrs. Jones was "in extremis" and "hardly compos mentis," she was "as little able competently to decide for herself as any child would be." For this reason, Judge Wright felt justified in applying the analogy of the case involving parental refusal of blood for children where, as we have seen, the court will routinely order the transfusion. Since Mrs. Jones was known to be a Jehovah's Witness and had expressed her refusal to have a blood transfusion before she lost competency, it would appear that she was really a "formerly competent adult" and not in the same position as a child. Thus it is not certain that this argument of Judge Wright should remain valid. However, the argument is consistent with the view that wishes stated while conscious and competent may be overridden if the patient rejected treatment before knowing that death would be the result.

27. The state may have a twofold interest: preventing psychological harm to the child from loss of its mother, and preventing expense that will ensue if the child becomes a public charge. See Cantor, "A Patient's Decision to Decline Life-Saving Medical Treatment," pp. 251–54.

28. Raleigh Fitkin-Paul Morgan Memorial Hospital v. Anderson, 42 N.J. 421, 201 A.2d 537 (1964), *cert. denied*, 337 U.S. 985 (1964). Also see Robert M. Byrn, "An American Tragedy: The Supreme Court on Abortion," *Fordham Law Review* 41 (1973): 844–49.

29. *In re* Charles P. Osborne, 294 A.2d 372 (D.C. Cir. 1972).

30. Sharpe and Hargest, "Lifesaving Treatment for Unwilling Patients," p. 699, note that the state might have a stronger interest if it were the life of a sole surviving parent at stake.

31. *In re* Charles P. Osborne, 294 A.2d 372 (D.C. Cir. 1972).

32. In "Constitutional Law: Transfusions Ordered for Dying Woman Over Religious Objections," *University of Pennsylvania Law Review* 113 (1964): 294, it is also argued that the interest of the state is difficult to defend when the surviving parent does not object to the spouse's decision.

33. Bouvia v. Superior Court of Los Angeles County, California Court of Appeal, Second District, 1986. 179 Cal. App. 3d 1127, 225 Cal. Rptr. 297, (Ct. App.), *review denied* (June 5, 1986), p. 304.

34. *In re* Quinlan, 70 N.J. 10, 355 A.2d 647 (1976), *cert. denied sub nom.* Garger v. New Jersey, 429 U.S. 922 (1976), *overruled in part, in re* Conroy, 98 N.J. 321, 486 A.2d 1209 (1985), p. 45; Bartling v. Superior Court (Glendale Adventist Medical Center, et al., Real Parties in Interest), 163 Cal. App. 3d 186 (Cal. App. 2nd 1984, p. 221.

35. Amundsen 1978.

36. Judicial Council, American Medical Association, 1986, p. 13.

37. Ibid., p. 12.

38. Veatch 1986b, pp. 129–31; Veatch 1987, pp. 129–49.

39. New York City Health and Hospitals Corporation v. Paula Stein, 335 N.Y.S.2d 461 (1972).

40. This case became rather complicated because of a change in the New York State Mental Hygiene Law at about the same time. A new regulation was scheduled to take effect on January 1, 1973, that expressly permitted mental patients to refuse not only electroshock treatments, but also "surgery . . . major medical treatment in the nature of surgery, or the use of experimental drugs or procedures." It was apparently significant that, in July 1972 when the Stein case was being considered the parties were aware of the new regulation and the hospital chose "to proceed in accordance with the spirit of the new recodification." This is somewhat puzzling since the new codification expressly grants all mental patients (presumably including those who are not competent to exercise the refusal) the right to refuse these four specific classes of treatment. Yet the decision granting Mrs. Stein's refusal was not based on a general right to refuse these treatments, but on a specific determination that she was competent to refuse and that the therapy "is not clinically indicated." Under the new regulation it would seem that finding Mrs. Stein to have the capacity to consent knowingly or withhold her consent would be extraneous.

41. *In re* Maida Yetter, 62 Pa.D. and C.2d 619 (1973).

42. Harriet Pilpel, "Minor's Rights to Medical Care," *Albany Law Review* 36 (1972): 462–87; Judith Areen, et al., *Law, Science and Medicine* (Mineola, New York: The Foundation Press, 1984), pp. 1274–75; Angela R. Holder, "Minors' Rights to Consent to Medical Care," *Journal of the American Medical Association* 257 (24): 3400–3402.

43. *New York Post*, July 9, 1971.

44. *In re* Green, 292 A.2d 387 (Pa. Sup. Ct. 1972).

45. *In re* Sampson, 37 A.D. 2d 668, 323 N.Y.S.2d 253 (1971).

46. David J. Sharpe, Salvatore Fiscina, and Murdock Head, *Law and Medicine—Cases and Materials* (St. Paul, Minnesota: West Publishing Co., 1978), pp. 218–19; Walter Wadlington, Jon R. Waltz, and Roger B. Dworkin, *Law and Medicine—Cases and Materials* (Mineola, New York: The Foundation Press, 1980), pp. 168–70.

47. Powell v. Columbian [sic] Presbyterian Medical Center et al. 49 Misc. 2d 215, 267 N.Y.S. 2d, 450 (Sup. Ct. 1965).

48. U.S. v. George, 33 U.S.L.W. 2518 (D.C., Conn., March 24, 1965).

49. See addendum in Ramsay v. Ciccone, 310 F. Supp. 600 (Mo., 1970): "A prisoner in need of medical treatment (including medical attention and surgical treatment) cannot, without leave and assistance of his keepers, at will go to a public or private facility to secure medical treatment and cannot at will call in a practitioner to treat him in prison. (If he is indigent he

might not be able to secure medical treatment in or out of prison with leave of his keepers.) Having custody of the prisoner's body and control of the prisoner's access to medical treatment, the prison authorities have a duty to provide needed medical attention."

50. Peek v. Ciccone, 288 F. Supp. 329 (W.D. Mo. 1968).

51. Smith v. Baker, 326 F. Supp. 787 (W.D. Mo. 1970).

52. Veale v. Ciccone, 281 F. Supp. 1017 (W.D. Mo. 1968).

53. Haynes v. Harris, 344 F. 2d. 462 (8th Cir. 1965). See also Petition of Baptista, 206 F. Supp. 288 (W.D. Mo. 1962).

54. Leach v. Shapiro, 13 Ohio App. 3d 393, 469 N.E.2d 1047 (Ct. App. 1984); Frances Okun v. The Society of New York Hospital, Supreme Court of the State of New York, County of New York, Summons, Index Number 13167/84, June 1, 1984; "Ohio Battery Suit: Galvin v. University Hospitals," *Society for the Right to Die Newsletter* (Fall 1986), p. 5.

Chapter 5. Deciding to Refuse Treatment: Incompetent Patients

1. Sharpe, Fiscina, and Head, *Law and Medicine—Cases and Materials*; Wadlington, Waltz, and Dworkin, *Law and Medicine—Cases and Materials*.

2. President's Commission 1983, p. 126.

3. Judith Areen, *Law, Science and Medicine* (Mineola, N.Y.: Foundation Press, 1984), p. 355.

4. Jackson and Youngner 1979.

5. Hastings Center 1987; President's Commission 1983, p. 127.

6. *In re* Eichner, 52 N.Y. 2d 363, 420 N.E.2d 64.

7. Ibid., pp. 72–73.

8. *In re* Storar, N.Y. 420 N.E.2d 64 (1981); Leach v. Shapiro, 13 Ohio App. 3d 393, 469 N.E.2d 1047 (Ct. App. 1984); Corbett v. D'Alessandro, 487 So. 2d 368 (Fla. Ct. App. 1986); Severns v. Wilmington Medical Center, Inc., 421 A.2d 1334 (Del. 1980); Brophy v. New England Sinai Hospital, Inc. 398 Mass. 417, 497 N.E.2d 626 (1986); *in re* Lydia E. Hall Hospital, 116 Misc. 2d 477, 455 N.Y.S.2d 706 (Sup. Ct. Nassau County 1982), 117 Misc. 2d 1024, 459 N.Y.S.2d 682 (Sup. Ct. Nassau County 1982).

9. Superintendent of Belchertown State School v. Saikewicz, 373 Mass. 728, 370 N.E.2d 417 (1977).

10. Ibid., p. 431.

11. Ibid.

12. Ibid., p. 428. In fact, we may be able to learn something about Mr. Saikewicz's uniqueness, even if he is severely retarded. He reportedly showed unusual aversion to injections, even in comparison to others similarly situated. In making the substituted judgment, one should possibly take that into account. For the most part, however, the surrogate would have to make the judgment with no concrete data about the patient's unique values.

13. *In re* Storar, N.Y., 420 N.E.2d 64 (1981), p. 72.

14. Ibid., p. 73.

15. Veatch 1984.

16. See Wisconsin v. Yoder, 406 U.S. 205 (1972); Pouce v. Society of Sisters, 268 U.S. 510 (1925).

17. Brophy v. New England Sinai Hospital, Inc., 398 Mass. 417, 497 N.E.2d 626 (1986).

18. *In re* Jobes, 210 N.J. Super. 543, 510 A.2d 133 (Super Ct. Ch. Div. April 23, 1986), *review denied* (N.J. March 10, 1986), *cert. granted* (N.J. Sept. 10, 1986), No. A–108/109, slip. op. (N.J. June 24, 1987).

19. *In re* Conroy, 98 N.J. 321, 486 A.2d 1209 (1985).

20. *In re* Dinnerstein, 6 Mass. App. Ct. 466, 380 N.E.2d 134 (App. Ct. 1978).

21. Barber v. Superior Court, 147 Cal. App. 3d 1006, 195 Cal. Rptr. 484 (Ct. App. 1983).

22. *In re* Eichner (*in re* Storar), 52 N.Y.2d 363, 420 N.E.2d 64, 438 N.Y.S.2d 266, *cert. denied*, 454 U.S. 858 (1981).

23. *In re* Quinlan, 137 N.J. Super. 227, 348 A.2d 801, p. 806.

24. Ibid., p. 814.

25. Ibid., p. 819.

26. Ibid.

27. Ibid., p. 822.

28. See the discussion of the distinction in Byrn 1975, pp. 17–19.

29. *In re* Quinlan, 137 N.J. Super. 227, 348 A.2d 801, p. 818. Both these views are in turn inconsistent with the statement in the opinion, "The judicial power to act in the incompetent's best interest in this instance selects continued life. . . ." Ibid., p. 822.

30. *In re* Quinlan, 70 N.J. 10, 355 A.2d 647 (1976), *cert. denied sub nom.* Garger v. New Jersey, 429 U.S. 922 (1976), *overruled in part, in re* Conroy, 98 N.J. 321, 486 A.2d 1209 (1985), p. 665.

31. Ibid., p. 666.

32. Ibid.

33. Ibid., pp. 662–64.

34. Ibid., p. 663.

35. Ibid.

36. Ibid.

37. Ibid., p. 664.

38. Ibid.

39. Ibid.

40. *In re* Eichner, N.Y., 420 N.E.2d 64 (1981), p. 70.

41. *In re* Quinlan, 70 N.J. 10, 355 A.2d 647 (1976), p. 653.

42. Ibid., p. 664.

43. *In re* Conroy, 98 N.J. 321, 486 A.2d 1209 (1985), p. 362; see also *in re* Heir, 18 Mass. App. 200, 464 N.E.2d 959 (Ct. App.), *review denied*, 392 Mass. 1102, 465 N.E.2d 261 (1984).

44. *In re* Quinlan, 70 N.J. 10, 355 A.2d 647 (1976), *cert. denied sub. nom.* Garger v. New Jersey, 429 U.S. 922 (1976), *overruled in part, in re* Conroy, 98 N.J. 321, 486 A.2d 1209 (1985), p. 671.

45. Superintendent of Belchertown State School v. Saikewicz, 373 Mass. 728, 370 N.E.2d 417 (1977), p. 434.

46. Ibid., p. 420.

47. Ibid., p. 431.

48. *In re* Dinnerstein, 6 Mass. App. Ct. 466, 380 N.E.2d 134 (App. Ct. 1978).

49. Ibid., p. 138.

50. *In re* Custody of a Minor, 379 N.E.2d 1053 (Mass. Supreme Judicial Ct., July 10, 1978).

51. Ibid., p. 1058.

52. *In re* Phillip Becker, 92 Cal. App. 3d 796, 156 Cal. Rptr. 48 (1979), *cert. denied sub nom.* Bothman v. Warren B., 445 U.S. 949 (1980).

53. Guardianship of Phillip Becker, No. 101–981, at 4 (Cal. Super. Ct., Aug. 7, 1981), *aff'd*, 139 Cal. App. 3d 407, 420, 199 Cal. Rptr. 781, 789 (1983).

54. *In re* Phillip Becker, 92 Cal. App. 3d 796, 156 Cal. Rptr. 48 (1979), *cert. denied sub nom.* Bothman v. Warren B., 445 U.S. 949 (1980).

55. Ibid., p. 801, 156 Cal. Rptr. at 51.

56. Ibid., pp. 801–02, 156 Cal. Rptr. at 51.

57. Guardianship of Phillip Becker. No. 101–981, slip op. p. 19 (Cal. Super. Ct., Aug. 7, 1981).

58. Guardianship of Phillip Becker, No. 101–981, p. 4 (Cal. Super. Ct., Aug. 7, 1981), *aff'd*, 139 Cal. App. 3d 407, 420, 199 Cal. Rptr. 781, 789 (1983).

59. Ibid., pp. 414–18, 188 Cal. Rptr., pp. 785–87.

60. Ibid., pp. 416–19, 188 Cal. Rptr., pp. 786–88.

61. People *ex rel.* Wallace v. Labrenz, 411 Ill. 613, 104 N.E.2d 769 (1952). For other relevant cases reaching similar conclusions see Morrison v. State, 252 S.W.2d 97 (C.A. Kansas City, Mo., 1952); Hoener v. Bertinato, 67 N.J. Super. 517, 171 A.2d 140 (1961); *in re* Santos, 16 A.D.2d 755, 227 N.Y.S.2d 450, *appeal dismissed* 232 N.Y.S.2d 1026 (1962): Application of Brooklyn Hospital, 45 Misc. 2d 914, 258 N.Y.S.2d 621 (1965); *in re* Clark, 21 Ohio Op. 2d 86, 185 N.E.2d 128 (C.P. Lucas 1962); *in re* Vasko, 238 App. Div. 128, 263 N.Y.S. 522 (1933).

62. State v. Perricone, 37 N.J. 463, 181 A.2d 751, *cert. denied* 371 U.S. 890 (1962).

63. People v. Pierson, 176 N.Y. 201, 68 N.E. 243 (1903).

64. David A. Andelman, "Parents Who Refused Treatment for Girl, 8, Overruled by a Judge," *New York Times*, May 26, 1972, p. 39.

65. George E. Hall, "Court-Ordered Blood Transfusion upon an Adult Patient," *The New Physician*, Feb. 1972, pp. 89–90.

66. Holman 1972.

67. John F. Kennedy Memorial Hospital v. Delores Heston and Jane Heston, 279 A.2d 670, N.J. Super Ct. 1971.

68. A similar case has already been mentioned (Collins v. Davis, 254 N.Y.S.2d 666 [1964]). A patient sought medical attention and then became unconscious. With an operation there was a good chance of saving his life; without one he would die. The patient's wife refused to give her consent for unspecified reasons, which were, in her opinion, justifiable, but in the opinion of the court they were unsound. The case did not involve a person who for religious or other reasons had refused to seek medical attention. The court ruled that once the patient came into the hospital, it was the responsibility of the hospital and its doctors to treat him. Like the mother of Dolores Heston, this patient's wife was not permitted to refuse the life-saving treatment.

69. Hazelton [sic] v. Powhatan Nursing Home, Inc., No. CH 98287 (Va. Cir. Ct. Fairfax County Aug. 29, 1986), order signed (Sept. 2, 1986), (Fortkort, J.), *appeal denied*, Record No. 860814 (Va. Sept. 2, 1986).

70. See also Mike Sager, "Nine-Year-Old Dies After Four Months in Coma," *Washington Post*, sect. B, col. 1 (Sept. 17, 1980), p. 6; *in re* Peter, N.J. Supreme Ct., No. A–78 (June 24, 1987); *in re* Torres, 357 N.W.2d (Minn. 1984); *in re* Vogel, 134 Misc. 2d 395, 512 N.Y.S.2d 622 (Sup. Ct. Nassau County 1986), notice of appeal filed (App. Div. 2d Dep't. Dec. 22, 1986).

71. Baker 1969. See also Young 1963.

72. Heinemann's Appeal, 96 Pa. 112, 42 Am. Rep. 532 (Ct. of App. 1880). The case is described in Baker 1969, p. 303.

73. Mitchell v. Davis, 205 S.W.2d 812 (Tex. Civ. App. 1947).

74. *In re* Rotkowitz, 175 Misc. 948, 25 N.Y.S.2d 624 (Dom. Rel. Ct. 1941).

75. *In re* Sampson, 328 N.Y.S.2d 686, 278 N.E.2d 918 (Ct. App. 1972). See also Oakley v. Jackson, 1 K.B. 216 (1914), cited in Baker 1969, p. 304; *in re* Carstairs, 115 N.Y.S.2d 314 (Dom. Rel. Ct. 1952), cited in Baker 1969, pp. 306–07.

76. *In re* Tuttendario, 21 Pa. Dist. 561 (Quar. Sess., Phila. Co. 1911). This decision also emphasized that "neglect" required "malicious intent" which was clearly lacking: "We have not yet adopted as a public policy that Spartan rule that children belong not to their parents, but to the state. As the law stands, the parents forfeit their natural right of guardianship only in cases where they have shown their unfitness by reason of moral depravity." Now, however, it is clear that we also have not adopted the equally Spartan rule that children do belong to their parents. Malicious intent (clearly lacking in the blood transfusion cases) must be abandoned as a required condition for neglect. See also *in re* Hudson, 13 Wash. 2d 673, 126 P.2d 765 (1942).

77. *In re* Frank, 41 Wash. 2d 294, 248 P. 553 (1942).

78. *In re* Seiferth, 127 N.Y.S.2d, *rev'd.*, 284 App. Div. 221, 137 N.Y.S.2d 35 (1955). This case is also discussed in Baker 1969, p. 302.

79. *In re* Infant Doe, No. GU 8204-00 (Cir. Ct. Monroe County, Ind. April 12, 1982, *writ of mandamus dismissed sub nom.* State *ex rel.* Infant Doe v. Baker, No. 482 S 140 [Indiana Supreme Ct., May 27, 1982]) (Case mooted by child's death); President's Commission 1983, p. 224.

80. Weber v. Stony Brook Hospital, 467 N.Y.S.2d 685 (A.D. 2 Dept. 1983).

81. Ibid., p. 686.

82. Ibid.

83. Ibid., p. 687.

84. See Swinyard 1971, pp. 17-18.

85. For examples of the debate about care of spina bifida infants, see Lorber 1971; Lorber 1974; Lorber 1973; Smith and Smith 1973; Stein, Schut, and Ames 1974, p. 556; Cook 1971; Zachary 1968, p. 274; Freeman 1974; Report by a Working Party 1975, p. 88; Eckstein 1974; and especially Swinyard 1971.

86. Robertson 1975, p. 213.

87. Ibid. Robertson is imprecise in his definition of the term *involuntary euthanasia.* He makes no use of the moral and legal differences between active killing and simply letting die, nor of the cases where treatment may acceptably be refused on grounds that it is not sufficiently reasonable. The grounds for approving the refusal may be found in Robertson's own wording. When he says that there is a legal duty to provide necessary medical assistance to the helpless minor, the implication is that it is not required to provide "unnecessary" assistance. That opens the debate about the definition of *necessary.* It is my contention that grave burden to the patient should be sufficient to classify the treatment as unnecessary. Clearly there is no homicide for failing to provide unnecessary treatment. Robertson fails to take up this argument. Also see the debate between Robertson and me in Swinyard 1971.

88. One very similar case is that of the newborn son of Sgt. and Mrs. Robert B. T. Houle who was born with several severe deformities, including a tracheoesophageal fistula, as well as the prospect of permanent physical and mental damage. The physician is quoted as saying that the infant's "probable brain damage has rendered life not worth preserving." See McCormick 1974. Upon the parents' refusal of treatment, the court ordered treatment for the infant, but the child died after surgery (*New York Times,* Feb. 25, 1974, p. 13):

Chapter 6. Dying Morally: Public Policy

1. The letter is by Robert S. Morison, the late professor in the Department of Sociology, Cornell University.

2. The legislation carried the title "Death with Dignity." This wording was in the 1970 version.

3. Amundsen 1978.

4. Feifel, et al. 1967a.

5. Kübler-Ross 1969, p. 20.

6. Lord Brock 1970.

7. Ibid., p. 663.

8. Fox and Swazey 1974, pp. 280-315.

9. *In re* Quinlan, 70 N.J. 10, 355 A.2d 647 (1976), p. 671.

10. New Jersey Guidelines for Prognosis Committees. No date.

11. Teel 1975.

12. Levine 1977; Veatch 1977.

13. President's Commission 1983, pp. 160-70.

14. Youngner, et al. 1983, p. 448.

15. "Nondiscrimination on the Basis of Handicap, Procedures and Guidelines Relating to Health Care for Handicapped Infants, Final Rule," 1984, p. 1642; U.S. Department of Health

and Human Services 1985b, p. 14880; U.S. Department of Health and Human Services 1985a, pp. 14893–901.

16. Cranford and Doudera 1984; Weinstein, ed. 1986.

17. Freedman 1981; Fleischman and Murray 1983; Cohen 1982; McCormick 1984; Kelly and McCarthy, eds. 1984.

18. Veatch 1977; Veatch "The Roles and Functions of Hospital Ethics Committees," in Weinstein, ed. 1986, pp. 1–15.

19. Veatch 1983b, p. 1.

20. The New York State Task Force on Life and the Law 1986; Meisel, Pinkus, and Snyder 1986; Beth Israel Hospital 1983.

21. "Guidelines for 'No-Code' Orders in Los Angeles County Department of Health Services' Hospitals," 1983; Committee on Policy for DNR Decisions, Yale-New Haven Hospital 1983; American Hospital Association, General Council Special Committee on Biomedical Ethics, *Values in Conflict: Ethical Issues in Hospital Care* (Chicago: American Hospital Association, 1985).

22. The Hastings Center 1987.

23. The statement by Robert S. Morison was presented to a meeting of the Research Group on Death and Dying at the Institute of Society, Ethics and the Life Sciences; Stead 1972, p. 47.

24. President's Commission 1983, p. 146.

25. Martyn and Jacobs 1984, p. 786; Fowler 1984, p. 1015; D.C. Code, sec. 21–2081 (1987 supp.).

26. The Catholic Hospital Association 1982.

27. Corbett v. D'Alessandro. 487 So. 2d 368 (Fla. Dist. Ct. App. 1986).

28. In the Montana version, the declaration would have to have been filed with the county clerk at least fifteen days before "euthanasia administration." The versions in all three states contained strong penalties for willful violation of the intent of the bill. In Idaho, the draft stated, "a person who willfully conceals, destroys, falsifies, or forges" a declaration is guilty of first-degree murder. In the Montana version, the penalty is life imprisonment. It is strange that in both states concealing the document, which is really refusing to go along with the requested euthanasia, is punishable in the same way that forging the document is. This represents either very bad writing or a strong conviction that individuals have the right to have their death hastened. In the Oregon version, there were different penalties—life imprisonment for falsifying a document to suggest a patient does desire euthanasia, but only ten years or $5,000 fine or both for falsifying the document to state a patient does not want it.

29. California Natural Death Act. Ca. Stat. Chapter 1439, Code, Health and Safety, sections 7185–95.

30. These paragraphs are based on the 40 statutes as well as valuable summaries in Society for the Right to Die 1985, and Mishkin, 1986.

31. Arkansas Death with Dignity, Ark. Stat. 82–3801 (1977).

32. New Mexico Right to Die Act, N.M. Stat. Ann. 24–7–1 (1978).

33. New Mexico S.B. 15 (1984).

34. North Carolina Right to Natural Death Act, N.C. Gen. Stat. 90–320, 1977, amended 1979, 1981, 1983; Oregon Rights with Respect to Terminal Illness, Or. Rev. Stat. 97.050, 1977 amended 1983.

35. Va. Code Ann. 54–325.8:6 (1984).

36. Virginia Natural Death Act, Va. Code Ann. Stat. 54–325.8:1.

37. President's Commission 1983, pp. 313–17.

Chapter 7: She'll Be Happier If She Never Knows

1. Oken 1961.

2. Meyer 1968, p. 176.

3. Richard B. Brandt, *Ethical Theory: The Problems of Normative and Critical Ethics* (Englewood Cliffs, N.J.: Prentice-Hall, 1959); Michael D. Bayles, ed. *Contemporary Utilitarianism* (Garden City, N.Y.: Doubleday, 1968); Ernest Albee, *A History of English Utilitarianism* (New York: Collier Books, 1962); David Lyons, *Forms and Limits of Utilitarianism* (Oxford: Oxford University Press, 1965); The Hastings Center, Institute of Society, Ethics and the Life Sciences, "Values, Ethics, and CBA in Health Care," *The Implications of Cost-Effectiveness Analysis of Medical Technology,* edited by the Office of Technology Assessment, Congress of the United States (Washington, D.C.: Office of Technology Assessment, 1980), pp. 168–85; Alasdair MacIntyre, "Utilitarianism and Cost-Benefit Analysis: An Essay on the Relevance of Moral Philosophy to Bureaucratic Theory," *Values in the Electric Power Industry,* edited by Kenneth Sayre (South Bend, Ind.: University of Notre Dame Press, 1977), pp. 217–37; Tom L. Beauchamp, "Utilitarianism and Cost/Benefit Analysis: A Reply to MacIntyre," *Ethical Theory and Business,* edited by Tom L. Beauchamp and Norman E. Bowie (Englewood Cliffs, N.J.: Prentice-Hall, 1979), pp. 276–83.

4. W. D. Ross, *The Right and the Good* (Oxford: Oxford University Press, 1939).

5. William Frankena, *Ethics,* 2d ed. (Englewood Cliffs, N.J.: Prentice-Hall, 1973), p. 47; Beauchamp and Childress, eds. 1983, p. 107.

6. Joseph Fletcher, *Situation Ethics: The New Morality* (Philadelphia: Westminster Press, 1966).

7. John Stuart Mill, "Utilitarianism," in *Ethical Theories: A Book of Readings,* edited by A. I. Melden (Englewood Cliffs, N.J.: Prentice-Hall, 1967), pp. 391–434.

8. Jeremy Bentham, "An Introduction to the Principles of Morals and Legislation," in *Ethical Theories: A Book of Readings,* pp. 367–90.

9. Immanuel Kant, *Groundwork of the Metaphysic of Morals,* pp. 67–68.

10. Kant 1909 [1797], pp. 361–65. I shall discuss below the possible differences between the outright lie and merely withholding information.

11. Ross, *The Right and The Good,* p. 21.

12. Fitts and Ravdin 1953, p. 903.

13. Ibid.

14. Henry Sidgwick, *The Methods of Ethics* (New York: Dover Publications, 1966 [1874]).

15. See Bayles, *Contemporary Utilitarianism,* and especially Lyons, *Forms and Limits of Utilitarianism.*

16. John Rawls, "Two Concepts of Rules," *The Philosophical Review* 44 (1955): 3–32.

17. Piatt 1946.

18. Oken 1961, p. 1127.

19. Robert N. Wilson, *The Sociology of Health: An Introduction* (New York: Random House, 1970), pp. 18, 20.

20. Lund 1946.

21. Meyer 1968, p. 173.

22. Lund 1946, p. 958.

23. May 1972, pp. 484–85.

24. Fitts and Ravdin 1953. For a summary of the shift in physician attitudes see Veatch and Tai 1980.

25. Oken 1961, pp. 1120–28.

26. Kelly and Friesen 1950

27. Samp and Curreri 1957.

28. Branch 1956.

29. Cappon 1962.

30. "Over 65," *Medical World News* 11 (No. 50, December 11, 1970): 32G.

31. Blumenfield, Levy, and Kaufman 1978–79.

32. Friedman 1970.

33. Mount, Jones, and Patterson 1974, p. 743.

34. Travis, Noyes, and Brightwell 1974, p. 21.

35. Rea, Greenspoon, and Spilka 1975, pp. 293–94.

36. Novack, et al. 1979.

37. Blumfield, Levy, and Kaufman 1979, pp. 306–10; Greenwald and Nevit 1982; and Channon and Ballinger 1984. Cf. Hatfield, et al. 1983–84.

38. Blumfield, Levy, and Kaufman 1979, pp. 307–08.

39. Hatfield, et al. 1983–84, p. 56.

40. Kelly and Friesen, 1950.

41. W. A. Crammond, "Psychotherapy of the Dying Patient," *British Medical Journal* (August 17, 1970): 389–93.

42. Meyer 1968, p. 169.

43. See ibid., p. 174.

44. Ibid., p. 172.

45. Kübler-Ross 1969, pp. 34–43.

46. Ibid., pp. 38–41.

47. Ibid., pp. 28–29.

48. Feifel, et al. 1967.

49. Hatfield, et al. 1983–84, p. 51.

50. Howells and Field 1982.

51. Kelly and Friesen 1950.

52. Aitken-Swan and Easson 1959.

53. Peck 1972.

54. Rea, Greenspoon, and Spilka (1975, p. 293) found no significant differences among medical specialties, but they were working with small groups (only twelve psychiatrists) and with physicians who had all shifted signficantly toward favoring disclosure. Greenwald and Nevit (1982, p. 593) found differences among internists, radiologists, and surgeons, but did not include psychiatrists in their study. Novack, et al. (1979) did not separate out psychiatrists but found no significant differences among nonpsychiatric specialties. All of their physicians groups strongly supported disclosure.

55. Fitts and Ravdin 1950.

56. Judicial Council, American Medical Association 1986, p. ix. The matter is made more complicated by the fact that in the interpretations of the Council on Ethical and Judicial Affairs a more traditional Hippocratic qualification seems to be added. The AMA Council says, "Informed consent is a basic social policy for which exceptions are permitted . . . when risk-disclosure poses such a serious psychological threat of detriment to the patient as to be medically contraindicated."

Several things should be noted about this retreat to paternalism. First, while the blunt commitment to honesty is the position adopted by the AMA House of Delegates, the therapeutic privilege exception is an interpretation added by the Council on Judicial Affairs. One might argue that it does not necessarily represent the position of the full House of Delegates. Second, the exception clause does not permit withholding of information whenever the physician believes it would be harmful to the patient to disclose, but only when the psychological threat is so serious as to be "medically contraindicated." It is not at all clear what it means for something to be "medically contraindicated." It sounds like a factual medical determination when, in fact, it is only a value judgment by physicians that the disclosure ought not to take place. Nevertheless, the tone is one of requiring substantial burden of proof on the clinician before information is withheld on this basis. Third, it should be noted that if "medical contraindication" implies that the patient would be so incapacitated as to be incapable of making a reasoned decision, then it would seem to follow that the patient should be declared incompetent and a guardian should be appointed to whom the disclosure would be made. Declarations of incompetency are matters of legal determination, not something that can be done by the individual clinician. Finally, even if one concludes that the Judicial Council permits withholding of diagnostic information on these traditional paternalistic grounds, it does not follow that it is either moral or legal to do so. Lay people and physicians standing in other ethical traditions (such as Judeo-Christianity or secular liberalism) may remain morally committed to the necessity of disclosure of a terminal diagnosis even in cases where the AMA Judicial Council's ethical system would permit withholding. From the legal point of view, the law may require disclosure of information adequate to offer a reasoned consent even in those cases where the AMA's council believes that nondisclosure is permissible.

57. World Medical Association, "International Code of Medical Ethics," in *Encylcopedia of Bioethics*, edited by Warren T. Reich (New York: The Free Press, 1978), p. 1750.

58. Judicial Council, American Medical Association 1986, p. ix. As noted above, the AMA's Council on Ethical and Judicial Affairs issues interpretations that often refine and sometimes modify the broader principles adopted by the AMA's House of Delegates. They have done so regarding confidentiality. While in the area of informed consent the council provided for a limited therapeutic privilege exception based on concern for the welfare of the patient, in the area of confidentiality the council's exception clause has a totally different basis, one that would not be relevant in the case of advanced disclosure of a terminal diagnosis to relatives. The council believes that exceptions to the confidentiality rule are appropriate when there are "overriding social considerations" such as "where a patient threatens to inflict serious bodily harm to another person and there is a reasonable probability that the patient may carry out the threat" (p. 21). That position, though plausible, is controversial. There are many other medical ethical systems that would formulate the social exception differently. In the case of disclosure of terminal diagnosis to relatives, however, the concern is not about threat of harm to others; it is about danger to the patient. Even though the council advocates a therapeutic privilege regarding informed consent, it does not do so regarding confidentiality.

This is in direct contrast to the earlier AMA position, which incorporated a therapeutic privilege as well as a social danger justification for violating confidentiality. The older confidentiality principle stated, "A physician may not reveal the confidence entrusted to him in the course of medical attendance, or the deficiencies he may observe in the character of his patients, unless he is required to do so by law or unless it becomes necessary in order to protect the welfare of the individual or of the society." Judicial Council, American Medical Association, *Opinions and Reports of the Judicial Council* (Chicago: American Medical Association, 1971), p. vii.

59. Ludwig Edelstein, "The Hippocratic Oath: Text, Translation and Interpretation," in *Ancient Medicine: Selected Papers of Ludwig Edelstein*, edited by Owsei Temkin and C. Lilian Temkin (Baltimore, Md.: The Johns Hopkins University Press, 1967), p. 6.

60. World Medical Association, "Declaration of Geneva," *World Medical Journal* suppl. 3 (1956): 10–12. Reprinted in *Encyclopedia of Biothetics*, p. 1749.

Chapter 8. The Newly Dead

1. Based on Bailey, et al. 1985; McCormick 1985a; Rosner 1985.

2. See Miller 1971, p. 4, for some of the complexities of that history.

3. Task Force on Organ Transplantation and the United Network for Organ Sharing, unpublished data.

4. ACS/NIH Organ Transplant Registry, Winter Newsletter, 1975–76.

5. United Network for Organ Sharing, unpublished data.

6. Task Force on Organ Transplantation 1986, p. 17.

7. Ibid.

8. Task Force on Organ Transplantation, 1985; Wish 1986; Copeland, et al. 1984.

9. Task Force on Organ Transplantation, unpublished data.

10. United Network for Organ Sharing, unpublished data.

11. Project on Organ Transplantation 1985, p. 6.

12. There is an exception. There is now a reported case of a heart transplant from a living donor. It resulted from the purposeful removal of the functioning heart of a living cystic fibrosis victim in order to implant in that patient the heart and lungs as a unit, a technically better procedure even though only the lungs were defective. This made the heart-lung recipient's original heart available for implantation in another patient. This source of hearts from living donors will obviously be very limited.

13. Task Force on Organ Transplantation 1986, p. 17; Copeland, et al. 1984.

14. Swazey and Fox 1970, pp. 315–57.

15. Task Force on Organ Transplantation 1986, p. 35.

16. Ladimer 1970, p. 5.

17. Task Force on Organ Transplantation–United Network for Organ Sharing, unpub. data.

18. Task Force on Organ Transplantation 1986, p. 18.

19. Gunby 1984.

20. Grundfest-Broniatowski and Novick 1986.

21. Task Force on Organ Transplantation–United Network for Organ Sharing, unpub. data.

22. I am indebted to Hans Jonas for many of these suggestions. See also Gaylin 1974.

23. May 1973, p. 3.

24. Romans 12:1.

25. Jakobovits 1959, pp. 134–52; Rosner 1972, pp. 132–54.

26. Augustine, "De Cura Pro Mortius," *Nicene and Post-Nicene Fathers*, 1st ser., vol. 3, ed. Philip Schaff, trans. H. Browne (Grand Rapids, Mich.: William B. Eerdmans, 1956), cited in May 1973, p. 12.

27. Wolstenholme 1966; Lyons 1970; Elkinton 1973; Nelson 1973; Project on Organ Transplantation 1985; Task Force on Organ Transplantation 1986; Rosner and Bleich, eds. 1979, pp. 351–74; Ashley and O'Rourke 1982, pp. 308–12.

28. McCormick 1985a.

29. Rosner 1985.

30. Samuel Gorovitz, "Will We Still be 'Human' If We Have Engineered Genes and Animal Organs?" *Washington Post*, Dec. 9, 1984, pp. C1, C4; Veatch 1986b.

31. Capron 1985; Annas 1985.

32. "Report of the National Institutes of Health," 1985, p. 22.

33. Ibid., p. 25.

34. Ibid.

35. Regan 1985, p. 9.

36. Veatch 1985; Veatch 1986, pp. 129–31; Veatch 1987, pp. 87–189.

37. Task Force on Organ Transplantation 1986, p. 16; Cotton and Sandler 1986, p. 59; United States House of Representatives 1984, pp. 2, 240; Gunby 1983; Project on Organ Transplantation 1985.

38. Public Law 98–507, October 19, 1984. *National Organ Transplant Act* 98 Stat. 2339, Title III.

39. Ibid., Title II.

40. Fox and Swazey 1978, pp. 226–65.

41. Childress 1970; Green 1976; Outka 1974.

42. Task Force on Organ Transplantation 1986, p. 87.

43. Ibid.

44. Ibid., p. 70.

45. Ibid., p. 92.

46. Ibid., p.74.

47. Marcia Chamber, "Tough Transplant Questions Raised by 'Baby Jesse' Case," *New York Times*, June 15, 1986.

48. See Veatch 1987.

49. Starzl, et al. 1987.

50. Rapaport 1987.

51. Veatch 1986b, 156–64.

52. Bart, et al. 1981, p. 383.

53. Project on Organ Transplantation, 1985, p. 6.

54. Ibid., p. 7. Cf. Public Law 98–507, October 19, 1984. *National Organ Transplant Act* 98 Stat. 2339.

55. Sadler, Sadler, and Stason 1968.

56. Dukeminier and Sanders 1968.

57. Ibid., p. 416.

58. Matas and Veith 1984; Matas, et al. 1985; Stuart, Veith, and Cranford 1981; Kennedy 1979.

59. Matas and Veith 1984; Stuart, Veith, and Cranford 1981; Starzl 1984.

60. Manninen and Evans 1985, p. 3112; Task Force on Organ Transplantation, Meeting Minutes, November 18–19, 1985, p. 3; Stuart, Veith, and Cranford 1981, p. 238.

61. Gallup Organization, Inc. Attitudes and Opinions of the American Public Toward Kidney Donation. Gallup Survey 1983, cited in Task Force on Organ Transplantation, 1986, p. 38. Cf. Stuart, Veith, and Cranford 1981.

62. Stuart, Veith and Cranford (1981) cite Austria, Czechoslovakia, Denmark, Finland, France, Greece, Israel, Italy, Norway, Poland, Spain, Sweden, and Switzerland.

63. Ibid. Countries with this pattern include Argentina, Australia, Belgium, Canada, Germany, Great Britain, India, Ireland, Japan, the Netherlands, New Zealand, South Africa, South Korea, and Thailand.

64. All but India, Japan, and South Korea.

65. Task Force on Organ Transplantation 1986, p. 28; cf. Project on Organ Transplantation 1985, p. 17.

66. The terms are Paul Ramsey's from his important chapter "Giving or Taking Cadaver Organs for Transplant," in Ramsey 1970, pp. 198–215.

67. Task Force on Organ Transplantation 1986, pp. 199–213. California, Oregon, Indiana, Kentucky, Maine, New York, and Washington.

68. Ibid., p. 34.

69. Peters 1986.

70. Task Force on Organ Transplantation, Meeting minutes, November 18–19, 1985, p. 3. Another survey found much less disparity (53% vs. 50%), but still more willingness to donate a relative's organs.

71. I proposed these during hearings of the House Subcommittee on Investigations and Oversight of the Committee on Science and Technology in April 1983.

72. Project on Organ Transplantation 1985, p. 21.

73. United States House of Representatives 1984, pp. 259–66; Project on Organ Transplantation 1985, pp. 3–4.

74. United States House of Representatives 1984, pp. 256–58; Walter Williams, "Vital Organs—Let the Market Decide," *Washington Times*, April 19, 1984; Peters 1984; Chapman 1983.

75. Judie Glave, "Doctors Decry Plan to Buy, Sell Kidneys," *Washington Post*, Sept. 24, 1983, p. A7; Fost 1983.

76. United States House of Representatives 1984, pp. 242–45, 274–83.

77. Ibid., p. 283.

78. Matas and Veith 1984; Caplan 1984b; Ellen Goodman, "Life For Sale," *The Washington Post*, Oct. 1, 1983, p. 23; United States House of Representatives 1984, pp. 308–82.

79. Ibid., pp. 335–39.

80. Task Force on Organ Transplantation, "Statement on the Commercialization of Organ Transplantation," January 1986; Caplan 1984b; Project on Organ Transplantation 1985, pp. 3–4.

81. Public Law 98–507, October 19, 1984. *National Organ Transplant Act* 98 Stat. 2339.

82. Meyers 1970, p. 101; and Sadler and Sadler (1968) provide the basis for this summary. See also Peters 1986, pp. 243–47.

83. Meyers 1970, p. 102.

84. Respected readers of early drafts of this chapter challenged me to abandon these paragraphs. How, they ask, can one have a duty toward nonliving things? A duty to a corpse or a duty to the environment might, they argued, be formulated more carefully as a duty to the living in relationship to that corpse or environment, that is, as a duty to the community. As an example, one critic suggested there is a duty to the community not to cause disease by putrefaction. After careful reflection I still affirm, as starkly as possible, a duty to the corpse as well as to the environment.

85. May 1973, p. 7.

86. David Henlin, *Death as a Fact of Life* (New York: Norton, 1973), p. 57. Cf. Jakobovits 1959, pp. 126–52. I am unable to locate the original quotation.

Chapter 9. Natural Death and Public Policy

1. See Byrn 1975.

2. See Steinfels and Veatch, eds. 1975, especially the essay by Paul Ramsey entitled "The Indignity of 'Death with Dignity,'" pp. 81–96, and the responses by Robert S. Morison and Leon Kass.

3. That he was indeed poking fun at the philosophical gamesmanship that distinguishes between killing and letting people die, there can be no doubt from the other lines of his updating of God's message to Moses:

Thou shalt not steal; an empty feat,
When it's so lucrative to cheat.
Thou shalt not covet; but tradition
Approves all forms of competition.

4. Illich 1974.

5. Cassell 1973.

6. Ronald Bayer and Daniel Callahan, "Medicare Reform: Social and Ethical Perspectives," *Journal of Health Politics, Policy and Law* 10 (1985): 534.

7. Gordon, Gerjuoy, and Anderson, eds. 1979; Veatch 1979.

8. Parker and Gerjuoy 1979; Hochschild 1973.

9. Walford 1983.

10. Haflick 1985; see also Woodhead, Blackett, and Hollaender 1985; Parker and Gerjuoy 1979; and Shock 1985.

11. Gordon, Gerjuoy, and Anderson, eds. 1979.

12. Childress and Callahan 1978.

13. Marya Mannes, *Last Rights: A Plea for the Good Death* (New York: William Morrow, 1974).

14. "A Plea for Beneficent Euthanasia," *The Humanist* 34 (July–Aug. 1974): 4–5.

15. Engelhardt 1979; Morison 1978; Engelhardt 1975b; Callahan 1979; and Callahan 1987.

16. As Edward Schneider, Deputy Director of the National Institute on Aging, put it, "Natural Death or dying from natural aging was ignorance. If you look at the statistics, the number of people dying from natural death has gone down drastically as we actually found out what they were dying from. Now any diagnosis of natural death is because the physician is too lazy to find out what the person really died from. You don't die from old age; you die from

disease." Quoted in Larry Thompson, "Age Won't Kill You," *The Washington Post* (Health), July 9, 1986, p. 13.

17. Caplan 1981.

18. See, for example John Finnis, *Natural Law and Natural Rights* (Oxford: Oxford University Press, 1980), and Ernst Troeltsch, "Das stoische-christliche Naturrecht und die moderne profane Naturrecht," in *Gesammelte Schriften, IV* (Tübingen: Verlag J. C. B. Mohr [Paul Siebeck], 1925), pp. 166–91.

19. Claude Lévi-Srauss, *The Raw and the Cooked* (New York: Harper and Row, 1969).

20. Parsons and Lidz 1967.

21. Veatch 1971.

22. G. E. Moore, *Principia Ethica* (Cambridge: Cambridge University Press, 1903); W. K. Frankena, "The Naturalistic Fallacy," in *Readings in Ethical Theory* (New York: Appleton-Century-Crofts, 1952), pp. 103–14; Roderick Firth, "Ethical Absolutism and the Ideal Observer," *Philosophy and Phenomenological Research* 12 (1952): 317–45; Robert M. Veatch, "Does Ethics Have an Empirical Basis?" *Hastings Center Studies* 1 (1973): 50–65.

23. Moore, *Principia Ethica*, p. 10; Frankena persuasively refutes Moore's argument, though, by claiming that what really must be attacked is defining something into moral categories by demonstrating that it fits empirically into a certain nonmoral category without defending the claim that such a definition is justified; Frankena, "The Naturalistic Fallacy," pp. 103–14.

24. Parsons and Lidz 1967, p. 138.

25. Hayflick 1973, p. 442.

26. Harman 1969.

27. Neugarten 1972; Gordon, Gerjuoy, and Anderson, eds. 1979.

28. Troeltsch, "Das stoische-christliche Naturrecht."

29. I am, of course, using the term *idealist* and *realist* not in their technical philosophical meanings, but rather to contrast one who is guided by ideals and one who is influenced by more practical considerations.

30. Epicurus, "Epicurus to Monoeceus," in *Ethical Theories*, edited by A. I. Melden (Englewood Cliffs, N.J.: Prentice-Hall, 1967), p. 144.

31. I am indebted to Bernard Williams for much of the argument presented in this paragraph. See his essay "The Makropulos Case: Reflections on the Tedium of Immortality," in Williams 1973.

32. Walt Whitman, "When Lilacs Last in the Dooryard Bloom'd," *Leaves of Grass*.

33. See Choron 1963, p. 45.

34. See Williams 1973, pp. 89–90.

35. Ibid., p. 91.

36. Ibid., p. 95.

37. Ramsey 1974.

38. Morison 1974, p. 66.

39. Veatch 1986b; Veatch 1985; and Veatch 1987.

Bibliography

Ad Hoc Committee of the Harvard Medical School to Examine the Definition of Brain Death. 1968. "A Definition of Irreversible Coma." *Journal of the American Medical Association* 205:337–40.

Agich, George J. 1976. "The Concepts of Death and Embodiment." *Ethics in Science and Medicine* 3:95–105.

Aitken-Swan, Jean, and E. C. Easson. 1959. "Reactions of Cancer Patients on Being Told Their Diagnosis." *British Medical Journal* 1 (March 21): 779–83.

Alexander, Leo. 1949. "Medical Science Under Dictatorship." *New England Journal of Medicine* 241:39–47.

American Hospital Association, General Council Special Committee on Biomedical Ethics. 1985. *Values in Conflict: Ethical Issues in Hospital Care.* Chicago: American Hospital Association.

Amundsen, Darrel W. 1978. "The Physician's Obligation to Prolong Life: A Medical Duty without Classical Roots." *Hastings Center Report* 8 (Aug.): 23–30.

Annas, George. 1985. "Baby Fae: The "Anything Goes" School Of Human Experimentation." *Hastings Center Report* 15 (No. 1, Feb.): 15–17.

Areen, Judith. 1987. "The Legal Status of Consent Obtained from Families of Adult Patients to Withhold or Withdraw Treatment." *Journal of the American Medical Association* 258 (No. 2, July 10): 229–35.

Aries, Philippe. 1974. *Western Attitudes toward Death: From the Middle Ages to the Present.* Baltimore: Johns Hopkins University Press.

Arts, W. F. M., H. R. Van Dongen, J. Van Hof-Van Duin, and E. Lammens. 1985. "Unexpected improvement after prolonged posttraumatic vegetative state." *Journal of Neurology, Neurosurgery, and Psychiatry* 48:1300–1303.

Ashley, Benedict M., and Kevin D. O'Rourke. 1982. *Health Care Ethics: A Theological Analysis.* 2d ed. St. Louis: The Catholic Health Association of the United States.

Bailey, Leonard L., Sandra L. Nehlsen-Cannarella, Waldo Concepcion, and Weldon B. Jolley. 1985. "Baboon-to-Human Cardiac Xenotransplantation in a Neonate." *Journal of the American Medical Association* 254 (No. 23, December 20): 332–29.

Baker, James A. 1969. "Court Ordered Non-emergency Medical Care for Infants." *Cleveland/Marshall Law Review* 18:297–98.

Baron, C. H. 1979. "Medical Paternalism and the Rule of Law." *American Journal of Law and Medicine* 4 (Winter): 337–65.

Bart, K., E. Macon, A. Humphries, et al. 1981. "Increasing the Supply of Cadaveric Kidneys for Transplantation." *Transplantation* 31:383–87.

Bates, Kevin W. 1982. "Live or Let Die: Who Decides an Incompetent's Fate?" *In re Storar* and *In re Eichner. Brigham Young University Law Review.* (No. 2): 387–400.

Baughman, William H., John C. Bruha, and Francis J. Gould. 1973. "Euthanasia: Criminal, Tort, Constitutional and Legislative Considerations." *Notre Dame Lawyer* 48:1202–60.

Bayer, Ronald, Daniel Callahan, John Fletcher, Thomas Hodgson, Bruce Jennings, David Monsees, Steven Sieverts, and Robert Veatch. 1983. "The Care of the Terminally Ill: Morality and Economics." *The New England Journal of Medicine* 309 (December 15): 1490–94.

Beauchamp, Tom L. 1979. "A Reply to Rachels on Active and Passive Euthanasia." *Medical Responsibility: Paternalism, Informed Consent, and Euthanasia.* Edited by Wade L. Robison and Michael S. Pritchard. Clifton, N.J.: The Humana Press, pp. 181–94.

Beauchamp, Tom L., and James F. Childress. 1983. *Principles of Biomedical Ethics.* 2d ed. New York: Oxford University Press.

Becker, Lawrence C. 1975. "Human Being: The Boundaries of the Concept." *Philosophy and Public Affairs* 4:334–59.

Beecher, Henry K. 1970. "The New Definition of Death, Some Opposing Views." Unpublished paper presented at the meeting of the American Association for the Advancement of Science, December.

Berrol, Sheldon. 1986. "Considerations for Management of the Persistent Vegetative State." *Archives of Physical Medical Rehabilitation* 67:283–85.

Beth Israel Hospital. 1983. "Guidelines: Orders Not to Resuscitate." President's Commission for the Study of Ethical Problems in Medicine and Biomedical and Behavioral Research. *Deciding to Forego Life-Sustaining Treatment: Ethical, Medical, and Legal Issues in Treatment Decisions.* Washington, D.C.: U.S. Government Printing Office, pp. 501–05.

Biorck, Gunnar. 1968. "Thoughts on Life and Death." *Perspectives in Biology and Medicine* 14 (Summer): 527–43.

Bleich, J. David. 1979. "Neurological Criteria of Death and Time of Death Statutes." *Jewish Bioethics.* Edited by Fred Rosner and J. David Bleich. New York: Sanhedrin Press, pp. 303–16.

Blumenfield, Michael, Norman Levy, and Diane Kaufman. 1978–79. "The Wish to be Informed of a Fatal Illness." *Omega* 9 (No. 4): 323–26.

———. 1979. "Current Attitudes of Medical Students and House Staff Toward Terminal Illness." *General Hospital Psychiatry* 1 (No. 4, Dec.): 306–10.

Boase, T. S. R. 1972. *Death in the Middle Ages: Mortality, Judgment and Remembrance.* New York: McGraw-Hill.

Branch, C. .H. 1956. "Psychiatric Aspects of Malignant Disease." *CA: Bulletin of Cancer Progress* 6:102–04.

Brant, Jonathan. 1981. "Last Rights: An Analysis of Refusal and Withholding of Treatment Cases." *Missouri Law Review* 46 (No. 2): 337–70.

Brierley, J. B., J. A. H. Adams, D. I. Graham, and J. A. Simpson. 1971. "Neocortical Death after Cardiac Arrest." *Lancet* 2 (Sept. 11): 560–65.

Brock, Lord. 1970. "Euthanasia." *Proceedings of the Royal Society of Medicine* 63 (No. 7, July): 661–63.

Brown, Norman K., Roger Bulger, Harold Laws, and Donovan J. Thompson. 1970. "The Preservation of Life." *Journal of the American Medical Association* 211:76–81.

Buchanan, Allen. 1981. "The Limits of Proxy Decision Making for Incompetents." *U.C.L.A. Law Review* 29:393.

Byrn, Robert M. 1975. "Compulsory Lifesaving Treatment For The Competent Adult." *Fordham Law Review* 44:1–36.

Byrne, Paul A., Sean O'Reilly, and Paul M. Quay. 1979. "Brain Death—An Opposing Viewpoint." *Journal of the American Medical Association* 242:1985–1990.

Callahan, Daniel. "Natural Death and Public Policy." 1979. *Life Span: Values and Life-Extending Technologies.* Edited by Robert M. Veatch. San Francisco: Harper and Row, pp. 162–75.

———. 1983. "On Feeding the Dying." *The Hastings Center Report* 13 (No. 5): 22.

———. 1987. *Setting Limits: Medical Goals in an Aging Society.* New York: Simon and Schuster.

Cantor, Norman L. 1973. "A Patient's Decision to Decline Life-saving Medical Treatment: Bodily Integrity versus the Preservation of Life." *Rutgers Law Review* 26 (No. 2): 228–64.

———. 1985. "*Conroy,* Best Interests, and the Handling of Dying Patients." *Rutgers Law Review* 37 (No. 3): 543–77.

———. 1987. *Legal Frontiers of Death and Dying.* Bloomington: Indiana University Press.

Caplan, Arthur L. 1981. "The 'Unnaturalness' of Aging—A Sickness Unto Death?" *Concepts of Health and Disease.* Edited by Arthur L. Caplan, H. Tristram Engelhardt, Jr., and James J. McCartney. Reading, Mass.: Addison-Wesley, pp. 725–37.

———. 1984a. "Ethical Issues in the Sale of Human Organs for Transplantation." *Bioethics Reporter* (Jan.): 6–8.

———. 1984b. "Ethical and Policy Issues in the Procurement of Cadaver Organs for Transplantation." *New England Journal of Medicine* 311 (No. 15, Oct. 11): 981–83.

———. 1985. "Ethical Issues Raised by Research Involving Xenografts." *Journal of the American Medical Association* 254 (Dec. 20): 3339–43.

———. 1986. "Requests, Gifts, and Obligations: The Ethics of Organ Procurement." *Transplantation Proceedings* 18 (No. 3, Suppl. 2, June): 49–56.

Cappon, Daniel. 1962. "Attitudes of and Towards the Dying." *Canadian Medical Association Journal* 87 (Sept. 29): 693–700.

Capron, Alexander M. 1978. "Legal Definition of Death." *Brain Death: Interrelated Medical and Social Issues.* Edited by Julius Korein. *Annals of The New York Academy of Sciences* 315:349–59.

———. 1985. "When Well-Meaning Science Goes Too Far." *Hastings Center Report* 15 (No. 1, Feb.): 8–9.

Capron, Alexander M., and Leon R. Kass. 1972. "A Statutory Definition of the Standards for Determining Human Death: An Appraisal and a Proposal." *University of Pennsylvania Law Review* 121:87–118.

Cassel, Eric. 1973. "Permission to Die." *BioScience* 23:475–78.

Catholic Health Association of the United States, The. 1982. "Christian Affirmation of Life." St. Louis: The Catholic Health Association of the United States.

Channon, Lorna D., and Susan F. Ballinger. 1984. "Death and the Preclinical Medical Student II: Attitudes Toward Telling the Terminal Patient the Prognosis." *Death Education* 8 (No. 5–6): 399–404.

Chapman, David E. 1983. "Retailing Human Organs Under the Uniform Commercial Code." *The John Marshall Law Review* 16 (No. 2, Spring): 393–417.

Childress, James F. 1970. "Who Shall Live When Not All Can Live?" *Soundings* 53 (No. 4, Winter): 339–54.

Childress, James F., and Sidney Callahan. 1978. "Regulating an Anti-Aging Drug." *Hastings Center Report* 8 (June): 19–20.

Choron, Jacques. 1963. *Death and Western Thought*. New York: Macmillan.

Clarke, Alex M. 1982–83. "The Choice to Refuse or Withhold Medical Treatment: The Emerging Technology and Medical-Ethical Consensus." *Creighton Law Review* 13 (No. 3): 719–42.

Cohen, Cynthia B. 1982. "Interdisciplinary Consultation on the Care of the Critically Ill and Dying: The Role of One Hospital Ethics Committee." *Critical Care Medicine* 10 (Nov.): 776–84.

Collins, Vincent J. 1977. "Considerations in Prolonging Life: A Dying and Recovery Score." *Death, Dying and Euthanasia*. Edited by Dennis J. Horan and David Mall. Washington, D.C.: University Publications of America.

Committee on Policy for DNR Decisions, Yale–New Haven Hospital. 1983. "Report on Do Not Resuscitate Decisions." *Connecticut Medicine* 47:477–83.

Conference of Royal Colleges and Faculties of the United Kingdom, The. 1976. "Diagnosis of Brain Death." *The Lancet* 2:1069–70.

Congregation for The Doctrine of The Faith. 1980. *Declaration On Euthanasia*. Rome: The Sacred Congregation for the Doctrine of the Faith, May 5.

Converse, Ronald. 1975. "But When Did He Die: Tucker v. Lower and the Brain-Death Concept." *San Diego Law Review* 12:424–35.

Cook, Richard C. 1971. "Spina Bifida and Hydrocephalus." *British Medical Journal* 4 (Dec. 25): 759–99.

Copeland, Jack G., Robert B. Mammana, James K. Fuller, David W. Campbell, Mary J. McAleer, and Janice A. Sailer. 1984. "Heart Transplantation: Four Years' Experience with Conventional Immunosuppression." *Journal of the American Medical Association* 251 (No. 12, March 23/30): 1563–66.

Cotton, Raymond S., and Andrew L. Sandler. 1986. "Regulation of Organ Procurement and Transplantation." *Journal of Legal Medicine* 7 (No. 1, March): 55–84.

Cowie, Deborah J. 1981. "Legislation and Death: Do They Mix?" *Albany Law Review* 46:174–97.

Crane, Diana. 1973. "Physicians' Attitudes Toward the Treatment of Critically Ill Patients." *BioScience* 23:471–74.

Cranford, Ronald E. 1978. "Minnesota Medical Association Criteria: Brain Death—Concept and Criteria. Part I." *Minnesota Medicine* 61:561–63.

Cranford, Ronald E., and Harmon L. Smith. 1979. "Some Critical Distinctions Between Brain Death and the Persistent Vegetative State." *Ethics in Science and Medicine* 6 (Winter): 199–209.

Cranford, Ronald E., and A. Edward Doudera. 1984. "The Emergence of Institutional Ethics Committees." *Institutional Ethics Committees and Health Care Decision Making*. Ann Arbor, Mich.: American Society of Law & Medicine, pp. 5–21.

Davis, Patricia K. 1978. "Constitutional Law—Right of Privacy—Qualified Right to Refuse Medical Treatment May Be Asserted for Incompetent Under Doctrine of Substituted Judgment." *Emory Law Journal* 27 (No. 2): 425–60.

Davis, Sonya M. 1980. "The Refusal of Life-saving Medical Treatment vs. the State's Interest in the Preservation of Life: A Clarification of the Interests at Stake." *Washington University Law Quarterly* 58 (No. 1): 85–116.

Detsky, Allan S., Steven C. Stricker, Albert G. Mulley, and George E. Thibault. 1981. "Prognosis, Survival, and the Expenditure of Hospital Resources for Patients in an Intensive-Care Unit." *New England Journal of Medicine* 305:667–72.

Dillon, William P., Richard V. Lee, Michael J. Tronolone, Sharon Buckwald, and Ronald J. Foote. 1982. "Life Support and Maternal Brain Death During Pregnancy." *Journal of the American Medical Association* 248: (Sept. 2): 1089–91.

Dinello, Daniel. 1971. "On Killing and Letting Die." *Analysis* 31 (Jan.): 83–86.

Dukeminier, Jesse, and David Sanders. 1968. "Organ Transplantation: A Proposal for Routine Salvaging of Cadaver Organs." *New England Journal of Medicine* 279:413–19.

Eckstein, Herbert B. 1974. "Severely Malformed Children: The Problem of Selection." *British Medical Journal* (May 5): 284.

Elkinton, J. Russell. 1973. "Ethical and Moral Problems in the Use of Artificial and Transplanted Organs." *To Live and To Die.* Edited by Robert H. Williams. New York: Springer-Verlag, pp. 123–33.

Engelhardt, H. Tristram, Jr. 1975a. "Defining Death: A Philosophical Problem for Medicine and Law." *American Review of Respiratory Disease* 112:587–90.

———. 1975b. "The Counsels of Finitude." *Hastings Center Report* 8 (April): 29–36.

———. 1979. "Is Aging a Disease?" *Life Span—Values and Life-Extending Technologies.* Edited by Robert M. Veatch. San Francisco: Harper and Row, pp. 184–94.

———. 1986. *The Foundations of Bioethics.* New York: Oxford University Press.

Feifel, Herman, et al. 1967. "Physicians Consider Death." *Proceedings of the American Psychological Association,* pp. 201–02.

Fitts, William T., Jr. and I. S. Ravdin. 1953. "What Philadelphia Physicians Tell Patients with Cancer." *Journal of the American Medical Association* 153:901–04.

Fleischman, Alan R., and Thomas H. Murray. 1983. "Ethics Committees for Infant Doe?" *Hastings Center Report* 13 (Dec.): 5–9.

Fletcher, George P. "Prolonging Life." *Washington Law Review* 42:999–1016.

Fletcher, John. 1980. "Ethics and the Costs of Dying," *Genetics and the Law II.* Edited by Aubrey Milunsky and George J. Annas. New York: Plenum, pp. 187–209.

Fletcher, Joseph. 1968. "Elective Death." *Ethical Issues in Medicine.* Edited by E. Fuller Torrey. Boston: Little, Brown, pp. 139–57.

———. 1969. "Our Shameful Waste of Human Tissue: An Ethical Problem for the Living and the Dead." *Updating Life and Death.* Edited by Donald R. Cutler. Boston: Beacon Press, pp. 1–30.

———. 1973. "Ethics and Euthanasia." *To Live and To Die.* Edited by Robert H. Williams. New York: Springer Verlag, pp. 113–22.

Ford, John C. 1964. "Refusal of Blood Transfusions by Jehovah's Witnesses." *Catholic Law* 10:212–26.

Fost, Norman. 1983. "The New Body Snatchers: On Scott's *The Body as Property.*" *American Bar Foundation Research Journal,* pp. 718–32.

Fowler, Mark. 1984. "Appointing an Agent to Make Medical Treatment Choices." *Columbia Law Review* 84 (May): 985–1031.

Fox, Renée C., and Judith P. Swazey. 1978. *The Courage to Fail: A Social View of Organ Transplants and Dialysis.* Chicago: University of Chicago Press.

Frederick, Richmond Stanfield. 1972. "Medical Jurisprudence—Determining the Time of Death of the Heart Transplant Donor." *North Carolina Law Review* 51:172–84.

Freedman, Benjamin. 1981. "One Philosopher's Experience on an Ethics Committee." *Hastings Center Report* 11 (April): 20–22.

Freeman, John M. 1974. "The Shortsighted Treatment of Myelomeningocele: A Long-Term Case Report." *Pediatrics* 53 (March): 311–13.

Friedman, Henry J. 1970. "Physician Management of Dying Patients: An Exploration." *Psychiatry in Medicine* 1 (No. 4, Oct.): 295–305.

Gatch, Milton McC. 1969. *Death: Meaning and Mortality in Christian Thought and Contemporary Culture.* New York: Seabury Press.

Gaylin, Willard. 1974. "Harvesting the Dead: The Potential for Recycling Human Bodies." *Harper's Magazine* 249 (Sept.): 23–28.

German Surgical Society. 1968. "Definition of the Signs and Time of Death: Statement by the Commission on Reanimation and Organ Transplantation." *German Medical Monthly* 13:359.

Gervais, Karen Grandstand. 1986. *Redefining Death.* New Haven: Yale University Press.

Gordon, Theodore, Herbert Gerjuoy, and Mark Anderson, eds. 1979. *Life-Extending Technologies: A Technology Assessment.* New York: Pergamon Press.

Graber, Glenn C. 1979. "Some Questions about Double Effect." *Ethics in Science and Medicine* 6 (No. 1): 65–84.

Green, Michael B., and Daniel Wikler. 1980. "Brain Death and Personal Identity." *Philosophy and Public Affairs* 9 (No. 2, Winter): 105–33.

Green, Ronald M. 1976. "Health Care and Justice in Contract Theory Perspective." *Ethics and Health Policy.* Edited by Robert M. Veatch and Roy Branson. Cambridge, Mass.: Ballinger Publishing, pp. 111–26.

Greenwald, Harold P., and Michael C. Nevit. 1982. "Physician Attitudes Towards Communication with Cancer Patients." *Soc. Sci. Med.* 16 (No. 5): 591–94.

Grundfest-Broniatowski, S., and A. Novick. 1986. "Pancreas Transplantation—1985." *Transplantation Proceedings* 18 (No. 3, Suppl. 2, June): 31–39.

"Guidelines for 'No-Code' Orders in Los Angeles County Department of Health Services' Hospitals." 1983. *Deciding to Forego Life-Sustaining Treatment: Ethical, Medical, and Legal Issues in Treatment Decisions.* The President's Commission for the Study of Ethical Problems in Medicine and Biomedical and Behavioral Research. Washington, D.C.: U.S. Government Printing Office, pp. 510–11.

Gunby, Phil. 1983. "Panel Ponders Organ Procurement Problem." *Journal of the American Medical Association* 250 (July 22/29): 455–56.

———. 1984. "Organ Transplantation Improvements, Demands Draw Increasing Attention." *Journal of the American Medical Association* 251 (No. 12, March 23/30): 1521–23, 1526.

Halley, M. M., and W. F. Harvey, 1968a. "Law-Medicine Comment: The Definitional Dilemma of Death." *Journal of the Bar Association of the State of Kansas* 39:179.

———. 1968b. "Medical and Legal Definitions of Death." *Journal of the American Medical Association* 204:423–25.

Harber, Stephen. 1985. "Withholding Food and Water from a Patient—Should It Be Condoned in California?" *Pacific Law Journal* 16 (No. 3): 877–93.

Harman, D. 1969. "Prolongation of Life: Role of Free Radical Reactions in Aging." *Journal of the American Geriatric Society* 17:721–35.

Hastings Center. 1987. *Guidelines on the Termination of Life-Sustaining Treatment and the Care of the Dying.* Briarcliff Manor, N.Y.: The Hastings Center.

Hatfield, C. B. and R. E. Hatfield, P. H. S. Geggie, et al. 1983–84. "Attitudes about Death, Dying, and Terminal Care: Differences Among Groups at a University Teaching Hospital." *Omega* 14 (No. 1): 51–63.

Hayflick, Leonard. 1973. "The Biology of Human Aging." *The American Journal of the Medical Sciences* 265 (June): 432–45.

———. 1985. "Theories of Biological Aging." *Experimental Gerontology* 20 (No. 3–4): 145–59.

Healy, Edwin F. 1956. *Medical Ethics*. Chicago : Loyola University Press.

Hendin, David. 1973. *Death as a Fact of Life*. New York: W. W. Norton.

High, Dallas M. 1972. "Death: Its Conceptual Elusiveness." *Soundings* 56 (Winter): 438–58.

Hill, Robert Everage. 1980. "Euthanasia: The Right to be 'Let' Alone." *Southern University Law Review* 7 (No. 1): 101–12.

Hochschild, R. 1973. "Effects of Various Drugs on Longevity in Female C57BL/6J Mice." *Gerontologia* 19:271–80.

Holck, Frederick, ed. 1974. *Death and Eastern Thought*. Nashville, Tenn.: Abingdon.

Holman, Edwin J. 1972. "Adult Jehovah's Witnesses and Blood Transfusions." *Journal of the American Medical Association* 219:273–74.

Horan, Dennis J., and Edward R. Grant. 1984. "The Legal Aspects of Withdrawing Nourishment." *The Journal of Legal Medicine* 5 (no. 4): 595–632.

Howells, Kevin, and David Field. 1982. "Fear of Death and Dying Among Medical Students." *Social Science and Medicine* 16:1421–24.

Illich, Ivan. 1974. "The Political Uses of Natural Death." *Hastings Center Studies* 2 (No. 1, Jan.): 3–20.

Ingvar, D. H., and L. Widen. 1972. "Brain Death—Summary of a Symposium." *Lakartidningen* 34:3804–14.

Jackson, David, and Stuart Youngner. 1979. "Patient Autonomy and 'Death with Dignity.'" *New England Journal of Medicine* 301 (Aug. 31): 404–08.

Jakobovits, Immanuel. 1959. *Jewish Medical Ethics*. New York: Block Publishing.

Jonsen, Albert R., and Michael J. Garland, eds. 1976. *Ethics of Newborn Intensive Care*. Berkeley: University of California Press.

Jordan, Shannon M. 1985. *Decision Making For Incompetent Persons: The Law and Morality of Who Shall Decide*. Springfield, Ill.: Charles C. Thomas.

Judicial Council, American Medical Association. 1986. *Current Opinions of the Council on Ethical and Judicial Affairs of the American Medical Association—1986: Including the Principles of Medical Ethics and Rules of the Council on Ethical and Judicial Affairs*. Chicago: American Medical Association.

Kant, Immanuel. 1909 [1797]. "On the Supposed Right to Tell Lies from Benevolent Motives." Translated by Thomas Kingsmill Abbott and reprinted in Kant's *Critique of Practical Reason and Other Works on the Theory of Ethics*. London: Longmans, pp. 361–65.

Kass, Leon R. "Death as an Event: A Commentary on Robert Morison." *Science* 173:698–702.

Kaste, Markku, Matti Hillbom, and Jorma Palo. 1979. "Diagnosis and Management of Brain Death." *British Medical Journal* 1 (Feb. 24): 525–27.

Kelly, Gerald. 1950. "The Duty of Using Artificial Means of Preserving Life." *Theological Studies* 11:203–20.

———. 1958. *Medico-Moral Problems*. St. Louis: The Catholic Hospital Association.

Kelly, Margaret John, and Donald G. McCarthy, eds. 1984. *Ethics Committees: A Chal-*

lenge for Catholic Health Care, St. Louis, Mo.: The Pope John XXIII Medical-Moral Research and Education Center and The Catholic Health Association of the United States.

Kelly, William D., and Stanley R. Friesen. 1950. "Do Cancer Patients Want to Be Told?" *Surgery* 27:822–26.

Kennedy, Ian McCall. 1971. "The Kansas Statute on Death—An Appraisal." *New England Journal of Medicine* 285 (Oct. 21): 946–49.

———. 1979. "The Donation and Transplantation of Kidneys: Should the Law be Changed?" *Journal of Medical Ethics* 5:13–21.

Kohl, Marvin. 1974. *The Morality of Killing: Sanctity of Life, Abortion and Euthanasia*. New York: Humanities Press.

———, ed. 1975. *Beneficent Euthanasia*. Buffalo, N.Y.: Prometheus Books.

———, ed. 1978. *Infanticide and the Value of Life*. Buffalo, N.Y.: Prometheus Books.

Korein, J., and M. Maccaria. 1971. "On the Diagnosis of Cerebral Death: A Prospective Study on 55 Patients to Define Irreversible Coma." *Clinical Electroencephalography* 2:178–97.

Korein, J., P. Braunstein, G. Ajax, M. Wichter, I. Kricheff, A. Lieberman, and J. Pearson. 1977. "Brain Death: I. Angiographic Correlation with the Radioisotopic Bolus Technique for Evaluation of Critical Deficit of Cerebral Blood Flow." *Annals of Neurology* 2:195–205.

Kricheff, I. I., R. S. Pinto, A. E. George, P. Braunstein, and J. Korein. 1978. "Angiographic Findings in Brain Death." *Brain Death: Interrelated Medical and Social Issues*. Edited by Julius Korein. *Annals of The New York Academy of Sciences*, 315:168–83.

Kübler-Ross, Elisabeth. 1969. *On Death and Dying*. New York: Macmillan.

Kutner, Luis. 1979. "Euthanasia: Due Process for Death with Dignity; the Living Will." *Indiana Law Journal* 54 (No. 2) 201–28.

Ladimer, Irving. 1970. *The Challenge of Transplantation*, Public Affairs Pamphlet No. 451.

Lamb, David. 1985. *Death, Brain Death and Ethics*. Albany: State University of New York Press.

Law Reform Commission of Canada. 1981. *Criteria for the Determination of Death*. Ottawa, Ont.: Minister of Supply and Services.

Levine, Carol. 1977. "Hospital Ethics Committees: A Guarded Prognosis." *Hastings Center Report* 7 (June): 25–27.

Lief, Harold I. and Renée C. Fox. 1963. "Training for Detached Concern in Medical Students." *The Psychological Basis of Medical Practice*. Edited by Harold I. Lief, et al. New York: Harper and Row, pp. 12–25.

Lifton, Robert J. 1986. *Nazi Doctors*. New York: Basic Books.

Lorber, J. 1971. "Results of Treatment of Myelomeningocele." *Developmental Medicine and Child Neurology* 13 (No. 3): 279–303.

———. 1973. "Early Results of Selective Treatment of Spina Bifida Cystica." *British Medical Journal* 4 (Oct. 27): 201–04.

———. 1974. "Selective Treatment of Myelomeningocele: To Treat or Not to Treat?" *Pediatrics* 53 (March): 307–08.

Lubitz, J. and R. Prihoda. 1984. "The Use and Costs of Medicare Services in the Last Two Years of Life. *Health Care Financing Review* 5:117–31.

Lund, Charles C. 1946. "The Doctor, the Patient and the Truth." *Annals of Internal Medicine* 24:957–58.

Lynn, Joanne, ed. 1987. *The Choice to Forgo Life-Sustaining Food and Water: Medical, Ethical, and Legal Considerations*. Bloomington: Indiana University Press.

Lynn, Joanne, and James F. Childress. 1983. "Must Patients Always be Given Food and Water?" *The Hastings Center Report* 13 (Oct.): 17–21.

Lyons, Catherine. 1970. *Organ Transplants: The Moral Issues*. Philadelphia: Westminster Press.

Magnet, Joseph E., and Eike-Henner W. Kluge. 1985. *Withholding Treatment from Defective Newborn Children*. Quebec: Brown Legal Publications.

Manninen, Diane L., and Roger W. Evans. 1985. "Public Attitudes and Behavior Regarding Organ Donation." *Journal of the American Medical Association* 253 (No. 21, June 7): 3111–15.

Mansson, Helge Hilding. 1972. "Justifying the Final Solution." *Omega* 3:79–87.

Martyn, Susan R., and Lynn Balshone Jacobs. 1984. "Legislating Advance Directives for the Terminally Ill: Living Will and Durable Power of Attorney." *Nebraska Law Review* 63 (No. 4): 779–804.

Matas, Arthur J., and Frank J. Veith. 1984. "Presumed Consent for Organ Retrieval." *Theoretical Medicine* 5:155–66.

Matas, Arthur J., John Arras, James Muyskens, Vivian Tellis, and Frank J. Veith. 1985. "A Proposal for Cadaver Organ Procurement: Routine Removal with the Right of Informed Consent." *Journal of Health Politics, Policy and Law* 10 (No. 2, Summer): 231–44.

May, William F. 1972. "The Sacral Power of Death in Contemporary Culture." *Social Research* 39:463–88.

———. 1973. "Attitudes toward the Newly Dead." *Hastings Center Studies* 1 (No. 1): 3–13.

McCormick, Richard A. 1974. "To Save or Let Die: The Dilemma of Modern Medicine." *Journal of the American Medical Association* 229 (July 8): 172–76.

———. 1984. "Ethics Committees: Promise or Peril?" *Law, Medicine & Health Care* 12(4):150–55.

———. 1985a. "Was There Any Real Hope for Baby Fae?" *Hastings Center Report* 15 (No. 1, Feb.): 12–13.

———. 1985b. "Caring or Starving? The Case of Claire Conroy." *America* (April 6): 269–73.

McCormick, Richard A., and Paul Ramsey, eds. 1978. *Doing Evil to Achieve Good: Moral Choice in Conflict Situations*. Chicago: Loyola University Press.

McGinley, Tony. 1980. "The Right of Privacy and the Terminally-Ill Patient: Establishing the 'right-to-die.'" *Mercer Law Review* 31 (No. 2): 603–15.

Meilaender, Gilbert. 1984. "On Removing Food and Water: Against the Stream." *The Hastings Center Report* 14 (No. 6): 11–13.

Meisel, Grevnik A., R. L. Pinkus, and J. V. Snyder. 1986. "Hospital Guidelines for Deciding About Life-Sustaining Treatment: Dealing with Health 'Limbo.'" *Critical Care Medicine* 14 (March): 239–46.

Mellerio, F. 1971. "Clinical and EEG Study of a Case of Acute Poisoning with Cerebral Electrical Silence, Followed by Recovery." *Electroencephalography Clinical Neurophysiology* 30:270–71.

Meyer, Bernard. 1968. "Truth and the Physician." *Ethical Issues in Medicine*. Edited by E. Fuller Torrey. Boston: Little Brown, pp. 159–77.

Meyers, David W. 1970. *The Human Body and the Law.* Chicago: Aldine.

Micetich, Kenneth, Patricia Steinecker, and David Thomasma. 1983. "Are Intravenous Fluids Morally Required for a Dying Patient?" *Archives of Internal Medicine* 143:975–78.

Miller, George W. 1971. *Moral and Ethical Implications of Human Organ Transplantation.* Springfield, Ill.: Charles C. Thomas.

Mishkin, Barbara. 1986. *A Matter of Choice: Planning Ahead For Health Care Decisions.* Washington, D.C.: American Association of Retired Persons.

Mohandas, A., and Shelley N. Chou. 1971. "Brain Death: A Clinical and Pathological Study." *Journal of Neurosurgery* 35 (Aug.): 211–18.

Moore, Maureen L. 1983. "Their Life is in the Blood: Jehovah's Witnesses, Blood Transfusions and the Courts." *Northern Kentucky Law Review* 10 (No. 2): 281–304.

Morison, Robert S. 1971. "Death: Process or Event?" *Science* 173:694–98.

———. 1978. "Misgivings about Life-Extending Technologies." *Daedalus* 107:211–26.

———. 1974. "The Last Poem: The Dignity of the Inevitable and Necessary." *Hastings Center Studies* 2 (No. 2, May): 63–66.

Mount, Balfour M., Allan Jones, and Andrew Patterson. 1974. "Death and Dying: Attitudes in a Teaching Hospital." *Urology* 4 (Dec.): 741–47.

Nelson, James B. 1973. "Organ Transplants: Their Human Dimensions." In *Human Medicine: Ethical Perspectives and New Medical Issues.* Minneapolis: Ausburg, pp. 149–70.

Netherlands Red Cross Society. 1971. *Summary of the Report of the Ad Hoc Committee on Organ Transplantation.*

Neuggarten, Bernice. 1972. "Social Implications of a Prolonged Life Span." *The Gerontologist* 12 (Winter): 438–40.

New Jersey Guidelines for Prognosis Committees. No date. "Guidelines for Health Care Facilities to Implement Procedures Concerning the Care of Comatose Non-Cognitive Patients."

New York State Task Force on Life and the Law, The. 1986. *Do Not Resuscitate Orders: The Proposed Legislation and Report of the New York State Task Force on Life and the Law.* N.P.: The New York State Task Force on Life and the Law.

Nilges, Richard G. 1984. "The Ethics of Brain Death: Thoughts of a Neurosurgeon Considering Retirement." *The Pharos of Alpha Omega Alpha* 47 (Spring): 34–35.

"Nondiscrimination on the Basis of Handicap, Procedures and Guidelines Relating to Health Care for Handicapped Infants, Final Rule." 49 *Federal Register* No. 8, 1622, January 12, 1984 (Part 84): 1622–55.

Novack, Dennis H., Robin Plumer, Raymond L. Smith, Herbert Ochitil, Gary R. Morrow, and John M. Bennett. 1979. "Changes in Physicians' Attitudes Toward Telling the Cancer Patient." *Journal of the American Medical Association* 241 (March 2): 897–900.

"Ohio Battery Suit: Galvin v. University Hospitals." 1986. *Society for the Right to Die Newsletter* (Fall): 5.

Oken, Donald. 1961. "What to Tell Cancer Patients: A Study of Medical Attitudes." *Journal of the American Medical Association* 175:1120–28.

Outka, Gene. 1974. "Social Justice and Equal Access to Health Care." *Journal of Religious Ethics* 2 (Spring): 11–32.

Pallis, Christopher. 1983. "ABC of Brain Stem Death: The Position in the USA and Elsewhere." *British Medical Journal* 286 (Jan. 15): 209–10.

Paris, John J. 1986. "When Burdens of Feeding Outweigh Benefits." *Hastings Center Report* 16 (Feb.): 30–32.

Paris, John J., and Anne B. Fletcher. 1983. "Infant Doe Regulations and the Absolute Requirement to Use Nourishment and Fluids for the Dying Infant." *Law, Medicine and Health Care* 11 (No. 5): 210–13.

Paris, John J., and Frank E. Reardon. 1985. "Court Responses to Withholding or Withdrawing Artificial Nutrition and Fluids." *Journal of the American Medical Association* 253 (No. 15, April 19): 2243–45.

Parker, Robert J., and Herbert Gerjuoy. 1979. "Life-Span Extension: The State of the Art." *Life Span—Values and Life-Extending Technologies.* Edited by Robert M. Veatch. San Francisco: Harper and Row, pp. 3–26.

Parsons, Talcott, and Victor Lidz. 1967. "Death in American Society." *Essays in Self-Destruction.* Edited by Edwin S. Schneidman. New York: Science House, pp. 133–70.

Parsons, Talcott, Renée C. Fox, and Victor Lidz. 1972. "The 'Gift of Life' and Its Reciprocation." *Social Research* 39:367–415.

Pearson, J., J. Korein, J. H. Harris, M. Wichter, and P. Braunstein. 1977. "Brain Death: II. Neuropathological Correlation with the Radioisotopic Bolus Technique for Evaluation of Critical Deficit of Cerebral Blood Flow." *Annals of Neurology* 2:206–10.

Peck, Arthur. 1972. "Emotional Reactions to Having Cancer." *CA: A Cancer Journal for Physicians* 22 (Sept.–Oct.): 2984–91.

Peters, David A. 1984. "Marketing Organs for Transplantation." *Dialysis & Transplantation* 13 (Jan.): 40–41.

———. 1986. "Protecting Autonomy in Organ Procurement Procedures: Some Overlooked Issues." *The Milbank Quarterly* 64 (No. 2): 241–70.

Piatt, Louis M. 1946. "The Physician and the Cancer Patient." *Ohio State Medical Journal* 42:371–72.

Pope Pius XII. 1958. "The Prolongation of Life: An Address of Pope Pius XII to an International Congress of Anesthesiologists." *The Pope Speaks* 4 (Spring): 393–98.

President's Commission for the Study of Ethical Problems in Medicine and Biomedical and Behavioral Research. 1981. *Defining Death: Medical, Legal and Ethical Issues in the Definition of Death.* Washington, D.C.: U.S. Government Printing Office.

President's Commission for the Study of Ethical Problems in Medicine and Biomedical and Behavioral Research. 1983. *Deciding to Forego Life-Sustaining Treatment: Ethical, Medical, and Legal Issues in Treatment Decisions.* Washington, D.C.: U.S. Government Printing Office.

Project on Organ Transplantation. 1985. *Ethical, Legal and Policy Issues Pertaining to Solid Organ Procurement.* New York: Hastings Center.

Public Law 98–507, October 19, 1984. *National Organ Transplant Act,* 98 Stat. 2339.

Rachels, James. 1975. "Active and Passive Euthanasia." *New England Journal of Medicine* 292:78–80.

———. 1979. "Euthanasia, Killing, and Letting Die." *Medical Responsibility: Paternalism, Informed Consent, and Euthanasia.* Edited by Wade L. Robison and Michael S. Pritchard. Clifton, N.J.: The Humana Press, pp. 153–68.

———. 1986. *The End of Life: Euthanasia and Morality.* Oxford: Oxford University Press.

Ramsey, Paul. 1970. *The Patient as Person.* New Haven: Yale University Press.

———. 1974. "The Indignity of 'Death with Dignity.'" *Hastings Center Studies* 2 (No. 2, May): 47–62.

Rapaport, Felix T. 1987. "A Rational Approach to a Common Goal: The Equitable Distribution of Organs for Transplantation [Editorial]." *Journal of the American Medical Association* 257 (No. 22, June 12): 3118–19.

Rea, M. Priscilla, Shirley Greenspoon, and Bernard Spilka. 1975. "Physicians and the Terminal Patient: Some Selected Attitudes and Behavior." *Omega* 6 (No. 4): 291–302.

Regan, Tom. 1985. "The Other Victim." *Hastings Center Report* 15 (No. 1, Feb.): 9–10.

Report by a Working Party. 1975. "Ethics of Selective Treatment of Spina Bifida." *Lancet* 1 (Jan. 11): 85–88.

"Report of the Medical Consultants on the Diagnosis of Death to the President's Commission for the Study of Ethical Problems in Medicine and Biomedical and Behavioral Research." 1981. President's Commission for the Study of Ethical Problems in Medicine and Biomedical and Behavioral Research. *Defining Death: Medical, Legal and Ethical Issues in the Definition of Death.* Washington, D.C.: U.S. Government Printing Office, pp. 159–66.

"Report of the National Institutes of Health on Baby Fae." 1985. *Spectrum* 16 (No. 1): 19–26.

Reynolds, Frank E., and Earle H. Waugh, eds. 1976. *Religious Encounters with Death: Essays in the History and Anthropology of Religion.* University Park: Pennsylvania State University Press.

Rhoden, Nancy. 1985. "Treatment Dilemmas for Imperiled Newborns: Why Quality of Life Counts." *Southern California Law Review* 58 (No. 6, Sept.): 1283–1347.

Riley, Gerald, James Lubitz, Ronald Prihoda, and Mary Ann Stevenson. 1986. "Changes in Distribution of Medicare Expenditures Among Aged Enrollees, 1969–82. *Health Care Financing Review* 7 (No. 3): 53–63.

Robertson, John. 1975. "Involuntary Euthanasia of Defective Newborns: A Legal Analysis." *Stanford Law Review* 27 (Jan.): 213–67.

Rosner, Fred. 1972. *Modern Medicine and Jewish Law.* New York: Yeshiva University Press.

———. 1985. "Artificial and Baboon Heart Implantation: The Jewish View." *Archives of Internal Medicine* 145 (July): 1330.

Rosner, Fred, and David J. Bleich, eds. 1979. *Jewish Bioethics.* New York: Sanhedrin Press.

Rosoff, S. D., and R. S. Scwab. 1968. "The EEG in Establishing Brain Death: A 10-Year Report with Criteria and Legal Safeguards in the 50 States." *Electroencephalography and Clinical Neurophysiology* 24:283–84.

Sadler, Alfred M., and Blair L. Sadler. 1968. "Transplantation and the Law: The Need for Organized Sensitivity." *Georgetown Law Journal* 57 (No. 1, Oct.): 9–13.

Sadler, A. M., B. L. Sadler, and E. Blythe Stason. 1968. "The Uniform Anatomical Gift Act." *Journal of the American Medical Association* 206 (Dec. 9): 2501–06.

Samp, Robert J., and Anthony R. Curreri. 1957. "A Questionnaire Survey on Public Cancer Education Obtained from Cancer Patients and Their Families." *Cancer* 10:382–84.

Scitovsky, Anne A. 1984. "The High Cost of Dying: What Do the Data Show?" *Milbank Memorial Fund Quarterly* 62 (No. 4): 591–608.

Scitovsky, A. A., and A. M. Capron. 1986. "Medical Care at the End of Life: The Interaction of Economics and Ethics." *Annual Review of Public Health* 7:59–75.

Sendak, Lawrence R. 1978. "Suicide and the Compulsion of Lifesaving Medical Procedures: An Analysis of the Refusal of Treatment Cases." *Brooklyn Law Review* 44 (No. 2): 285–316.

Sharpe, David J., and Robert F. Hargest, 3d. 1968. "Lifesaving Treatment for Unwilling Patients." *Fordham Law Review* 36:695–706.

Shaub, Henry Z. 1980. "The Right to Refuse Medical Treatment: Under What Circumstances Does It Exist? *Duquesne Law Review* 18 (No. 3): 607–28.

Shelp, Earl E. 1986. *Born To Die? Deciding The Fate of Critically Ill Newborns*. New York: Free Press.

Sherlock, Richard. 1987. *Preserving Life: Public Policy and the Life Not Worth Living*. Chicago: Loyola University Press.

Shock, Nathan W. 1985. "The Physiological Basis of Aging." *Frontiers in Medicine—Implications for the Future*. Edited by Robert J. Morin and Richard J. Bing. New York: Human Sciences Press, pp. 300–312.

Siegler, Mark, and Alan J. Weisbard. 1985. "Against the Emerging Stream: Should Fluids and Nutritional Support Be Discontinued?" *Archives of Internal Medicine* 145: 129–31.

Silverman, Daniel, Richard L. Masland, Michael G. Saunders, and Robert S. Schwab. 1970. "Irreversible Coma Associated with Electrocerebral Silence." *Neurology* 20:525–33.

Smith, G. Keys, and E. Durham Smith. 1973. "Selection for Treatment in Spina Bifida Cystica." *British Medical Journal* 4 (Oct. 27): 189–97.

Society for the Right to Die. 1985. *The Physician and the Hopelessly Ill Patient: Legal, Medical and Ethical Guidelines*. New York: Society for the Right to Die.

Solnick, Paul B. 1984. "Withdrawal and Withholding of Life-Support in Terminally Ill Patients. Part 1." *Medicine and Law* 3:4309–32.

Somers, Anne R. 1982. "Long-Term Care for the Elderly and Disabled." *New England Journal of Medicine* 307:222.

Starzl, Thomas E. 1984. "Implied Consent for Cadaveric Organ Donation [Editorial]." *Journal of the American Medical Association* 251 (No. 12,, March 23/30): 1592.

Starzl, Thomas E., Thomas R. Hakala, Andreas Tzakis, Robert Gordon, Anderi Steiber, Leonard Makowka, Joeta Klimoski, and Henry T. Bahnson. 1987. "A Multifactorial System for Equitable Selection of Cadaver Kidney Recipients." *Journal of the American Medical Association* 257 (No. 22, June 12): 3073–75.

Stead, Eugene. 1972. "A Physician's Instructions on Final Care." *Medical World News* 13 (April 7): 47.

Stein, Sherman C., Luis Schut, and Mary D. Ames. 1974. "Selection for Early Treatment in Myelomeningocele: A Retrospective Analysis of Various Selection Procedures." *Pediatrics* 54 (Nov.): 553–56.

Steinfels, Peter, and Robert M. Veatch, eds. 1975. *Death Inside Out*. New York: Harper and Row.

Stendahl, Krister. 1965. *Immortality and Resurrection*. New York: Macmillan.

Strand, John G. 1976. "The 'Living Will': The Right to Death with Dignity?" *Case Western Reserve Law Review* 26 (No. 2): 485–526.

Stuart, Frank P., Frank J. Veith, and Ronald E. Cranford. 1981. "Brain Death Laws and Patterns of Consent to Remove Organs for Transplantation from Cadavers in the United States and 28 Other Countries." *Transplantation* 31 (April): 238–44.

Sullivan, Joseph V. 1973. *Catholic Teaching on the Morality of Euthanasia*. Washington: Catholic University of America Press.

Sullivan, Michael T. 1973. "The Dying Person—His Plight and His Right." *New England Law Review* 8:197–216.

Swazey, Judith P., and Renée C. Fox. 1970. "The Clinical Moratorium: A Case Study of Mitral Valve Surgery." *Experimentation with Human Subjects.* Edited by Paul E. Freund. New York: George Braziller, pp. 315–57.

Swinyard, Chester A. 1971. *The Child with Spina Bifida.* New York: Institute of Rehabilitation Medicine.

Task Force on Death and Dying of the Institute of Society, Ethics and the Life Sciences. 1972. "Refinements in Criteria for the Determination of Death: An Appraisal." *Journal of the American Medical Association* 221:48–53.

Task Force on Organ Transplantation. 1985. *Report to the Secretary and the Congress on Immunosuppressive Therapies.* Washington, D.C.: United States Department of Health and Human Services, October.

———. 1986. *Organ Transplantation: Issues and Recommendations.* Washington, D.C.: United States Department of Health and Human Services.

Teel, Karen. 1975. "The Physician's Dilemma: A Doctor's View: What the Law Should Be." *Baylor Law Review* 27:6–9.

The Tibetan Book of the Dead. 1973. Trans. W. Y. Evans-Wentz. 1973. New York: Causeway Books.

Thomson, Judith Jarvis. 1976. "Killing, Letting Die and the Trolley Problem." *The Monist* 59 (April): 204–17.

Tomlinson, Tom. 1984. "The Conservative Use of the Brain-Death Criterion—A Critique." *Journal of Medicine and Philosophy* 9:377–93.

Toole, James F. 1971. "The Neurologist and the Concept of Brain Death." *Perspectives in Biology and Medicine* 14:599–607.

Travis, Terry A., Russell Noyes, Jr., and Dennis R. Brightwell. 1974. "The Attitudes of Physicians Toward Prolonging Life." *International Journal of Psychiatry in Medicine* 5 (No. 1): 17–26.

Twycross, Robert G. 1982. "Ethical and Clinical Aspects of Pain Treatment in Cancer Patients." *Acta. Anaesth. Scand.* Supplement. 74:83–90.

Ueki, K., K. Takeuchi, and K. Katsurada. 1973. "Clinical Study of Brain Death." Presentation No. 286. Fifth International Congress of Neurological Surgery. Tokyo, Japan.

U.S. Department of Health and Human Services. 1985a. "Infant Care Review Committees—Model Guidelines." *Federal Register: Notices* 50 (No. 72, April 15): 14893–901.

———. 1985b. "Child Abuse and Neglect Prevention and Treatment Program: Final Rule: 45 CFR 1340." *Federal Register: Rules and Regulations* 50 (No. 72, April 15): 14878–892.

United States House of Representatives. 1984. *Procurement and Allocation of Human Organs for Transplantation: Hearings Before the Subcommittee on Investigations and Oversight of the Committee on Science and Technology.* 98th Congress, First Session, November 7, 9, 1983. Washington, D.C.: U.S. Government Printing Office.

Veatch, Robert M. 1971. "Doing What Comes Naturally." *Hastings Center Report* 1 (No. 1, Sept.): 1–3.

———. 1976. *Value-Freedom in Science and Technology: A Study of the Religious, Ethical and Other Socio-Cultural Factors in Selected Medical Decisions Regarding Birth Control.* Missoula, Montana: Scholars Press.

———. 1977. "Hospital Ethics Committees: Is There a Role?" *Hastings Center Report* 7 (June): 22–25.

————. 1978. "The Definition of Death: Ethical, Philosophical, and Policy Confusion." *Brain Death: Interrelated Medical and Social Issues.* Edited by Julius Korein. *Annals of The New York Academy of Sciences,* pp. 307–21.

————, ed. 1979. *Life Span: Values and Life-Extending Technologies.* San Francisco: Harper and Row.

————. 1981. *A Theory of Medical Ethics.* New York: Basic Books.

————. 1982. "Maternal Brain Death: An Ethicist's Thoughts." Editorial in *Journal of the American Medical Association* 248 (Sept. 3): 1102–03.

————. 1983a. "Definitions of Life and Death: Should There Be Consistency?" *Defining Human Life.* Edited by Margery W. Shaw and A. Edward Doudera. Ann Arbor, Mich.: AUPHA Press, pp. 99–113.

————. 1983b. "Ethics Committees: Are They Legitimate?" *Ethics Committee Newsletter* 1 (Nov.): 1–2.

————. 1984a. "Limits of Guardian Treatment Refusal: A Reasonableness Standard." *American Journal of Law and Medicine* 9 (4, Winter): 427–68.

————. 1984b. "The Ethics of Institutional Ethics Committees." *Institutional Ethics Committees and Health Care Decision Making.* Edited by Ronald E. Cranford and A. Edward Doudera. Ann Arbor, Mich.: American Society of Law and Medicine, pp. 35–50.

————. 1985. "From Fae to Schroeder: The Ethics of Allocating High Technology." *Spectrum* 16 (No. 1): 15–18.

————. 1986a. "The Ethics of Xenografts." *Transplantation Proceedings* 18 (No. 3, Suppl. 2, June): 93–97.

————. 1986b. *The Foundations of Justice: Why the Retarded and the Rest of Us Have Claims to Equality.* New York: Oxford University Press.

————. 1987. "Distributive Justice and the Allocation of Technological Resources to the Elderly." *Life-Sustaining Technologies and the Elderly: Working Papers, Volume 3: Legal and Ethical Issues, Manpower and Training, and Classification System for Decision-making.* Washington, D.C.: U.S. Congress, Office of Technology Assessment, pp. 87–189.

————. 1988. "The Definition of Death: Problems for Public Policy." *Dying: Facing the Facts.* 2d edition. Edited by Hannelore Wass, Felix M. Berardo, and Robert A. Neimeyer. Washington, D.C.: Hemisphere Publishing Corporation, pp. 29–53.

Veatch, Robert M., and Ernest Tai. "Talking About Death: Patterns of Lay and Professional Change." *Annals of the American Academy of Political and Social Science* 447 (January 1980): 29–45.

Veith, Frank J., Jack M. Fein, Moses S. Tendler, Robert M. Veatch, Marc A. Kleiman, and George Kalkinis. 1977. "Brain Death: I. A Status Report of Medical and Ethical Considerations." *Journal of the American Medical Association* 238:1651–55.

Vorys, Yolanda V. 1981. "The Outer Limits of Parental Autonomy: Withholding Medical Treatment from Children." *Ohio State Law Journal* 43 (No. 3): 813–29.

Walford, Roy. 1983. *Maximum Life Span.* New York: W. W. Norton.

Walker, A. Earl. 1981. *Cerebral Death.* Baltimore-Munich: Urban & Schwarzenberg.

Walker, A. Earl, Earl L. Diamond, and John Moseley. 1975. "The Neuropathological Findings in Irreversible Coma." *Journal of Neuropathology and Experimental Neurology* 34:295–323.

Walker, A. Earl, et al. 1977 "An Appraisal of the Criteria of Cerebral Death—A Summary Statement." *Journal of the American Medical Association* 237:982–86.

Walker, A. E., and G. F. Molinari. 1977. "The Clinical Applicability of Sedative Drug Surveys in Coma." *Postgraduate Medicine* 61 (April 4): 105–09.

Walshe, Thomas M., and Cheryl Leonard. 1985. "Persistent Vegetative State." *Archives of Neurology* 42:1045–47.

Warren, David G. 1972. "Developing a New Definition of Death." *Health Law Bulletin* (No. 35, July): 3.

Weinstein, Bruce D., ed. 1986. *Ethics in the Hospital Setting: Proceedings of the West Virginia Conference on Hospital Ethics Committees.* Morgantown: The West Virginia University Press.

Weir, Robert. 1984. *Selective Nontreatment of Handicapped Newborns.* Oxford: Oxford University Press.

Williams, Bernard. 1973. "The Makropulos Case: Reflections on the Tedium of Immortality." In *Problems of the Self.* Cambridge: Cambridge University Press, pp. 82–100.

Williams, Robert H. 1973. "Propagation, Modification, and Termination of Life: Contraception, Abortion, Suicide, Euthanasia." *To Live and To Die.* Edited by Robert H. Williams. New York: Springer-Verlag, pp. 80–97.

Wish, J. B. 1986. "Immunologic Effects of Cyclosporine." *Transplantation Proceedings* 18 (No. 3, Suppl. 2, June): 15–18.

Wolstenholme, G. E. W. ed. 1966. *Ethics in Medical Progress: With Special Reference to Transplantation.* Boston: Little, Brown.

Woodhead, Avril D., Anthony D. Blackett, and Alexander Hollaender. 1985. *Molecular Biology of Aging.* New York: Plenum Press. [*Basic Life Sciences* 35 (1985).]

Working Party. 1979. *The Removal of Cadaveric Organs for Transplantation: A Code of Practice.* Health Depts. Great Britain and Ireland: H. M. Stationary's Office.

Young, Stephen Grant. 1963. "Parent and Child—Compulsory Medical Care Over Objections of Parents." *West Virginia Law Review* 65:184–87.

Youngner, Stuart J., David L. Jackson, Claudia Coulton, Barbara J. Juknialis, and Era Smith. 1983. "A National Survey of Hospital Ethics Committees." President's Commission for the Study of Ethical Problems in Medicine and Biomedical and Behavioral Research. *Deciding to Forego Life-Sustaining Treatment: Ethical, Medical, and Legal Issues in Treatment Decisions.* Washington, D.C.: U.S. Government Printing Office, pp. 443–57.

Zachary, R. B. 1968. "Ethical and Social Aspects of Treatment of Spina Bifida." *Lancet* 2 (Aug. 24): 274–76.

Legal Cases

In re Baptista, 206 F. Supp. 288 (W.D. Mo. 1962).

Barber v. Superior Court, 147 Cal. App. 3d 1006, 195 Cal. Rptr. 484 (Ct. App. 1983).

Bartling v. Superior Court (Glendale Adventist Medical Center, et al., Real Parties in Interest), 163 Cal. App. 3d 186 (Cal. App. 2d 1984).

Barnette v. Potenza 359 N.Y.S.2d 432 (1970), 79 Misc. 2d 51.

In re Phillip Becker, 92 Cal. App. 3d 796, 156 Cal. Rptr. 48 (1979), *cert denied sub nom.* Bothman v. Warren B., 445 U.S. 949 (1980).

Guardianship of Phillip Becker, No. 101–981, at 4 (Cal. Super Ct., Aug. 7, 1981), *aff'd.*, 139 Cal. App. 3d 407, 420, 199 Cal. Rptr. 781, 789 (1983).

Berkey v. Anderson. Cal. App. 3d 790, 805, 82 Cal. Rptr. 46.

Application of Brooklyn Hospital, 45 Misc. 2d. 914, 258 N.Y.S.2d 621 (1965).

In re Estate of Brooks, 32 Ill.2d 361, 205 N. E.2d.435 (1965).

Bouvia v. County of Riverside, No. 159780 (Cal. Super. Ct. Dec. 16, 1983).

Bouvia v. Superior Court of Los Angeles County, California Court of Appeal, Second District, 1986. 179 Cal. App. 3d 1127, 225 Cal. Rptr. 297, (Ct. App.), *review denied* (June 5, 1986).

Brophy v. New England Sinai Hospital, Inc. 398 Mass. 417, 497 N.E.2d 626 (1986).

Canterbury v. Spence, 464 F.2d 772 (D.C. Cir.), *cert. denied,* 409 U.S. 1064 (1972).

Cantor v. Weiss, No. 626 163 (Cal. Super. Ct. Los Angeles County Dec. 30, 1986) (Newman, J.).

In re Carstairs, 115 N.Y.S.2d 314 (Dom. Rel. Ct. 1952).

In re Chetter (LaSala), No. 1086/87 (N.Y. Sup. Ct. Nassau County May 1, 1987) (Becker, J.).

In re Clark, 210 N.J. Super. 548, 510, A.2d 136 (Super. Ct. Ch. Div. 1986).

Cobbs v. Grant 520 P.2d 1 (Cal. 1972).

Collins v. Davis, 254 N.Y.S.2d 666 (1964).

In re Conroy, 98 N.J. 321, 486 A.2d 1209 (1985).

Cooper v. Roberts 286 A.2d 647 (Pa. 1971).

Corbett v. D'Alessandro. 487 So. 2d 368 (Fla. Dist. Ct. App. 1986), *review denied,* 492 So. 2d 1331 (Fla. 1986).

Delio v. Westchester County Medical Center, 134 Misc. 2d 206, 510 N.Y.S.2d 415 (Sup. Ct. Westchester County 1986), 516 N.Y.S.2d 677, *rev'd,* 129 A.D.2d1 516 N.Y.S.2d 677 (1987).

In re Dinnerstein, 6 Mass. App. Ct. 466, 380 N.E.2d 134 (App. Ct. 1978).

In re Infant Doe, No. GU 8204–00 (Cir. Ct. Monroe County, Ind. April 12, 1982), *writ of mandamus dismissed sub nom.* State *ex rel.*

Infant Doe v. Baker, No. 482 S. 140 (Ind. Supreme Ct., May 27, 1982) (Case mooted by child's death).

Dow v. Permanente Medical Group 90 Cal. Rptr. 747 (Cal. 1970).

In re Eichner (*In re* Storar), 52 N.Y.2d 363, 420 N.E.2d 64, 438 N.Y.S.2d 266, *cert. denied,* 454 U.S. 858 (1981).

Erickson v. Dilgard, 44 Misc. 2d 27, 252 N.Y.S.2d 705 (Supp. Ct. 1962).

People v. Eulo, 63 N.Y.2d 341, 472 N.E.2d 286, 482 N.Y.S.2d 436 (1984).

In re Farrell, 212 N.J. Super. 294, 514 A.2d 1342 (N.J. Super. Ct. Ch. Div. 1986), *motion for direct certification granted* (N.J. July 11, 1986).

Foster v. Tourtellotte, No. CV 81–5046–RMT (C.D. Cal. Nov. 16, 17, 1981), 704 F.2d. 1109 (9th Cir. 1983).

In re Frank, 41 Wash. 2d 294, 248 P.2d 553 (1942).

Gilbert v. State, 487 So. 2d 1185 (Fla. App. 4 Dist. 1986).

U.S. v. George, 33 U.S.L.W. 2518 (D.C., Conn., March 24, 1985).

In re President and Directors of Georgetown College, Inc., 333 F.2d 1000 (D.C. Cir.), *cert. denied sub nom.* Jones v. President and Directors of Georgetown College, Inc., 377 U.S. 978 (1964).

In re Green, 292 A.2d 387 (Pa. Sup. Ct. 1972).

In re Guardianship of Grant, No. 52509–5 (Wash. Nov. 20, 1986) (order with opinion to follow).

Griswold v. Connecticut, 381 U.S. 479, 88 S. Ct. 1678, 14 L.Ed.2d 510 (1965).

In re Lydia E. Hall Hospital, 116 Misc. 2d 477, 455 N.Y.S.2d. 706 (Sup. Ct. Nassau County 1982); 117 Misc.2d 1024, 459 N.Y.S.2d 682 (Sup. Ct. Nassau County 1982).

Hazelton [sic] v. Powhatan Nursing Home, Inc., No. CH 98287 (Va. Cir. Ct. Fairfax County Aug. 29, 1986), order signed (Sept. 2, 1986), (Fortkort, J.), *appeal denied*, Record No. 860814 (Va. Sept. 2, 1986).

Heinemann's Appeal, 96 Pa. 112, 42 Am. Rep. 532 (Ct. of App. 1880).

In re Heir, 18 Mass. App. 200, 464 N.E.2d 959 (Ct. App.), *review denied*, 392 Mass. 1102, 465 N.E.2d 261 (1984).

Hoener v. Bertinato, 67 N.J. Super. 517, 171 A.2d 140 (1961).

In re Hudson, 13 Wash. 2d 673, 126 P.2d 765 (1942).

Hunter v. Brown, 4 Wash. App. 899, 484 P.2d 1162 (1972).

In re Jobes, 210 N.J. Super. 543, 510 A.2d 133 (Super Ct. Ch. Div. April 23, 1986), *review denied* (N.J. March 10, 1986), *cert. granted* (N.J. Sept. 10, 1986), No. A–108/109, slip. op. (N.J. June 24, 1987).

John F. Kennedy Memorial Hospital, Inc. v. Delores Heston and Jane Heston, 58 N.J. 576, 279 A.2d 670 (N.J. Sup. Ct. 1971).

Leach v. Akron General Medical Center, 68 Ohio Misc. 1, 22 Ohio Ops. 3d 49, 426 N.E.2d 809 (Com. Pl. 1980).

Leach v. Shapiro, 13 Ohio App. 3d 393, 469 N.E.2d 1047 (Ct. App. 1984).

In re L.H.R., 253 Ga. 439, 321 S.E.2d. 716 (1984).

Martin v. Stratton 515 P.2d 1366 (Okla. 1973).

Mitchell v. Davis, 205 S.W.2d 812 (Tex. Civ. App. 1947).

Morrison v. State, 252 S.W.2d 97 (C.A. Kansas City, Mo., 1952).

Natanson v. Kline, 186 Kan. 393, 350 P.2d 1093, *clarified*, 187 Ka. 1986, 354 P.2d 670 (1960).

Oakley v. Jackson, 1 K.B. 216 (1914).

Frances Okun v. The Society of New York Hospitals, Sup. Ct. of the State of New York. County of New York. Summons, Index Number 13167.84, June 1, 1984.

In re Charles P. Osborne, 294 A.2d 372 (D.C. Cir. 1972).

Peek v. Ciccone, 288 F. Supp. 329 (W.D. Mo. 1968).

State v. Perricone, 37 N.J. 463, 181 A.2d 751, *cert. denied*, 371 U.S. 890 (1962).

In re Peter, N.J. Supreme Ct., No. A–78, slip. op. (June 24, 1987).

In re Phelps, No. 459–207 (Milwaukee County Ct., filed July 11, 1982).

People v. Pierson, 176 N.Y. 201, 68 N.E. 243 (1903).

In re Application of Plaza Health and Rehabilitation Center (N.Y. Sup. Ct., Onondaga County Feb. 2, 1984) (Miller, J.).

Frince v. Massachusetts, 321 U.S. 158, 166–7 (1944).

Pouce v. Society of Sisters, 268 U.S. 510 (1925).

Powell v. Columbian [sic] Presbyterian Medical Center, et al., 49 Misc.2d 450 (Sup. Ct. 1965).

In re Quakenbush, 156 N.J. Super. 282, 383 A.2d 785 (1978).

In re Quinlan, 137 N.J. Super. 227, 348 A.2d 801 (Super. Ct. Chancery Div., 1975).

In re Quinlan, 70 N.J. 10, 355 A. 2d 647 (1976), *cert. denied sub nom.*, Garger v. New Jersey, 429 U.S. 922 (1976), *overruled in part*, in re Conroy, 98 N.J. 321, 486 A.2d 1209 (1985).

Raleigh Fitkin-Paul Morgan Memorial Hospital v. Anderson, 42 N.J. 421, 201 A.2d. 537 (1964), *cert. denied*, 337 U.S. 985 (1964).

Ramsay v. Ciccone, 310 F. Supp. 600 (Mo., 1970).

In re Requena, 213 N.J. Super. 443, 517 A.2d 869 (Super Ct. App. Div. 1986) (per curiam).

In re Rodas, No. 86PR139 (Colo. Dist. Ct. Mesa County, Jan. 22, 1987) (Buss, J.).

Roe v. Wade, 410 U.S. 113 (93 S.Ct. 705, 1973).

In re Rotkowitz, 175 Misc. 948, 25 N.Y.S.2d 624 (Dom. Rel. Ct. 1941).

Superintendent of Belchertown State School v. Saikewicz, 373 Mass. 728, 370 N.E.2d 417 (1977).

In re Sampson, 328 N.Y.S.2d 686, 278 N.E.2d 918 (Ct. App. 1972).

In re Santos, 16 A.D.2d 755, 227 N.Y.S.2d 450, *appeal dismissed*, 232 N.Y.S.2d 1026 (1962).

Satz v. Perlmutter, 362 So. 2d 160 (Fla. Dist. Ct. App. 1978), *aff'd*, 379 So. 2d 359 (Fla. Sup. Ct. 1980).

Schloendorff v. Society of New York Hospital, 211 N.Y. 125, 105 N.E. 92 (1914).

In re Seiferth, 127 N.Y.S.2d, *rev'd.*, 284 App. Div. 221, 137 N.Y.S.2d 35 (1955), 285 A.D. 221.

In re Severns, 425 A.2d 156 (Del. Ch. 1980).

Severns v. Wilmington Medical Center, Inc., 421 A.2d 1334 (Del. 1980).

Smith v. Baker, 726 F. Supp. 787 (W.D. Mo. 1970).

New York City Health and Hospitals Corporation v. Paula Stein, 335 N.Y.S.2d 461 (1972).

In re Storar. See *In re* Eichner.

In re Torres, 357 N.W.2d 332 (Minn. 1984).

In re Triarsi, No. 86–14241 (N.Y. Sup. Ct. Suffolk County Aug. 21, 1986) (Yachim, J.); N.Y.L.J. Sept. 18, 1986, at 12, col. 5.

In re Tuttendario, 21 Pa. Dist. 561 (Quar. Sess., Phila. Co. 1911).

In re Vasko, 238 App. Div. 128, 263 N.Y.S. 522 (1933).

Veal v. Ciccone, 281 F. Supp. 1017 (W.D. Mo. 1968).

In re Visbeck, 210 N.J. Super. 527, 510 A.2d 125 (Super. Ct. Ch. Div. 1986).

In re Vogel, 134 Misc. 2d 395, 512 N.Y.S.2d 622 (Sup. Ct. Nassau County 1986), *notice of appeal filed* (App. Div. 2d Dep't Dec. 22, 1986).

People *ex. rel.* Wallace v. Labrenz, 411 Ill. 613, 104 N.E.2d 769 (1952).

State v. Watson 191 N.J. Super. 464 (1983).

Weber v. Stony Brook Hospital, New York State, Supreme Court, Appellate Division, 489 N.E. 2d 1193.

Weber v. Stony Brook Hospital, 467 N.Y.S.2d 685 (A.D. 2 Dept. 1983).

Wilkinson v. Vesey 295 A.2d 676 (R.I. 1972).

Wisconsin v. Yoder, 406 U.S. 205 (1972).

In re Maida Yetter, 62 Pa.D. and C.2d 619 (1973).

In re Custody of a Minor, 379 N.E.2d 1053 (Mass. Supreme Judicial Ct., July 10, 1978).

Index